Subcultural Mosaics
and Intersubjective Realities

<u>Assessment</u>

<u>negative</u>: • privileging ethnographic research,

- better to present the ethnographic
  approach as one possible method
  to acquire _{certain} insights and _{certain} knowledge
- it depends on the kind of
  knowledge one is seeking, which
  approach is more appropriate or
  "better"

<u>positive</u>:

- the book is needed for an
  emerging field like the third
  sector to make sure that the
  following do not control the
  research agenda:
- logical positivists, their preeminence
  manifested by the resources
  spent on the National
  Taxonomy of Exempt Entities
  (NTEE)

- economists
- lawyers

Subcultural Mosaics
and Intersubjective Realities

An Ethnographic Research Agenda
for Pragmatizing the Social Sciences

Robert Prus

State University of New York Press

Published by
State University of New York Press, Albany

© 1997 State University of New York

For information, address State University of New York Press,
State University Plaza, Albany, NY 12246

Production by Cynthia Tenace Lassonde
Marketing by Fran Keneston

Library of Congress Cataloging-in-Publication Data

Prus, Robert C.
    Subcultural mosaics and intersubjective realities : an
ethnographic research agenda for pramatizing the social sciences /
Robert Prus.
        p.   cm.
    Includes bibliographical references and index.
    ISBN 0-7914-3239-4 (alk. paper). — 0-7914-3240-8 (pbk. : alk.
paper)
    1. Symbolic interactionism.   2. Participant observation.
    3. Social sciences—Methodology.   I. Title.
HM29.P726   1997
    302—dc20   96-32485
                                                                    CIP

10 9 8 7 6 5 4 3 2 1

This book is dedicated to my wife, Lorraine, and our daughters, Kitzi, Mitzi, and Robin

And in Memory of
Carl Couch (1925–1994)
Fred Davis (1925–1993)
and Anselm Strauss (1916–1996)
who have helped further our educations

Contents

Preface

In devising an agenda for their department (circa 1900), the original four sociologists at the University of Chicago adopted the viewpoint that their city should be approached as a dynamic social laboratory (Kurtz, 1984).[1] Envisioning the world of human group life as our field of operations, the present volume extends this vision by encouraging social scientists to venture out into every realm of human endeavor that one might encounter.

This book is divided into three major sections: "Establishing the Conceptual Foundations," "Pragmatizing the Social Sciences," and "Pursuing the Ethnographic Venture." While the first section provides a set of theoretical premises and a conceptual framework for approaching the study of human group life "in the making," the second section outlines a research agenda intended to indicate how social scientists may ethnographically access and synthesize materials across wide ranges of human endeavor. The last section deals with the practical matters of conducting field research and developing ethnographic research reports.

Throughout this volume, there is a heavy emphasis on *respecting the life-world of the other*. Recognizing that human group life takes its shape in the "doing" or "accomplishing" of activity, a primary concern is that of achieving what Blumer (1969) terms "intimate familiarity" with one's subject matter, namely, the world of human lived experience. In pursuing this objective, it is necessary to establish intersubjectivity with the other, a task that social scientists may accomplish effectively only through sustained ethnographic inquiry. This requires (a) an enduring focus on the actual forging of human activity, (b) an appreciation of the human struggle for existence as this is manifested in everything from the most basic to the most expressive or playful aspects of human association, and (c) engaging the other in extended dialogue and other interchanges so that one might access (and grasp) the experiences of the other in a more complete sense.

Building on the broader interpretivist/constructionist, ethnographic, and pragmatist traditions, particularly as these have been developed within symbolic interaction, this book provides an agenda for reorienting the social or human sciences. In addition to laying out a set of assumptions (i.e., linguistically achieved intersubjectivity,

better: broadening

xi

multiple perspectives, reflectivity, activity, negotiation, and emergence)
that centrally respect the unique (and uniquely enabling) features of
the human condition, consideration is given to a reformulation of the
"cultural problematic." The present view of culture implies an explicit
recognition of multiple life-worlds in (even what seem the most
"simple" of) human societies.

By viewing community life as a *subcultural mosaic* that is more
or less continuously "in the making" (wherein people engage [the
world]* within the context of a plurality of intersubjective realities),
a systematic research agenda for attending to the entire realm of
human involvement is developed, one that is intended to open every
single arena of endeavor to ethnographic inquiry.

Beyond showing how most areas of contemporary life in western
society are highly amenable to ethnographic research, this material
also provides an essential bridge (via generic social processes and
substantive pragmatic features of the human struggle for existence
and expression) that facilitates research and analytical comparison
both within *and* across societies.

As I look back, I'm not sure exactly how the ideas for this present
volume began to crystallize. This statement clearly is predicated on
the necessity of studying human activity in the making, but it very
much reflects a number of concerns about the ways in which social
scientists have been pursuing the study of the human condition.

First, within the social sciences more generally, there has been
an enduring disregard of both what may be termed "the intersubjective
other" and the "ongoing accomplishment of human activity." Over the
past several years, I have been troubled by the neglect of human
enterprise (and the human struggle for existence) that has been so
rampant among those adopting a "postmodernist" viewpoint. However,
and more consequentially, I have also been dismayed by the enduring
tendency of those adopting a conventionalist (positivist/structuralist)
viewpoint in the social sciences to ignore the ways in which people
experience (make sense of and engage on an ongoing basis) the life-
worlds in which they find themselves. On a somewhat different front,

---

* Although readers may find it distracting on occasion, I've [bracketed] terms (e.g., the
world, objects, deviance) in certain instances to emphasize aspects of the problematic
and constructed nature of [reality] as it is humanly experienced (socially interpreted
and meaningfully engaged). For a fuller statement pertaining to "reality as an intersubjectively accomplished human essence" beyond that provided in this volume, see
Prus (1996). In the last two chapters of that book, the interactionist/intersubjectivist
approach taken in the present volume is contrasted with conventionalist (positivist/
structuralist) and postmodernist viewpoints on the human condition.

the Marxists and others taking a "reformist" orientation may distance themselves from some other versions of structuralism, but (other than promoting their own agendas) typically they too have trivialized both (human) intersubjectivity and the practical accomplishment of group life.

Second, I also have become increasingly cognizant of ethnographic research as the essential means of achieving a thorough, detailed, and "empirical" familiarity with the intersubjective other. Quantitative analysis may be useful for certain things (as in physical science applications and related studies of biomedical conditions involving humans), but even where humans most centrally focus on [physical objects] as with scientists, engineers, technicians, or practitioners at large, we would want to be attentive to the intersubjectively developed understandings and technologies with which they work as well as their ongoing interpretations of the instances they encounter. Even before one counts (e.g., "How much money do you have in your wallet or purse?"), one has to think. Minimally, this means invoking some motivated (meaningful) focusing practices, a set of categories, definitions of particular instances of [objects] within these categories,[2] and some rules or procedures (and symbols) of enumeration. As a "rule of thumb," one might suggest that the more humans are actively (mindfully and interactively) involved in something, the less valuable quantitative analysis is in attempting to account for those things.

Third, I have become more acutely aware of the necessity of developing concepts (generic or transsituational social processes) that not only would allow scholars to compare (and contrast) human activities across wide ranges of substantive contexts, but that also explicitly recognize human interpretive processes, enterprise, and interchanges of all sorts.[3]

The present statement was also inspired by some interactionist research on "subcultures."[4] As forums for the development of activities, perspectives, identities, relationships, and the like, subcultures represent the pivotal settings in which humans engage the world in a more direct, meaningful, and "here-and-now" basis. Human group life always takes place in the here and now, even though the here and now is informed by aspects of the past and often encompasses anticipations of the future.

As readers examine the subsequent material, it will become apparent that both the notions of subcultures presented here and the matters pertaining to people's participation in these realms of the here and now have been formulated around generic social processes. However, since people "objectify" (Berger and Luckmann, 1966), and often develop particular fascinations around, substantive areas, people sometimes have difficulty anticipating or envisioning processes that transcend substantive contexts. So long as scholars also accept these objectifications or acquire more particularistic fascinations themselves, they may be unable to benefit from research in other fields even though that work may very well address a variety of conceptual issues with which they themselves are struggling.

Somewhat in conjunction with this, I also began to realize that a great many people would like to do ethnographic research in particular settings but, lacking more direct (substantive) prototypes or conceptual frames on which to build, find themselves at a loss about how to proceed at a very fundamental level. With these notions in mind, I began to lay out a research agenda (or set of agendas) that could deal with virtually any area of human enterprise, with chapters 4, 5, and 6 eventually taking their present shape.

These chapters introduce a framework around which ethnographic inquiry on a wide range of substantive fields may be pursued. However, it is anticipated that this material may also enable scholars to access, benefit from, dialogue with, and contribute to a more extensive, emergent, ethnographically informed literature revolving around basic or transcontextual social processes.[5]

With this agenda in mind, I largely disregarded quantitative, speculative, moralistic, or prescriptive analyses of the human condition because these materials do not adequately attend to the ways in which human group life is accomplished in practice (see Blumer, 1969; Prus, 1996).

This is not to deny the "scholarly merit" of these statements, but rather to point to a rather pervasive tendency on the part of social scientists more generally to avoid direct, sustained contact with those about whom they speak. Although often interesting and useful for some applications, demographic and survey data, experimental data, historical materials, or archaeological or contemporary artifacts should not be envisioned as constituting the primary "data" for learning about the human condition. It is necessary to engage our subject matter in much more direct, meaningful (i.e., intersubjective), and pervasive manners in order that we might develop theory that is attentive to the life-worlds experienced by those in the human community.

People doing ethnographic research in particular substantive areas would likely find it instructive to attend to this broader body of literature so that they can outline the general thrusts of work that has been done in this or that area and perhaps use this as a basis for distinguishing the contributions of their work from these other statements. However, since this literature sheds proportionately so little light on the ways in which humans actively define, shape, and adjust to [the world] about them, I focused primarily on those materials that deal with the ways in which people engage aspects of "the world at hand." While this subsequent quest for resource materials has been frustrated by the lack (and my own limited awarenesses) of ethnographic inquiries in many areas, those ethnographic forays that have become heavily interfused with other agendas (moralisms, control, and advocacy positions, as well as fictionalizations and entertainment motifs) also were of very little value.

In contrast, those ethnographies that "respect the ethnographic other" or examine the life-worlds of others as (legitimate or not to be tampered with) domains unto themselves, and especially those providing extended first-hand statements from others in those life-worlds, have been truly invaluable in assembling this volume. Regardless of the eras or the substantive arenas in which they were produced, these pieces of work provided the bedrock foundations for the research agenda developed here. Enabling readers to gain more comprehensive understandings of the practices of humans engaging the world on a here-and-now basis, each and every one of these studies is like a treasure chest unto itself.

In this regard, those interested in studying the human condition, especially newcomers to the field, are strongly encouraged to read and acquire (for ongoing reference) as many ("Chicago-style" or "interactionist") ethnographies as they possibly can. One can learn things from "textbooks," but even those that have been most carefully crafted typically provide very limited appreciations of human group life "in the making." There simply is no substitute for the insights into human behavior attainable through careful, sustained ethnographic inquiry, particularly when these materials are read mindfully of the contexts in which they were developed and in comparison with (not moralization about) one's awarenesses of the various social worlds in which one and those of one's close acquaintance are involved.

Beyond the ethnographic works of the sort just discussed, there are a great many people to whom I am more personally indebted in developing this material. Since this project reflects many years of involvement in the academic community (particularly in the interactionist and ethnographic research traditions), I know that I will miss thanking many who have contributed to this volume in one or other ways. Nevertheless, I would like to express my gratitude to at least some of these people by name. It is in this spirit that I acknowledge Patricia and Peter Adler, Cheryl and Daniel Albas, Leon Anderson,

Michael Atkinson, Hans Bakker, Eleen Baumann, Joel Best, Herbert Blumer, Craig Bryson, Robert A. Campbell, Kathy Charmaz, Tina Chester, Carl Couch, Jim Curtis, Lorne Dawson, Helen Rose Ebaugh, Bob Farmer, Scott Grills, Rick Helmes-Hayes, Robert Hiscott, Dick Henshell, Rosanna Hertz, Styllianoss Irini, John Johnson, Peter Labella, Ron Lambert, John Lofland, Stan Lyman, Elizabeth McNulty, Richard Mitchell, Danny Miller, Tom Morrione, Adie Nelson, Clint Sanders, Stan Saxton, Marvin Scott, C. R. D. Sharper, Eldon Snyder, Chuck Tucker, Keith Warriner, Audrey Wipper, Jackie Wiseman, and Daniel Wolf.

As three longstanding friends and practitioners in the field, Mary Lorenz Dietz, William Shaffir, and I wrote chapters 7 and 8 together, and I am grateful for their contributions to this volume. We had originally developed these statements for a conference on ethnographic research, but they seemed to fit so nicely with the flow of the present volume that we decided to insert them here.

I would also like to thank Chris Worden and Zina Lawrence (editors) at SUNY Press for their interest in work dealing with the accomplishment of human group life, and Cindy Lassonde (production editor) and James Peltz (copy editor) for their assistance through the latter stages of this project. This is the second book I will have published with this press, and I have very much enjoyed working with the SUNY staff.

Finally, my wife, Lorraine, deserves some special recognition with respect to this volume. She has been a major source of inspiration and assistance throughout this project. Lorraine has read and commented on numerous drafts of this material and since she seems endlessly interested in everything that people do this book has benefitted greatly from her interest, thoughtfulness, and care.

Endnotes:

1. The Sociology department at the University of Chicago was chaired by Albion Small, but also included Charles Henderson, George Vincent, and W. I. Thomas.

2. When you want to see how much "money" you have on you, do you actually count your coins? I often don't. I've also observed that people often don't bother to count their smaller bills when they want to see if they have enough money to pay for something (more costly): "Forget that, I can see that I'm not even close." Did you count any credit or bank cards (i.e., the limits to which you have access) as money? Most vendors are happy to count that as "real money," too.

3. For those concerned about maintaining the idiographic or unique features of ethnographic research, it may be useful to appreciate, as Blumer (1928) observes, that concepts enable people to acknowledge, compare and contrast instances of phenomena. Likewise, any attempt to clearly define and (especially) convey the "truly unique" almost inevitably results in the development of some representational [concept] that presumably could be applied to other (if only hypothetical) instances of this phenomenon, were such things to exist.

4. Although the emphasis has been on "deviant subcultures," it should be recognized that since the interactionists approach [deviance] as a matter of audience definitions (rather than as an objective condition), their views on subcultures are quite generic in thrust.

5. One interesting, unanticipated, and yet rather humbling personal result of this project has been a much greater appreciation of all realms of human enterprise; to more explicitly see *everything* that humans do as interesting and relevant for a fuller comprehension of the human condition. Although not as informed in any area of human endeavor as I would desire, working on this agenda has provided an opportunity to read more extensively in the ethnographic tradition and to learn more about people and the wide ranges of activities in which they engage. Hopefully, others will share in this enthusiasm for comprehending the human condition as they engage the ethnographic enterprise.

Part I

Establishing the Conceptual Foundations

1

Studying the Human Condition:
An Interactionist Approach to the
Ethnographic Venture

At Greenview [a stripper bar], we started talking with Doug, a used
car dealer. On learning that we were from the university, he asked
what we were doing there. I didn't know where he fitted into things
there, so I said, "We heard about this place at Spring Gardens [which
over the years had become a very rough bar] and thought we should
check it out. I thought maybe we could learn something about
people." He replied, "Yeah, that's a good idea. All those things you
learn in books, and I've read a lot of books myself, they don't do
you any good when you're dealing with people. . . . A lot of people,
writers and university people, they think that they are better than
anybody else. Then they just don't find out what's happening in
people's lives. If you want to learn about people, real people, you
have to go to places like this. You have to go to the upper levels and
to the lower levels, places like this and Sunset, the hookers' bar,
or maybe Spring Gardens, where you were, it's one of the roughest
places in town. (notes) (Prus and Irini, 1980:237)

This book is premised on the viewpoint that the social sciences have
as their primary mission the task of attending to the ways in which
the human condition manifests itself in the day-to-day world in which
people find themselves. This means that those in the social sciences
should not only strive to develop stocks of knowledge (conceptual
schemes and substantive information) pertinent to every realm of
human conduct, but that these scholars should also use every accessible instance of human behavior as <u>foundational material</u> on which
to develop and inform an emergent social science.

Unfortunately, to date, social scientists have only been marginally
attentive to this agenda. Instead of appreciating the uniquely enabling
and actualizing features of the human condition, social scientists have

3

largely modeled themselves (theoretically and methodologically) after the physical sciences. While neither denying the accomplishments of, nor taking issue with the viability of existing practices within, the physical or natural sciences, it is posited that a different notion of "scientific inquiry" is necessary for studying the human condition. What is required is a transformation or a revitalization of the social sciences from a positivistically oriented (emphasizing objectification, quantification, causation) realm of inquiry to one that centrally attends to the actualities of human lived experience.[1]

better: broaden

Interestingly, perhaps, if not rather ironically, the approach proposed here should not only make the social sciences relevant to a great many realms of human group life that have been largely disregarded, but it should also help demystify the social sciences for people in general. This is not to suggest that we do away with concepts, theory, data, or methodological rigor, but rather provide the means by which those in the social sciences may build more enduring, two-way bridges between their specialized stocks of knowledge and the day-to-day, human life-worlds they purport to study.

here author is inclusive

In maintaining this position, we are pursuing the pragmatist agenda, the task of developing knowledge that is directly pertinent to the world of human lived experience. At the same time, however, we are extending this agenda by locating the pragmatist concern of understanding the accomplishment of everyday life within a context that is theoretically, methodologically, and substantively informed in ways that the early pragmatists were unable to achieve.[2] The emphasis is on enabling inquiry and fostering a conceptually developed but substantively informed stock of knowledge.

The position taken here is a relativist one in the sense that no way of life is endorsed over others. At the same time, however, human group life is not viewed as completely arbitrary.[3] Rather, at base is an acknowledgement of the fundamental human struggle for existence, the primacy of intersubjectivity (or symbolic communication) to the human condition, and the necessity of people actively engaging the world (as they know it to be). Likewise, while appreciating that people may define and act toward "the world" in a great many ways, the emphasis is on understanding and conceptualizing the ways in which human group life is accomplished in practice. The approach taken, thus, is thoroughly humanist in the sense that it focuses intensively on all facets of human experience, endeavoring to do so from the participants' viewpoints in every instance. It does not, however, attempt to prescribe moralities or life-styles for anyone.[4] Other than insisting on a social science that intensively focuses on the practical accomplishment of human lived experience, the emphasis is neither on condemning nor encouraging any particular way of life.

While drawing much inspiration from the early pragmatists, especially George Herbert Mead and Charles Horton Cooley, this statement is also heavily indebted to the conceptual works of Wilhelm Dilthey (hermeneutic, intersubjectivist, or interpretivist tradition), Georg Simmel (forms of association), and the "constructionist tradition" associated with Alfred Schutz (1962, 1964) and Peter Berger and Thomas Luckmann (1966). This material is also informed by the ethnographic tradition in anthropology, but it draws most centrally on the writings of Herbert Blumer and "the (ethnographically oriented) Chicago School of symbolic interaction."[5]

Having traced the theoretical and methodological roots of symbolic interactionism elsewhere in some detail (Prus, 1996:33–172), as well as having compared and contrasted interpretivist analysis with both positivist approaches to the physical and social sciences (Prus, 1996: 3–9, 203–16; Prus and Dawson, 1996) and postmodernist tendencies (Dawson and Prus, 1993a, 1993b, 1995; Prus,1996:217–33; Prus and Dawson, 1996), the central premises which undergird this approach will be addressed in a more direct manner at this point. The baseline position is that *the matters of intersubjectivity and human enterprise* (as discussed later) *are fundamental to **all** comprehensions of the human condition. This includes all scientific (natural and social sciences) experience (observation, conceptualization, and inquiry) as well as any other realm of meaningful human involvement.*[6]

Theoretical and Methodological Foundations

Symbolic interaction rests in the last analysis on three simple premises. The first premise is that human beings act toward things on the basis of the meanings they have for them. . . . The second premise is that the meaning of such things is derived from, or arises out of, the social interaction that one has with one's fellows. The third premise is that these meanings are handled in, and modified through, an interpretative process used by the person in dealing with the things he encounters. (Blumer, 1969:2)

The position developed herein may be best envisioned as an extension of "Chicago-style" symbolic interactionism, and is most adequately grounded in Blumer's (1969) collection of papers (some dating back to 1931).[7] Very much a student of George Herbert Mead

(1863–1931), Herbert George Blumer (1900–1987) not only promotes a *thoroughly intersubjectivist conception of human group life*, but by attending to Charles Horton Cooley's notion of *sympathetic introspection* (now more commonly referred to as ethnographic inquiry, participant-observation, or field research), Blumer incorporates into Mead's conceptual scheme a methodology that centrally respects or attends to the experiential essences of the human condition.

Like Mead before him, Blumer emphasizes that *human life is group life*. However, even more sharply than his predecessors, Blumer draws attention to the misplaced tendency on the part of mainstream (positivist) social scientists to attempt to explain human behavior by invoking "factors" or "variables" (typically in the form of individual qualities or structural conditions) to account for this or that state of human behavior. Blumer argues that human behavior is not the outcome of some set of factors (internal or external) or variables *acting on* people, but rather represents ongoing social constructions. Human behavior represents instances of meaningful formulative processes that only come about as people make sense of the world and take themselves (and others) into account in developing lines of action toward the situations in which they find themselves.

Unlike other [objects] of human awareness,[8] Blumer contends that people are "minded beings." Through their interactions with others, people develop notions of objects, including themselves. By attending to the viewpoints of the other (as expressed through language [and other shared gestures]) and applying these notions to "the world about them," including themselves, people acquire capacities for self-awareness. In the process of delineating and making indications toward objects, people achieve (self-)reflectivity or become "objects unto themselves." As objects of their own awareness, people can communicate with themselves about themselves. They can take themselves into account in developing lines of action toward this and that [thing]. Viewed in this manner, the self is a community essence. Thus (as with Mead and Dilthey), Blumer thoroughly rejects the idea of the subjectivist or individually developed self. There can be no self without the other. Like many other biological life-forms, people can "learn" things through conditioning effects, but without achieving a sense of intersubjectivity, without tapping into the viewpoint of the other, there would be no meaningful notion of mind, self, reflectivity, thinking, imagining, anticipating, strategizing, assessing, or creating.

If they were able to survive, somehow, on their own, humans would likely develop [images] of some sort of the [things] around them, but in the absence of the concepts that people acquire through association with others, any images so experienced are apt to have minimal if any comprehensible shape? In contrast to other biological species that appear predisposed to act toward [situations] with minimal if any "symbolic interchange" on the part of others, *[Objects] become meaningful to humans only because people acquire a means of communicating or sharing understandings or viewpoints from (and then with) others.* Only by achieving a sense of mutuality with the other, only by taking the perspective of the other, do humans begin to acquire a sense of mind or some preliminary ways of making sense of the situation at hand.

Intersubjectivity occurs through an acknowledgement or sharing of the gestures, symbols, or language of the other. Only in acquiring some familiarity with the images and practices that are meaningful to others is one able to relate to others in the community in comprehensible terms. By adopting the viewpoint of the other, people may begin to envision themselves as objects amidst the other objects to which people in their community refer. This achievement of symbolic mutuality represents the foundational essence of the self. This is not to deny subsequent creativity on the part of individuals, but rather to stress that people's senses of individuality or "independence of thought" presuppose or are based on the preliminary achievement of intersubjectivity with others.

Society, thus, consists of people with selves, interacting with one another by means of shared symbols, embarking on lines of action that are mindful of the world of objects signified by those symbols. As objects unto themselves (i.e., of their own awareness), people are not only able to adjust their lines of activity relative to other objects (and other people), but they are also able to reflect upon (or envision in some respect) their involvements in these situations prior to, during, and after acting toward any particular set of objects.

In contrast to the tendency on the part of many social scientists to view human behavior as the product of various instincts, forces, factors, or variables acting upon or from within individuals, the perspective taken here envisions human behavior as a community-informed, reflective, constructed phenomenon. The result is a theory of community, agency, and enterprise that contrasts sharply with the positivist emphasis on factors thought to predispose people to act in this or that manner.

While critical of those in the social sciences who fail to appreciate the fundamentally social essence of human behavior, Dilthey, Mead, and Blumer do not wish to dispense with the conceptual rigor or methodological precision that they associate with the notion of science.

However, they envision the human essence to be so different from other objects that people might study as to make it entirely inappropriate to subject the study of the human condition to the models and methods of the physical sciences. Likewise, Dilthey, Mead, and Blumer do not deny "the physical environment" in which humans exist, but they emphasize the fundamentally interpretive, community-based, or inter-subjective essence of all meaningful human activity, including all activity directed toward (known and defined) aspects of the physical environment. Instead of attempting to imitate the practices of the physical sciences simply because of the many successes they have achieved in their subject domains, Dilthey, Mead, and Blumer stress the point that those in the social sciences have the more fundamental obligation of respecting the *social essence* of the human condition.

Whereas Dilthey and Mead established the conceptual foundations for a social science that was thoroughly intersubjective in its thrust, it was not until Blumer more squarely synthesized this conceptual emphasis with ethnographic inquiry (also known as sympathetic intro-spection, field research, or participant-observation) that the social sciences were provided with a methodology that could adequately attend to the intersubjective and enterprising features of the human condition.

Compared to the conceptual precision and methodological rigor attainable in many realms of the physical sciences, Blumer (1928) observes that Cooley's method of sympathetic introspection (i.e., ethnography) might not appear very "scientific" from certain viewpoints. However, since humans live in interpreted life-worlds and human behavior involves the study of active, interpreting, interacting agents, *the study of human group life generates some highly unique problems for researchers, problems that simply cannot be managed by modeling human inquiry on the methods of the physical sciences.*

Blumer clearly had reservations about sympathetic introspection as a conventional mode of "scientific research." In particular, he acknowledges the problems associated with achieving comprehensive intersubjectivity with other people in the course of ethnographic inquiry and the related matters of establishing evidence and developing viable concepts.[10] Still, above all things, Blumer contends, if social scientists are to achieve scientific integrity, they must respect the nature of their (human) subject matter. On this basis, he concludes, ethno-graphic inquiry is the *only* feasible way that one may achieve intimate familiarity with human group life as it is actually accomplished:

> No one can catch the process merely by inferring its nature from the overt action which is its product. To catch the process,

the student must take the role of the acting unit whose behavior he is studying. Since the interpretation is being made by the acting unit in terms of objects designated and appraised, meanings acquired, and decisions made, the process has to be seen from the standpoint of the acting unit. It is the recognition of this fact that makes the research work of such scholars as R. E. Park and W. I. Thomas so notable. To try to catch the interpretive process by remaining aloof as a so-called "objective" observer and refusing to take the role of the acting unit is to risk the worst kind of subjectivism—the objective observer is likely to fill in the process of interpretation with his own surmises in place of catching the process as it occurs in the experience of the acting unit which uses it. (Blumer, 1969:86)

Intensively concerned that social scientists develop concepts that are both sensitive to the phenomenon being studied and foster ongoing comparisons (and contrasts), Blumer encourages a constant receptivity and openness on the part of researchers. He insists that social scientists have an obligation to adjust their preconceptions to the instances of the phenomenon that they encounter in the course of conducting their inquiry. Emphasizing the necessity of developing concepts that are attentive to individual instances of the features of human behavior under consideration, Blumer also stresses the desirability of conducting and analyzing (ethnographic) research in ways that foster conceptual comparisons. Most centrally though, he is concerned that all conceptualizations, inquiries, and comparisons on the part of social scientists be informed by the enacted aspects of human group life.

Mindful of developments in the sociology of science over the past few decades that depict the fundamentally social essence of all knowledge productions,[11] it is tempting to contend that Herbert Blumer was fifty years or more ahead of his time. However, the more accurate (and somber) position is that Blumer was both in step with his time and our time. The problem is that, at present, the social sciences more generally are at least a century behind Dilthey's (1833–1911) intersubjectivist (or hermeneutic) legacy. Because Blumer's work has not yet become more widely acknowledged in mainstream social science, it has only been partially effective in helping us catch up. In imitating or modeling themselves after the physical sciences, those promoting a positivistically oriented social science (with an emphasis on objectivity, quantification, and causation) have failed to attend adequately both to the intersubjective essence of the human condition and the ongoing enterprise that characterizes human community life.[12]

The scholars (e.g., Auguste Comte, Emile Durkheim, Max Weber, John Stuart Mill, Wilhelm Wundt) who set the early (essentially positivist) agenda for the social sciences developed notions that were attentive to the human condition in certain respects, but in attempting to make the study of the human condition amenable to the method-ological (and theoretical) orientations that have been developed in the physical sciences, they violated the essential interpretivist, interactive, and enterprising features of the human condition (Prus, 1996:3–9, 205–16).

As a result, those in the social sciences have been laboring on an enterprise that was extremely ill-fated from its inception. Masses of books and papers (reflecting both "learned speculation" and reams of quantitative data) have been generated, but these have rather limited relevance to the ongoing accomplishment of everyday life. Focusing on factors (or variables) purported to cause or contribute to this or that outcome, minimal attention has been given to (a) people's achievement of meaningful communication, (b) people's definitions of situations, (c) the human capacity for reflective thought, (d) the ways in which people actually formulate (implement, monitor, and adjust) their lines of action, (e) the manners in which people interact (including instances of influence and resistance) with one another, (f) the ways in which people form and attend to relationships with one another, or (g) the ways in which these facets of human group life are accomplished by people in processual terms.

Despite the seemingly straightforward and unpretentious (i.e., rigorously grounded in the world of everyday life) agenda established by Herbert Blumer and others working in the interactionist tradition, this viewpoint has encountered considerable motivated resistance on the part of those in the social science. As noted elsewhere (Prus, 1992b, 1996:209–12), those working in positivist paradigms have developed a variety of deeply entrenched practices (e.g., disciplines, departmental programs, professional associations, service industries, publication venues, control of granting agencies) that serve to perpetuate positivist versions of the social sciences.[13] As well, more personal concerns with maintaining professional competencies, achieving career advance-ment, and acquiring prestige also engender motivated resistances to an intersubjectively informed social science.

While some positivistically trained scholars have made or are in the process of making the transition to an intersubjectivist social science, others may be concerned that their personal situations might be significantly jeopardized were the social sciences to be transformed into a social constructionist program. Unlike the more common

(margin handwritten note: shortcoming of positivism?)

practice of learning another variation of a statistical technique, for instance, the shift to an intersubjectivist social science will necessitate a rather abrupt redefinition of theoretical emphasis as well as a distinct methodological break with prevailing practices.[15] It is worth observing, too, that those scholars in positions most able to foster a rapid and smooth transition to an intersubjectivist agenda are often those more steeped in, and committed to perpetuating, the positivist paradigm. In the chapters that follow, a reorientation of exactly this sort for the social sciences is proposed. Hopefully, it will be seen as relevant, accessible, and enabling rather than frightening or obstructionist in thrust.

Outlining the Premises

As a means of framing the foundational features of an interactionist approach (as developed most explicitly by George Herbert Mead and Herbert Blumer) in a form that may be more accessible to newcomers to the field,[15] the following discussion is organized around seven premises, which although discussed one at a time, are very much interrelated in the ongoing accomplishment of everyday life.[16]

1. *Human Group Life Is Intersubjective.* The notion of inter-subjectivity draws our attention to the primacy of the group in the conceptualization and study of human lived experience. Not only are people born into group situations on a physiological basis, but so too are they born into social life-worlds that preexist them.[17] It is impossible to ascertain just how humans may have first developed a capacity for achieving mutuality or a sharing of meanings or references to this or that phenomenon, but every human group of which we have relevant information possesses a language or set of symbols that not only enables them to communicate within community contexts, but which is also used as a primary tool to enable human offspring and other newcomers to gain some comprehension of the world at hand. Although the actual symbols (and the meanings associated with particular symbols) may vary greatly from community to community, human group life centrally reflects a shared linguistic or symbolic reality that sustains human association and takes its shape as people interact with one another. All meaningful essences, including the more solitary experiences of (linguistic) members of human groups, derive from or are built on comprehensions of "the reality of the other."

2. *Human Group Life Is (Multi) Perspectival.* While language enables people to communicate with one another and to share

definitions of reality with others, each human group is faced with the prospects of making sense of the world and developing lines of action toward the world that enables both baseline survival and the pursuit of any secondary objectives. It is in the process of making and acknowledging indications about aspects of the world that groups develop and sustain perspectives (also worldviews, symbolic realities, frames of reference, interpretive frameworks, orientations). Without contesting the viability of any claims or "stocks of knowledge" that people develop, it is important to recognize that people inevitably prioritize viewpoints (and interpretations thereof) whenever they begin to act in meaningful fashions.

The notion that human group life is multiperspectival acknowledges the diverse, almost limitless, meanings that people may attach to [objects] both across groups and over time. Rather than posit the existence of a singular, stimulus, or objective reality that people experience in some uniform manner, it is recognized that people *actively* distinguish [objects], develop meanings for particular objects, and develop styles of relating to those objects as they interact with one another.

Neither the identification of [things] as "objects" nor the meanings that people attach to objects are predetermined or automatic. Objects are problematic in their emergence (i.e., human awareness or delineations), the duration of their recognized existence, and the directions (e.g., categories, attributes, valuings) given to them by this or that group of people. However, when groups of people establish consensus among themselves on the existence and meanings of particular objects, they tend to envision these definitions of situations as "real" or "objective."[18]

Since the adoption of certain worldviews may enable members of some groups of people to do things that others may not, it is essential to attend carefully to the symbolic realities of any group(s) under consideration. It is these viewpoints that represent the paramount realities for understanding people's participation in the situations at hand. Thus, people are seen to operate in versions of (multiple) realities which they share, albeit imperfectly, with others at an "intersubjective" level.

3. *Human Group Life Is Reflective.* Through interaction with others, and taking the viewpoint of the other with respect to oneself, people become "objects unto themselves" or objects of their own awareness. By attending to the perspective of "the other" (what Mead [1934] terms "role-taking"), people are able to attribute meanings to their own "essences" and to develop lines of action which take themselves (and

other objects) into account. Enabling people to see themselves from the standpoint of the other and to "converse with themselves about themselves," the acquisition of (self-)reflectivity fosters meaningful initiative (i.e., human agency, enterprise, intentionality) as people develop their activities in manners which take themselves into account. As reflective entities, people may pursue activities on their own as well as incorporate suggestions and resist unwanted inputs from others.

While reflectivity presupposes a sharing of perspectives, it denotes people's capacities to interpret or make sense of situations on an ongoing basis, to monitor and assess their own experiences, and to attend to the situated viewpoint of particular others. Beyond enabling people to interpret and reinterpret their situations on a more or less continual basis, it is this capacity for reflectivity, as well, that allows people to be creative, strategic, and deceptive with respect to their dealings with others.

Human group life presupposes human agency or the capacity for people to embark on meaningful intentional behavior. While people may sometimes be exempt from accountability because of age (e.g., of comprehension, responsibility) or other circumstances (e.g., illnesses, mistakes), people typically expect that others also "know that they can exercise some control or direction over their own behaviors." The notion of reflectivity does not presume an automatic "rationality" or "wisdom," although an appreciation of human agency provides the basis on which assessments of these sorts may be invoked by people in this or that situation.[19]

4. *Human Group Life Is Activity-based.* Humans are action-oriented beings. While some people may live rather sedentary life-styles, either by preference or default, the sheer quest for survival necessitates highly focused sets of undertakings on the part of humans more generally. As well, the realm of human activity is readily extended to any arena of object awareness, with important implications for each realm of awareness. While people's actions are meaningful only with respect to their preexisting perspectives, these viewpoints are apt to undergo transformations of sorts as people go about implementing particular lines of action.

A great deal of human activity entails physical activity, but human activity encompasses a great deal more than the physiological movements that may be evident to an outside observer. Human activity is rooted in intersubjective communication and the related notion of perspectives, but it also reflects the human capacity for reflectivity and denotes an emergent, situated process unto itself.

Human activities vary greatly in both complexity and completeness, but activity not uncommonly implies: encounters with ambiguity and (interpretive) sense-making endeavors; anticipations of options, performances, and outcomes; behavioral implementations, situational monitoring, and ongoing assessments of these endeavors; and after-performance (re)assessments of situations, along with subsequent anticipations and adjustments. As well, although some activities may be more private and solitary in focus, a great deal of human activity is developed in ways that are mindful of others. In addition to the human undertakings that involve the explicit coordination or interchanges of activity with others, a great many seemingly solitary activities are conducted in ways that are attentive to others (e.g., things done in anticipation of or following encounters with others; activities intended to assist, entertain, deceive, or obstruct others in some manner).

Considerations of the "doing," implementing, or constructing of action (or what Blumer calls "the active forging" of human behavior) involve a highly sustained focus on the ways in which people assemble their activities in process, how people work their ways through situations, both in a solitary fashion and in conjunction with others in a more direct, interactive sense. There is no requirement that the activity in question need be successful as intended, nor need it be viewed as wise or rational by others or even by the actors, themselves, over time. Activity draws our attention to the matter of ongoing enterprise, to the constituent notions of defining, anticipating, invoking, encountering resistance, accomplishing, experiencing failure, redefining, reassessing, and adjusting, on both interactive as well as more solitary behavioral levels.

5. *Human Group Life Is Negotiable.* Although the term *negotiation* often implies an adversarial stance, this concept may be used more basically to refer to situations in which people (as reflective entities who define their own situations from this or that viewpoint) strategically pursue particular interests in their interactions with others.

Acknowledging people's abilities to shape the life-worlds that others experience, to influence and resist the influences of others, this premise makes the interactive dimension of human reflectivity especially explicit. Since people may have (a) similar, supportive interests in some cases, as well as (b) parallel but competitive or antagonistic viewpoints in some instances, or (c) mixed agendas (with respect to the other) on yet other occasions, matters of cooperation, competition, conflict, and compromise are all highly consequential for understanding the alignments (and adjustments) that people develop with respect to others. While attending to the interests, intents, and tactics of the people under consideration, there is no presumption of inherent self-interestedness. People may knowingly contribute to, or intensively pursue, agendas (for the good of specific others or the community at large) that clearly jeopardize their own financial situations, physical well-being, and the like.

It is also worth noting that although alignments presume some degree of mutuality or acknowledgement, one or more parties to the interactive setting may be much more concerned about the inter-actional outcomes of the encounter than may others (e.g., consider a child about to ask a parent for a new toy). At the same time, however, it is essential to recognize that all parties to an encounter may adopt on a sequential or concurrent basis the roles of both tacticians *and* targets as any interchanges take place and the people involved attempt to achieve (also maintain, forego, or reestablish) what they deem more appropriate circumstances.

6. *Human Group Life Is Relational.* Like other objects of their awareness, humans define one another in developing (and maintaining) lines of action toward each other. As people distinguish others in their community and envision tentative lines of action toward others, people's associations (bonds, affiliations, networks) and related activities become more particularized, selective, or focused. This premise not only acknowledges the differing identities (i.e., self and other definitions; images and reputations) that people attach to one another, but it is also mindful of the loyalties, disaffections, and other inter-actional styles that emerge between and among people in the course of human interaction.

Since a great many of the activities in which people engage are made meaningful and shaped in certain manners because of people's attentiveness to specific others in the setting, an acknowledgment of people's involvements and embeddedness in particular groups within the broader community is essential in enabling analysts to comprehend people's viewpoints and activities. More generally, however, the notion of relatedness points to the fundamental necessity of locating and comprehending all of people's experience (and activities) within the community (of the other).

7. *Human Group Life Is Processual.* Although some sense of process (change, continuity, and disruption) seems applicable to the study of all phenomena (e.g., consider matters of origins, development, sequencing, stability, disintegration), the concept of process seems

especially consequential for comprehending the human condition. On the one hand, there is the widespread recognition that people change physiologically (aging, experiencing and satisfying hunger, becoming ill and well, and so forth). On the other hand, the struggle for human existence is built on an attentiveness to continuity and change in the broader environment (e.g., seasons, cycles, patterns of development). For our purposes, though, a third sense of process is pivotal, one that acknowledges the historical flow or sequencing of people's experiences across the range of life-world situations in which they find themselves. The concept of process, thus, cuts across all of the other premises, including intersubjectivity, particularized worldviews, reflectivity, activity, negotiated interchange, and relationships.

Reflecting the development, sharing, and shaping of symbolic realities, intersubjectivity is very much an ongoing process. Likewise, people's perspectives (or notions of objects, object meanings, and object-relevant behaviors) develop and change over time. As an ongoing dimension of human group life, reflectivity not only is interdependent with the flow of people's associations with others, but is most centrally experienced and expressed dynamically as people engage in instances of definition, interpretation, intentionality, assessment, and minded adjustments over time. Likewise, reflectivity assumes its significance as "human agency" in process terms as people go about their activities. Representing the implementation of the perspectives that people acquire through association with others and their senses of (reflective) self-agency, activity is fundamentally tied to process.

Denoting (experiential and behavioral) sequences of definitions, anticipations, implementations, assessments, and adjustments, that are built up over time (consider techniques, practices, skills, stocks of knowledge and manners of engaging objects), human activity represents particularly compelling instances of emergence and transition. Human interchange is steeped in process. Not only do people define situations (and selves), work out tentative lines of action, make indications to others, and interpret the indications of others on an ongoing basis, but they also make ensuing adjustments to others (in the form of subsequent definitions, plans, and indications) as their encounters unfold.

Relationships, as well, are best understood in processual terms (or as having natural histories) with respect to their emergence, intensification, dissipation, and possible reconstitution, as people distinguish and define specific others and attempt to develop their life-worlds in conjunction with those with whom they associate. Not only may we follow people's involvements in particular situations over time, but we may also consider the ways in which "their careers" are interwoven—concurrently and sequentially—with the careers or involvements of their associates. In sum, then, the primary conceptual and methodological implication of this processual emphasis is this: since all aspects of group life take place in dynamic terms or take their shape over time, *it is essential that the human condition be conceptualized and studied in manners that are acutely mindful of the emergent nature of human lived experience.*

Conceptual and Methodological Implications

Matters of methodology will be given more explicit consideration in chapter 7, but it may be instructive to comment briefly on some of the conceptual and methodological implications of the interactionist paradigm, mindful of the premises just discussed. This will be done within the context of introducing the subsequent chapters in this volume.

First, the interactionist approach or paradigm attends centrally to *the study of human lived experience as the paramount reality in the pursuit of a social science.* Denoting aspects of intersubjectivity, perspectives, reflectivity, activity, negotiation, relationships, and process, the study of the human condition requires a theory and methodology that respects the distinctive nature of human group life. This means that the most feasible way of learning about human lived experience is through *interactive inquiry* into human life-worlds. This is not possible to accomplish either by administering questionnaires to people (about their beliefs, attitudes, behaviors, background characteristics, and the like), by running people through experimental settings, or by giving people "personality tests." Likewise, "content analyses" of documents, messages, photographs, videotapes, or other artifacts are not adequate on their own. These forms of data do not enable researchers to achieve intersubjectivity with the other. Access to more materials pertinent to the situation may enable researchers to ask more instructive questions of the people involved in their production, but these materials in themselves do not allow researchers to access people's perspectives, capacities for reflectivity, activities, interactions, or relationships in any substantial sense.[20] These types of data are woefully inattentive to the ways in which human behavior is accomplished (in process) by living, thinking, acting, and interacting beings.

What is required is an active appreciation of the lived situations of the other, and this can be attained most effectively by venturing out into the life-worlds of those being studied and interacting extensively with those involved therein. Indeed, one can acquire a viable understanding of the lived experiences of the other only through the sustained pursuit of intersubjectivity or a mutuality of experience with the other. This may be achieved most effectively through ongoing participation in the life-worlds being studied and through extended open-ended conversations with those whose activities and experiences are being considered.

Clearly, an important message emerging from this introductory chapter and the volume more generally is that social scientists (instructors, researchers, and students) have a primary obligation to respect the fundamentally social essence of the human condition, and that can be accomplished only by achieving intersubjectivity with the other. This means attending to the human capacity for symbolic interchange, the acquisition and use of perspectives, reflectivity, the social construction of activity and interaction, and the development of relationships in process terms.

Still, while appreciating the necessity of examining and understanding human behavior within the particular contexts in which it occurs, the objective is not to pile up isolated or disconnected studies on a variety of life-worlds. Thus, the present volume is also intended to focus attention on the importance of developing a body of concepts that allows us to access, comprehend, and compare the life-worlds of others as we go about doing research across a range of settings. It is to these interrelated tasks of (a) learning about the various manifestations of human experience (by actively pursuing intersubjectivity with the other) and (b) developing a set of concepts applicable to the study of the human condition across communities, that the rest of this volume is directed.

Readers are apt to find much that resonates with their own lived experiences in chapter 2, "Subcultural Mosaics and Intersubjective Realities," but this statement redefines the social science project in some very consequential manners. Although maintaining an attentiveness to the more broadly shared aspects of the general culture, this chapter reconceptualizes "culture" in a way that rather uniquely enables sociologists, anthropologists, and other social scientists to focus on the various realms of human enterprise that constitute the human community. While attending to the "transcontextual intersubjectivities" that provide the basis for notions of a "shared broader culture," this chapter considers the ways in which culture as an element of the human condition both takes its shape from, and gives shape to, the vast realms of meaningful enterprise that characterize the human community. Despite various practical and more particularistically motivated tendencies toward cultural consistency and continuity, it is argued that community life is realized through people's involvements, activities, and interchanges in shifting configurations of subcultural ventures. Thus, consideration is given to a multidimensional, processual conceptualization of culture, one which recognizes the fundamental or essential nature of the great many subcultural enterprises that constitute human group life in local as well as more global realms. Beyond challenging the prevailing, totalizing notions of "culture" and providing some terminology that people may use to delineate and represent a variety of interlinked life-worlds, the subcultural mosaic represents a unique, processually grounded manner of integrating vast realms of human enterprise.

Chapter 3, "Subcultural Involvements," establishes a further foundation for pursuing the subcultural mosaic by presenting readers with a set of "generic social processes." This "conceptual tool kit" not only outlines a set of action-oriented concepts that may be applied to any new realm of study, but also provides scholars with a means of achieving transcontextuality with the existing ethnographic literature. Beyond enabling scholars to build on both the concepts and substantive insights that have been generated in several decades of ethnographic research in the Chicago tradition, this material also provides researchers with a means of (comparatively) assessing their immediate work and theoretically synthesizing it with the works of others who've examined similar processes in contexts that may be quite different in substantive terms. Thus, for instance, concepts such as acquiring perspective, developing identities, and building relationships may not only be instructive in developing studies of dating couples, religious cults, biker gangs, feminist associations, police departments, or work groups, but may also enable researchers to compare and contrast people's experiences and practices along these lines across these (and countless other) realms of involvement in conceptually meaningful and productive manners.

Representing an agenda for pragmatizing the social sciences, chapters 4, 5, and 6 build squarely on the conceptual material developed in the preceding discussions of subcultural mosaics and generic social processes. Focusing on matters of *achieving intersubjectivity, managing place and space, maintaining presence, encountering the interpersonal other, managing morality, emphasizing community presence,* and *experiencing the self,* these chapters outline a research agenda that addresses the ongoing accomplishment of human community life. In addition to recasting many of the more conventional research topics in the social sciences in manners more amenable to ethnographic inquiry, this material also draws attention to a great many presently overlooked realms of human activity. While by no means exhaustive, this research agenda is intended to make the social science venture relevant to each and every area of human behavior. By attending to the human enterprise entailed in the subcultural mosaic, readers are presented with a conceptual scheme that lends itself to considerable cross-contextual insights as well as providing an analytical frame for synthesizing both seemingly substantively disconnected research and so called micro and macro levels of analysis.

Pursuing the matters of researcher accessibility to the subcultural mosaic, chapters 7 and 8 outline a set of research and writing practices that may be used in conjunction with the research agenda presented here. Chapter 7, "Doing Ethnographic Research," considers the ways in which ethnographic inquiry is accomplished in practice. It's a discussion of field research that Mary Lorenz Dietz, Bill Shaffir, and I developed mindful of the sorts of messages we try to convey to our own graduate and undergraduate students. In attempts to achieve what Herbert Blumer terms "intimate familiarity with one's subject matter" (i.e., particular "life-worlds"), ethnographers rather uniquely pursue the tasks of (a) attending to various facets of the social worlds of the other as fully and carefully as they are able; (b) noting, probing, recording, and analyzing the situations they encounter; and (c) attempting to convey these notions to outsiders in careful, balanced, representative manners.

Like people (more generally) venturing into and achieving acceptance in other settings, researchers in the field also very much face the prospects of both accessing particular groups of people and maintaining a viable, working presence in those arenas over time. Thus, ethnographers find themselves attempting to come to terms with (i) the perspectives or worldviews characterizing the people in the settings in which they find themselves, (ii) the sets of self and other identities that people in those settings invoke, (iii) the activities that take place in those arenas, (iv) the relationships that develop between the participants in those life-worlds, (v) the emotionalities that people in those contexts express, and (vi) their modes of achieving communicative fluency. With these matters in mind, chapter 7 considers the ways in which ethnographers access, comprehend, study, and analyze the life-worlds into which they venture. Beyond a more standardized textual account of these issues, however, we've inserted sets of comments pertaining to our own experiences and observations with respect to various aspects of the research enterprise. Hopefully, this will help newcomers to the field appreciate the very human aspects of stage fright, ambiguity, adjustment, resistance, frustration, and readjustment that field research entails.

Chapter 8, "Writing Ethnographic Research Reports," builds on many of the notions developed in chapter 7, but follows it one step further as we (Prus, Shaffir, and Dietz) try to indicate how people might go about "producing an ethnographic text." This statement is not intended as a magic potion for creating ethnographic accounts, but rather represents a reference point for people embarking on this undertaking. Simply put, it is a statement dealing with the things that we routinely attempt to convey to our own students when they ask us how they might go about writing up their studies. Noting the sorts of objectives, practices, and dilemmas that undergird the production of ethnographic texts, we try to walk newcomers through the process. Thus, consideration is given to titles, introductions, literature reviews, methodological statements, data and analysis, conceptual contributions, and the like, indicating some of the different ways these may be developed or combined in practice.

Newcomers should be cautioned, however, that the style of research introduced here (that is, an interactive, open-ended, inquiry into the life-worlds of the other) also is apt to be one of the more challenging, difficult, and frustrating ventures on which one may embark. This approach requires considerable patience, self discipline, and perseverance. As well, since ethnographic research involves other people in a very direct interactive manner, one faces the task of obtaining cooperation from others on an ongoing basis. The matters of accessing others, gaining and maintaining their acceptance over a period of time, and achieving openness in dealing with them typically require considerable interpersonal flexibility, persistence, and congeniality.

Further, researchers attempting to study the life-worlds of others are apt to find themselves having to fend off the critiques of positivist social scientists and (more recently) deal with confusions generated by the postmodernists,[21] as well as the efforts of any variety of moralists or control agents who may attempt to tell researchers how they should proceed and what questions they should be asking of the other. Researchers may also find themselves explaining their projects to, or pursuing funding from, bureaucrats who want or are pressured into obtaining "quick (and usually highly simplistic) fixes" to some problem they are encountering.

The approach introduced here is by no means perfect, even when executed by the most competent researchers under the most ideal circumstances. Ethnographic research involves people and all the complexities that they develop in the course of coming to terms with their daily lives. The world of human lived experience cannot be reduced to nice, neat little boxes, charts or tables. Not only is every ethnography apt to be a labor-intensive undertaking, but the matter of building an intersubjective social science will also be a slow and challenging process.

Still, despite these drawbacks, those venturing into this mode of research are apt to find it one of the most fascinating and intellectually stimulating pursuits they might entertain. As well, because of its simultaneous open and situated nature, ethnographic research has the potential to be the most conceptually stimulating and rigorously grounded (i.e., empirical) mode of inquiry in the social sciences. And, when informed by interactionist premises, it also is the method that most thoroughly respects (i.e., is attentive to) the emergent nature of human lived experience:

> *It's not so much that they don't want to explain their situations, but until you've instilled that confidence in you as a person, they don't want to open up all that's good and bad about their business. . . . Once you get to know that businessman and show him that you're up front with him, then he'll let you know, "I'm having trouble in this area." They don't want you to go to another businessman and tell him, "Joe Blow down the street is really having troubles selling so and so's." Once you've established confidence with him, then he's not afraid to let you know what his problem is. . . . With repeat people, the more you work with them, the more you realize what it is that they really want to push. You begin to understand more about their businesses. . . . You have to listen. That's number one! The clients really do want to let you know about their businesses, because otherwise you can't help them. And I think that a lot of salesmen find that one of their biggest downfalls, they talk too much. And if you're talking, you're not listening. What you have to do is listen. (promotions-radio) (Prus, 1989a:88)*

Endnotes:

1. See Prus (1996:3–9, 203–16) for an extended consideration of the foundations of positivist social science and its relationship to the quest for intersubjectivity in the social sciences. Since the present discussion builds extensively on materials developed in that volume more generally, I will be

making references to that statement in order to avoid needless duplication of text.

2. Although pragmatism has become somewhat broadly diffused as a concept, the pragmatists were generally opposed to "rationalist" or "determinist" (i.e., positivist) philosophy and wanted to develop conceptualizations of human behavior that attended to the actual practices of people on a day-to-day basis. Charles Peirce, William James, John Dewey, Charles Horton Cooley, and George Herbert Mead are especially notable among the early pragmatists. Morris (1970) provides one of the best accounts of the pragmatist movement. For other literature and a summary statement on pragmatism which more specifically focuses on the development of symbolic interactionism, see Prus (1996:46–59).

3. Attending to the practical accomplishment of human activity, the pragmatist viewpoint breaks sharply with the postmodernist tendency to reduce all human productions to linguistic text. While centrally acknowledging the linguistic base of the human community, the approach taken here recognizes the privileging of claims that are essential for meaningful human activity to take place. For more extended critiques of the notion of an allegedly postmodernist social science, see Dawson and Prus (1993a, 1993b, 1995), Best (1995), Charmaz (1995), Sanders (1995), Schwalbe (1995), and Prus (1996:217–43). Stoddart's (1986) and Lofland's (1995) statements are also relevant to many of the more general issues addressed here. Prus and Dawson (1996) more explicitly discuss Blumer's notion of obdurate reality and the "privileging of presence" in developing ethnographic research. Also see note 12 in this chapter.

4. For a further elaboration of the fundamental intersubjectivity of the *human* community, see Prus (1996). For a more specific commentary on "humanist" positions (as commonly expressed) see Prus (1996:234–35n).

5. Chicago interactionism (and Blumer's own work) was also significantly shaped by the contributions of W. I. Thomas and Florian Znaniecki, Ellsworth Faris, Robert Park and Ernest Burgess, Everett Hughes, and a set of trail-blazing student ethnographers such as Nels Anderson, Clifford Shaw, Paul Cressey, and Francis Donovan (see Prus, 1996:113–34) as well as those (e.g., Anselm Strauss, Erving Goffman, Gregory Stone, Fred Davis, John Lofland and Jacqueline Wiseman) who were to follow in their footsteps. However, it was Herbert Blumer who most singularly articulated the basic premises and methodological orientations of what was to become known as symbolic interaction.

6. This position is developed in considerable detail in Prus (1996).

7. While I have provided a fuller discussion of Blumer's approach to the study of human behavior and his devastating critiques of mainstream social science elsewhere (Prus, 1996:127–32, 144–45, 245–50), scholars interested in the study of human behavior are well advised to read Blumer's (1969) collection of papers on symbolic interaction. Nowhere else is the theory of symbolic interaction (and the interrelated critiques of the positivist social science) so effectively developed.

8. An [object] is any item, thing, distinction, concept, behavior, or image to which people may refer (i.e., become aware of, attend to, point to, acknowledge, consider, discuss, or otherwise act toward). However, even when people attend to things on a more solitary basis, objects are best seen as problematic, intersubjectively informed constructions:

> Rather than endowing [objects] with inherent meanings or assuming that certain shapes, colors, masses, sizes, and the like, exist in pre-defined terms, the position taken here (Mead, 1934:78) is that people bring [objects] into existence by the ways in which they attend to, distinguish, define, and act toward these [experiential essences]. This is not to deny that [things] are "out there" or that particular [things] may impinge on people or resist people's efforts to do [things]. Indeed, the capacity for things to act on (and resist) people is central to Blumer's (1969) notion of an "obdurate reality" and the human struggle for existence. However, people's awarenesses of [things], the ways in which they view (delineate, categorize, appreciate) these [objects], and the manners in which people act toward the [objects] they've distinguished from other [things] are all problematic in scope, emphasis, and particulars. (Prus, 1996:11–12)

9. Don Evans's work (Evans, 1987, 1988, 1994; Evans and Falk, 1986) with deaf children provides particularly powerful portrayals of the problems that linguistically deprived or limited individuals have in forming, retaining, and communicating images that are readily accessible to (and often taken for granted by) those actively involved in the spoken world.

10. In no way should Blumer's observations about the limitations of ethnographic inquiry be seen as redeeming quantitative research in the social sciences. To the contrary, these problems are especially pronounced (and confounded!) by those embarking on survey and experimental research or "content analysis" in which the opportunities for achieving intersubjectivity with the other are severely limited. Although the data obtained in these manners is much more readily standardized and statistically processed (providing a surface impression of scientific rigor), the vital matter of achieving intersubjectivity is so problematic in these methodological ventures that the ensuing concerns of establishing evidence and developing viable concepts must be considered highly suspect from the viewpoint of adequately representing the human condition.

11. More sustained examinations of the physical sciences enterprise indicates that "science," like other realms of human endeavor, is very much a social product and a social process. While taking particular inspiration from the writings of Thomas Kuhn (1962) and Harold Garfinkel (1967), the sociologists most active in developing this new (or post-Mertonian) sociology of science include Barnes (1974), Barnes and Edge (1982), Knorr-Cetina (1981, 1983, 1995), Collins and Pinch (1982, 1993), Latour (1987), Star (1989), Clarke

and Gerson (1990), Pickering (1990, 1992, 1993, 1994), and Clarke and Fujimura (1992). For a more extended consideration of the linkages of this material with the interactionist/constructionist literature, see Prus (1996:94–98, 212–16).

12. Those adopting "postmodernist" and related viewpoints have also been critical of positivist social science, but they have contributed very little to the development of an intersubjective social science. While drawing attention, variously, to a relativistic, linguistically developed set of social worlds, those generating (e.g., Foucault, 1967, 1970, 1972; Derrida, 1976, 1978; Lyotard, 1984, 1985) and promoting (e.g., see Denzin and Lincoln, 1994), postmodernist/ poststructuralist viewpoints have concurrently become entangled in a series of cynical, subjectivist, expressive, and moralistic viewpoints and agendas. The result (in the proverbial "nutshell") is a massive production of messy, contradictory, often self-enchanting texts which fail to appreciate (a) the human struggle for existence, (b) the interactive essence of human group life, (c) the enterprising nature of the human condition, (d) the necessity of attending to the ways in which human group life is accomplished, or (e) the value of concepts and intellectual responsibility in the development of scientific enterprise. See Dawson and Prus (1993a, 1993b, 1995), Best (1995), Charmaz (1995), Sanders (1995), Schwalbe (1995), Prus (1996), and Prus and Dawson (1996) for more extended considerations of the viability of postmodernism for an intersubjective social science.

13. Focusing on resistances to change in the sphere of music, Becker (1995) makes a somewhat parallel case for the inertia associated with prevailing practices in the art world more generally.

14. As indicated elsewhere (Prus, 1996:212–16), the base-line premises undergirding the intersubjectivist and positivist paradigms are so different in emphasis that they do not lend themselves to viable synthesis (see references, therein, to the efforts of Max Weber, Norman Denzin, and Randall Collins) except under a recognition of the fundamental primacy of intersubjectivity. As a result, we may expect to see some scholars endorsing versions of theoretical and methodological pluralism. This tactic may allow some scholars to flip (theoretically and methodologically) back and forth in their own work, albeit in conceptually contradictory fashions, while in other cases this viewpoint may be invoked as a strategy to enable some people to pursue positivist social science without having to directly reconcile their current endeavors with the epistemological (conceptual relatedness of theory and method) issues at hand.

15. See Prus (1996) for a much fuller statement on the roots, foundational essences, variants, and controversies (positivist and postmodernist) of symbolic interaction. For other statements on symbolic interaction, see Mead (1934), (especially) Blumer (1969), Shibutani (1961), Laurer and Handel (1977), Charon (1979), Karp and Yoels (1979), Strauss (1993), and Morrione (n.d.).

16. Herbert Blumer (1969:2) uses three premises in developing his statement on symbolic interaction, while Anselm Strauss (1993) identifies nineteen premises. In earlier statements (Prus, 1987, 1989a, 1989b, 1994b),

I've used five premises to outline the conceptual core of interactionist thought (numbers 2, 3, 5, 6, and 7), but more recently (see Prus, 1996) have considered it important to emphasize the intersubjective (1) and activity-based (4) aspects more centrally than I had done in the past. Clearly, the overall content is much more important than the actual number of premises. While different readers may find one or other renderings of this material more helpful in enabling them to conceptualize interactionist thought, the material presented in this discussion is highly consistent with the other two authors, and indeed, Anselm Strauss (1993) and I have both benefitted enormously from Blumer's foundational statements on symbolic interactionism.

17. The matter of being born into preexisting cultural contexts has rather profound implications for people's senses of "reality" as well as their notions of the objects that exist in their life-worlds (Mead, 1934; Berger and Luckmann, 1966; Blumer, 1969; Prus, 1996, especially 11–18, 52–59, 150–52).

18. See Schutz (1962, 1964) and Berger and Luckmann (1966) for particularly valuable elaborations of the "objectification" (and typification) process as this pertains to people's sense of reality and their "stocks of knowledge."

19. For a fuller elaboration on rationality as a social process (i.e., problematic, reflective, negotiable), see Schutz (1962) and Prus (1989b:139–48).

20. Sometimes, as with archeological artifacts and longstanding historical documents, researchers may be forced to contextualize human productions without the benefit of engaging the participants in more direct interchanges, but it is important to appreciate the unavoidably speculative nature of these endeavors (even when working with what seems a great deal of "data"). There may also be other instances wherein social scientists, working on a more contemporary plane, can only "speculate" because ethnographic data is inaccessible for one reason or another. However, it is essential that scholars avoid building a social science on extended realms of speculation, however "learned" this may seem. For this reason, it is crucial that those studying "human behavior (and group life) in the contemporary scene" endeavor to engage the people involved in various aspects of its production in extended interchange so that they might more effectively achieve intimate familiarity with their subject matter.

21. See note 12 regarding postmodernism.

2

Subcultural Mosaics and Intersubjective Realities: Acknowledging Ambiguity, Activity, and Accomplishment

Although "culture" is seen as an essential, if not the central, feature of the social sciences, the concepts of culture with which most social scientists work (explicitly and implicitly) are not only inadequate for depicting the essence of the human condition, but they have also served to obstruct the more meaningful and productive analysis of human group life. The problem has originated, it seems, somewhat jointly as a consequence of attempting to approach the study of the human condition by invoking the positivist viewpoint (models and methods) of the physical sciences on the one hand and the tendency to envision culture in totalizing or integrated terms on the other. The two issues are interrelated, but the present statement focuses primarily on the latter, or "the cultural problematic." While the interpretivist (also hermeneutic, intersubjectivist, interactionist) critique provides the essential foundation for developing a social science that is genuinely attentive to human lived experience,[1] a somewhat parallel reformulation of the notion of culture is in order if we are to move toward a more thoroughgoing intersubjective social science. The concept of culture has been much overlooked or taken for granted by social scientists, but most current images of culture imply totalizing or integrating tendencies, which while seemingly innocent on the surface, nevertheless have served to discourage a more complete acceptance (and development) of a hermeneutic social science.

The approach taken here builds on a thoroughly intersubjectivist (vs. positivist/structuralist) vision of the human condition and a fundamental attentiveness to the ongoing accomplishment of activity in the human community. Introduced as an alternative to mainstream, totalizing images of culture, the subcultural mosaic (which may be envisioned as denoting a multiplicity of life-world involvements that constitute people's experiences of "society" at any given point in time) discussed here not only challenges the adequacy of prevailing images of culture for the study of human group life, but lays the foundation for an agenda that could revitalize the social sciences.

Reformulating the Cultural Problematic

[S]ubcultures evolve their own little communities or social worlds, each with its own local myths . . . , own legendary heroes . . . , own honorary members . . . , its own scale of reputations . . . , and its own social routine. . . . (Simmons, 1969:88–89)

[A]ny group of persons—prisoners, pilots, patients [in mental hospitals]—develop a life of their own that becomes meaningful, reasonable, and normal once you get close to it. (Goffman, 1961:ix–x)

In what was to become the dominant theoretical statement on culture for several decades, Alfred Louis Kroeber and Clyde Kluckhohn (1952) presented a massive review and assessment of the 160-plus definitions of culture they could locate in the social sciences. While tracing the origins of the term *culture* to eighteenth-century German scholarship (*kultur*; denoting the cultivation process, somewhat akin to the notion of civilization), Kroeber and Kluckhohn credit E. B. Tylor (1871:1) with the first explicit, contemporary usage definition of the term *culture* to refer to *that complex whole which includes knowledge, belief, art, law, morals, custom, and any other capabilities and habits acquired by man as a member of society.*

Kroeber and Kluckhohn depict a variety of emphasis in subsequent definitions of culture by anthropologists, sociologists, psychologists, and philosophers, designating these variously as descriptive, historical, normative, psychological, structural, genetic (products of association), and incomplete. Although considerable variation exists in these images of culture, a great many of these definitions assume, if not emphasize, the *totalizing*, integrating, or homogenizing aspects of culture (as opposed to variants within cultures). The following definitions of culture are somewhat prototypic in that sense:

. . . that complex whole which includes all habits acquired by man as a member of society. (Ruth Benedict, 1931:806 [in Kroeber and Kluckhohn, 1952:81])

It [culture] is the integral whole consisting of implements and consumers' goods, of constitutional characters for various social groupings, of human ideas and crafts, beliefs and customs. (Branislaw Malinowski, 1944:36 [in Kroeber and Kluckhohn, 1952:83])

Culture is the configuration of learned behavior and results of behavior whose component elements are shared and transmitted by members of a group. (Ralph Linton, 1945a:32 [in Kroeber and Kluckhohn, 1952:119])

Among the less integrative definitions of culture are the following:

. . . all social activities in the broadest sense, such as language, marriage, property system, etiquette, industries, art, etc.. (C. Wissler, 1920:3 [in Kroeber and Kluckhohn, 1952:81])

Culture is all behavior mediated by symbols. (R. Bain, 1942:87 [in Kroeber and Kluckhohn, 1952:137])

Culture is that name of a distinct order . . . of phenomena, namely, those things and events that are dependent upon the exercise of a mental ability, peculiar to the human species, that we have termed "symbolling." (Leslie White, 1949a:363 [in Kroeber and Kluckhohn, 1952:137])

However, as far as I can discern, the larger literature with which Kroeber and Kluckhohn deal presumes an overarching singularity or synthesis of culture as opposed to generating images of internal cultural diversity (disjunctures, integrations, and irrelevancies) that are bound together by virtue of mutuality of human interchange (as the mainstay of the human condition). Likewise, while Kroeber and Kluckhohn's discussion of "cultural relativism" (1952:345–54) is very thoughtful, they have given little consideration to "internal cultural (mosaic) relativism."

Even Florian Znaniecki who, rather uniquely for his time, envisions culture in constructionist and relativist terms, speaks as if culture were fairly homogeneous at each instance of societal existence:

The progress of knowledge about culture demonstrates more and more concretely the historical relativity of all human values, including science itself. The image of the world which we construct is a historical value, relative like all others, and

a different one will take its place in the future, even as it has
itself taken the place of another image . . . history shows that
it is relative and changing. (Znaniecki, 1919, especially 15–16
[in Kroeber and Kluckhohn, 1952:58–59])

Perhaps, in attending to matters such as the definitions of culture, the functions of culture, the variability of culture across time and space, the evolution (and diffusion) of culture, and the like (see White, 1973), anthropologists have been collectively diverted from further consideration of (subcultural) diversities within particular societies. In any event, there has been a tendency for anthropological fieldworkers to depict other societies in more singular, global terms; perhaps as a means of more dramatically comparing and contrasting these life-worlds with the seeming "dominant culture" of their home communities.[2]

Somewhat mindful of the dilemmas that anthropologists have been encountering in the field while working with more unified notions of culture, Kuper (1992) presents a set of conference papers on the problematics of conceptualizing society from a more integrationist viewpoint. Of the six highly diverse papers presented in that volume, one by Fredrik Barth is particularly relevant to the ensuing discussion.

In moving toward a theory of action which somewhat (albeit in a very limited and seemingly unwittingly fashion) parallels Blumer's conceptualization of symbolic interaction, Barth (1992) argues that "society" should *not* be viewed (variously) as (1) an aggregate of social relations, (2) an aggregate of institutions, or (3) a whole composed of parts. *Nor*, he contends, is it appropriate to (4) declare the entire world one society, a modern world system, (5) attempt to abstract society from the material context, or (6) use *society* as a term implying a homogenized essence of the social life-world.

In discarding these fallacies or misconceptions (his terms), Barth wants to emphasize (a) an attentiveness to interactional processes; (b) an awareness of disorder and incongruities in human associations; (c) the uneven connection between events and their interpretations; and (d) the problematic nature of all knowledge claims. Assessing the viability of cultural homogeneity or integration even with respect to the most primitive and pristine communities with which anthropologists may have contact, Barth says,

I would argue . . . that the anthropological construct of the
local community is itself a stifling, pervasive artifact of the
traditional anthropological fiction of society, which has often
perverted our understanding and representation of the realities

*of life in small communities and prevented the anthro-
pological fieldworker from noticing, depicting, and drawing
the required conclusions from evidence which is pervasively
accessible. (Barth, 1992:29)*

The solution to comprehending the ethnographic other, Barth
contends, revolves around the study of activity:

*If we wish to make our concept of 'society' useful to our
analysis of social relations and social institutions, as they
are manifest in the actions of people, we need to think of
society as the context of actions and the result of actions but
not as a thing—or it will persist as an ossified object in the
body of our developing social theory. (Barth, 1992:31)*

Although also recognizing culture as a consequential feature of
human group life, *sociologists* likewise have largely ignored the significance of culture diversities (and human activities) within societies for
the study of human lived experience. Generally speaking, those inspired
by Durkheim, Marx, and Weber have failed to attend to the human
enterprise entailed in accomplishing (defining, initiating, sustaining, and
dissipating) activities in any realm of human involvement. In the quest
for centralizing themes in society, these scholars and those following
them have disregarded the many realms of activity that characterize
human group life on a day-to-day basis. Likewise, those writing within
postmodernist/poststructuralist or cultural studies "traditions," while
more attentive than fundamentalist Marxists to multiple disciplines
of discourse (Foucault, 1977), local cultures (Lyotard, 1984), or to
diversities in historical epochs, class, race, and gender, have nevertheless continued to perpetuate notions of structural determinism.[3]

In contrast to those who have envisioned culture either as denoting
integrated systems of values and structures (functionalists, structural-
ists), oppressive modalities at either a grand level (Marxists, cultural
studies) or within microcosms of discourse (postmodernists), this
statement considers the multiplicities of life-worlds—connected and
disjointed, situated and transcontextual—that constitute human lived
experience, the realms in which people live, think, and act.

Acknowledging the Subcultural Mosaic

In developing this discussion of the subcultural mosaic, this chapter
draws central direction from the interpretivists (interactionists, reality

constructionists, ethnomethodologists) in sociology. It is this group of scholars (Dilthey [Ermarth, 1978]; Mead, 1934; Blumer, 1969; Schutz, 1962, 1964; Berger and Luckmann, 1966; Garfinkel, 1967) who have most explicitly attended to the human capacity for developing multiple intersubjectively informed frames of reference for engaging the world about them. Still, even these scholars have tended to consider one "life-world" at a time rather than ask about the implications of a multiplicity of life-worlds for comprehending people's experiences in particular communities. Likewise, although these and other social scientists working in the interpretive tradition have viewed group life generically (see Prus, 1987, 1994b, 1996) and have recognized people's involvements in different life-worlds on a sequential or concurrent basis, they have not adequately emphasized the extent to which people's experiences in the various subcultures, subcommunities, or plurality of life-worlds that constitute any given society represent the key to a cultural comprehension of that society.

In a somewhat related manner, sociologists (predominantly interactionists) working in the realm of deviance have long made reference to deviant "life-styles," "life-worlds," "subcultures," and the like (e.g., Thrasher, 1927; Shaw, 1930; Cressey, 1932; Sutherland, 1937; Becker, 1963; Lofland, 1966; Simmons, 1969; Prus and Sharper, 1977; Fine and Kleinman, 1979; Fine, 1983; and Sanders, 1989), but most of these studies have used terms of this sort primarily as a tool for contrasting particular "deviant" life-worlds with mainstream society. Although recognizing the existence of a great many diverse life-styles or subcultures (deviant and otherwise), even those engaging in ethnographic research have tended to take the subcultural mosaic for granted since most of their research focuses on one life-style setting at a time.[4]

While he does not pursue this theme very fully, in discussing "the methodological position of symbolic interaction," Herbert Blumer (1969:35–39) provides what may be envisioned as a foundational statement for the subcultural mosaic:

> *Let me begin by identifying the empirical world of human beings. This world is the actual group life of human beings. It consists of what they experience and do, individually and collectively, as they engage in their respective forms of living; it covers the large complexes of interlaced activities that grow up as the actions of some spread out to affect the actions of others; and it embodies the large variety of relations between the participants. . . . If one is going to respect the social world, one's problems, guiding conceptions, data, schemes of*

*relationship, and ideas of interpretation have to be faithful
to that empirical world. This is especially true in the case
of human group life because of the persistent tendency of
human beings in their collective life to build up separate
worlds, marked by an operating milieu of different life situations and by the possession of different beliefs and conceptions for handling these situations. One merely has to think
of the different worlds in the case of a military elite, the clergy
of a church, modern city prostitutes, . . . a gambling syndicate,
a university faculty, and so on endlessly. The modes of living
of such groups, the parade of situations they handle, their
institutions and their organizations, the relations between
their members, the views and images through which they see
their worlds, the personal organizations formed by their
members—all these and more reflect their different empirical
worlds. One should not blind oneself to the recognition of
the fact that human beings in carrying on their collective life
form very different kinds of worlds. To study them intel-
ligently, one has to know these worlds, and to know the
worlds one has to examine them closely. (Blumer, 1969:35,
38–39)*

Subsequently, the most explicit and sustained conceptual discussion of the notion that society is best understood from the viewpoint
of people operating in diverse sets of social worlds has come from
Anselm Strauss (1982, 1984, 1993):[5]

*The concept of social life worlds in the sociological and
interactionist sense is where I would begin thinking about
contemporary society. I shall argue that if the concept of
social worlds is made central to a conceptualization of
society, then a radically different view emerges. This view
is at odds with predominant models of society. . . . The
concept does require that we conceive of persons in modern
society as characteristically having membership in a multiplicity of worlds, ranging from a few memberships to a very
great number indeed. Thinking in terms of social worlds, their
activities, and their members is, I am arguing, immensely
useful in understanding the nature of the contemporary
world. . . .
    In each social world, at least one primary activity (along
with related clusters of activity) is strikingly evident; such*

as climbing mountains, researching, collecting. There are sites
where activities occur: hence space and landscape are relevant.
Technology *(inherited or innovative modes of carrying out the
social world's activities) is always involved. . . . In social
worlds at their outset, there may be only temporary divisions
of labor, but once under [way],* organizations *inevitably evolve
to further one aspect or another of the world's activities . . .
for instance, site finding, manufacturing, marketing, and the
teaching of technical skills. . . . Organizational building,
extending, defending, invading, taking over, and converting.
(Strauss, 1993:211–13)*

Given his (Blumerian-informed) emphasis on the production of action,
Strauss's materials on social worlds very much resonate with the
present statement, and his work has a great deal of potential for those
interested in understanding the processes by which social worlds
emerge and are sustained in the context of other social worlds. Still,
neither Strauss nor his students (e.g., Adele Clarke, Joan Fujimura,
Elihu Gerson, Susan Leigh Star) have pursued the study of the ongoing
accomplishment of activity in and across these life-worlds as fully
as they might have. Consequently, Strauss's formulations do not
provide as much direction as one might hope with respect to fieldwork
applications.

On another front, Harrison Trice (1993), who focuses on occupational and organizational contexts, also proposes that scholars explicitly
recognize that organizations are constituted of pluralities of occupational subcultures. Thus, he concludes his book by observing that (a)
occupations are to be studied as cultural realities, (b) occupational
cultures represent distinct subcultures within organizations, (c) organizations are primarily multicultural in nature, (d) subcultures imply
relationships and adaptations, and (e) occupational cultures are
continually in flux. While informed by some of the same literature,
Trice's orientation is considerably more structuralist (and typologically)
oriented than is the approach adopted here. Nevertheless, the material
developed in the present volume shows how researchers may examine
multi-subcultural notions of the sort to which Trice refers in actual
ethnographic research in organizational and occupational (as well as
an almost endless range of other) contexts.

At a more grounded, empirical level, the existence of a plurality
of subcultures is apparent in many ethnographic studies (e.g., Anderson,
1923; Shaw, 1930; Sutherland, 1937; Becker, 1963; Davis, 1963; Lofland,
1966; Lesieur, 1977; Prus and Sharper, 1977, 1991; Schneider and

Conrad, 1983; Steffensmeier, 1986; Haas and Shaffir, 1987; Sanders, 1989; Charmaz, 1991; Wolf, 1991; MacLeod, 1993; Fine, 1996). While primarily relying on single sets of actors, these studies offer readers an opportunity to envision some of the ways in which participants from particular life-worlds engage one another in intersecting settings. The coming together and interrelatedness of a plurality of subcultures or groups of interactants within particular settings is more explicit still in Cressey's (1932) study of taxi-dance halls, Wiseman's (1970) depiction of skid row agencies, and Roebuck and Frese's (1976) account of an after-hours bar. These works provide readers with more sustained accounts of the ways in which people in two or more distinct areas of endeavor jointly work out aspects of their lives in conjunction with one another.

Although we did not use the term, subcultural mosaic, the underlying notion of communities consisting of a plurality of diversely integrated subcultures became particularly impressed upon me when Styllianoss Irini and I were doing a study of "the hotel community" (Prus and Irini, 1980 [also see Irini and Prus, 1982; Prus, 1983]). Like most other researchers in the social sciences, I had been inclined to focus on one group, subculture, or category of people at a time, but this project indicated how limited this view was for conceptualizing people's activities, interconnectedness, and flux within community contexts. While we didn't anticipate doing so at the outset, we found ourselves attending to a great variety of activities, involvements, viewpoints, relationships, interchanges, and interrelatedness of people participating in a multitude of subcultures (variously as hookers, desk clerks, exotic dancers, musicians, bar staff, security people, rounders, and some rather diverse sets of patrons) within a larger community setting. Once one permeates the "deviant mystique" (Prus and Grills, n.d.), it also becomes evident that people's interactions in this setting are not so different from those taking place in the other (community) contexts in which people find themselves. Thus, the conceptual material we developed in the hotel community served as a sensitizing analytical frame for subsequent studies of marketing, sales, and consumer behavior (Prus, 1989a, 1989b, 1993b, 1994a; Prus and Frisby, 1990; Prus and Dawson, 1991), and economic development (Prus and Fleras, 1996).

The present statement on subcultural mosaics is very much informed by Blumer, Strauss, and others (particularly those working in the interactionist/ethnographic tradition), but it also builds on a set of *generic social processes* that reflects this same realm of scholarship.

While discussed in greater depth in chapter 3, generic social processes refer to:[6]

> ... the transsituational elements of interaction; to the abstracted, transcontextual formulations of social behavior. Denoting parallel sequences of activity across diverse contexts, generic social processes highlight the emergent, interpretive features of association. They focus our attention on the activities involved in the "doing" or accomplishing of human group life. (Prus, 1996:142)

Although central to the analysis of contemporary, urbanized societies, the conceptual frame introduced here seems no less relevant to highly isolated rural groups or bands of people. The approach taken is attentive to the meanings, interactions, and accomplishment of ongoing community life regardless of context.

By locating human endeavor within the context of generic social processes, the material presented here offers social scientists a means of developing analytical frames that both are applicable to highly situated inquiries and explicitly foster transcontextual comparisons. In addition to opening up and providing a means of synthesizing a great many realms of life in contemporary society, this statement also offers a means of resolving some dilemmas encountered by ethnographers in anthropology (particularly as this pertains to notions of cultural complexity and diversity, idiographic life-worlds, and cross-cultural comparisons).

The term **subcultural mosaic** refers to the multiplicity of subcultures, life-worlds, or group affiliations that constitute people's involvements in societies or communities at any point in time. While it may be useful to assign names to societies and communities as general reference points, and it may be instructive to consider some broad unifying themes within these contexts, it is essential that social scientists approach the notion of a central, overarching culture with considerable caution. Indeed, from the point of understanding human lived experiences and the accomplishment of community life, it seems counterproductive for social scientists to maintain a more totalizing image of culture.

Rather than envision any society or community (from the most elementary and homogeneous human communities to the most complex and diversified societies) as characterized by a dominant or highly pervasive culture, it is posited that *any society or community consists of people acting in a mosaic (or set, configuration, amalgamation,* matrix, or *collage) of diverse subcultures or life-worlds that exist in temporal, dialectic (and in many cases only indirectly connected) relationships to each other.*

This is *not* to deny certain tendencies toward cultural unity, such as that implied by central group identities and geographical co-presence,[7] groupwide assemblies, centralized communication forums, or overlapping memberships of people within particular subcultures. Likewise, no attempt is made to deny the existence of a basic (and essential) language that enables people within a society to attain a sense of intersubjectivity through an appreciation of "the generalized other" (Mead, 1934) and thereby achieve typical notions of "common sense" or a broadly based "taken-for-granted" reality (Schutz, 1962).[8]

As well, there typically are advantages for those even in the most autonomous and secretive of subcultures in the broader community to maintain some (even intentionally misdirected or deceptive) dialogue or relationship with others in the community, lest they be deprived of opportunities to sustain an existence in that setting. Still, despite these and some other tendencies toward unity, it will be argued that the great predominance of community life takes its shape through people's involvements, activities, and interchanges in shifting configurations of subcultural ventures.

People may orient themselves toward aspects of the broader culture in certain respects (e.g., attending to intersubjectively established notions of language, time, or prevailing monetary currencies), but people live, think, and act within a set of subcultural contexts (and the variants that they collectively develop and experience with others).[9] In the process, they may acknowledge as well as redefine the significance of any feature of the broader culture. Subcultural participants (within their more particularized life-worlds) may alter or challenge any aspect (viewpoints, activities, identities, relationships, linguistic practices, expressions of emotionality, and the like) that they associate with the broader community culture, as well as develop more unique sets of cultural configurations unto themselves. However, these people also coexist within broader contexts and typically incorporate a great many features of that broader community into their own theaters of operation.

Thus, this statement is not intended as a denial of transcontextual intersubjectivities within societies, but rather emphasizes the widespread pervasiveness of subcultural involvements within societies. Accordingly, it is proposed that *the study of human group life in any community is most adequately accomplished when social scientists are acutely attentive to people's multiple life-world involvements, because it is within these subcultural contexts that human activity takes place.*

The recognition of the centrality of a subcultural matrix for understanding human group life seems a simple claim, and yet, if taken seriously, it could have wide-sweeping implications for the ways in which social scientists approach the study of human group life. It also may foster a more explicit blending of "macro" and "micro" levels of analysis in a manner that attains considerable theoretical and methodological coherence as this pertains to the study of human lived experience.[10]

Culture as "Something in the Making"

Rather than view culture as a unified object or an objective condition, it is proposed that **culture** *be seen as "something in the making,"* as a multidimensional set of human processes, practices, and products whose interlinkages are problematic and tenuous.

Culture is an intersubjective or community-based essence that derives its existence from the development of shared meanings or the abilities of people to attend to one another, to convey understandings to the other, and to acknowledge the viewpoint of the other. It hinges on people's abilities to make indications [of things] to self and others and to achieve a mutuality of focus and sensation. Intersubjectivity is contingent, as well, on people's abilities to retain images of [objects] encountered and to develop (symbolic) representations of those images. It is this ability of people to retain images and achieve more enduring representations that can be conveyed to, and experienced by, others that allows humans to develop more sustained cultures.

Although people may reshape the physical environment in highly diverse manners and generate various physical artifacts, *culture exists most fundamentally as an (intersubjectively) enacted phenomenon, a symbolically experienced set of human endeavors or enterprises.* Culture is *a linguistically mediated process,* but it is much more than a linguistic phenomenon. Culture encompasses people's (linguistically developed, conveyed, and sustained) *stocks of knowledge* in a most comprehensive sense (i.e., people's language, definitions of "objects," techniques and modes of acting toward objects [including tools and technologies], and styles of relating to others and oneself), but culture is most effectively realized as people *do things* (i.e., in the course of engaging in meaningful activity).

Signifying viewpoints and tentative lines of action, *culture is also a uniquely enabling phenomenon;* while people may disattend or challenge earlier notions of culture, the stocks of knowledge which people have developed to this and that point in time allow individuals in those communities to make sense of, and act toward [the world] in which they find themselves. People may develop very different ways of acting toward [the world out there] on a community-to-community basis, but the linguistically mediated realities (and stocks of knowledge) that people (in each community) collectively create to this and that point of their existence are essential for the comprehension of human lived experience.

Not only does (shared) language allow individual members of particular communities to distinguish [objects] from [other objects], but language also enables those individuals to bring into existence entire (but particular) worlds of objects and to locate themselves and others within those notions of "reality." This point is made especially effectively by Mead (1934:78):

> *Symbolization constitutes objects not constituted before, objects that would not exist except for the context of social relationships wherein symbolization occurs. Language does not simply symbolize a situation or object which is already there in advance; it makes possible the existence or appearance of that situation or object, for it is a part of the mechanism whereby that situation or object is created.*

While cultural notions may become "objectified" at a rudimentary level whenever two or more people (appear to) agree on indications [of objects] and an associated set of sensations or meanings, the *objectification process* (see Berger and Luckmann, 1966) can be seen to become intensified (enduring) when people (a) attach names to these [objects]; (b) share these notions with contemporaries; (c) transmit these notions to newcomers (and subsequent generations); (d) continue to act toward those particular objects in the manner indicated; (e) adjust their activities to accommodate or acknowledge these notions; (f) more explicitly recognize these practices on a collective or community-wide basis; and (g) envision collective and individual interests or uses for perpetuating these practices.

Insofar as the term *culture* may be applied to the entire range of human endeavor in any given society, there may be a tendency on the part of some analysts to assume a more unified or dominant culture than may be merited. In this respect, it is essential to distinguish hypothetical images of (mainstream) culture of a given society (often expressed as some tendency toward the [artificially generated] statistical mean) from those human productions (e.g., language, shared identities, common practices) which foster senses or realms of trans-contextual intersubjectivities within community contexts.

While emphasizing the existence of a multiplicity of life-worlds, the notion of a subcultural mosaic does not deny possible integration of cultural themes on either a situated or enduring basis. It does, however, draw attention to the *human enterprise* entailed in developing and sustaining particular cultural themes within community contexts. Thus, while people may disattend to any linkages between two or more cultural themes (e.g., religion and owning property or driving cars), or more explicitly attempt to separate two or more cultural themes (e.g., commercialism, religion, and sexuality), they may also find it strategically advantageous to integrate (and justify the synthesis of) two or more cultural themes. Sometimes, people merge or blend two or more themes at certain points in time (consider the practices of moralists, politicians, and lawyers) in attempting to make their definitions of the situation more compelling to others.[11] This also may occur on a more sustained basis. Consider retailers catering to certain cultural themes (such as weddings, birthdays, parties, or recreational pursuits) to generate and perpetuate sales. Likewise, on a more cyclical basis, merchants, parents, and children (each pursuing their role-related interests) all may foster commercialism with respect to Christmas, Easter, and Halloween, for instance. However, other than the fact that people in the same broader community are interrelating or synthesizing things, there may be no necessary connection between any two (cultural) themes in a given setting. There may be certain practical advantages for "members at large" to engage in certain activities that serve to foster "cultural integration" or "cultural continuity," but social scientists who fail to acknowledge the fuller—*disconnected* and *integrated*—range of cultural themes operative in any community may be generating analytical impediments for understanding human group life.

This is not to suggest that social scientists ignore the objectification process or people's tendencies to homogenize, integrate, and perpetuate various cultural themes; quite the contrary, for these denote important aspects of human group life. However, *unless students of human behavior attend to the many different life-worlds that make up (the subcultural mosaic of) a society, they are apt to miss a great deal of human lived experience as this pertains to both the human struggle for existence and the development of any other matters to which people in particular human groups may attend.* Quite simply, to do so is apt to result in an extensive simplification and truncation of "the human culture" developed in any society.

Attending to Subcultural Enterprises

If societies are to be envisioned as subcultural mosaics, matrixes, collages, amalgamations, or configurations of sorts, some further discussion of the concept of subculture or social life-world is necessary. The term *subculture* is generally used herein to refer to a *set of interactionally linked people characterized by some sense of distinctiveness (outsider and insider definitions) within the broader community.*[12] Subcultures typically develop around some form of activity, but imply reflectivity, interaction and continuity over time.

While contingent on communication between the participants, subcultural communication is not limited to face-to-face interaction (consider mail, telephone, and computer linkages), nor need it imply direct interaction between all members of the subculture (others may provide interactive linkages). Thus, while a great many subcultures are built directly on face-to-face interactions, it is not necessary that those involved in any particular subculture reside in the same geographic setting or even know of each other's existence.

Some subcultures may be very small (two-person groups), although others may encompass virtually all members of some larger identifiable community. Even in these latter cases, though, it should be appreciated that any subculture will represent only one theme in the lives of the participants. Further, even while organized around particular life-themes, subcultures need not be homogenous within. Indeed, not only may participants be quite heterogeneous in many regards, but they may also assume a variety of roles with respect to any particular subcultural theme.[13] Subcultures are also amenable to factions and splinterings within; hence, the notion of "subcultural variants" is a noteworthy aspect of the subcultural mosaic, and recognizes that participants may develop subthemes pertinent to more encompassing realms of activity.[14]

Subcultures may develop around any set of pursuits that the participants find meaningful in some respect, but they are also characterized by the development of somewhat unique *perspectives, identities* (of insiders and outsiders), *activities, relationships, commitments, styles of emotional expressiveness,* and *modes of communication* (jargon, styles of talk). These matters will be discussed in more detail later, but even in the seemingly most elementary societies, we may expect to find a multitude of subcultural themes that people develop both in the course of pursuing the human struggle for existence and as they generate secondary activities, interests, and associations with respect to one another.

Each realm of enterprise, each subset of interactants, each shared variant of understandings (perspectives), each set of activities, each package of mutually acknowledged identities, each realm of commitment, each context of emotional expression, and each particular style of communication serves to define aspects of people's life-worlds that, even in more transient instances, provide departures and breaks from any (presumed) overarching culture.

The subcultures operative in any given community exist in multidimensional, uneven, and shifting relationships to one another.[15] Any two or more subcultures may exist concurrently or sequentially in a historical sense. Likewise, they may be interconnected by reference to overlapping perspectives, activities, relationships, and the like, or they may be quite removed from one another in any of these regards. A (particular) subculture may be subsumed by another (broader) subculture, or exist independently of the other. A subculture may be envisioned as supportive of another subculture, or it may be viewed in oppositional, competitive, or unrelated terms. All of the participants in some subcultures may agree extensively on exactly who the other participants may be, while in other instances, participants may be uncertain about who the other "members" might be or even whether they themselves might be defined as genuine members of that subcultural venture.[16]

The participants in some subcultures may be more exclusionary in their composition, while others may attempt to include everyone in their enterprises. Subcultures may also operate with varying degrees of voluntary (vs. involuntary) participation and may invoke wide ranges of strategies designed to deal with troublesome instances both from within and outside the association at hand. In relative terms, as well, some subcultures may be envisioned as more central or consequential in the broader community than others, some subcultures may become more enduring features of community life, and some subcultures may make heavier demands on their participants.

Likewise, while the members of some subcultures may strive for autonomy within the broader community, those involved in certain subcultures may attempt to control other subcultures in the community.[17] Some subcultures may operate very casually or informally, while others may become highly "objectified" as a consequence of the ways in which the participants develop, present, and attempt to maintain their perspectives, practices, identities, and so forth.

Working Notions of Subcultural Variants

Given the endless assortment of contexts (and levels) in which the concept *subculture* may be applied, it may be worthwhile to suggest some terms that may enable researchers and other analysts to work more effectively within the notion of a subcultural mosaic. Readers are cautioned that these terms are suggestive and inevitably will lend themselves to some diversity of application. Thus, while the working definitions provided here may foster some continuity across research settings, those employing these terms have an obligation to define the context in which these or similar terms are used and to use them consistently within those frames of reference. Readers, accordingly, should be attentive to the situated applications or contexts in which these terms are used.

Local, Embedded, and Translocational Associations. Although matters of location represent only one feature of subcultural involvements, it seems fitting to suggest some terms that people may find useful in attending to matters of physical presence. *Local subcultures* refer to more or less sustained and focused gatherings of people that operate within particular settings (e.g., church X in a community; a local police department; family X, Y, or Z in a neighborhood; a city baseball league; the patrons and staff at bars 1, 2, or 3; two friends A and B; and the like).

Embedded or *nested subcultures* are those groups that operate within local subcultures (e.g., cliques within a local church or a traffic division in the police department; two siblings in family X; the members of baseball team K; the staff community at bar 1). Likewise any triad may be seen to consist of three embedded (dyadic) subcultures (assuming that each of the three people involved interacts somewhat autonomously with the other two).

In many instances, the application of the term *local* or *embedded* to a particular unit of association will reflect the focal point of the analyst in the setting. A friendship dyad, thus, may denote a local subculture for some purposes, but would be an embedded or nested subculture were the dyad to become incorporated into or located within a larger grouping.[18] For example, two children who develop and sustain a friendship at school (where the school could be defined as the local subculture in this case) would represent an embedded subculture, whereas two children who play together after school, largely unsupervised (nonembedded), could be seen to represent a local subculture on their own.

The local-embedded distinction need not be critical for understanding the relationships that ensue in some settings, but it does provide analysts with a distinction that may be very useful in other contexts. Further, whereas the term *local subculture* may imply more autonomy than does the notion of *situated* or *embedded subculture*, it may be best to envision autonomy as relative, problematic, and processual in all instances. Since all subcultures are located within broader communities, outsiders may impose themselves on particular subcultures in a variety of ways (e.g., support, control, elimination) during the course of their existence.

Translocal subcultures refer to those associations that transcend local subcultures in some manner. As with notion of an embedded or nested subculture, depending on the way in which the term *local subculture* has been used, translocal subcultures may imply a broader base of involvement in a particular geographical community or may reflect more widespread regional subcultural linkages. Thus, the term may be used to refer to a city school system or a city police department, which may be seen both to encompass and be largely constituted by the (local) schools or (local) precincts under its jurisdiction. In a somewhat parallel fashion, when one focuses on a particular (local) department or set of (local) departments in an academic setting, then the host university may be seen as a translocal subculture.

In other instances, the terms *regional* and *transregional, national,* and *transnational subcultures* may be applied to indicate an increasingly broader geographical or organizational interconnectedness of participants in some focal pursuit. Clearly, some subcultures exist on several geographical and organizational planes, implying various horizontal as well as vertical linkages. In all instances, however, it is the connectedness of interactants that provides the essential foundation of the larger (translocal, regional, or transnational) subculture in question, while examinations of more localized and embedded subcultures within and the communicative interlinks between these various elements are apt to shed more light on the ongoing accomplishment of community life. It is useful to keep in mind, too, that while people involved in subcultures embedded in other subcultures (e.g., transnational corporations) may see themselves as "the locals," so may those (embedded) in the "head offices" of these associations view themselves as the "locals." Depending on the definition of their project, analysts may define either one of these or some other group as the "local subculture" for this or that purpose.

While subcultures are most commonly envisioned as bounded or encompassed by broader, singular societies, it is important that social scientists also attend to *transnational* or *transsocietal subcultures*, those subcultures that transcend particular societies or geographical domains. Images of multinational corporations are relevant here, but so too are those (mega-transsocietal subcultures) associations which pursue transsocietal or global agendas with respect to religion (e.g., Roman Catholicism), politics (communism), health care (Red Cross), human rights and welfare (United Nations), marketing (multinational corporations), and so forth.[19] On a less prominent (micro-transsocietal) scale, one might also recognize that many individuals from different (home) societies may be involved in a variety of transnational networks or subcommunities. Here, one may consider migrant family members who live in one nation but also maintain contact with families and friends in the country "back home"; pen pals or (more recently) computer-networked correspondents located in different countries; or a group of scientists who maintain contact with colleagues on an international level through publications, direct correspondence, or face-to-face conferences and other meetings. Although geographically separated from one another, these people may maintain (subcultural) contact through the media, personal travel, and other interpersonal communications venues. These involvements (business, religion, politics, family, friendship, scientific relations) may rather uniquely transcend local or home cultures, but they can be readily examined as further instances of subcultures in an analytical sense. They do, however, point to another limitation of attempts to explain behavior in reference to holistic notions of culture, at least in more contemporary society.[20] As well, lest some be tempted to attribute transnationality to some magical "postmodernist" development,[21] it might be appreciated that subcultural agendas (religious, political, family ties) of these sorts may well have transcended particular societies for as long as people have had the means of carrying or conveying messages to people in other geographical sectors of the world.

Totalizing, Focused, and Interfused Subcultures. On another level, researchers may sometimes find it useful to distinguish *totalizing subcultures*, or those that encompass virtually all areas of participants' lives, from more *focused subcultures*. Total institutions (Goffman, 1961) such as mental hospitals, prisons, convents, and the like may most sharply epitomize totalizing subcultures, but somewhat parallel tendencies may also be noted among people involved in cults, marriages (Whitehurst, n.d.), some work roles,[22] and recreational pursuits, wherein involvements imply a more encompassing way of life. Other subcultural involvements may be much more focused or delimited, as when groups of people assemble to pursue certain kinds of activities with the implied understanding that this activity most likely will not significantly spill over into other realms of their lives. However, as Goffman (1961) so effectively observes, cooperation is problematic even in totalizing institutions, while people may develop very intense fascinations with (and totalizing involvements in) activities that would seem on the surface to represent highly focused involvements.[23]

It also may be useful in some settings to utilize the notion of *interfused subcultures* to refer to circumstances in which people find themselves more or less simultaneously involved in or actively engaged in managing two or more situationally coexistent subcultures. Adler and Adler's (1991) study of the dual life-worlds of college athletes represents an instance of interfused subcultures, as does Baroody-Hart and Farrell's (1987) account of prison artists. Representing the site of several situationally coexistent subcultures (e.g., hookers, strippers, bar staff, patrons, thieves), the bar/hotel community (Roebuck and Frese, 1976; Prus and Irini, 1980) may also be envisioned as another instance of a interfused subculture. What is most consequential about interfused subcultures are the multiplicity of "central" activities and the problematic and shifting nature of people's opportunities, involvements, and emphases within more or less concurrent time-frames.

Cyclical, Occasional, and Supportive Subcultural Phenomena. Three other subcultural distinctions which some analysts may find useful are those involving cyclical, occasioned, and supportive endeavors. *Cyclical subcultures* refer to those realms of involvement that entail a seasonal or calendar dimension of sorts. In contemporary North America more generally, these recurrent, collectively sustained, subcultural themes would include such things as Christmas, Easter, Thanksgiving, Halloween, Independence day (U.S.A.), Mother's Day, New Year's, and Valentine's Day. At more of a local community level, any variety of festivals and events represent annual or seasonal instances in which certain (subcultural) practices may be invoked. In smaller groups, people may attend to "anniversaries" of sorts, birthdays, and other (recurrent) "special" days or occasions. Calendars have long provided an important means of "objectifying dates" in Western society, while any variety of religious, political, financial, recreational, or sentimental interests that people associate with particular cyclical events may generate the motivated continuity and enterprise necessary to sustain these matters over periods of relative inactivity (one should not, however, overlook more enduring, behind-the-scenes preparations).

Occasioned subcultural involvements are somewhat akin to cyclical pursuits, but denote people's (usually temporarily defined) participation in certain kinds of situations. People who are getting married, dealing with funerals, spending time in the hospital, selling a house, going on holidays,[24] and the like typically find themselves in association with other people who either are also occasioned in the setting in directly parallel or interlinked roles or, who on a more sustained basis, facilitate particular activities on the part of others.

A consideration of impending weddings affords access to an occasioned subculture, which not only has endured for some time despite a continual flow (entries and exits) of the seemingly most central figures through this situation, but also appears likely to continue for some time.[25] Depending somewhat on the period of engagement and people's wedding plans, not only the couple to be married but many of their relatives and friends also may find themselves becoming rather involved in the wedding subculture. On a very general level, this occasion may become the focus of considerable attention in many conversations with others in the community (who relive their own experiences, offer advice [e.g., have a church wedding; have a big reception; elope!], and the like), as well as those involved in the wedding party, the reception, and other events (e.g., showers) as guests, coordinators, and financial sponsors.

In contemporary society, one also finds an assortment of "service specialists" (ministers, jewellers, bridal boutiques, florists, caterers, hairstylists, photographers, and the like) who have organized themselves (sometimes exclusively, sometimes partially) around the wedding subculture. And, whereas bridal parties may come and go, these service specialists not only provide continuity to those they successively encounter, but may also promote the wedding subculture in various ways (e.g., media, bridal shows, display windows) on their own. Although less elaborated, one may make a similar case for those experiencing (as participants and facilitators) the divorce subculture (Waller, 1930; Hunt, 1966; Vaughan, 1986). While the participants represent the essential grist for occasioned subcultural mills in these and other instances, those involved as service specialists or facilitators may also establish *supportive subcultures* around their enterprises. Thus, although a particular bridal boutique or a catering business may be seen as a local subculture, people involved in various "facilitating industries" may also form translocal (possibly national and international) subcultures or associations for other forms of interaction and promotion of their particular realms of enterprise.

Toward a Conclusion

While struggling on the one hand with attempts to adopt the methods of the physical sciences to the study of human group life, and with agendas designed to alter the course of human group life on the other, scholars in the social sciences over the past century also have been working (implicity and explicitly) with totalizing images of culture that distort the actualities of human experience. All three of these orientations have served to obstruct the central mission of the social sciences, namely, to develop a comprehensive, intimately informed body of knowledge about the human condition.

At base, the concept of a subcultural mosaic represents a relatively simple reformulation of ideas that have long been implied in Chicago (interactionist) ethnography, but the implications of making this viewpoint explicit are rather substantial. In contrast to tendencies on the part of those in the social sciences to envision human community life (and associated research agendas) as represented variously by, or in combinations of, (a) an integrated set of institutions (structural-functionalism), (b) complexes of structures and factors (positivism, structuralism), (c) theories of oppression (Marxism), or (d) cynical and playful expressivity (postmodernism), *the subcultural mosaic* draws attention to the primacy of human intersubjectivity and the inter-related practical (and problematic) accomplishment of activity. By conceptualizing human group life as entailing a subcultural mosaic, as opposed to a totalizing culture, social scientists may overcome a seemingly innocuous but very consequential element that has impeded the development of a genuinely intersubjectivist social science.

Although ethnographers engaged in subcultural research are apt to have worked with implicit appreciations of a subcultural mosaic, even they are apt to find it particularly valuable to deal with this notion on a more explicit level. Minimally, it enables researchers both to attain a sharper contextual focus and to achieve conceptual trans-contextuality with research on other life-worlds.

An appreciation of the subcultural mosaic also suggests that ethnographic research is much more essential for understanding "mainstream" (sub)cultural life-styles than has commonly been assumed. As will become more evident in chapters 3, 4, and 5, the concept of the subcultural mosaic also opens up vast domains of ethnographic inquiry. It provides social scientists with a vital entry point for theoretically, methodologically, and substantively examining the great many realms of enterprise that constitute the pragmatically lived features of the human community.

Endnotes:

1. The interpretivist critique was introduced to the social sciences most centrally by Wilhelm Dilthey (Ermarth, 1978), but is expressed most effectively by Herbert Blumer (1969). For an elaboration of the development of the interpretive tradition in the social sciences and an extended consideration of mainstream (positivist) social science, see Prus (1996).

2. Part of the reason that anthropologists have had so much difficulty permeating other societies is that they've not only had to acquire linguistic and other interactional capacities for achieving intersubjectivity with the ethnographic other, but they've encountered subcultural mosaics that have been developed (and mixed) rather independently of those in their home societies. Even when they've focused on specific "institutions," anthropological fieldworkers have tended to assume that the community in question could be characterized by centralizing qualities or overarching rationalities. By attending to processes and the human production of action, the concept of *subcultural mosaic* enables scholars to avoid pitfalls of this sort while enabling them to appreciate the rich diversity of pursuits entailed in the human struggle for existence in any community.

3. While clearly reacting against Marxist conceptualizations of materialism, hegemony, and sovereign control of cultural productions (viewed as bogus, grand narratives), Foucault and Lyotard have continued to perpetuate notions of cultural homogeneity and organizational determinism within disciplinary power sites and local (predominantly institutional) settings. These "sites" and "settings," however, appear to represent multiple instances of hegemonic microcosms in which those thusly caught up are dominated (body and mind) in a totalizing sense. For further elaborations of the practical limitations of postmodernist thought for the social sciences, see Dawson and Prus (1993a, 1993b; 1995), Best (1995), Charmaz (1995), Sanders (1995), Prus (1996), and Prus and Dawson (1996). Although arguing that each historical era is characterized by its own peculiar cultural mix, with respect to (the social constructs of) class, race, gender, and such, those engaged in "cultural studies," likewise, have essentially replaced Marx's grand sweeping images of material determinism with a plurality of "factors" (or "structures") that they allege define the central essences of cultural contexts.

4. Further, while generally appreciating the parallel or generic processes characterizing people's experiences in deviant life-worlds (e.g., Goffman, 1961, 1963; Becker, 1963; Lofland, 1969), only a few of those working in this tradition have made explicit reference to the simultaneous and overlapping coexistence of persons in different deviant subcultures (D. Arnold, 1970; Miller, 1978; Prus

and Irini, 1980). Howard Becker (1966:viii) makes passing reference to the notion of a mosaic in introducing Shaw's *The Jack-Roller* (1930), but has not, as far as I know, developed this notion further.

5. Although noting some parallels with Berger and Luckmann's (1966) concept of "symbolic universes," Strauss (1993:159) traces his indebtedness to Shibutani (1955) and the Chicago school of symbolic interaction more generally, but also seems (Strauss, 1984:123–24) to have been inspired specifically by Kling and Gerson (1978) and Becker (1982).

6. As I've indicated elsewhere (Prus, 1987), the formulation of the material on generic social processes also has benefitted from Strauss's work (particularly Glaser and Strauss [1967] on the formulation of "grounded theory," and Strauss [1970]).

7. Insofar as people (as insiders and outsiders) define some group as constituting a distinctive collection of people, some notion of cultural homogeneity is perpetuated by this sense of inclusiveness. As well, when people occupy the same designated geographical territories, they may begin to sense a commonality of place by virtue of a greater awareness of, and opportunities for contacts with, others in that area.

8. The most consequential element fostering a sense of common culture is a (shared) language. To the extent that there is any "common-sense"—making capacity in the broader community, it is contingent on intersubjective realization, and this is possible only because people find some means of conveying meanings and comprehending (even if imperfectly) one another. Notions of these sorts form the core of an overarching culture, and are important in that respect. However, what is concealed are the underlying subcultures which develop around *the different activities entailed in implementing ongoing community life*. It is not enough to observe that most people in a community might agree on how to tell time, that water is something to drink, or that theft is wrong. If we are to understand human group life, we need to see how community life is accomplished in practice, and here the notion of a common culture is of limited assistance. Further, while language may represent the key feature linking the members of the broader community, language should not be confused with the ongoing accomplishment of human activity. Language enables people to function (distinctively) as humans, as minded, interacting beings, but the practical tasks entailed in the human struggle for existence, as well as the pursuit of any variety of secondary interests, take people into yet other realms of human enterprise, with each realm of human activity implying another subcultural theme (and other notions of communicative fluency).

9. Compared to the number and diversity of life-styles to which contemporary urban dwellers are apt to be exposed, a small, highly isolated band of people without any access to modern technology may seem "subculturally impoverished." However, even though their opportunities for cultural homogeneity or cultural closure may seem greater, it should not be assumed that they do not develop a series of subcultures within their own life-worlds.

First, even though their options may be more limited, we should not assume that everyone participates in every activity. Likewise, when virtually all members participate in shared activities, we should not assume that everyone is equally involved (or attains or remains at the same level of participation). Even where the very same people are involved in all of the activities characterizing a particular community, they are apt to assume somewhat different roles with respect to each of the activities involved and may be seen in different ways (by themselves and others) with respect to each set of activities in which the common group engages. Not only are people likely to develop differing skills and interests, and have variable amounts of available time in which to pursue particular activities, but they are also apt to be differentially received by others in the setting (especially over time).

The notion of an overarching culture is even more difficult to sustain in contemporary urban society, at least as a central concept for explaining human lived experience. While formal education systems may be established to generate a common linguistically adept and knowledgeable society, this only pertains to limited realms of people's lives. People using the media (e.g., newspapers, books, radio, movies, television) may also contribute to the maintenance of a common culture in some respects. However, the media may also serve to generate an awareness of a multiplicity of subcultures within the community as well as cater to an assortment of subcultural ventures within the broader community. Even in highly constrained (uniform message) settings, it should not be assumed that people will either consistently attend to these sources or interpret those messages in the same (or intended) fashions. When more diverse messages and multiple avenues of the media are available to people, they may assume more active roles in selecting out those to which they will attend. Thus, while the media may foster shared awarenesses across wide cross-sections of people, the media may be used with any variety of (subcultural) applications in mind and interpreted in an even larger assortment of manners by those encountering these messages on their own or in the context of ongoing interaction with others.

10. See Prus (1996) for a fuller discussion of the foundational (and epistemological) basis on interpretivist (especially symbolic interactionist) theory and methodology as this compares and contrasts with both positivist (structuralist) and postmodernist orientations to the social sciences.

11. Depicting the definitional, constructionist foundations of "social problems," Blumer (1971) provides a valuable indication of the ways in which people bring various cultural themes together in promoting their definitions of situations (and, conversely, resisting the viewpoints of others). Garfinkel's (1956) discussion of "degradation ceremonies" affords another powerful illustration of situated blendings of mixed cultural themes (e.g., morality, culpability, integrity), as do Klapp's (1962, 1964) portrayals of "heroes, villains, and fools" and (related) "symbolic leaders."

12. Subcultures should not be confused with "categories of people" (e.g., children, females, rich), although people may form subcultures by drawing

members from within particular categories of people (see Daniel Wolf's [1991] examination of outlaw bikers and Charlotte Wolf's [1994] portrayal of conversion to feminism). As Fine and Kleinman (1979) emphasize, subcultures imply an interlocking (interacting) group culture that is quite distinct from simple typification practices. People sometimes attribute subcultural qualities to particular categories of people and may in the process encourage some conscious identification and interaction along these lines, but only those people who become caught up in more direct, focused interchanges with others may be seen as involved in subcultures.

13. Beyond differing interests in pursuing particular activities, people's (differing) involvements in other activities may facilitate or restrict their opportunities to engage in particular subcultures. As well, while all members may participate in certain activities, subcultures typically entail a variety of tasks which need not (and possibly cannot) be performed by all participants. As well, in addition to those more directly involved in the activities at hand, some people may be involved essentially as facilitators of sorts. Consider, for instance, parents who enroll, fund, and "taxi" their children to various recreational (subcultural) pursuits.

14. This brings us to the question of how far one can reasonably extend the concept of subculture or subcultural variants. Although all "linguistically socialized" individuals (as self-reflective, self-communicating entities) may be seen as able to create variants on cultural themes on a solitary basis, and may later share these notions with others, the term *subculture* seems best not pushed beyond the dyad (representing the most basic unit for the actual sharing or interchange of symbols).

15. Readers are also referred to Strauss's (1993:215–19) insightful discussion of the relationships of subworlds to one another, wherein he attends to matters of origin, distinction, and intersections of life-worlds.

16. Albeit brief, I found Simmons's (1969:88–92) discussion of subcultures very helpful in formulating my thoughts in this area.

17. Those involved in moral crusades and control agency work may be seen to engage in *impositional subcultures* of sorts. Some missions are much more broadly defined and enduring than others, but the people involved in these ventures generally intend that their directives will have more "pervasive" or "transcontextual" applications. Consider antiabortion and antismoking campaigns on the one hand and, on the other, control agents such as school teachers, police officers, and judges, who assume the task of protecting, enabling, or overseeing people's life-styles within broader domains.

18. On some occasions, researchers may find it useful to invoke the term *microsubculture*, referring to small group associations, as well as make references to *dyadic* and *triadic subcultures* more specifically in the course of their analysis. Depending on one's frame of reference, each instance may represent a local (e.g., a local dyadic or local micro-) or an embedded (e.g., embedded triadic or embedded micro-) subculture.

19. The term *megasubculture* may be employed to indicate comparatively vast subcultures or those widely diffused within some large (possibly global) geographical region. The term may be useful in referring to large-scale conglomerates and other vast corporate "empires," as well as other more molar or massive associations (political, religious, recreational). Communication and coordination may seem especially problematic in these multiple-layered and wide-ranging subcultural contexts, but it should be appreciated that only by developing reasonably effective communication channels and coordination practices have these enterprises been able to grow, develop, and maintain themselves over extended periods of time. On the reverse side, it may be acknowledged that the more fundamental difficulties people have achieving communication and coordination with others have resulted in the demise of countless small group associations. For social scientists, the more fundamental issue revolves around the problematics and processes of communication and coordination across the fuller range of human association, hopefully devoid of megasubcultural mystique.

20. In a somewhat parallel fashion, Hannerz (1992) uses the term *global ecumene* to refer to the networks of networks that overlap any number of societies. While addressing some limitations associated with cultural homogeneity for understanding contemporary life-styles and people's experiences therein, Hannerz's statement provides little in the way of more precise conceptual or methodological suggestion.

21. Space limitations prohibit a more expansive discussion of the practical limitations of postmodernist thought for the social sciences. See Dawson and Prus (1993a, 1993b; 1995), Best (1995), Charmaz (1995), Sanders (1995), Prus (1996:217–43), and Prus and Dawson (1996).

22. Consider work roles such as those of physicians (Haas and Shaffir, 1987), bar staff (Roebuck and Frese, 1976; Prus and Irini, 1980), and store managers (Prus, 1989b) that lend themselves to more totalizing involvements in their respective settings.

23. Readers may refer to people's involvements in gambling (Lesieur, 1977), fantasy role games (Fine, 1983), shopping (Prus and Dawson, 1991), shuffleboard (Snyder, 1994) as denoting cases in which recreational pursuits may become highly centralized features in people's lives.

24. People's involvements in holidays, vacations, tourist ventures, and the like may vary greatly, but it may be very instructive to begin to examine people's involvements in these "events" in subcultural terms. In addition to those directly involved as participants, it would be very worthwhile to attend to those involved in supporting subcultures (e.g., travel agencies, the hospitality industry, tourism guides, etc.).

25. I am drawing here, in a most rudimentary fashion, on some very interesting work that Tina Westlake Chester (1995) has been doing on the wedding experience.

3

Subcultural Involvements: Experiencing, Forming, and Coordinating Subcultural Associations

The majority of gangs develop from the spontaneous play-group. . . .
(I)n the course of business or pleasure, a crowd, in the sense of a
mere gathering of persons, is formed. . . . On this basis of interests
and aptitudes, a play-group emerges. . . . Such a play-group may
acquire a real organization. Natural leaders emerge, a relative
standing is assigned to various members and traditions develop. It
does not become a gang, however, until it begins to excite disapproval
and opposition, and thus acquires a more definite group conscious-
ness. . . . This is the real beginning of the gang, for now it starts to
draw itself more closely together. It becomes a conflict group. . . .
The ganging process is a continuous flux and flow, and there is little
permanence in most of the groups. New nuclei are constantly
appearing and the business of coalescing and recoalescing is going
on everywhere in the congested areas. Both conflict and competition
threaten the embryonic gangs with disintegration. . . . Some new
activity of settlement, playground or club frequently depletes its
membership. (Thrasher, 1927 [1963:25–31])

Although one often finds great diversity from subculture to subculture within the broader society, each subculture may be seen as a forum or setting in which several basic facets of people's lives may take shape. The life-worlds implied by subcultures denote settings in which people typically work out aspects of perspectives, identities, activities, relationships, expressions of emotionality, and communicative styles.

Subcultures represent interactional contexts in which various aspects of earlier or outside life-styles may be disregarded or challenged and various alternatives introduced, developed, sustained, and dropped as people's associations take place over some time frame. Thus, while subcultures are fundamentally enabled by the more encompassing *transcontextualizing intersubjectivities* (most especially through the common language) of the larger community, each subculture affords participants an opportunity to achieve another "paramount" or "operational" reality.

Participants in these various life-worlds may deliberately strive to be different from others (outsiders) on a sustained or sporadic basis, but, in many other cases, "differences" emerge rather incidentally with respect to outsiders as the people involved attend to this or that pursuit or subtheme within an associational context. Any variety of interests and practices may be entertained and managed in any way that the participants at hand deem appropriate. There is no reason to presuppose that the participants in any subculture are of one mind on any matters that surface during their association. Thus, as with the broader community in which particular subcultures are embedded, one may expect sporadic if not more enduring instances of cooperation, competition, conflict, and compromise within each subculture. Likewise, alliances may be formed and factions may emerge (i.e., embedded within local subcultures). Shifting membership and individual disengagement may be expected to occur rather commonly, as may reconciliations, realignments, and reinvolvements.[1] Subcultures may endure for extended periods of time, fold quickly, or perhaps become ruptured or wither away as factions develop, people's interests change, or members leave in other ways. On occasion too, subcultures may be reconstituted where there is (some memory of and) a renewed collective vision of their value to the people at hand.

Since subcultures exist within larger subcultural mosaics, and individual participants are typically involved in several associations, the matter of "identifiable differences" (denoting any basis on which people may make distinctions) becomes important for appreciating ongoing association or more enduring subcultural affiliations. While participants sometimes intend that their association will be viewed as unique, they need not embark on any elaborate or intensive identity work to achieve recognition as a unit (consider two young neighborhood children who have begun to play together on an intermittent but somewhat sustained basis). Both insiders and others (outsiders) are more likely to view associations in more concrete terms when they associate some noteworthy qualities (e.g., noise, trouble, happiness) with this or that associational nexus. Insiders may pursue associations with particular others, find themselves encouraged to associate with particular others, or feel that they have no feasible alternative but to associate with particular others. Regardless of the route (or mixed routings) of their involvements, however, a sense of "identifiable differences" or a recognition that "something" distinguishes these associations from other associations is consequential for promoting continuity. It does not matter, in this respect, whether the subculture is viewed in friendship, recreational, task, or other terms, or whether or not people may want to remain involved in some particular subcultural context, a sense of distinctiveness draws attention to a particular associational forum as a setting in which certain kinds of things are done by a specific group of people.

People involved in (particular) subcultures for longer periods of time have their existing subcultural stocks of knowledge on which to draw with respect to subsequent association and activities. However, newcomers are typically expected to be attentive to the identifiable differences that longer-term participants have come to envision as more fundamental to their (particular) subcultures. Since much of the "understandings and practices" that typify subcultures as unique entities may be developed and sustained rather casually in these associational contexts, many aspects of subcultural life may be taken-for-granted (Schutz, 1962) or treated more implicitly by regular participants. Indeed, many aspects of subcultural routines may become problematic only when these are disregarded, questioned, or threatened by outsiders or newcomers to the group. In other instances, and perhaps as a consequence of challenges that have emerged or desires (and ensuing resistances) to promote the subculture as a way of life more generally, participants may develop more explicit methods (e.g., philosophies, jargon, attire, practices, ceremonies, training programs) for fostering particular aspects of their ways of life.

If one accepts the notion that *community life is made up of a series of diverse subcultures or life-worlds that people experience on a day-to-day basis*, then social scientists ought to direct attention to the ways in which people (1) become involved and sustain participation in specific subcultural settings, (2) experience particular subcultural involvements in a more complete sense, and (3) form and coordinate (subcultural) associations. Albeit developed in a fairly compacted manner around a set of "generic social processes,"[2] it is on these matters that the remainder of this chapter is focused. Acknowledging basic or transsituational social processes of human association such as "being involved," "acquiring perspectives," "doing activity," and "building relationships," generic social processes represent sets of sensitizing concepts for approaching the study of human groups.

Becoming Involved in Subcultural Enterprises

Since subcultures consist of people acting in association with others with respect to some focal set of activities, they also represent the forums in which "careers" or strands of people's involvements in particular settings unfold.[3] Two or more people may establish life-worlds that begin and end with certain associations (e.g., friendship, marriage, partnership), but the existence of other subcultures may both predate specific people's involvements in the setting and extend well beyond their departure. For more enduring subcultures of this latter sort, it is not unusual to find, on a more or less simultaneous basis, that some people may be beginning involvements (as participants) at the same time that others are becoming more intensively involved, dropping out, or possibly becoming reinvolved. Indeed, while some subcultures are highly stable membership-wise, there may be considerable flux in other subcultures as people come and go on a more or less continuous basis.

As well, whereas newcomers are often seen as targets for the recruitment and socialization efforts of existing participants, it is much more accurate to view all parties (newcomers and longer-term participants) as targets and tacticians with respect to one another. Thus, for instance, although outsiders (analysts included) might find that the practices of particular groups offend their moralities and tend to presume that newcomers are inducted into these sorts of practices unwittingly or against their will, closer examinations of these situations often reveal that many newcomers have no such reservations and sometimes have actively pursued earlier developed fascinations with particular life-styles. Likewise, longer-term participants may find themselves subject to various influence efforts on the part of "newcomers" (consider, for example, instances of parents becoming involved in particular recreational or "dining" pursuits in attempts to please or pacify their children).

The existence of the subcultural mosaic also implies that everyone in the community is involved in multiple subcultures on a simultaneous and sequential basis. Thus, while we may endeavor to follow someone's involvements (career-wise) in a specific subculture, people are rather routinely faced with the task of managing or juggling diverse sets of involvements at any given point in time. Further, insofar as people's involvements in particular subcultures are interwoven with those of the other people with whom they interact at this or that point in time, analysts may find it productive to attend to (a) the ways in which specific people's lives intersect with those of particular others across and within particular subcultural situations and (b) the ways in and extent to which people's involvements in particular situations are sustained and discouraged through their interactions with specific others.[4]

In discussing people's careers of involvement, it is important to explicitly acknowledge people's varying interests and skills, as well as their differing opportunities to become involved (and more fully participate) in each particular subculture. Thus, even when the very same people are involved in identical sets of (i.e., the very same) subcultures, their participation in each context may be very uneven, reflecting varying levels of skills, commitment, duration, acceptance by the others in the setting, and so forth.[5]

Since subcultures consist of people getting involved in, continuing and intensifying particular pursuits within, developing disenchantments with, and becoming disengaged from, the situation under consideration, as well as possibly becoming reinvolved in those same pursuits, an appreciation of people's experiences with the subcultural mosaic would be fostered by a good working familiarity with what may be termed the *involvement* or *career contingency process*. At the same time, though, it is only by developing greater familiarity with the major dimensions of subcultural routines that analysts may more fully appreciate what these involvement processes entail. Thus, following an overview of the routings and considerations that people may take into account in developing "careers" as participants in those situations, attention is focused more directly on the ways in which people experience (and accomplish) their involvements in various (subcultural) situations.

Whereas people's experiences with subcultures will be considered in more detail shortly, it may be useful at this point to briefly emphasize the multidimensional nature of subcultural involvements. Subcultures may be most notably defined by activities, but the life-worlds that develop around those activities are also characterized by sets of perspectives, identities, relationships, commitments, emotional expressions, and linguistic influences. Because a fuller appreciation of these notions is typically only developed through sustained participation in those settings, people becoming involved with particular subcultures are apt to have only a partial image of any of these notions. With more exposure to the group, however, newcomers tend to find that they are not only expected to come to terms with all of these aspects of the situation, but that each of these subfields provides themes and situations that they may define as appealing and disenchanting over the terms of their involvement in those subcultures.

Attending to the *how* (vs. *why*) of involvements, a processual approach to people's involvements focuses on the careers of people's participation in particular situations (Becker, 1963; Prus, 1987, 1996:153–55). While people may become involved in multiple, shifting, and potentially incompatible subcultures, each involvement may be envisioned with respect to four somewhat interrelated processes: (a) initial involvements, (b) continuities, (c) disinvolvements, and (d) reinvolvements.[6]

Getting Started (Initial Involvements)

As suggested below, there are three major routings by which people commonly become involved in subcultures. It should be noted, however, that people may combine these routings in various manners. They may also have reservations about particular involvements. Likewise, while people may vary greatly in the extent to which they consider particular reservations or reluctances to be consequential, an inability to ignore or neutralize pertinent reservations may deter participation in settings that people might have considered viable in other respects. Getting started, thus, seems contingent on people:[7,8]

- Engaging in "seekership" (pursuing self-attributed interests)
- Being recruited (others attempt to foster interest, encourage participation)
- Experiencing "closure" (perceiving pressing obligations, limited choices)
- Managing reservations (overcoming doubts, stigma, risks) (Prus, 1996:153–54)

Sustaining and Intensifying Involvements (Continuities)

Although people may begin to participate in subcultures along one or more of several dimensions, more enduring continuity (and intensification of involvement) is dependent on a fuller range of participation, reflecting matters of:[9]

- Internalizing perspectives (viewpoints consistent with particular involvements)
- Achieving identity (self and other definitions consistent with particular involvements)
- Accomplishing activities (competence and composure in the focal setting)

- Managing emotionality (exhibiting and experiencing appropriate affective styles)
- Acquiring linguistic fluency (learning and effectively using communication formats)
- Making commitments (making investments, developing dependencies)
- Developing relationships (experiencing positive bonds with others in the setting)
- Foregoing alternative involvements (neglecting options, "bridgeburning")

Becoming Disinvolved

Continuity and disengagement represent distinct processes in some respects, but they are often closely intertwined in actual practice. Sometimes, people's departures from subcultures are both abrupt and extensive. On many other occasions, though, the situation is much less clear. Not only may people's involvements in situations be partial and rather uneven (along the several dimensions just noted), but people may also question the viability of their involvements along any of these dimensions at any point in time. This suggests that people may experience doubts about their continued involvement throughout their careers as participants, and that even more acute doubts or disenchantments with respect to any one of these areas may be inadequate in themselves to foster detachment. Still, disinvolvement seems more likely when people find themselves:[10]

- Questioning the viability of perspectives (facing obstacles, dilemmas)
- Reassessing identity (consistent with desired images?)
- Finding activities troublesome (boring, unpleasant, cumbersome)
- Encountering emotional difficulties (e.g., becoming distraught, withdrawn, distrusting)
- Lacking linguistic fluency (encountering difficulties communicating with other participants)
- Being freedup from existing commitments (free to "relocate")
- Severing relationships (conflict, animosity, exclusion)
- Encountering opportunities for alternative involvements[11]

Becoming Reinvolved

Should people find that disinvolvements (and/or subsequent involvements) are less satisfactory than they had anticipated, they may entertain reinvolvement in an earlier situation. This seems more likely as people begin:[12]

- Defining opportunities for reinvolvements in former situations as more feasible
- Noting greater changes to self or situation that would justify reinvolvement
- Finding that they have less extensively organized their routines around their present involvements (i.e., disentanglement is more easily accomplished) (Prus, 1996:155)

Experiencing Subcultural Life-Worlds

Regardless of whether people in particular subcultures might operate in more explicit or more casual manners, social scientists interested in the ways in which these associations are experienced and sustained would likely find it instructive to attend more specifically to several key dimensions or generic social processes around which subcultures (as associational forums) develop. It is here that we begin to appreciate the centrality of perspectives, identities, activities, relationships, emotional experiences, and communication styles for people's ongoing involvements in particular subcultures.

Acquiring Perspectives

Denoting interpretive frameworks or viewpoints (also worldviews, paradigms, versions of reality) for making sense of the world, the perspectives that people develop through association with others provide the orientational content of group life. In more general terms, perspectives encompass people's traditions (as well as "fads" and "fashions"), senses of rationality, political and religious beliefs, and generalized fascinations and disaffections, as well as language and other symbols. Perspectives include people's definitions of objects, their rules, their notions of practices, lines of authority, consensual understandings, and other "rules of thumb" that humans develop in the groups under consideration.

While subcultures rather centrally build on preestablished perspectives within the host or broader community, the participants develop variants (including explicit rejections) of some of these broader intersubjective themes. Subcultures vary greatly in the extent to which the viewpoints that define particular association as unique within the community are shared, articulated, promoted, and acted upon by the participants. However, whereas the perspectives that more distinctively define the subculture under consideration may be the focus of considerable ambiguity and conflict within the subculture on some occasions, it is those "differences" (internally and externally recognized) that set specific associations apart, as meaningful entities, within the broader community.

The matter of working out (i.e., defining, negotiating, and renegotiating) the particular perspectives that purportedly typify this or that subculture at any point in time merits further consideration on its own (see the later section on forming and coordinating associations in this chapter), but it is essential that analysts attend to the processes by which participants learn about, reconcile, and work with the potentially contradictory set of viewpoints they encounter in particular subcultural contexts and in the broader subcultural mosaic in which they are embedded on a day-to-day basis. The following list highlights these subprocesses:[13]

- Encountering perspectives (definitions of reality) from others
- Assessing (new, incoming) perspectives and resisting unwanted viewpoints
- Developing images of objects (including images of other people and oneself)
- Learning (cultural) patterns of objects (e.g., rules of thumb, norms, fashion)
- Defining situations (i.e., applying perspectives to the "cases at hand")
- Dealing with ambiguity (lapses and limitations in existing explanations)
- Resolving contradictions (dilemmas within and across paradigms)
- Extending or improvising on existing perspectives
- Promoting (and defending) perspectives to others
- Rejecting formerly held viewpoints
- Adopting new viewpoints (Prus, 1996:151–52)

Achieving Identity

The names or other identity tags (e.g., gender designations, identification numbers) that people may be assigned at birth serve to generate more particularized demarcations or labels within the broader community in which they are located. However, each particular subculture in which people subsequently find themselves offers opportunities for people to attain other identities that may, but need not, recognize or build upon the names that have been associated with these same people (i.e., targets) in other contexts. Further, beyond their own identities in each subcultural context, people are expected to come to terms with the identities (i.e., labels, definitions, reputations, stereotypes) that have become associated with others in the group (e.g., family, friends, club members) with which these individuals are associated.

The ensuing identity work reflects ongoing assessments and negotiations as the parties involved jointly develop (suggest, use, tolerate, resist) sets of self and other definitions (and reputations) mindful of the more particularized circumstances in which they find themselves. Where the subcultures are larger or more multifaceted in nature, participants may also find that their identities are subject to some alteration and adjustment as they move laterally or vertically from embedded subculture to embedded subculture within those larger subcultural contexts. Since people's identities (especially reputations) take shape over time, it seems instructive to envision these definitions in process or career terms. At the same time, it is important to acknowledge the identity shifts that normally occur as people move from one set of relational others to the next. The subprocesses following attend to notions of this sort:

- Encountering definitions of self from others
- Attributing qualities to self (self-definitions)
- Comparing incoming and self-assigned definitions of self
- Resisting unwanted identity imputations
- Selectively conveying information about self to others
- Gleaning information about others
- Assigning identities to others
- Promoting specific definitions of others
- Encountering resistance from others
- Reassessing identities imputed to others (Prus, 1996:152–53)[14]

Doing Activity

People's activities acquire some meaning or sense of purpose relative to both the perspectives from which activities are envisioned and the identities of the participants involved, but the matter of human enterprise defines much of the consequential essence of subcultural life. This is because subcultures represent arenas in which people *do things*, and the things they do can have important implications for themselves as well as for others in the community. For our purposes, as analysts, it is useful to distinguish three subfields or realms of activity: (a) performing activities, (b) influencing others, and (c) making commitments.

The performing of activity highlights the "problematics of accomplishment." No assumption is made about people acting "wisely" or "rationally" in any objective sense. As indicated elsewhere (Prus, 1989b, especially 139–42), people may anticipate, plan, rehearse, and implement behavior on their own as well as anticipate, coordinate, and adjust their activities mindfully of others, but matters of ambiguity and uncertainty, as well as encountered resistance on the part of others, can render human endeavor particularly problematic. In contrast to much contemporary social science, which rather myopically focuses on antecedent conditions or factors and outcomes, *the emphasis on performing activity puts the focus squarely on the enterprise (successful and otherwise) that undergirds the practical accomplishment of human group life.* This emphasis on the social production of action enables scholars to respect the emergent nature of the human community as it takes its shape on a day-to-day basis. The processes relevant to performing activity are:[15]

- Making (preliminary) plans
- Getting prepared
- Managing stage fright (reservations, if any)
- Developing competence (stock of knowledge, tactics, applications)
- Engaging objects in particular instances
- Coordinating events with others (team members and others)
- Achieving and working with "routines"
- Dealing with ambiguity, obstacles, resistances, and distractions
- Conveying images of competence (displaying ability, composure)
- Encountering competition
- Making ongoing assessments and adjustments

The second and often related aspect of "doing activities" involves the *influence (and resistance) or persuasion process.* This reflects people's attempts to "gain the cooperation or commitments of others" with respect to both "one-to-one" and more diversified "group" situations. As minded (Mead, 1934) or intersubjective entities, people are quite capable of implementing meaningful behavior on their own, but the concept of subculture takes us more directly into realms of influence and negotiation. A great many aspects of the influence process involving subcultures are pitched at an interpersonal level, but some influence work in subcultural settings reflects media communications. In all instances, however, social scientists interested in the influence process would want to be attentive to the ways in which (and extent to which) those embarking on influence work deal with the following processes:[16]

- Formulating (preliminary) plans
- Role-taking (inferring/uncovering the perspectives of the other)
- Promoting interest in one's objectives
- Generating trust
- Proposing specific lines of action
- Encountering resistance
- Neutralizing obstacles
- Seeking and making concessions
- Confirming agreements
- Assessing "failures" and recasting plans (Prus, 1996:158)

If subcultures are to survive and take some sort of shape, then it is necessary that some of the participants assume initiative in sustaining particular sets of associations. Participant interests in perpetuating specific associations may be similar or diverse, but if the groupings are to achieve some continuity and focus, then some sort of *commitments*, investments, or pursuits are required on the part of (at least) some associates. As well, since subcultures entail some cooperative behavior on the part of at least two people (dyadic subcultures), then some mutuality of focus is also a prerequisite condition.

Denoting but one of several ventures in which individuals may be involved, each subculture may be seen as potentially competing with a variety of other (often shifting) subcultural involvements for people's commitments (time, resources, sacrifices). Viewed thusly, we may ask not only about the extent to which individuals have begun to make or sustain commitments to particular subcultures in a more direct sense, but also about the extent to which they have begun to organize their other involvements around particular subcultural involvements. In conjunction with this (and beyond the commitments that people initiate on their own), we may ask about the roles that people play (influence processes just discussed) in endeavoring to encourage and intensify the commitments that others may make to particular subcultural involvements. Mindful of the subcultural mosaic or the sets of multiple life-worlds in which specific subcultures are situated, the subprocesses relevant to an appreciation of people's commitments to particular subcultures include:[17]

- Exploring and assessing options
- Dealing with (any) earlier commitments
- Avoiding commitments ("elusive targets")

- Minimizing or diversifying investments ("hedging bets")
- Organizing routines around particular activities
- Neglecting other options ("closure by default") (Prus, 1996:158)

Experiencing Relationships

The selectivity and continuity of association entailed by "interpersonal bonds" or "affiliational networks" signifies another vital element in social life. This is especially consequential with reference to subcultures, wherein particularized relationships represent the fundamental human links that enable subcultures to persist. Relationships imply perspectives, identities, and activities (including performances, influence, and commitments), all of which can be powerful elements in shaping the associations that people develop with one another. However, relationships also entail some selectivity (affection and disaffection) of association, the related processes of intimacy and distancing, and matters of ongoing coordination (including conflict, compromise, and cooperation) within the context of focused interchange.

Since they entail process, relationships also can be envisioned as having natural histories or careers (i.e., initial involvements, continuities, disinvolvements, reinvolvements). Nevertheless, relationships also provide a testimony to the interlinkages of people's careers or involvements in particular (subcultural) settings. While people may endeavor to reshape the relationships they have with those with whom they feel obliged to interact for various reasons, other relationships entail a greater openness and hinge more centrally on the affections and disaffections that people develop with respect to one another.

As with the broader community more generally, analysts involved in studying subcultures would want to be attentive to the wide ranges of relationships that may develop between subcultural insiders, as well the diversity of relationships that participants may develop with various outsiders. Given the great many relationships in which people find themselves on an ongoing and emergent basis, the following processes seem especially pertinent for understanding the affiliational linkages that people establish with others both inside and outside any particular subculture:[18]

- Getting prepared for generalized encounters
- Defining self as available for association
- Defining (specific) others as desirable associates
- Making approaches/receiving openings from others
- Encountering (and indicating) rejection/acceptance

- Assessing self and other for "goodness of fit"
- Developing interactional styles (in each relationship)
- Managing openness and secrecy
- Developing understandings, preferences, loyalty
- Managing distractions (and outside commitments)
- Juggling (multiple) relationships
- Severing relationships (disentanglement)
- Renewing relationships (Prus, 1996:159)

Still other aspects of "developing relationships" will become evident in the following discussions of experiencing emotionality and developing communicative fluencies.

Experiencing Emotionality

Since a great deal of affectivity takes place within particular relationships and an attentiveness to people's emotional experiences may help social scientists to better understand the relationship process, it is tempting to blend these two discussions. However, because some emotional experiences entail more solitary dimensions and others clearly transcend particular relationships, people's affective experiences warrant consideration on their own.

Three processes that seem central to an appreciation of emotionwork in subcultural settings are (a) learning to define emotional experiences, (b) developing techniques for expressing and controlling emotional experiences, and (c) experiencing emotional episodes and entanglements. Because readers can refer to Prus (1996:173–201) for considerably more detail with respect to the substance and subprocesses each of these notions entail,[19] I will only briefly allude to these aspects of human lived experience and their implications for understanding subcultural routines.

As with other aspects of human community life, people appear to *learn notions of what it means to be emotional* from contact with other people. In learning about the cultural moralities and significances of the life-worlds in which they find themselves, people acquire notions of affective human states as well as the sorts of experiences people have with these states. While people's broader senses of emotionality reflect the understandings of the generalized other (Mead, 1934) that they attain through an assortment of group affiliations, more particularistic experiences with and expressions of emotionality (e.g., modesty, disgrace, fear, happiness, indignation, pride) may be encouraged through association with specific (subcultural) others.

In addition to acquiring stocks of knowledge (and "rules of thumb") regarding the existence and nature of emotional situations and states, people also *learn how to do emotional activity.* At a performance level, people not only learn (sometimes through explicit instruction) how to monitor their own situations and behaviors, but they also learn how to express and manage particular emotional themes and states. As well, people generally learn ways of monitoring, assessing, and influencing (affecting) the emotional states that others may experience. As with perspectives on emotionality, people may encounter variants (sometimes quite pronounced) on modes of expressing emotionality in the company of different (subcultural) associates. Consider, for instance, the adjustments that even the more "rambunctious" children typically make as they move from playgrounds to classrooms.

As with other (symbolic) interactions, emotional interchanges may be viewed best in process terms. One cannot predict just how particular encounters will work out despite the postures assumed by one or other parties, but we may ask about people's initial involvements, continuities, and intensifications, as well as discontinuities and dissipations and reinvolvements in particular emotional episodes of both a more solitary and a more interactive nature. As well, heightened attentiveness to specific subcultural contexts seems appropriate, for it is within these interactional frames that a great many of people's emotional entanglements emerge, take place, and intensify or dissipate.

Developing Communicative Fluency

Denoting a shared set of symbols, language is the single most important feature fostering a tendency toward a unified or centralized culture, but somewhat ironically it is also the feature of community life that most singularly enables people to develop and sustain subcultures that may be highly diverse in their emphasis.[20]

While the existence of a generally shared language enables the development of any particular subculture, it is important to acknowledge that *each set of activities in which people engage represents a realm around which extensions or variants of that linguistic base may be developed.* Subcultures are able to achieve initial viability because participants share a preexisting communication forum. However, any matters pertaining to (a) differing experiences (or challenges), (b) developments in concepts and technologies, (c) concerns with autonomy (and secrecy), or (d) interests in achieving particular communication contents (themes) within or outside the group at hand may represent occasions for creating more distinctive expressions.[21]

Regardless of the forms of communication employed by subcultural participants (e.g., verbal, gestural, graphic, electronic), the processes of "encountering" and "generating" messages have a generic quality. Thus, while scholars focusing on particular subcultures will want to attend to the specific communicative practices (e.g., jargon, contact styles, mediums) employed by people in those contexts, they will also find it instructive to attend to the various subprocesses entailed in generating and encountering messages:

Generating Messages
Anticipating communications with others
Presenting messages (making indications) to others
Assessing comprehension (on the part of other) of messages sent
Encountering feedback (including communication obstacles or resistances) from others
Continuing (including reformulating messages) communications
Terminating messages

Encountering Messages
Noticing and identifying communicative efforts from others
Interpreting communicative endeavors, either on a solitary or group (interactive) basis
Dealing with ambiguity and confusion
Disregarding or screening out undesired communications
Attending (more intently) to communications of interest
Pursuing (interactively) communications of interest
Applying messages to situations at hand
Evaluating or assessing communications

Forming and Coordinating (Subcultural) Associations

The matter of forming or generating associations with others is fundamental to the notion of subcultures or social life-worlds. This discussion centrally builds on the generic social processes just outlined, but the forming of associations is also contingent on people recognizing the advantages of incorporating others into their objectives. Associations can vary greatly in size, duration, formality, and the like, but generally involve attempts to obtain the cooperation of others with respect to ventures that people feel unwilling to pursue (or unable to accomplish) on their own. Not all of these joint ventures will be developed very far or successfully, but three subprocesses seem relevant in a great many cases: (a) establishing associations, (b) objectifying associations, and (c) encountering outsiders.

As a caveat, it should be noted that people's activities in subcultural contexts may vary significantly with respect to these three subprocesses, reflecting (i) the developmental states of the subcultures in which they find themselves, (ii) any specializations that may already be practiced therein, and (iii) people's relative interests in perpetuating the subcultures in question. First, while some people may attempt to initiate groups and others may wish to more firmly locate existing subcultures in the community more generally, many subcultures are quite well established at the time that particular members encounter them. In instances of the latter sort, the participants may have well-developed sets of routines for recruiting and socializing newcomers, they may have established considerable presence (awareness, legitimation) in the community at large, and they may have well-formulated sets of guidelines and practices for dealing with both insiders (internal relations) and outsiders. Although open to change, much of the "organizational structure" may already be in place, and the participants involved in those associations may concentrate on sustaining these routines. In other cases, participants may endeavor to build subcultures from the ground up, so to speak, and find themselves more fully involved in the preliminary planning or rudimentary stages with respect to all three subprocesses. In still other cases, participants may define their roles in more selective manners, such that while some people may pursue certain aspects of these three subprocesses, others may focus on tasks intended to further their subculture in other ways. The individual participants in any life-world are also apt to be differentially interested in perpetuating that subculture. Some people may take much more active roles than others in promoting (and possibly reshaping) aspects of the subculture in one or other ways. Scholars dealing with matters of establishing associations, objectification processes, and encounters with outsiders, thus, should be attentive to subcultural developmental states, activity specializations within life-worlds, and differing levels of enterprise that insiders assume as they contribute to the continuity of particular subcultures within the broader community.

Establishing Associations

The matter of generating subcultural affiliations draws attention to the task of, and enterprise involved in, incorporating others into a collective entity (i.e., group, venture, team, side, agency, organization, gang, committee, department, office, crew, mob, band, tribe, or cult). People involved in more fleeting alignments may circumvent or truncate some processes, but those involved in longer-term ventures seem likely to pursue activities of this sort. Thus, the following notions are particularly pertinent to the emergence and development of subcultures:[22]

- Anticipating the value of collective enterprise
- Involving others in the venture (recruitment, screening, minimizing reservations)
- Justifying the group (developing perspectives, moral viewpoints)
- Celebrating the venture (witnessing, recognizing, emphasizing—within the group)
- Defining the team (membership criteria, positions, responsibilities)
- Establishing communication forums (interpersonal, media)
- Pursuing resources for the group
- Arranging member assemblies (encounters, practices)
- Providing instruction for members (perspectives, techniques)
- Monitoring members
- Assessing member performances
- Motivating and disciplining members
- Rejecting and reinstating members
- Facing internal upheaval (splintering, factions, challenges from within)
- Facing generalized loss of interest
- Dealing with dissolution
- Attempting to revitalize cooperative ventures (Prus, 1996:161)

Objectifying Associations

Effectively, everything that people do (in establishing associations and encountering outsiders) with a particular association in mind may be seen to "objectify" (Berger and Luckmann, 1966) or more firmly establish the presence of the group entity within the community, but we can also consider the objectification process on a more explicit level.[23] While the participants of some associations may plan for their group to remain unnoticed within the larger community, those involved in other associations may be keenly interested in establishing a prominence for their groups that is more obvious to outsiders within the community. Even those groups who wish to "go undercover" for a variety of reasons may adopt certain practices to make their associations appear more evident or "more real" to their members. Those desiring greater recognition within the broader community may be even more outreaching in their efforts.

On an *insider* basis, people interested in objectifying or having their (subcultural) associations envisioned as a more consequential element in the community may engage in practices of these sorts:[24]

- Developing a group identity (name, logo, flag)
- Stipulating justifications for existence and operations
- Creating identity markers for members (uniforms, appearances, signs)
- Defining exclusiveness (selectivity, oaths, codes, jargon)
- Establishing a public presence (announcements, advertising, rallies, protests)
- Legitimating the group publicly (endorsements, credentials, charters, licences)
- Demarcating territories and jurisdictions (buildings, places, locations) (Prus, 1996:162)

The objectification process also becomes intensified when *outsiders* (intentionally or otherwise) engage in "identity work" pertaining to particular associations. The outsiders involved may have rather diverse interests (curiosities, fascinations, entertainment, knowledge, fear, condemnation, control, elimination) with respect to the subculture in question, but insofar as they serve to identify, talk about, and act toward particular associations as if they were more unique, prominent, consequential, and the like, they may be seen to contribute to the "realism" of particular subcultural essences. Thus, outsider activities of the following sort are particularly noteworthy in generating profile for particular (subcultural) associations:

- Defining a set of people as constituting a group or interactive entity within the community
- Associating (assigning, acknowledging) specific names (and other identity markers) with the group
- Attributing particular properties (qualities and evaluations) to the group
- Discussing (talk, rumor, media messages) the group with others in the community
- Making more concerted efforts (from fascinations and facilitative activity to condemnations and control concerns) to attend to or deal with the group as an entity within the broader community (Prus, 1996:162)

Although any communicative tendencies along these lines may have the effect of more firmly establishing the identity or presence of a particular subculture in the community, the media may be centrally involved in this process on some occasions (Fine and Kleinman, 1979:11–15). However, since *the media* (denoting graphic and electronic messages) is a rather obscure term by itself, some qualifications are essential here, especially as these pertain to the media as (a) a third-party source of information, (b) an outsider control resource, and (c) an insider communication resource.

First, while those generating the media (as a third-party source of information) may foster an awareness of certain life-worlds, those producing media materials may very readily ignore other subcultures (including some keenly desiring media attention). When focusing on particular life-worlds, those using the media commonly draw attention to these situations by sharpening and dramatizing insider beliefs and practices and focusing on certain people (actors or "personalities") within. In the process, those developing media messages may intentionally or inadvertently contribute to subcultural intrigue or mystique, generate stigma and resentment or sympathy, and help establish featured individuals as "celebrities" (e.g., heroes, villains) of sorts. By enabling others to become aware of the existence, practitioners, and activities surrounding particular life-worlds, media depictions commonly foster a spread of ideas, and enhance opportunities for outsiders to imitate or pursue direct contact with subcultural participants. However, beyond the matter of informing outsiders about specific life-worlds, those developing media messages often pursue other agendas, including such things as promoting the sales of particular media products and formats, fostering generally acknowledged or more personal notions of morality, and using more intriguing subcultural materials in attempts to establish themselves (e.g., journalists, talk-show hosts) as celebrities of sorts in the broader community. As a consequence of these mixed agendas, media representations are apt to be problematic for those hoping to promote, control, or even openly comprehend particular subcultures.

As well, once outsiders learn about certain subcultures, they may attempt to use the media as a means of shaping or controlling the larger social environment in which they locate themselves. Where outsiders define certain subcultures as undesirable, they may sponsor certain kinds of media messages in attempts to discredit the practices and participants associated with specific subcultures. In other instances, outsiders may envision certain subcultures in more positive terms and may support media messages that encourage the development of those subcultural ventures or more firmly establish links with their own operations.

Subcultural insiders wishing to promote their own pursuits may also sponsor media messages as tools with which to recruit and socialize members as well as to legitimate their presence in the community at large (possibly challenging other subcultures in the process).[25] In all instances, regardless of whether the media are used as third-party sources of information, or as insider or outsider resources, their deployment with respect to a particular subculture can be seen to contribute to the community profile of that life-world. However, in the midst of all other issues to which people in a given community may attend, a subculture's prominence or recognition as a noteworthy presence is problematic over time as other focal points are introduced, fostered, and dropped in the community.

Encountering Outsiders

As subcultures become established within the community, participants may make contact with a variety of individuals and groups within the larger theater of operation. Outsiders may variously represent (a) targets (i.e., prospects, clients, customers, patrons, cases, suckers, marks, patients, inmates) for subcultural participants' enterprises, (b) potential partners for particular cooperative ventures, (c) threats or adversaries (competitors, enemies), or (d) more ambiguous members of the community at large. While the group's interests in particular individuals and groups can be quite wide-ranging, the following practices tend to be noteworthy more generally:[26]

- Representing the association('s interests)
- Making contact with outsiders (establishing co-presence, making the scene)
- Defining the theatre of operation (places, objectives, strategies)
- Identifying outsiders (targets, cooperators, adversaries, witnesses, nobodies)
- Pursuing associational objectives through the others (cooperation, influence work)
- Confronting outsiders (challenges, competitions, conflicts)
- Protecting (sometimes concealing) the association from outsiders
- Readjusting group routines to more effectively deal with outsiders (Prus, 1996:163)

While some subcultures are viewed in confrontational or adversarial terms virtually from their inception, and are subject to a variety of control or elimination tactics on the part of outsiders, some other subcultures may be very well received (and supported) overall within the broader community. However, even members of those subcultures seemingly defined in the most facilitative, desirable, or even necessary terms at this and that point in time are apt to find themselves subject to some competition if not more open adversity as people in the community at large pursue other (including parallel) interests and develop alternative viewpoints, technologies, and associations.[27] Thus, beyond attending to the ways in which the participants in this and that subculture approach and deal with outsiders, the reactions of outsiders to particular subcultural ventures and the ensuing adjustments that take place on the part of all of those involved deserve considerable attention on the part of social scientists.

Endnotes:

1. Strauss (1984, 1993:215–19) introduces similar notions under the rubric of "segmentation processes," which:

> *refer to how these subworlds originate, evolve, maintain themselves, distinguish themselves from others, break apart in further segmentation, also decline and vanish, and so on. . . . Segmentation processes include defining and building a legitimate core activity or activities; differentiating the subworld from others; the writing and rewriting of history; competing for resources; debating and maneuvering in arenas; and further segmenting. (215–16)*

2. This discussion of generic social processes builds rather directly on Prus (1987, and especially 1996:141–86). These formulations, in turn, are rooted in Simmel's (1950) notions of social forms (vs. content) and the works of several other scholars, such as Glaser and Strauss (1967), Blumer (1969), Lofland (1970), and Couch (1984) who have written more explicitly about these matters. However, the generic social processes outlined here also are integrally informed by a great many extended instances of ethnographic (particularly Chicago-style interactionist) research. Although he does not talk explicitly about "generic processes," the community of scholars working in this tradition more generally has also benefitted greatly from the transcontextual concepts developed by Erving Goffman (especially 1959, 1961, 1963), whose work in many ways is reminiscent of that of Simmel.

3. The concept of "careers" in subcultural contexts can be traced back to early Chicago-school ethnographies, including Shaw (1930) and Cressey (1932).

4. As indicated in Waller's (1930) study of divorce, Roebuck and Frese's (1976) study of an after-hours club, Lesieur's (1977) depiction of gambling, Prus and Irini's (1980) examination of the hotel community, and Adler and Adler's

(1991) consideration of college athletes, when people remain in specific settings for some period of time, their lives often become more interconnected with particular others (with respect to matters of perspectives, identities, activities, relationships, and commitments). As a consequence, disinvolvements often become problematic, even when participants might strongly desire to become disengaged from the focal setting.

5. Although readily evident, three other observations may be made in this context. First, it is worth noting that people may be much happier (or more discontent) in certain subcultural settings (or variants thereof) than others. This can have extremely important implications for their coming and going, as well as their anticipations and participation in those arenas. Consider the different senses of affectivity (and enthusiasm) that most students associate with school as opposed to holidays or playgroups. Many adults can readily identify with this example, both retrospectively and currently (often with respect to their work roles). Secondly, people can take on different roles, personas, and interactional styles in different contexts. Third, as self-reflective entities, people may become involved in concealing particular subcultural activities and involvements from others. Goffman's (1963) discussion of people "passing" and living "double lives" is particularly relevant here.

6. Among the monographs that address involvements or career contingencies in ethnographic inquiries are Shaw (1930), Cressey (1932), Sutherland (1937), Becker et al. (1961), Lofland (1966), Bartell (1971), Ditton (1977), Lesieur (1977), Prus and Sharper (1977), Prus and Irini (1980), Dietz (1983), Fine (1983), Haas and Shaffir (1987), Sanders (1989), Adler and Adler (1991), Faupel (1991), Waldorf et al. (1991), Wolf (1991), and MacLeod (1993).

7. In a more complete sense, one should also note the existence of "imposed" (e.g., physiological/medical complications) and "inadvertent" (accidental, unwitting) involvements.

8. The matter of initial involvements is given particular attention in Shaw (1930), Cressey (1932), Sutherland (1937), Becker et al. (1961), Becker (1963), Lofland (1966), Bartell (1971), Kando (1973), Ditton (1977), Lesieur (1977), Prus and Sharper (1977), Prus and Irini (1980), Fine (1983), Haas and Shaffir (1987), Sanders (1989), Van Zandt (1991), and Wolf (1991).

9. Albeit somewhat extended, this listing is adopted from Prus (1996:154). For materials that specifically attend to continuity of role involvements, see Shaw (1930), Cressey (1932), Sutherland (1937), Becker et al. (1961), Becker (1963), Lofland (1966), Bartell (1971), Ditton (1977), Lesieur (1977), Prus and Sharper (1977), Prus and Irini (1980), Fine (1983), Adler (1985), Snyder (1986), Steffensmeier (1986), Haas and Shaffir (1987), Biernacki (1988), Sanders (1989), Faupel (1991), Waldorf et al. (1991), Wolf (1991), MacLeod (1993), and Dietz (1994a).

10. See Ebaugh (1988) for a review of the literature on "Becoming an Ex," as well as an instructive, ethnographically informed attempt to formulate the generic social processes constituting disinvolvement. As with continuity and disinvolvement, it is most important to be attentive to the interlinkages of

disinvolvement and reinvolvement processes. The implication is that all of these notions are much more fluid, partial, and ambiguous than seems commonly supposed. For some ethnographic materials that attend to disinvolvement, see Ray (1961), Lesieur (1977), Prus and Sharper (1977), Prus and Irini (1980), Peyrot (1985), Biernacki (1988), and Waldorf et al. (1991).

11. The notion of "encountering opportunities for alternative involvements" may be more consequential for explaining disinvolvements than it might at first seem. While people seem most willing to entertain alternatives when they find themselves more disenchanted with a current situation, people frequently take things for granted until they see something that appears more advantageous. As well, those representing alternatives may attempt to generate focused (i.e., particularistically motivated) dissatisfaction on the part of the participants with respect to their present circumstances. See Festinger et al. (1956), Lofland (1966), Prus (1989a), Van Zandt (1991), and Wolf (1994).

12. Only a few studies have addressed the reinvolvement process in a substantial manner: see Ray (1961), Wiseman (1970), Lesieur (1977), Prus and Sharper (1977), Prus and Irini (1980), Biernacki (1988), and Waldorf et al. (1991). Taken together, these studies suggest that considerable vacillation (disinvolvement and reinvolvement) may represent commonplace experiences for people involved in, and attempting to disentangle themselves from, many situations.

13. Most extended ethnographies nicely illustrate themes pertaining to "the acquisition of perspectives," and almost inevitably address notions of identities, involvements, activities, and relationships as well, for these elements are very much interrelated in subcultural life-styles. Some book-length ethnographies that do a particularly effective job of conveying the ways in which people become exposed to, and familiar with, particular worldviews include Anderson (1923), Shaw (1930), Blumer (1933), Blumer and Hauser (1933), Sutherland (1937), Becker, Hughes et al., (1961, 1968), Goffman (1961), Davis (1963), Lofland (1966), M. Scott (1968), Wiseman (1970), Bartell (1971), Kando (1973), Prus and Irini (1980), Dietz (1983), Fine (1983), Kleinman (1984), Evans and Falk (1986), Haas and Shaffir (1987), Sanders (1989), Stebbins (1990), Adler and Adler (1991), Charmaz (1991), Van Zandt (1991), Wolf (1991), Jorgensen (1992), and MacLeod (1993).

14. While very much informed by Chicago-style ethnographic research (Prus, 1996:113–40), these notions also build directly on the dramaturgical works of Erving Goffman (1959, 1963) and Orrin Klapp (1962, 1964) as well as the "labeling theory" associated with Edwin Lemert (1951, 1967), Harold Garfinkel (1956), Howard Becker (1963), and others. For reviews of the literature on "identity work" as this pertains to type-casting, public designations, and resisting unwanted imputations, see Prus (1975a, 1975b, 1982). Ethnographic monographs that are particularly attentive to identity work and self-images include Edgerton (1967), Bartell (1971), Kando (1973), Prus and Irini (1980), Scott (1981), Dietz (1983), Evans and Falk (1986), Haas and Shaffir (1987), Sanders (1989), Charmaz (1991), and Wolf (1991).

15. The subprocesses listed here extend somewhat those found in Prus (1996:157). The following monographs provide some of the more focused materials on how people accomplish activities: Anderson (1923), Shaw (1930), Maurer (1964), Emerson (1969), Bartell (1971), Letkemann (1973), Hargreaves et al. (1975), Ditton (1977), Lesieur (1977), Prus and Sharper (1977, 1991), Prus and Irini (1980), Ross (1980), Knorr-Cetina (1981), Dietz (1983), Fine (1983), Mitchell (1983), Albas and Albas (1984), Powell (1985), Steffensmeier (1986), Haas and Shaffir (1987), Prus (1989a, 1989b), Adler and Adler (1991), Charmaz (1991), Faupel (1991), Waldorf et al. (1991), Wolf (1991), MacLeod (1993), and Wright and Decker (1994).

16. While notions of negotiation are evident in a great many Chicago-style ethnographies, matters pertaining to persuasion (influence and negotiation processes) are more explicit in the following studies: Sutherland (1937), Festinger et al. (1956), Davis (1959, 1961), Roth (1962), Lofland (1966), Emerson (1969), Wiseman (1970), Bartell (1971), Prus and Sharper (1977, 1991), Prus and Irini (1980), Ross (1980), Fine (1983), Haas and Shaffir (1987), Prus (1989a, 1989b), Sanders (1989), Prus and Frisby (1990), Van Zandt (1991), and Grills (1994).

17. For some ethnographic materials that attend more directly to the commitment-making process, see Lofland (1966), Bartell (1971), Kando (1973), Lesieur (1977), Prus and Sharper (1977), Prus and Irini (1980), Haas and Shaffir (1987), Prus (1989a, 1989b), Prus and Frisby (1990), Van Zandt (1991), and Wolf (1991).

18. The development, maintenance, and severance of relationships is given particular attention in the following monographs: Shaw (1930), Waller (1930), Hunt (1966), Lofland (1966), Bartell (1971), Lesieur (1977), Prus and Sharper (1977, 1991), Prus and Irini (1980), Fine (1983), Adler (1985), Steffensmeier (1986), Vaughan (1986), Prus (1989a, 1989b), Fishman (1990), Van Zandt (1991), Wolf (1991), and Lyman (1993). Lemert's (1962) analysis of "paranoia and the dynamics of exclusion" deserves special recognition as one of the best accounts of interpersonal relationships.

19. As indicated in that statement (Prus, 1996:174–76), although few ethnographic studies have been explicitly focused on emotionality per se, a great deal of Chicago-style ethnography addresses matters of emotionality in consequential fashions. Consider, for instance, (a) people's experiences with *stigma, shame, disrespectability, or embarrassment* (Waller, 1930; Davis, 1961; Goffman, 1963; Edgerton, 1967; Prus and Irini, 1980; Schneider and Conrad, 1983; Sanders, 1989; Lyman, 1993), (b) *intimacy and distancing* (Waller, 1930; Cressey, 1932; Bartell, 1971; Prus and Irini, 1980; Vaughan, 1986; Hopper, 1993), (c) *ambiguity, ambivalence, and confusion* (Shaw, 1930; Lofland, 1966; M. Scott, 1968; Gubrium, 1975b; Fine, 1983; Schneider and Conrad, 1983; Haas and Shaffir, 1987; Sanders, 1989; Charmaz, 1991; Sandelowski et al., 1991; Wolf, 1991; Weger, 1992; Karp, 1993, 1996; March, 1994), or (d) *enthusiasm, devotion, fascination, and excitement* (Blumer, 1933; Blumer and Hauser, 1933; Lofland,

1966; Bartell, 1971; Lesieur, 1977; Fine, 1983; Mitchell, 1983; Prus, 1989a; Sanders, 1989; Wolf, 1991).

20. Interestingly, because people are differentially exposed to, and involved in the comprehension, use, and promotion of, a particular language, even within the same "society," language represents a "subcultural realm of involvement" in its own right, with participants becoming variously involved in perpetuating, articulating, using, and resisting this communication device. Like other subcultural instances, we can ask about people's careers as users of, or participants in, particular languages (as well as their perspectives on that language, their identities, activities, relationships, and sense of emotionality as these pertain to the use of this language). At the same time, it is only with the possession of a(n intersubjectively accomplished) language of some sort that one acquires a base for assessing that or any other language to which one may be exposed.

21. Insofar as they focus on somewhat unique life-worlds, almost every Chicago-style ethnography provides some insight into the development, tutelage, and usage of jargon, lingo, argot, or other expressions that people use in conceptualizing, communicating about, and acting toward various [objects] in their realms of endeavor. See, for example, studies of hobos (Anderson, 1923), professional thieves (Sutherland, 1937; Maurer, 1964), religious groups (Lofland, 1966; Shaffir, 1974; Ebaugh, 1977; Van Zandt, 1991), deaf children (Evans and Falk, 1986), medical students (Haas and Shaffir, 1987), entertainers (Becker, 1963; Prus and Irini, 1980; MacLeod, 1993), horse racing and gambling (M. Scott, 1968; Lesieur, 1977), bikers (Wolf, 1991), and drug users (Becker, 1963, 1967; Biernacki, 1988; Faupel, 1991; Waldorf et al., 1991).

22. For instances of materials that ethnographically depict the ways in which people attempt to establish groups or associations of sorts, see Sutherland's (1937) and Maurer's (1964) professional thieves; Karsh et al.'s (1953) union organizers; Rubington's (1968) bottle-gangs; Lofland's (1966) and Van Zandt's (1991) religious cults; Prus and Sharper's (1977) road hustlers; Adler's (1985) drug dealers; Prus and Frisby's (1990) party plans; Wolf's (1991) outlaw bikers; and Grill's (1994) political recruitment practices.

23. In a somewhat related manner, Strauss (1982) discusses five processes that contribute to the legitimation of social life-worlds. These (with my shorthand definitions in parentheses) are: discovering and claiming worth (drawing attention to valuable, noteworthy features of the subculture); distancing (maintaining a sense of distinctiveness, exclusivity for the subculture); theorizing (developing an ideology, set of justifications for the subculture); standard-setting, embodying, evaluating (defining and maintaining criteria for subcultural practices); and boundary-setting and boundary-challenging in arenas (identifying and dealing with outsiders).

24. For illustrations of "objectification" practices on the part of groups wishing to become known in the community at large, see Karsh et al. (1953), Goffman (1961), Lofland (1966), Wiseman (1970), Gusfield (1981, 1989), Prus (1989a,b), Van Zandt (1991), and Grills (1994). For examples of internal

objectification practices among those wishing to remain unnoticed in the larger community, see Sutherland (1937) and Prus and Sharper (1977). Still other groups may desire or flirt with a semi-public recognition (e.g., taxi-dance hall operators [Cressey, 1932]; street gangs [Keiser, 1969]; drug dealers [Adler, 1985]; fences [Steffensmeier, 1986]; action bars [Roebuck and Frese, 1976; Prus and Irini, 1980]; and outlaw bikers [Wolf, 1991].

25. For ethnographic material involving people's use of the media to promote insider agendas and discredit competitor subcultural endeavors, see Prus (1989b: especially 201–242 and 286–300) and Prus and Fleras (1996). Similar processes are also worth examining in religious (Lofland, 1966; Van Zandt, 1991) and political (Grills, 1989, 1994; Atkinson, 1995) arenas, amongst others. Although only minimally ethnographic in thrust, the most sustained considerations of the role of the media from an (essentially) interactionist viewpoint can be found in the work of Altheide (1974, 1985), Altheide and Snow (1979), and Altheide and Johnson (1980). Also, see "enhancing communications (and the media)" in chapter 5.

26. Those interested in the ways in which members of groups (and organizations) make contact with and deal with outside parties (e.g., targets, clients, suspects, etc.) may wish to examine: Cressey (1932), Sutherland (1937), Goffman (1961), Emerson (1969), Wiseman (1970), Prus and Sharper (1977), Prus and Irini (1980), Ross (1980), Haas and Shaffir (1987), Grills (1989, 1994), Prus (1989b), Van Zandt (1991), Wolf (1991), and MacLeod (1993).

27. Consider, for instance, the notion of "knowledge as a social problem in academia" (Kuhn, 1970; Prus, 1992), or the difficulties that even those involved in the production of seemingly primary products (e.g., farmers, fishermen, loggers, miners) may encounter when pursuing their trade amidst the varying interests and activities of those who constitute the subcultural mosaic in their broader communities.

Part II

Pragmatizing the Social Sciences: A Research Agenda

4

Achieving Intersubjectivity, Managing Place and Space, and Maintaining Presence

Building on notions of subcultural mosaics, generic social processes, and ethnographic research, chapters 4, 5, and 6 outline a research agenda for the social sciences that attends to the ongoing accomplishment of human group life. Theoretically based in a processually oriented interactionism and methodologically grounded in ethnographic inquiry, this agenda is intended to encourage social scientists to attend to every single context in which human group life may take its shape—from the most basic of human activities to those that seem the most conceptually sophisticated, technologically developed, and organizationally complex. Focusing directly on the "doing" or accomplishing of human community life, this approach provides a theoretically coherent means of connecting a great many seemingly diverse and disjointed activities that take place on a community-wide, societal, and even global basis. Still, several qualifications are in order.

First, although the listing of topics presented here indicates a great number of departure points for inquiry, it should be emphasized that virtually all of these topics are so immense that they can be sketched out only in the most rudimentary terms. Each theme (and subtheme within) is integrated by virtue of a process-oriented, action-based dimension, but a great number of consequential subcultures may be embedded in any given subtheme.

It is also important that social scientists have some means of drawing linkages both within and across these areas of inquiry. The generic social processes discussed in chapter 3 provide a conceptual foundation that not only may be invoked in the study of any subcultural context, but that also constitute a basis for assessing and synthesizing findings across the range of human involvements. At the same time, however, people's interests in substantive areas often reflect a variety of group objectives, practical concerns, and personal intrigues in the context at hand. By presenting this research agenda, it is anticipated that this material may allow researchers to (a) tap into specific realms of human endeavor, while (b) maintaining a substantive focus for purposes of comprehending a larger realm of enterprise. As well, it is hoped that the conceptual base that undergirds this statement may enable researchers not only (c) to approach each realm of human activity in processually more informed manners, but also (d) to use each situated inquiry as a means of informing the academic community about aspects of a broader set of generic social processes.

Third, as readers examine the listings following, they will note some overlap of content areas and social processes. Many of the fields outlined here are interlinked with other arenas of human enterprise via (a) multiple subcultural involvements on the part of particular people, (b) the many interrelated realms of activity involved in every subcultural world, and (c) the existence of intersecting subcultures. Some of these interlinkages may have developed inadvertently, but others reflect deliberate attempts on the part of people involved in particular sectors of activity to become involved in other realms of enterprise. Along a somewhat similar line, it might also be observed that many human pursuits entail (d) a blending of several subcultural themes and products. Thus, extensive "subcultural loading" (involving the coordination of people involved in different times and places, realms of activity, associations, and mediums of exchange) may be entailed in accomplishing many tasks. Consider the diverse assortment of products (as well as activities and distribution networks) involved in assembling an airplane, building a house, or producing a textbook. Likewise, the common practice of "making a coffee or tea" (which even without cream and sugar still entails a container, a measuring or stirring device, water, heat, and processed and packaged coffee or tea) attests to both a sense of subcultural loading and the exchange mediums that people invoke in "producing" these items. Indeed, it is often only by tapping into extended networks of activities implied by the roles of suppliers, purchasing agents, retailers, and the like that people are able to conduct a great many activities in what seems a rather direct and simple manner.

Fourth, the ordering in which the research topics are presented is somewhat arbitrary and obscures some important interlinkages between these sets of pursuits. The actual headings selected are intended to convey consequential features of human group life, but other people may have cast these same sets of activities in different manners, perhaps using fewer or more major headings and emphasizing or subsuming certain sets of activities in ways not done here. Still, the essential value of the research agenda outlined rests on researchers and analysts attending to the ongoing accomplishment of human group life, as opposed to adopting a factors-oriented approach that neglects human enterprise in any setting.

In generating this listing, I have tried to be mindful of the most elementary human conditions for existence as well as to consider the diversity of contemporary practices and to anticipate future concerns. As much as possible, an attempt has been made to maintain historical-cultural developmental flows for the materials outlined here. However, the range of concurrent and interconnected concerns entailed in (a) the sheer human struggle for survival, coupled with the uneven development of both (b) baseline variants of human adjustment, and (c) the pursuit of relative "luxuries" or secondary interests, confound sequencings along temporal-developmental dimensions. Likewise, although these realms of activity are presented in more generic fashions, some materials that are specifically mindful of developments in contemporary Western society have also been introduced. Hopefully, this material may foster ethnographic inquiry in our own society, but it should be appreciated that other communities may develop practices along lines other than those noted here. As well, the listings are far from uniform in the detail in which they are developed. In large part, this reflects the limits of my own thoughtfulness and stocks (and lacks) of knowledge in particular areas. Much more important than the actual headings or topics, therefore, is the ongoing attentiveness of researchers and analysts to the processes by which people accomplish their activities on a here-and-now basis.

Finally, although some of the ethnographic research (particularly of an interactionist nature) that has been conducted in these areas is indicated, the citations provided are far from exhaustive or comprehensive. Not only am I apt to have missed many viable sources,[1] but the ethnographic work remaining is truly monumental in proportion to what has been accomplished to date. For this reason, too, researchers are strongly advised to read ethnographic research in subject areas other than those in which they have direct substantive interests. Although there is a general tendency for people to attempt to become substantive or area specialists, it is often the case that a great deal of, if not also the most, pertinent conceptual literature is apt to have been developed in substantively unrelated contexts that parallel researcher settings in processual (i.e., generic) terms. As well, beyond benefitting from the conceptual cross-fertilization that emerges in this manner, those who read ethnographies more extensively are apt to develop a stronger appreciation of the human condition in all of its manifestations.

Subcultural Mosaics: Examining Realms of Human Endeavor

In an attempt to present materials encompassing the major boundaries of human experience in a more manageable package, the research agenda has been organized around (i.e., reduced to) seven major themes: *achieving intersubjectivity; managing place and space; maintaining presence; encountering the interpersonal other; managing morality; emphasizing community presence; and experiencing the (intersubjective) self.*

While addressing general sets of human concerns, readers might be cautioned that these broad areas conceal a great deal of the diversity and interconnectedness (intersectedness or interwovenness) of the activities that constitute the (mosaic) essence of human group life. Thus, an appreciation of each subfield of human activity would seem, in some measure, to enable social scientists to better understand the nature of human group life in every other context. It should also be noted that the relative importances attributed to any of these realms of human engagement may vary greatly across subcultural communities as well as over time and across contexts within broader communities. It must be emphasized, however, that while these topics denote potential realms of inquiry and synthesis in the abstract, *it is not until people act and interact* mindfully of this or that pursuit that one may speak of subcultures *being invoked* or coming into play. No one knows just exactly what forms particular life-worlds may assume or how long they will last, but it is incumbent on social scientists to be attentive to the fundamentally intersubjective essence of every realm of human endeavor they consider, to concentrate their emphasis on people *doing* things within the context of "minded" (Mead, 1934) enterprise.[2]

One more note is in order. Because of the amount of material entailed in outlining the subcultural mosaic, the research agenda introduced here has been divided into three chapters. This is not done with the intention of privileging one set of topics over another or separating one set of subcultural themes from another. It simply represents an attempt to present this material in what hopefully will be a more accessible format.

Achieving Intersubjectivity

While a fuller appreciation of intersubjectivity or the achievement of mutual awareness with the other may be seen to encompass all of the experiences that might be entailed in the entire subcultural mosaic in which people find themselves, the matter of achieving "mindedness with the other" represents the essential departure point for the study of the human community.[3] In the themes most immediately following, attention is given to (a) symbolic interchange, (b) the development of stocks of knowledge, and (c) human encounters with [objects].

The achievement of intersubjectivity is the primary enabling feature of the human community, but it also must be emphasized that intersubjectivity cannot be comprehended as an element of the human condition apart from the entire range of activity in which humans engage. Thus, considerations of intersubjectivity both enlighten and are enlightened by close examinations of human involvements in *all* realms of the subcultural mosaic.

Managing Symbolic Interchange

The development and use of language is pivotal to the human accomplishment of intersubjectivity and group life as we know it. Denoting a shared symbolic system or a set of mutually acknowledged referents, language allows people to achieve life-worlds that are profoundly social and uniquely enabling. Further, once one acknowledges the intersubjective base of human experience and human behavior, it becomes strikingly apparent that human behavior cannot be reduced to the properties of individuals. It is this same intersubjective essence, as Dilthey (Ermarth, 1978) and Blumer (1969) emphasize, that also necessitates the development of a methodology for studying the human condition that is substantially different from that used to study any other (nonminded, nonsymboling, noninteracting) objects of human awareness.

However, since the accomplishment of intersubjectivity also entails a social process, it too lends itself to inquiry. In particular, social scientists may find it most instructive to consider the ways in which symbols are implemented, developed, transmitted, used, extended, rejected, and possibly replaced. As well, attention may also be directed toward the ways in which people with existing (linguistically informed) viewpoints deal with other (new to them) intersubjective worlds as these are encountered. Although intersubjective disjunctures, discontinuities, or contrasts may be more profoundly experienced by people (e.g., immigrants, missionaries, anthropological ethnographers) exposed to others using entirely different languages, each venture into another subcultural context is likely to entail some attentiveness and adjustment to new symbols as well as redefinitions of objects and activities that the newcomers had associated with other life-worlds. As people trying to comprehend the viewpoints of others, ethnographers may be especially attentive to such matters, but the practical accomplishment of intersubjectivity both within and across interactive contexts represents a fundamental and ongoing concern across the range of human association. Thus, processes of the sort following would seem to represent valuable points of inquiry.

Achieving Interpersonal Communication
 Anticipating Encounters
 Making Indications to Others / Observing and Assessing Responses
 Encountering Indications from Others
 Making Sense of the Other / Seeking Clarification
 Elaborating on Interchanges (and Themes Therein)
 Assessing Encounters
 Terminating Communications / Reinvoking Communications

Teaching Language (to Others)
 Dealing with Children[4]
 Encountering People Who Rely on Other Primary Languages
 Working with Sensory-Deprived People[5]
 Assessing People's Communicative Competencies
 Providing Remedial Instruction

Developing Linguistic Variants (and Alternative Modes of Symbolic Communication)
 Trying to Express New Experiences and Concepts, Share Information with Others[6]
 Pursuing Linguistic Autonomy in Group settings[7]
 Blending Linguistic Life-worlds

Experiencing New (Different) Linguistic Contexts
 Achieving Primary (Specific Language) Fluency
 Encountering Difficulties Acquiring Fluency
 Encountering Linguistic Diversity on a Solitary Basis
 Encountering Linguistic Diversity in the Company of Familiar (Symbolically Consonant) Others
 Attempting to Reframe New Life-worlds within Preexisting Perspectives
 Experiencing Communicative Incompetence in New Linguistic Settings
 Seeking / Obtaining Interpretive Assistance from Others
 Learning New Languages, Perspectives, Practices, Competencies

Losing (and Maintaining) Earlier Communicative Competencies
and Viewpoints

Developing Stocks of Knowledge

People's stocks of knowledge rest fundamentally on the human
capacity for achieving intersubjectivity through symbolic communication. However, as essential pragmatizing features of the human
condition, people's stocks of knowledge allow them to make sense
of, and act toward, "the world out there." While denoting (intersubjectively developed) symbolic or imaged productions of sorts, people's
stocks of knowledge importantly include all of their notions of [object]
awareness, definition, control, and usage.

Whereas the term *technology* is often associated with modern
"equipment" and "devices," a more fundamental sense of technology
would include all wisdoms and "tools" (conceptual and physical) that
people use to shape or manipulate aspects of their situations, including
their interactions with other people. People's (working) stocks of
knowledge are subject to ongoing testing, revision, and rejection, as
well as intentional and inadvertent disregard, but the most profound
gift that one generation of people may give to the next would seem
to be their stocks of knowledge. Like other aspects of human interchange, however, the transmission of knowledge is apt to be quite
uneven. Thus, we would want to be attentive to matters of generating,
recording, and transmitting—as well as receiving, evaluating, accepting,
and rejecting—"knowledge."[8]

While people's stocks of knowledge are commonly linked to
"educational associations" (especially schools and universities in
contemporary society), social scientists would be remiss were they
not also to attend to the production and diffusion of "folk" knowledge,
as well as other forums that may be invoked in developing and transmitting notions "about the world." Likewise, although stocks of
knowledge are often associated with abstract, secular forms of knowing,
researchers may also be mindful of more applied (craft-like, technical),
moral (religious, political), recreational (e.g., hobbies, sports, entertainment), and expressive (e.g., art, fashion, emotion) aspects of people's
"educations." Finally, recognizing the interactive nature of the educational experience, researchers would likely find it most productive to
consider the ways in which the targets of knowledge-related communications deal with these endeavors.

Focusing on (a) the development of folk and scientific knowledge,
(b) the problematics of stabilizing and maintaining information at an

intersubjective level, (c) the creation and maintenance of educational forums (and academic institutions), (d) the pragmatics of attending to conveyed stocks of knowledge, and (e) the ways in which people experience more formal "student" roles, the material following attempts to outline central features of people's experiences with (intersubjectively shared) stocks of knowledge.

Developing Folk and Scientific Knowledge[9,10,11]
    Defining Situated and Enduring Concerns about "Knowing"
    Learning through Trial, Consequences, and Adjustment
    Observing (Reflectively) Others
    Sharing Wisdoms
        Drawing inferences / Discussing thoughts with others
        Developing recipes or "rules of thumb"
        Fashioning conceptual and physical technologies
        Instructing others (providing definitions, illustrations, applications)
    Using and Reassessing Wisdoms and Technologies
        Encountering limitations / Recasting concepts
        Promoting other viewpoints and practices

Stabilizing and Maintaining Information
    Building on Verbal Communication (Routines and Instruction)
    Generating Collective Memories (Folklore, Records, Histories, Genealogies)
    Developing Graphic, Print, and Electronic Material (Indicators, Reminders, and Records)[12]

Developing, Funding, and Maintaining Educational Forums[13]
    Conceptualizing and Legitimating Particular Educational Forums
    Pursuing Funding (and Sponsors) for Particular Educational Forums
    Promoting Particular Educational Forums in the Community
    Implementing and Assessing Particular Educational Policies and Programs
    Locating, Assessing, Retaining, and Releasing Instructors[14]
    Providing Instruction (Instructor Activities and Experiences)[15]
        Presenting materials / Assessing student performance[16]
        Managing trouble
    Indicating Effectiveness of Forum
    Encountering Competition across Educational Forums

Acknowledging (and Disattending to) Stocks of Knowledge
    Accessing (Being Exposed to) Instructional Forums
    Attending to Incoming Information

Observing interest on the part of others
Experiencing curiosity
Desiring to become proficient, knowledgeable
Having problems to solve[17]
Viewing others as knowledgeable
Trying to evidence the learned (capable) self to others
Disattending to Incoming Information
Encountering conceptual problems
Being unable to discern significant from inconsequential aspects of messages
Not understanding central concepts
Being unable to envision applications
Experiencing Skepticism
Doubting the relevancy of incoming messages
Encountering inconsistencies
Defining learning as undesired (or nonessential) activity
Becoming diverted by other interests, viewpoints, or involvements[18]
Avoiding accountability
Finding alternative ways of dealing with learning situations

Experiencing Classroom (Student) Routines[19]
Gaining Entry / Getting to School / Attending Classes
Learning Things from School / Relating to Instructors
Doing (and Avoiding) Assignments[20]
Preparing for and Taking Tests
Socializing with Friends and Other Students at School (During Classes, Breaks)[21]
Avoiding School (or Specific Classes)[22]
Coping with Outside Involvements and Events
Managing Setbacks / Facing Program Failure / Leaving School Prematurely
Making the Grade / Graduating / Entering New Life-Worlds

Dealing with Objects

Insofar as humans "live in a world of [objects],"[23] the material outlined here is relevant across the entire range of human experience. Denoting anything that can be conceptualized, envisioned, indicated, pointed to, referenced, talked about, or even thought about, [objects] would include all environmental and biological phenomena; all tools, appliances, and devices of all sorts; as well as all clothing and other apparel, and all realms of fashion, ideas, concepts, and beliefs—in short, all things of human awareness. The human capacities for distinguishing, developing, using, owning, making, changing, trading, maintaining, disposing of, and salvaging objects introduce a vast array of themes for research in the social sciences. Interestingly, though, despite the profound significance of [objects] for an appreciation of the human condition, social scientists have been notably inattentive to the "world of objects."[24]

Although the materials presented here are also relevant to animals and other biological life-forms (including people), the differing ways in which people define and attend to particular [objects] as "life-forms" and "agents" introduces some additional complexities for the study of human-[object] relations. Insofar as people distinguish any "life-forms" (e.g., other mammals, birds, fish, reptiles, insects, plants, bacteria, and such) from more "inert substances" (e.g., rocks, wood, water), as people in contemporary Western society conventionally do, social scientists may also find it instructive to attend to the sets of activities that people develop around their differing images of [objects]. Although people's definitions of "life-forms" seem somewhat contingent on their prevailing states of technology, we should not overlook broader tendencies on the part of humans to endow [objects] that contemporary Westerners typically consider lifeless (e.g., rocks, clouds, sun, stars) with lifelike (and even human, agency-like) qualities. The last set of themes in this section addresses some issues along these lines, albeit with a contemporary Western world slant.

Defining, Using, and Valuing [Objects][25]

> Learning about and/or Delineating Particular [Objects] from Other [Objects]
>
> Reflecting on Particular Object Essences
>
> Conceptualizing Objects and Object Applications
>> Attending to others' modes of relating to objects
>> Envisioning object applications
>> Acquiring "wisdom" regarding object use and value
>> Discovering, innovating, and designing (prototypic[26]) objects and practices
>> Attending to necessity, utility, convenience, recreation, and entertainment[27]
>
> Developing Objects
>> Obtaining materials and resources (also funding projects, finding sponsors)
>> Shaping, designing and otherwise "engineering" objects[28]

Assembling and testing concepts (applying objects to the situations at hand)

Assessing and Valuing Objects[29]

Attending to others' and one's own definitions and experiences with objects

Evaluating and reconceptualizing object essences, features, applications

Being encouraged (recruited by others) to appreciate particular objects

Attempting to generate (and shape) valuings of objects on the part of others

Obtaining Objects

Finding (and Searching for) Objects

Making (also Assembling, Reshaping, Restoring) Objects

Receiving (Gifts), Sharing, Borrowing, Copying, or Stealing Objects (and Concepts)

Purchasing Objects (see "Trading Objects")

Keeping and Collecting Objects

Making, Packaging, and Distributing Objects

Producing Objects[30]

Financing "manufacturing" ventures (self-sufficiency, sponsors, investors)

Obtaining and assembling materials

Anticipating usages (self and/or others)

Establishing Cooperative Production Endeavors

Assembling and coordinating (communicating with, delegating, routinizing, managing) others

Encountering resistance from others

Dealing with individuals

Facing collective (emergent and organized) opposition

Sustaining a Focus (Interest, Enthusiasm) on Production / Becoming Distracted[31]

Packaging, Preserving, and Transporting Objects

Trading Objects[32]

Defining Eligible Items for, and Mediums of, Exchange[33]

Trading Occasionally (by Anyone)

Trading Systematically (Activities Assume Merchant, Dealer, or Vendor Proportions)[34]

Establishing trading practices and arenas

Obtaining stock (supplies for trade) / Defining prices and profits

Engaging in marketing and sales activities
   Selling on an interpersonal level
   Using displays, showrooms, exhibits, the media
   Building relationships / Collecting monies (goods) owed[35]
Ceasing trading activities
   Closing businesses / Going bankrupt
   Resuming trading activities
Facilitating Trade (Brokers, Financiers, Property Managers)
   Lending money / Financing supplies
   Establishing and managing trading arenas, exchange centers[36]
   Developing and providing bankruptcy services
Purchasing Objects (Buyer Activities)[37]
   Learning about objects (through others, media)
   Assessing objects for desirability
   Making deals for objects / Paying for objects
   Managing budgets and finances

Maintaining and Repairing Objects
   "Doing It Yourself" / Getting Help from Others
   Establishing and Maintaining Service and Repair Industries
      Serving industrial, commercial, agricultural, governmental,
      consumer sectors
   Using (and Dealing with) Service Specialists (Customer Experiences)

Disposing of Objects
   Using Up (Expendable) Objects / Gifting, Sharing, Lending, Trading
   (and Selling)
   Losing, Discarding, Leaving Behind, Dumping, Destroying Objects

Salvaging (Refurbishing/Rendering/Recycling) Objects[38]

Dealing with "Life-form" Objects
   Defining Life-form Objects (e.g., Attributing Biological Qualities
   to [Objects])
   Defining Life-form Object Capabilities and Usages
   Hunting, Capturing, Terminating Life-form Objects
   Breeding, Raising, Domesticating Life-form Objects
   Using, Experimenting with,[39] and Consuming (Various Uses) Life-
   form Objects
   Treating, Caring for, Rehabilitating, Protecting,[40] and Mystifying[41]
   Life-form Objects
   Personifying "Life-form" Objects[42]
   Turning Life-form Objects into "Pets"[43]
   Establishing Life-form Object-Related Industries[44]

Managing Place and Space

Recognizing that people are embodied entities that not only require certain kinds of environments for their existence, but also possess capacities to mindfully (and technologically) adapt to a great many diverse circumstances, it is important to pay close attention to all manners of adjustments that people make with respect to both the fundamental human struggle for existence and the pursuit of other activities within the contexts of place and space. Clearly, people's capacities for achieving symbolic interchange, their existing (and developing) stocks of knowledge, and their definitions and modes of acting toward [objects], figure prominently in the ways in which they approach matters of place and space.[45] At the same time, however, each encounter with "the environment" affords opportunities for assessing and possibly reshaping the (intersubjective) world of human lived experience.

Acknowledging the Physical (Geographical) Environment

While a great deal of the preceding material acknowledges or presumes aspects of the physical environment in one or other ways, social scientists may also wish to attend more explicitly to the ways in which people envision and endeavor to come to terms with the physical contexts in which they find themselves. This would include such things as attentiveness to (a) physical conditions and objects of all manners (including those defined as "resources" and "obstacles"); (b) considerations of short-term and local, as well as more enduring and widespread, climatic conditions; (c) timing and sequencing of environmental phenomena;[46] and (d) any concerns with the impact of human (and other life-forms) activity on the environment in both short-term and long-run dimensions.[47]

As with objects more generally, it is essential that researchers attend to the delineations, definitions, and meanings that people associate with various aspects of the world about them. This would include the ways in which people envision, use, and shape any feature of their "environments," as well as their attempts to adjust to what they envision as disasters in these settings.

Attending and Adjusting to Aspects of the Environment
   Discerning and Defining Environmental Phenomena
   Using (Renewable and Nonrenewable) Environmental Objects to
      Accomplish Tasks
   Monitoring, Tracking, and Theorizing about Environmental
      Phenomena

Anticipating, Predicting, and Endeavoring to Control Environmental Phenomena

Attempting to Preserve (and Revitalize) Aspects of the Environment[48]
Developing Concerns about Maintaining (and Restoring) Environmental Conditions
Defining and Developing Desired Lines of (Environmentally-defined) Action
    Assuming self initiative
    Dealing with others (influence work, resistance, limitations)

Encountering and Dealing with Environmental Disasters
Defining Situations as Troublesome and Worthy of Attention[49]
Mobilizing for Action
    Embarking on solitary remedial activity
    Engaging in cooperative remedial ventures[50]
Forming and Implementing Plans
Encountering and Dealing with Resistance from Others
"Rebuilding" Surroundings and Resuming Other "Routines"
Anticipating Subsequent (identical, parallel, vaguely defined) Disasters
    Seeking safer havens or sites of activity
    Constructing shelters or other structures
    Attending to other (presumably) disaster related activities (and safety precautions)
    Establishing and maintaining disaster and emergency programs (and agencies)

Obtaining and Maintaining Spaces and Accommodations

Because people are entities that both require and use space, notions of places and shelters or territories and amenities represent important themes in both the human struggle for existence and the pursuit of secondary interests. Migrant groups may be seen to invoke more fleeting notions of space and land usages, but, for those who are more geographically fixed, matters of property claims, land development, and styles of usage often become enduring (and highly objectified) concerns. Government planners, demographers, geographers, and social ecologists, among others, have given extended attention to population distributions and people's living arrangements for centuries, but very little consideration has been directed toward *the human enterprise* that pervades every single aspect of space definition and use within the context of human group life.

Since the material following could be applied across wide ranges of "properties" (from "wilderness areas" to all sorts of residential, agricultural, government, military, religious, recreational, commercial, and corporate arrangements and practices), the themes listed below lend themselves to a great many new research sites for ethnographic inquiry. It is also hoped that these headings may provide analytical focal points of sorts around which people examining matters of space and accommodations in an assortment of contexts may begin to achieve further conceptual dialogue pertaining to the subprocesses involved therein.

Claiming and Maintaining Spaces
    Defining, Challenging, and Protecting Spaces
    Establishing Property and Land Usage Claims[51]
        Overseeing property claims and land uses / Invoking administrative authority
        Establishing policies for spaces and usages / Monitoring and enforcing space policies
        Encouraging (and discouraging) development[52]
    Constructing Facilities[53]
        Planning, financing, assembling, landscaping
        Servicing and repairing facilities

Using (and Sharing) Spaces and Facilities[54]
    Furnishing, Decorating, Rearranging and Cleaning Facilities
    Attending to Decorum[55]
    Adjusting to and Dealing with Others (and Their Concerns with Space and Propriety)

Buying, Selling, and Brokeraging Spaces and Facilities
    Buying and Selling Properties (see "Trading Objects")
    Brokeraging Real Estate (Lands and Facilities) / Operating Real Estate Agencies

Developing, Maintaining, and Using Temporary Spaces and Facilities
    Developing, Renting and Managing Places (Business Ventures)
        Renting houses, apartment buildings, land, storage areas[56]
        Running motels, hotels and other more transient accommodations
        Operating transportation facilities (moving companies and facilitators)
    Renting (As a Tenant, Patron) Lands and Facilities[57]
        Searching for places (and assessing feasibility) / Negotiating arrangements

Moving in, adjusting to, and customizing "temporary locations"[58]

Dealing with property managers / Encountering other renters

Moving out

Providing and Using Public Places, Available Spaces,[59] and Recreational Facilities[60]

Achieving Mobility and Transportation

As entities that are capable of (a) achieving intentional self-mobility, (b) deliberately moving other items, and (c) envisioning ways of using other objects to transport people and other items, people provide social scientists with a plethora of research sites revolving around matters of mobility. In addition to practices and devices more directly associated with (seemingly) more simplistic or self-reliant transportation of people, human communities commonly develop extended sets of skills and industries around the transportation process.[61] Since a great deal of human activity revolves around the movement of objects, extended examinations of these practices represent valuable routings for learning more about the human condition.

Developing Modes of Mobility and Transportation

Envisioning Transportation Concepts and Technologies

Developing Transportation Devices (see "Making, Packaging, and Distributing Objects")[62]

Implementing transportation devices / Encountering difficulties and limitations in usage

Adjusting to, and improving upon, existing transportation devices

Facilitating Mobility (Transportation Industries)

Manufacturing Transportation Devices

Servicing and Supporting Transportation Devices

Developing (work-role) expertise as operators, instructors, technicians[63]

Supplying enabling materials (e.g., fuels, components), repair facilities, and procedures

Developing and maintaining roads and other travelways

Establishing and enforcing travel regulations[65]

Operating insurance industries[65]

Owning, Accessing, and Using Particular Modes of Transportation

Learning about, Accessing, and Obtaining Transportation Devices[66]

Developing Familiarity (and Skill) with Particular Modes of Transportation
Using and Sharing Transportation Devices[67]
Encountering Difficulties En Route
Maintaining and Servicing Transportation Devices
Experiencing Accidents with Transportation Devices
    Getting into accidents
    Dealing with injuries, damages, and losses
    Sorting out events (and culpability) / Encountering control agencies, insurance adjustors

Accommodating and Encouraging Mobility
Renting Transportation Devices (and Spaces on Transportation Devices)
Providing Accommodations and Other Amenities on Travelways
Promoting a Tourist Trade (developing local attractions, establishing travel agencies)

Maintaining Presence

Beyond achieving intersubjectivity and coming to terms with a precarious geospatial environment, the human struggle for existence is also contingent on people's abilities to locate sources of nourishment and establish cooperative ventures of various sorts. Thus, concerns with food substances, clothing, human services, and the often related "quest for objects" represent both consequential arenas of human enterprise and important realms of study for social scientists. As well, people's involvements in each of these sectors of activity contribute in an emergent manner to the symbolic interchanges, stocks of knowledge, and senses of objects that constitute particular instances of the human community.

Locating and Consuming Foods
(Including Liquids and Other Substances)

Since human survival presupposes the availability of viable foods (solids, liquids, and other ingestible substances), the processes and problematics of defining feasible and desirable foods are issues worthy of much consideration on the part of social scientists, as are the related matters of obtaining, distributing, preparing, preserving, and consuming foods.[68] Regardless of whether people pursue food for baseline survival or attend to various taste preferences, "luxuries," moral issues, and the like, the human enterprise revolving around food lends itself to a great many fruitful realms of inquiry. However, given people's capacities for innovations and the pursuit of diverse experience, it seems advisable to attend as well to other substances (illicit and otherwise) that humans may consume beyond those that might be deemed "healthy" in any context. Indeed, since the human processes involved in defining, obtaining, distributing, preserving, and consuming substances considered of interest beyond their material value would seem parallel to those processes involved in dealing with food deemed "healthy" in this or that context, much more may be gained by maintaining substance co-presence than by separating these into separate realms of inquiry and analysis.

Defining Food[69]
> Attending to and Assessing (Desirable / Undesirable) Potential Food Sources

Obtaining Food (Liquids and Other Substances)
> Accessing, Hunting, Gathering Food[70]
> Growing and Producing Food (Plants and Livestock)[71]
> Creating (Natural) Food Substitutes
> Trading and Purchasing Food (see "Trading Objects")
> Sharing, Borrowing, Mooching, Scrounging, Begging, and Stealing Food
> Utilizing (Client Activity) Subsidized Food Programs, Centers, Institutions

Distributing Food
> Gifting, Sharing, Lending Food
> Developing Food Supplier Networks[72]
> Trading (and Retailing) Food (see "Trading Objects")
> Opening and Operating Restaurants, Taverns, Catering Services[73]
> Establishing and Managing Subsidized Food Programs, Distribution Centers, Services

Preparing Food[74]
> Preparing Casual (Residential) Food / Defining and Preparing Exotic and Ceremonial Food
> Preparing Food in Restaurant, Catering, and Institutional Food Settings

Preserving Food
> Attending to Durability ("Shelf-life" or Spoilage of Particular Foods)
> Developing Knowledge of and Technologies for Preserving Food
> Preserving Practices in Domestic, Commercial, and Other Settings

Developing and Maintaining Food Preparation, Preservation, and Distribution Industries

Consuming Food[75]

> Learning about, and Attending to, Consumptive Practices, Proprieties, and Preferences
>
> Experiencing Openness and Practicing Restraint Regarding Consumption[76]

Developing and Using Clothing

The term *clothing* is used herein to refer to any item that people use to wrap, cover, protect, display, or enhance some part of their bodies. This would include such things as coats, pants, dresses, scarves, mitts, hats, footwear, and undergarments of all sorts, as well as armor and other protective gear (e.g., worn by firefighters, deep-sea divers, astronauts, medical personnel, or beekeepers). Although less conventionally defined as clothing, it also seems analytically instructive to include eye-wear, lotions, cosmetics, fragrances, jewelry, hairstyles and grooming-related appearances, and other adornments (e.g., marks, costumes) or markings (e.g., tattoos, scarring, body piercing) under the broader umbrella of clothing. As well, it is worth noting that while objects may be intended to be worn as clothing in some sense (e.g., laying on a store shelf or hanging in someone's closet at home), it is "in the wearing" that things achieve their fullest significance as "objects of clothing." It is essential, therefore, that analysts not disregard the ways in which people use, implement, or incorporate objects (as clothing) into their activities (and appearances—both given off and interpreted) on a more situated basis.

Clearly, different peoples may have quite different geographical conditions (including landscape, climate, and other [objects]) with which to contend in the mere quest for physical survival, but beyond these baseline clothing applications, attire of various sorts may be put to wide ranges of use (and expression). Clothing may be employed to provide protection or practical convenience, or may be used to generate desired images or entertainment of sorts. Items of clothing may also be used in conjunction with minimal physical activity or, conversely, employed to enable people to engage in intense physical exertion. Clothing may be strategically employed in military agendas or used sensuously in romantic encounters. People may associate certain attire with immorality or deep religious devotions. People may also use clothing as a means of "identifying with" or "standing out from" others. Clothing may also be used to sharpen people's role identities as well as to blur or conceal people's involvements or presence in community contexts. Further, because of the visual and other sensory images associated with items of clothing worn by particular people, these items are frequently used in identifying or distinguishing specific people (or categories of people) within a community.

As with other objects to which people may attend, the meanings or images that people associate with clothing and the lines of action that they may adopt with respect to particular objects (as clothing) seem limited primarily by their existing stocks of knowledge and their capacities for reflective interaction.

Like other objects, as well, things used as clothing commonly come to represent focal points of considerable creativity and enterprise, technology and production, trading, and other interchanges. While items of clothing (and styles of dress) often seem taken for granted or envisioned as "natural" by people born into communities, it is important to appreciate the developmental (i.e., conceptual, interactive, enterprising, and processual) aspects of things used in one or other manners as "clothing."

Conceptualizing Attire and Applications of Attire
  Learning about Clothing from Others
  Developing (Assembling, Testing, and Adjusting) Prototypes of Attire[77]
  Customizing Apparel (Adjusting Objects to Different People)
  Incorporating New Materials and Technologies into Existing Attire

Acquiring, Using, and Maintaining Particular Objects of Clothing[78]
  Making, Sharing, Borrowing, Stealing, and Trading Objects of Clothing[79]
  Developing Proficiencies in the Use of Particular Objects of Clothing
  Maintaining (Caring for and Repairing) Attire
  Building and Maintaining Viable "Wardrobes"[80] / Disregarding and Discarding Attire[81]

Encouraging Others to Adopt Particular Attire
  Portraying Attire and Providing Instructions in Clothing Use
  Generating Positive and Negative Definitions of Particular Objects (and Appearances)
  Developing Industries Around the Production, Promotion, and Use of Clothing[82]
  Fostering Attentiveness to New Fashions in Clothing[83,84]

Extending Attire Applications to Other Life-Form Objects[85]

Providing Person-Directed Services

Encompassing assistance that pertains to people's physical well-being and a variety of services of a more secondary nature, the material outlined in this section suggests another set of topics central to a fuller appreciation of the human condition. Although in contemporary Western society one finds a vast array of "service specialists" (practitioners, agencies, and institutions) who cater to human "clients" on a full-time, compensation-oriented basis, it is important to also attend to both the more fundamental nature (and roots) of these services and the more informal, often voluntary forms of assistance that people provide for one another even in seemingly "high technology" societies.[86]

Denoting an almost unending set of research sites, the realm of person-directed services also provides a wide assortment of contexts in which people more explicitly enter the sphere of [objects] to be managed in some regard by others. This is especially the case for considerations of primary health care, supportive care facilities, "last services," and other modes of personal assistance.

Focusing on entertainment as an aspect of person-directed service, the last item in this section also treats the clients as objects to be acted toward, but, as a service, entertainment is often (and especially in the media) delivered at a more generalized level. Thus, while entertainment may also be highly personalized in presentational thrust, it highlights some dimensions that tend to be less developed in other areas of person-directed services.

Engaging in Family and Casual Health Care Practices
Caring for the Young / Caring for the Elderly[87]
Attending to Illness, Injury, and Incapacitation

Practicing Folk and "Certified" Physical Health Treatments[88]
Developing, Testing, and Promoting Treatment Concepts, Techniques, and Products
Accessing and Practicing on Particular Cases
Assessing and Refining Treatments
Obtaining Supplies and Funding
Sharing Stocks of Knowledge with Others

Developing Health Support Technologies and Industries[89]
Developing Health-Care Products (Concepts, Procedures, Equipment, Substances)
Testing, Assessing, and Adjusting (Revising) Health-Care Products

Producing Health-Care Products / Promoting Health-Care Products
Encountering User Resistance and Product Competition
Terminating Health-Care Products

Establishing and Operating Health Facilities (Centers, Clinics, Hospitals)
Doing the Foundational Work
Conceptualizing health facilities (and defining abstract agendas)
Legitimating facilities (promoting concepts and gaining acceptance)
Pursuing, obtaining, and managing funding
Locating and training personnel
Operating Health Facilities
Developing (and changing) agendas
Assigning and maintaining staff
Accessing, classifying, and processing health-related cases[90,91]
Maintaining Health Facilities
Assessing effectiveness / Maintaining internal order
Portraying accountability[92]
Dealing with outside challenges and competition

Providing Supportive Care Facilities[93]
Establishing and Maintaining Care Arrangements for the Young, Aged, Infirm, Disabled
(see preceding material on "Establishing and Operating Health Facilities")

Providing Last (Postenabling) Services[94]
Dealing with Deceased and Other Affected (Concerned) Persons
Developing and Implementing Specialized Practices, Agencies, and Industries

Providing Services for Other Modes of Personal Assistance
Catering to Personal Appearances[95]
Assisting friends and associates
Operating commercial ventures (see "Trading Objects")
Establishing and Maintaining Personal Counseling and Other Remedial Services[96]
Assisting friends and associates
Operating commercial ventures (see "Trading Objects")

Providing Entertainment
Defining Entertainment (Positively Defined Interests, Fascinations) in the Setting

Entertaining Friends and Associates
Providing Focused (Specialized, Sustained) Entertainment[97]
  Developing entertainment, recreational themes
  Coordinating people, places, and routines to facilitate entertainment
  Marketing entertainment to prospective audiences (see "Trading Objects")
  Becoming entertainers (see involvement processes in chapter 3)
  Entertaining audiences (processes and problematics of doing performances)
  Working alone / Providing team-based performances
  Adjusting to target (audience) interests / Facing competitors
Using the Media to Convey Entertainment
Utilizing Entertainment Themes to Encourage People's Participation in other Agendas[98]

Obtaining Negotiables for Exchange

Without making claims about particular practices in any society, once people "envision objects in ownership terms" a consequential foundation is laid for exchange relationships (and the transfer of objects that this implies). Even here, however, people's concepts of objects that may be exchanged can vary immensely as may their notions of both "valued goods (and services)" and "abstract negotiables." Since matters pertaining to the trading of objects were considered earlier in this chapter, the emphasis here is on the task of attaining goods (and funds) with which to embark on trade.[99]

People sometimes obtain commodities for trade as a consequence of fortuitous circumstances and benefactors of various sorts, but for many others the task of obtaining negotiables very much represents a life-long challenge. Thus, more consequential than the exact forms that negotiables assume in particular settings is the matter of finding ways of acquiring desired goods. Social scientists may have directed little attention to the manners in which people obtain, conceptualize, and use money and other mediums of trade, but there is little doubt that a great deal of activity in some societies is organized around the acquisition of negotiables. Hopefully, the material following will help draw attention to the importance of these areas of human enterprise.

Finding and Receiving Negotiables
  Being Lucky (Finding, Accessing, Winning Valuables; Being "Born" into Fortune)
  Striving to be Lucky (e.g., Gambling, Looking for Signs)

Having Benefactor Relationships
    Receiving Gifts and Inheritances from Concerned Parties
    Tapping into Others' Resources (Finances and Other Objects)
        Sharing family resources / Marrying into resource situations
        Establishing partnerships / Finding (and presuming) sponsors

Obtaining Employment
    Encountering Occupational Subcultures[100,101]
        Encountering opportunities
        Looking for work (and pursuing skills, experience)[102]
        Experiencing closure (lack of workplace alternatives)
        Overcoming reservations (regarding particular work roles, settings)
    Learning Work Skills / Fitting into Work Settings
    Avoiding or Minimizing Work
    Experiencing Success
    Encountering Disenchantment or Failure on the Job
    Dealing with Transitory Work Situations[103]
    Obtaining Work-related Security / Seniority
    Negotiating Payment and Other Terms of Employment
        Developing work arrangements with employers on one's own
        Establishing worker collectives (and unions)[104]
            Promoting, recruiting, sustaining, utilizing, imposing collectives (and unions)
            Negotiating settlements[105] / Going on strike (and aftermath)
            Encountering power struggles within collectives / Experiencing disenchantment
            Deunionizing (or embarking on other collective dismantling) episodes
            Witnessing employment shifts (company goes bankrupt, closes, moves)
    Leaving Occupational Settings
        Quitting, being dismissed, or retiring
        Reentering the work world[106]

Embarking on Occasional Trading Practices and (Systematic) Business Activities[107]
    Trading (or Renting) Possessions (e.g., Private Arrangements, Garage Sales, Consignments)
    Engaging in Systematic Trading Practices (see "trading objects")

Arranging Loans (Business and Personal)[108]
    Appealing to Trust on the Part of Others / Providing Security

Repaying Loans / Defaulting on Loans
Experiencing Corporate or Personal Bankruptcy

Openly Soliciting Assistance from Others
(Approaching Private or Public Sources)[109]
    Soliciting for Oneself
    Canvassing for Others (Individuals or Associations)

Participating in Financial Relief Programs
(Unemployment, Welfare, Subsidies)[110]
    Learning of Financial Subsidies / Applying for Financial Subsidies
    Managing on (and Supplementing) Subsidies
    Terminating (and Losing) Subsidies

Achieving Gain through Adversarial Activities
    Gambling for Financial Gain[111]
    Entering Competitions (and Contests)
    Engaging in Theft and Related Enterprises[112]
    Dealing in Illicit Goods[113]
    Embarking on Interpersonal Intimidation (Robbery, Extortion, Blackmail)[114]
    Using the Courts for Financial Gain (Suing Spouses, Corporations, Others)

Endnotes:

1. Although somewhat uneven in their contents, the most valuable journals by far for ethnographic materials were the *Journal of Contemporary Ethnography, Qualitative Sociology,* and *Symbolic Interaction.* I did not make as much use of the anthropological literature as I had anticipated, in part reflecting the difficulty (and frustration) of attempting to sort through highly uneven mixes of agendas, conceptual orientations, and substantive foci. This is not to deny the value of specific pieces of work buried in this literature, but to point to my own relative lack of familiarity with this material and its rather diffuse nature. Hopefully, the conceptual scheme in the present volume, with its emphasis on activity, may help overcome some comparative conceptual problems should it be used in the study of human activity in other societies.
    In relative terms, the alleged "flagship journals" in sociology, namely the *American Sociological Review* and the *American Journal of Sociology* have contributed embarrassingly little to an intersubjective/ethnographic appreciation of the human condition over the last several decades. The major journals in psychology (e.g., the *American Journal of Psychology* and the *Journal of Personality and Social Psychology*) have been even less relevant in this regard.

2. In contrast to those who envision the study of human behavior in "objectivist" or "subjectivist" terms, the position taken here (Dilthey [Ermarth, 1978]; Mead, 1934; Schutz, 1962, 1964; Berger and Luckmann, 1966; Blumer, 1969; Prus, 1996) is that human behavior is an *intersubjectivist* phenomenon in a most comprehensive or pervasive sense.

3. For an overview of the roots of the intersubjectivist or interpretivist approach to the study of the human condition, as well as conceptual contrasts with structuralist and postmodernist approaches, see Prus (1996).

4. Since the acquisition of language is fused with the development of concepts (including rules), Strauss's (1952, 1954) work on children's conceptions of money is suggestive of the valuable work that may be conducted along these lines. For a case study of "children's negotiations of meanings in day care settings," see Mandell (1984). Also see Scott's (1969), Evans and Falk's (1986), and Evans's (1988, 1994) accounts of concept development and communication difficulties experienced by blind and deaf children, respectively.

5. Readers interested in the problematics and processes of providing instruction to and achieving communication with people with exceptional vision and hearing limitations are referred to R. Scott (1968, 1969), Higgins (1979), Kielhofner (1983), Evans and Falk (1986), Evans (1988, 1994). For an insightful account of the problems that formerly fluent individuals may have in communicating with "normals," see Robillard (1994).

6. Wierzbicka (1994) provides a thoughtful, cross-culturally informed, discussion of some of the problems associated with categorizing [objects]. Among sociologists, the ethnomethodologists (see Garfinkel, 1967; Mehan and Wood, 1975) have been particularly attentive to the problematics of concept development and communication.

7. The development of a secret or insider language or set of codes may enable participants to achieve (a) information control and strategic maneuvering, (b) freedom from outsider influence, and (c) expressive diversity. Among those involved in contemporary military operations, the matter of developing and deciphering (secret) codes has become a significant industry.

8. While perhaps not producing "primary culture" in quite the same way that those they study do, ethnographers may be seen to contribute to people's stocks of knowledge (or insights into the human condition) more generally by providing careful, sustained examinations of particular life-worlds. Likewise, although most ethnographers may not intend to produce "historical documents," the accounts that they assemble may very well have that quality for future scholars. Insofar as they develop some body of knowledge pertaining to the human condition, then ethnographers may be seen to generate primary culture as well. Clearly, these endeavors will be of most contemporary and long-term value when they are highly detailed, extensively grounded in the life-worlds of the ethnographic other, and respect the social essence of the human group (Blumer, 1969) as opposed to invoking moralistic, advocacy, or expressive agendas (for a more sustained critique of postmodernist and related agendas, see Prus [1996:217–33]).

9. Although "folk knowledge" is often associated with "primitive societies" or "earlier times," there are many realms of "folk" knowledge in any society. Consider the ways in which people learn about food, illness, sexuality, religion, transportation, clothing, shopping, entertainment, and the like. Indeed, each realm of human involvement seems informed by stocks of "folk knowledge." This also appears to hold true for people involved in highly specialized learning facilities, wherein both instructors and students develop (folk-informed) subcultures of their own (e.g., see Caplow and McGee, 1958; Haas and Shaffir, 1987). Virtually all Chicago-style ethnographies provide illustrations of the "acquisition of perspectives" (and the folk knowledge implied therein).

10. It may be advantageous to distinguish "scientific" and "folk" knowledge in some respects, but it also may be observed (Prus, 1996: especially 94–98 and 203–16) that the scientific enterprise is fundamentally intersubjective in its constitution and that "anyone who actively *(and reflectively)* engages aspects of one's environment may be seen to adopt some minimalist notion of a scientific stance" (Prus, 1996:214).

11. The study of science as an area of human endeavor is relatively underdeveloped compared to some other substantive realms, but readers may refer to Kuhn (1962), Barnes (1974), Knorr-Cetina (1981, 1983), Barnes and Edge (1982), Collins and Pinch (1982, 1993), Latour (1987), Mukerji (1989), Star (1989), Clarke and Gerson (1990), Pickering (1990, 1992, 1993, 1994), Clarke and Fujimura (1992), Barley and Bechkey (1994), Kohler (1994), Henderson (1995). Karen Knorr-Cetina (1995) provides an excellent review of this literature. Unfortunately, as observed elsewhere (Prus, 1996:94–98), little of this material is explicitly ethnographic in thrust.

12. Powell (1985) provides a valuable ethnographic account of the book-publishing industry. For an interesting case of "constructing the truth," see Tomlinson's (1986a) account of editing an encyclopedia. Using food preparations as an ethnographic context, Tomlinson (1986b) also provides an instructive commentary on the practical problems of "following written instructions."

13. In addition to competing with other "established forums," institutions of learning may also have to compete with parents who operate home-based schools (Knowles, 1991).

14. For some ethnographic accounts of academic life and endeavors, see Caplow and McGee's *The Academic Marketplace* (1958); Reid's (1982) statement on academic general practitioners in medical school; Laub's *Criminology in the Making* (1983); and Haas and Shaffir's (1987) study of medical school.

15. See, for instance, the work of Martin (1975), Hargreaves et al. (1975), and Haas and Shaffir (1987).

16. Dingwall (1987) develops an instructive inquiry around the question of how teachers justify letting students pass.

17. As Goldstein et. al.'s (1985) study of physicians pursuing holistic medical practices suggests, the matter of "having problems to solve" is apt to foster a greater receptivity to new forms of learning.

18. See Bernstein (1972) and Adler and Adler (1991) for instances of diversions in student life.

19. While addressing people's educational experiences more generally, readers may benefit from examining the ethnographic studies of Becker, Hughes et al. (1961, 1968), Bernstein (1972), Hargreaves et al. (1975), Albas and Albas (1984, 1988, 1994), Winfree et al. (1984), Fine (1985), Haas and Shaffir (1987), and Adler and Adler (1991).

20. Although focused more on types of work diversions than the ways in which people become involved in and sustain "student fritters" at the university level, Bernstein's (1972) work is still quite suggestive. For a consideration of some aspects of essay writing, see Grills (1985).

21. For some indications of peer culture in university settings, see Haas and Shaffir (1977, 1982, 1987), Kleinman (1983), Albas and Albas (1988), Adler and Adler (1991), and Granfield (1991, 1992).

22. Kalab (1987) provides a brief account of nonattendance practices in the university setting.

23. I've bracketed the term *objects* (i.e., [objects]) on some occasions to emphasize the problematic features of attentiveness, demarcation, definition, usage, and valuing that people might associate with particular [things] in their universes of intersubjective awareness and activity.

24. Archaeologists represent something of an exception in this regard, for they spend much of their time attempting to uncover meaningful human objects and develop interpretations of the ways in which these objects were used. However, lacking a more direct intersubjective base on which to develop more informed contexualizations of [objects], archaeological work is inevitably highly speculative. Somewhat ironically, we have comparatively few instances of attentiveness to the human use of objects on a more contemporary plane wherein it would be much easier to establish with intersubjective (ethnographic) confidence the ways in which objects are used in practice.

25. Although his statement reflects an uneven mixture of scholarly orientations to [objects], I found Belk (1988) very helpful in developing this discussion. Conceptually, however, this consideration of objects is centrally informed by Mead (1934), Schutz (1962), Berger and Luckmann (1966), Blumer (1969) and the Chicago (interactionist) ethnographic tradition. A careful reading of any ethnography in this tradition will reveal the importance of people coming to terms with (i.e., acquiring perspectives on and acting toward) the [objects] in that setting.

26. Hopefully, terms such as *prototype* and *engineering* do not obscure the very fundamental aspects of using, making, and reshaping objects on the parts of *all* peoples.

27. Nash's (1990) ethnographic consideration of "working at and working" computers is suggestive of the many ways that people may incorporate objects into their routines.

28. For some ethnographic entries into the world of high technology engineering and science lab practices, see Knorr-Cetina (1981), Kunda (1992), Barley and Bechky (1994), and Henderson (1995).

29. Although both the settings in which and the objects to which valuings are assigned are virtually limitless, consider the promotion of valuing of objects in the marketplace (Prus, 1989a, 1989b), the art world (McCall, 1977; Valentine, 1982; Gibbon, 1987), and the antique or collectors' world (Stenross, 1994).

30. Despite a rather massive literature "on work," relatively little attention has been given to the ways in which people actually make, produce, or assemble objects. Interestingly, though, a number of ethnographic studies have been developed around the production of art and theatre. See, for instance, Christopherson (1974), Lyon (1974), Faulkner (1976), McCall (1977), Mukerji (1977), Mast (1983), Dubin (1985), Schwartz (1986), Baroody-Hart and Farrell (1987), Gilmore (1987), and Friedman (1990).

31. Bernstein's (1972) consideration of student fritters and Nash's (1990) portrayal of computer fritters are instructive here.

32. While many of the points depicted here imply distinct roles of "buyers" and "sellers," it should be emphasized that both parties to an exchange should be seen as targets and tacticians on a more or less simultaneous basis. This holds even when people assume the highly institutionalized roles of "vendors" and "consumers" (see Prus, 1989a, 1989b, 1993a, 1993b, 1994a; Prus and Frisby, 1990; Prus and Dawson, 1991).

33. For an instructive conceptual discussion of the intersubjective essences of valuing and exchange, see Simmel's *The Philosophy of Money* (1907).

34. This material on trading objects derives much inspiration from some ethnographic examinations of vendor activities in the marketplace (Prus, 1989a, 1989b; Prus and Frisby, 1990). For some other statements on marketplace exchanges, see Bigus (1972), Unruh (1979b), Valdez (1984), Gilderbloom (1985), Smith (1989), Clark and Pinch (1995), and Peretz (1995). For valuable accounts of illicit trade worlds, see Cressey (1932), Roebuck and Frese (1976), Adler and Adler (1980), Prus and Irini (1980), Fields (1984), Adler (1985), Steffensmeier (1986), Ronai and Ellis (1989), Murphy et al. (1990), Williams (1991), and Tunnell (1993).

35. See Rock (1973) and Bass (1983) for some field research on credit collection activities.

36. Consider, for instance, the enterprise entailed in setting up and operating markets, malls, lending institutions, stock exchanges, and brokerages of various sorts.

37. For some ethnographic materials on consumer behavior, see Prus and Frisby (1990); Baumann (1991), Prus and Dawson (1991); Prus (1993a, 1993b, and 1994a); and Peretz (1995). Somewhat parallel practices on the part of people buying products for manufacture and resale are evident in Prus (1989b:133–72). As Steffensmeier's (1986) account of "fencing" indicates, those involved in illicit trade are faced with similar concerns.

38. Ralph's (1950) M.A. thesis on junk dealers provides a valuable ethnographic account of the salvaging industry in a major urban center.

39. For some ethnographic work on animal experimentation, see Arluke (1991, 1994).

40. In addition to practices designed to foster human functioning (see the later section on "person-directed" services), a number of industries have emerged around the preservation and functioning of other life-form objects. For an ethnographic encounter with veterinary clinics, see Sanders (1994).

41. Sutherland and Nash's (1994) account of the tendency on the part of those involved in the animal rights movement to view animals in mystical terms is pertinent here.

42. This would include such things as "talking with" these "life-forms" as well as presuming other modes of human reflectivity on their part. Also consider the practices of "naming" and "dressing" these objects.

43. Hickrod and Schmitt (1982), Robins et al. (1991), and Sanders (1993, 1994) provide some insightful ethnographic materials on pets and their owners.

44. Beyond the food production industries (agriculture, fisheries) catering to humans more directly, an assortment of industries have arisen around the tasks of feeding and maintaining a wide range of life-forms. Ethnographers have yet to attend to the human enterprise developed around this theme.

45. As a consequence of the contrasts in the ways that people approach *place* and *space* across societies, the anthropological literature affords analysts interested in these aspects of the human condition a great many insights into these matters. See, for instance, Malinowski (1922), Chagnon (1992), and Lee (1992).

46. People may develop quite different notions of "time," but some appreciation of change (and development) and repetition (cycles) of events (even if only as basic as night and day) seems fundamental to many aspects of the human condition. Ethnographically rooted examinations of people's perceptions, definitions, and uses of time (cycles and developments) merit greater attention on the part of social scientists, as does the development of devices (e.g., moon cycles, tides, calendars, clocks) for marking time, and human attentiveness to the temporal sequencing associated with all manners of planning, coordinating, and implementing activities. Albeit contextually focused, Calkins's (1970) account of time usage by patients in a rehabilitative facility is illustrative of some of the differing ways in which people may approach the concept of "temporality."

47. As well, while the quest for human survival depends on coming to terms with a more immediate planetary environment, researchers should also acknowledge people's attentiveness to the sun, moon, and other stellar objects. Space travel may be seen as a recent innovation but concerns with phenomena beyond the earth have been matters of longstanding interest to people and have been incorporated into human group life in many ways in different civilizations and over the centuries.

48. For instances of ethnographic research pertaining to pollution and related environmental mobilization and control endeavors, see Hawkins (1984), Gould (1993), Gould et al. (1993), and Alley (1994).

49. People's notions of "disasters" can vary greatly, from massive, immediate life-threatening situations to concerns with aesthetic aspects of

fleeting environmental conditions (e.g., consider the [rather ironic] "environmentally hazardous [to humans] war on dandelions"). As suggested by this sublisting, Blumer's (1971) statement on "social problems as collective behavior" is highly pertinent here, as is the somewhat parallel material on "constructing and regulating moralities" (chapter 5) more generally. Smith and Belgrave's (1995) ethnographic study of people's experiences with the devastation of Hurricane Andrew is indicative of the valuable work that could be done along these lines.

50. The material on "forming and coordinating associations" (chapter 3) is especially relevant here, as people find themselves seeking, offering, obtaining, and otherwise dealing with "help."

51. Rubin's (1987) consideration of "rule-making exceptions and county-land use" is instructive here.

52. For a preliminary statement from a much larger interactionist project on economic development (and the pursuit of corporate investors more specifically), see Prus and Fleras (1996).

53. Facilities would encompass any human-built or -used structures, regardless of end-purpose. Consider, for example, forums or places intended for residential, commercial, agricultural, educational, governmental, military, entertainment, or storage purposes. Since considerable enterprise often is entailed in preparing and shaping particular sites, researchers would also find it instructive to attend to the many industries that have developed around the construction of facilities. For instances of ethnographic work on building construction, see Reimer (1979) and Applebaum (1981).

54. Despite a pervasive concern with space and place, relatively few ethnographic inquires along these lines have been conducted. See Anderson's (1923) study of hobo life-worlds, Rollinson's (1990) account of single-room occupancy among elderly hotel tenants, Counts and Counts's (1992, n.d.) work on "RVers," Snow and Anderson's (1993) depiction of homeless street people, and Southard's (1996) portrayal of "homeless campers."

55. Goffman's (1959) material on impression management is most relevant, but much more is involved. For ethnographic accounts of cleaning and custodial work, see Hood (1988) and Ghidina (1992).

56. Gilderbloom (1985) provides an interesting account of landlords' concerns in setting rent prices.

57. Beyond people renting lands and facilities for agricultural and commercial enterprises, this would include those renting houses, apartments, and rooms as well as those staying at hotels and motels on a more transient basis.

58. Goffman's (1961) consideration of the adaptation practices of mental patients is instructive here.

59. Hobos (Anderson, 1923) and other temporarily and long-term homeless people (Snow and Anderson, 1993) represent interesting alternatives to more conventional life-styles in their uses of places and spaces, as do "RVers" (Counts and Counts, 1992, n.d.) and homeless campers (Southard, 1996). For a literature

review on the use of public spaces, see Lofland (1989). Dubin's (1985) study of commissioning (and funding) acceptable public artwork is also relevant.

60. For some instances of the development and use of recreational facilities, see Cressey (1932), Roebuck and Frese (1976), Prus and Irini (1980), Wolf (1991), and Counts and Counts (1992).

61. "Containers" such as bags, suitcases, pockets, pails, bottles, and cups attest to one category of implements used for transporting goods, but each of these devices implies certain concepts and technologies on the part of the people utilizing these forms of transportation. Other important (and seemingly elementary) ways of moving objects have been developed by invoking other (motion) notions, such as carrying, pushing, pulling, lifting, rolling, and prying. Still, the implementation of particular instances of these and other facilitating themes (e.g., gravity, floatation, flight, magnetism, and chemical combustion) typically represent an accumulation of collective wisdoms and technologies that particular peoples have developed over extended time frames. Although people may envision many mobility devices that others have developed as very simple in principle or application, it is important that analysts not take these modes of transportation for granted. In addition to attending to the practices that people have developed in other societies, it may be very useful, in this regard, to embark on field studies of children's experiences (images, concepts, applications, instructions, adjustments) with respect to matters of mobility as well as those of other newcomers to particular work or recreational settings.

62. See Gamst (1980) for an ethnographic portrayal of the railroad industry and the engineers who run the trains.

63. Davis's (1959) and Henslin's (1968) studies of cab drivers, Zurcher's (1965) work on sailors, Blake's (1974) and Ouellet's (1994) accounts of truckers, and Gamst's (1980) work on railroad engineers denote instances of people developing careers around transportation devices. While denoting another context of human mobility, Hunt's (1995) research on risk-taking among deep-sea divers is also instructive here.

64. For ethnographic materials dealing with traffic regulations and their enforcement, see Coleman (1976), Warren and Phillips (1976), and Richman (1983).

65. Ross's (1980) volume, *Settled out of Court*, is most instructive here.

66. Davis's (1959) and Henslin's (1968) studies of cab drivers provide some insights into the matter of renting out transportation devices.

67. Relevant here are the works of Blake (1974) and Ouellet (1994) on truckers, Nash (1975) on bus riding, Gamst (1980) on railroad engineers, and Counts and Counts (1992) on "RVers."

68. This definition of "foodstuffs" is intentionally broad and would include the use of alcohol, cigarettes, "illegal drugs," and other substances (also herbs and spices, medicines, chemicals, air) that people might bodily consume, regardless of any claimed or acknowledged "nutritional" or "health" values.

69. As with so many topics that fall under the research agenda presented in chapters 4–6, the matter of managing "foodstuffs" receives its sharpest

contrasts through considerations of anthropological accounts of people's practices across wide ranges of societies. Although somewhat fragmentary in many instances, the anthropological literature provides many exceptionally valuable insights into the food-related practices of different peoples (e.g., Malinowski, 1922; Lindenbaum, 1979; Chagnon, 1992, and Lee, 1992).

70. Thorlindsson (1995) provides an instructive ethnographic account of the "science" of fishing as invoked by skippers at sea. Also see Nelson's (1969) quasi-ethnographic depiction of hunting practices among the Eskimo.

71. For an ethnographic account of an agricultural venture (albeit marijuana as a cash crop), see Raphael (1985). Gardner's (1993) consideration of subsistence foraging is also suggestive here.

72. Pestello (1991) addresses some of the problems that develop around food distribution collectives.

73. For some ethnographic materials on the "hospitality industry," see Donovan (1920), Roebuck and Frese (1976), Prus and Irini (1980), Prus (1983), and Fine (1996). Given its generic emphasis, much of the conceptual material developed in Prus (1989a, 1989b) would also seem applicable to this realm of endeavor.

74. Fine (1985, 1996) provides some valuable material on both trade-school instruction and the actual preparation of restaurant cuisine, while Lu and Fine (1995) deal with the topic of ethnic authenticity in the presentation of Chinese food. Tomlinson (1986b) considers the problematics of attending to recipes in the process of preparing food.

75. Focusing on emergent preferences for Chinese food on the part of New York Jews, Tuchman and Levine (1993) provide an interesting case in the development of people's consumptive practices. Researchers focusing on drug use (Becker, 1963; Adler and Adler, 1978; Rosenbaum, 1981; Faupel, 1987, 1991; Biernacki, 1988; and Waldorf et al., 1991) and drinking (Rubington, 1968; MacAndrew and Edgerton, 1969; Spradley, 1970; Roebuck and Frese, 1976; Prus and Irini, 1980; Prus, 1983; Donner, 1993) also provide insightful discussions of the processes and problematics of consumptive practices as subcultural endeavors. Field research on other aspects of consumer behavior (Prus and Dawson, 1991; Prus, 1993b, 1994a) may suggest some interesting parallels to matters of selectively purchasing and consuming foods in homes and restaurant settings, as would the ethnographic literature on people's involvements (chapter 3) more generally.

76. The matters of developing food preferences and consuming (often with considerable encouragement from others in the setting) more food than one "comfortably requires" merits attention on the part of researchers, as does people's attentiveness to restraints of various sorts. People's self-initiated restraints in the consumption of "foodstuffs" may also assume several dimensions, reflecting such things as dieting practices, personal or group concerns with product abstinence, nutritional balancing practices, allergies and other health-related concerns, images of users or sources of certain products, and financial limitations. As well, people may find themselves subject to restraints

imposed by others (e.g., companions, family members) or attempt to impose limits on their associates.

77. While we often focus on "end products," it is important to acknowledge not only the tentative images and preliminary efforts that undergird the introduction of "new" objects of clothing within particular communities, but also the matter of obtaining and assembling supplies or "raw materials" and all of the underlying technologies that enable people in specific contexts to actually put these things together into a viable product.

78. It is one thing to "learn" that certain objects exist, but it may be quite a different matter to develop proficiency in the use of particular objects of clothing, either in ways that (more adequately) address their intended purposes or in ways that might achieve approval (e.g., meets group standards, shows social graces, portrays "style") in particular circles of associates.

79. Trading encompasses all manners of buyer-seller anticipations, activities, interchanges, and relationships. Prus's (1989a, 1989b) ethnographic study of marketing and sales activity is especially relevant here. Not only does this material outline a basic set of activities associated with marketing and selling a wide range of objects (e.g., foodstuffs, real estate, advertising, industrial products), but it is fairly extensively interfused conceptually and substantively (especially through extracts from interviews) with materials from vendors involved in buying, promoting, and selling a variety of objects of clothing (including shoes, jewelry, and cosmetics). See also Sanders (1989), Prus and Frisby (1990), Prus and Dawson (1991), Davis (1992), Prus (1993a, 1993b, 1994a), and Peretz (1995) for somewhat related works on vendors and customers.

80. Although people may approach the matter of collecting assortments of clothing (also shoes, jewelry, cosmetics, fragrances) in many ways, it should not be assumed that this is a "frivolous" pursuit. Indeed, researchers should be particularly mindful of (a) the diverse settings in which people may find themselves over periods of time, (b) *user* concerns with the adequacy of the objects of clothing to which they have access, and (c) the practices in which people engage in pursuing, assembling, implementing, and altering their stocks of clothing.

81. The matter of dealing with clothing that one no longer desires or finds usable for one or other reason lends itself to many interesting, but ethnographically unexplored, considerations with respect to the original owners and those subsequently involved with these items.

82. People interested in these topics may wish to examine Prus (1989a, 1989b) and Davis (1992).

83. Referring to novelties or changes (that may or may not be either widespread or enduring in effect), fashion in clothing would include not only "new looks" but also reflect people's attentiveness to "new" objects or object uses, as well as shifts in materials, technologies, colors, labels, suppliers, points of origin or manufacture, or any other noticeable realms of "change" (including people's emphasis).

84. Albeit massive with respect to clothing-related objects in contemporary society, the fashion industry is by no means limited to clothing (also see Davis, 1992). Consider the "fashion" associated with automobiles, furniture, housing styles, entertainment, religion, politics, education, medicine, and "technology" (in virtually all fields of human endeavor). The clear implication, in part, is that in attending to "fashion" with respect to clothing, one may gain valuable insights into fashion (influence work, continuity, and resistance) in a great many other realms of human activity, and vice-versa.

85. Seemingly paralleling applications of clothing for humans in many respects, this topic also lends itself to considerations that range from uses of certain attire to promote survival of particular life-forms to the means of expressing sentiments to be directed toward particular life-forms (e.g., "cute dog") or the humans associated with these particular life-forms. Attire also may be used to distinguish one animal from another (as in a pet show, a racing event, or even claims to ownership).

86. For some ethnographic research on volunteer work, see Stanton (1970), Daniels (1988), Marks (1990), and Wharton (1991).

87. Blum (1991) and Lyman (1993) provide insightful portrayals of family caregivers dealing with relatives diagnosed as having Alzheimer's disease.

88. The practices associated with medicine, dentistry, nursing, optometry, physiotherapy, acupuncture, naturopathy, and the like represent cases in point. For indications of some of the ethnographic work that has been conducted around the matter of providing physical health treatment, readers are referred to studies of medical students and physicians (Coombs and Powers, 1975; Haas and Shaffir, 1977, 1982, 1987; Reid, 1982; Yoels and Clair, 1994), paramedics (Palmer, 1983), nurses (Davis and Oleson, 1963; Davis, 1968; Rodabough and Rodabough, 1981; Grove, 1992), holistic healers (Goldstein et al., 1985; Semmes, 1991), acupuncturists (Kotarba, 1975), and family caregivers (Lyman, 1993). Writing about medical practitioners, patient care, patient views on medical treatment, and related topics, Friedson (1961, 1970a, 1970b, 1975, 1986) provides some valuable background material for those interested in these issues more generally.

89. The earlier discussion of "dealing with objects" is very relevant here. On a more substantive level, consider the development (and the trading practices) of companies involved in producing pharmaceuticals and other devices used by those "practicing" medicine, optometry, dentistry, and the like.

90. For some indication of ways in which cases are managed in medical settings, see Roth's (1962) study of a tuberculosis clinic, Emerson's (1970) account of gynecological examinations, Roth's (1972) consideration of an emergency hospital service, Yoels and Clair's (1994) account of an outpatient clinic, and Palmer's (1983) study of paramedics and emergency medical technicians. For instances of how hospital staff deal with dying patients, see Davis (1963), Glaser and Strauss (1965), Sudnow (1967), Hoffman (1974), Coombs and Powers (1975), and Rodabough and Rodabough (1981). Semmes (1991) provides an ethnographic account of patient-practitioner encounters in natural

health care contexts. Lindenbaum (1979) provides a valuable cross-cultural contrast.

91. Workers and clients may develop quite different notions of "appropriate treatment" in medical (Roth, 1962, 1972) and other "remedial" (e.g., Wiseman, 1970; Peyrot, 1985; Wharton, 1989) programs.

92. See Olson (1995) for a statement on "clinic record keeping" as a means of exhibiting accountability.

93. Among supportive care facilities, nursing homes (for the elderly) have received ethnographic attention (e.g., Gubrium, 1975a, 1975b, 1993; Marshall, 1975; Shields, 1988; Diamond, 1992).

94. The preceding listings on developing health support technologies and industries and establishing and operating health facilities are directly relevant (in parallel terms) to the range of services that people may generate around the matter of "providing last services." In addition to the roles of physicians (Coombs and Powers, 1975), nurses (Rodabough and Rodabough, 1981), coroners (Atkinson, 1971; Charmaz, 1975), ministers (Wood, 1975) and funeral directors (Unruh, 1979a; Cahill, 1995), some ethnographic attention has also been given to those dealing with death in nursing homes (e.g., Gubrium, 1975a, 1975b; Marshall, 1975; and Shields, 1988). For some historical and cross-cultural materials on "funeral practices," see Habenstein and Lamers (1960, 1981).

95. Consider the practitioners and industries revolving around hairstyles, cosmetics and fragrances, clothing, and jewelry, for instance. Many salespeople, especially those in the retail trade, see themselves as offering personal services (see Prus, 1989a; Sanders, 1989; Eayrs, 1993; and Peretz, 1995).

96. This would include those acting as counselors, consultants, psychiatrists (Daniels, 1970), and welfare and other "rehabilitative" control agents, as well as those working as lawyers, mediators, insurance agents, financial advisors, dieting consultants, fitness advisors, private investigators (Shulman, 1994), and the like. Ross's (1980) study of the insurance claims adjustment process is especially relevant here.

97. Consider commercialized entertainment and recreational themes such as magic (Stebbins, 1984, Prus and Sharper, 1991), occult tarot reading (Jorgensen, 1992), comedy (Salutin, 1973; Stebbins, 1990), music (Becker, 1963; MacLeod, 1993; O'Berick 1993), sexuality (Cressey, 1932; Prus and Irini, 1980; Ronai and Ellis, 1989), sports (Dietz and Cooper, 1994), and the hospitality industry (Donovan, 1920; Roebuck and Frese, 1976; Prus and Irini, 1980; Fine, 1996).

98. People embarked on educational, financial, religious, or business pursuits may use any variety of entertainment or recreational ventures in developing and sustaining interest in their primary objectives.

99. As Simmel (1907) suggests, money may be seen as a "liberating device" that enables its possessors to enter into exchange relationships with a wide range of others. While the "buying power" of money rests on the willingness of others in the community to objectify (or confirm) the integrity of particular (symbolic) mediums of exchange, abstracted currencies not only offer

considerable advantages of portability, but afford owners highly versatile forms of exchange.

100. Here, one may consider the related matter of "work worlds as sub-cultures." Agencies and corporations may be viewed as social worlds, as may smaller departments and work groups within.

101. Of the ethnographic work conducted to date, a good deal of this material focuses on occupations in one or other ways. Consider, for instance, research attending to education (Caplow and McGee, 1958; Hargreaves et al., 1975; Martin, 1975), religion (Lofland, 1966; Shaffir, 1974; Ebaugh, 1988; Wallace, 1992), medicine and health-related services (Roth, 1962, 1972; Glaser and Strauss, 1965; Sudnow, 1967; Davis, 1968; Kotarba, 1975; Palmer, 1983; Haas and Shaffir, 1987), marketing and sales (Prus, 1989a, 1989b; Peretz, 1995), factory work (Roy, 1953, 1959; Molstad, 1986), personal services (Donovan, 1920; Davis, 1959; Spradley and Mann, 1975; Prus and Irini, 1980; Paules, 1991), police work (Bittner, 1967; Davis, 1983; Meehan, 1992; McNulty, 1994; Mulcahy, 1995), court-related roles (Blumberg, 1967; Coleman, 1976; McConville and Mirsky, 1995), control-agency work (Emerson, 1969; Arnold, 1970; Wiseman, 1970; Peyrot, 1985), and entertainment (Becker, 1963; Stebbins, 1990; Prus and Sharper, 1991; Jorgensen, 1992; MacLeod, 1993), as well as a variety of work roles considered disrespectable or illegal in one or other ways, such as theft (Sutherland, 1937; Prus and Sharper, 1977), burglary (Wright and Decker, 1994), robbery (Einstadter, 1969; Desroches, 1995), fencing (Steffensmeier, 1986), drug dealing (Adler and Adler, 1980; Fields, 1984; Adler, 1985; Murphy et al., 1990; Williams, 1991; Tunnell, 1993), and sex-related trade (Cressey, 1932; Prus and Irini, 1980; Ronai and Ellis, 1989). Many more references to ethnographic works depicting aspects of occupational roles can be found in discussions of other topics in this volume or by consulting the bibliography at the end.

102. Although unemployed people approach the prospects of finding work with varying levels of enthusiasm and intensity, readers may find the work of Burman (1988) and Engbersen et al. (1993) relevant to the matter of "looking for work" more generally.

103. Rogers's (1995) consideration of the work worlds of "temps" (temporary employees) is suggestive here, as are studies of migrant workers (Nelkin, 1970), exotic dancers (Prus and Irini, 1980), comedians (Stebbins, 1990), club date musicians (MacLeod, 1993), and shift workers (Garey, 1995).

104. Karsh et al.'s (1953) account of the tactical maneuverings and recruit-ment practices involved in setting up a "new" union provides valuable insight into the multileveled influence-work involved in "selling" employees on this concept.

105. Friedman's (1994) ethnographic study of labor negotiations is instruc-tive here.

106. Since many people engage in multiple work roles (generally sequen-tially, but sometimes simultaneously as well), it is important to be attentive to the shifting nature of people's involvements in various occupational (similar

and dissimilar) contexts. Not only does this have important implications for understanding people's careers as workers more generally, but researchers may also find it instructive to consider the varying stocks of knowledge (gained through particular work-role settings) that people may incorporate in one or other ways in each subsequent realm of endeavor.

107. In addition to any variety of possessions that one might trade (including one's blood; see Kretzmann, 1992) or rent to others on a more occasional basis, it is also important to consider the vast array of goods and services that people may trade on a more systematic basis. All of these pursuits represent viable realms of ethnographic inquiry. Many of the processes outlined in the earlier discussion of "dealing with objects" are relevant here.

108. Despite the extensive reliance of people on "consumer credit" of various sorts (e.g., bank loans, credit accounts and cards, pawn shops, and [formal and informal] loans from relatives or friends) in our society, the matter of "arranging loans" has received very little attention from ethnographers. The related matter of "managing on a budget," likewise, has been almost totally neglected. Ironically, virtually every household (family or independent person) faces the prospect of juggling income and expenditures, and most people become involved in credit arrangements of some sort if only on an occasional basis. Business loans represent another area of untapped but rich ethnographic potential. Because people's finances are so extensively interwoven with their other activities (in both commercial and consumer contexts), an examination of the ways in which people manage money (and loans) is apt to offer insights into many other contemporary realms of human endeavor.

109. For a brief, but noteworthy consideration of aid in public settings, see Gardner (1986).

110. See Burman (1988), Engbersen et al. (1993), Rank (1994), and Rogers-Dillon (1995) for some ethnographic materials addressing matters of unemployment and involvement in relief programs of sorts, as well as considerations of other enterprises designed to enable people to deal with financial shortcomings.

111. Lesieur (1977) provides a particularly valuable account of gambling involvements.

112. For instances of people's involvement in the thief subculture, see Shaw (1930), Sutherland (1937), Letkemann (1973), Ditton (1977), Prus and Sharper (1977), Prus and Irini (1980), and Wright and Decker (1994). Also instructive, in an interconnected sense, are Roebuck and Frese's (1976) account of an after-hours bar, Lesieur's (1977) study of gambling, and Steffensmeier's (1986) study of a fence. Cressey's (1953) examination of embezzlement depicts peoples' involvements in theft on a more solitary basis.

113. Among the ethnographic studies of people involved in trading illicit goods are considerations of drug dealing (Adler and Adler, 1980; Fields, 1984; Adler, 1985; Murphy et al., 1990; Williams, 1991; Tunnell, 1993), fencing (Steffensmeier, 1986), and sexual liaisons (Cressey, 1932; Reiss, 1960; Prus and Irini, 1980; Luckenbill, 1985; Ronai and Ellis, 1989).

114. Einstadter (1969), Letkemann (1973), and Desroches (1995) provide ethnographic insights into robbery as a realm of enterprise.

5

Encountering the Other, Managing Morality, and Emphasizing Community Presence

This chapter continues in a very straightforward fashion an attempt to outline the subcultural mosaic in a manner that is amenable to sustained ethnographic inquiry. As such, it starts out directly with the matter of "encountering the interpersonal other."

Encountering the Interpersonal Other

Although the intersubjective essence of the human condition has been emphasized throughout, the matter of people interacting (and forming relationships) with one another is so consequential to an understanding of the human element that it both deserves extended attention on its own and serves as a vital precursor to the activities following. Encompassing a wide range of default and preferential associations, the themes addressed in this section represent both valuable entry points for ethnographic research and vital keys to understanding the human condition.

Some of the associations outlined here are notably bound in procreational contexts or revolve around matters of intimacy and sexuality, but the other forms of association are relatively content-free and may be applied to any variety of life-worlds. Social scientists, particularly social psychologists in both psychology and sociology, have given much attention to interpersonal relationships, but most of their work has been driven by the quest for factors presumed to cause (or dispose people toward) certain relationships rather than focused on the ways in which people develop and sustain relationships in actual practice.

In contrast, the immediate emphasis is on the processes by which people construct and manage relations with others. Consideration, thus, is directed not only toward the meanings that people associate

125

with particular encounters (and relationships) on both a general and ongoing basis, but also toward the ambiguity and enterprise (impressions, initiatives, influences, and resistances) involved in developing and sustaining associations with others over time. As well, the present statement acknowledges the full range of interaction (intimacy and distancing, cooperation, competition, compromise, conflict) and emotional expression that human relationships entail. Mindful of these considerations, the material following focuses on (a) acknowledging family life, (b) encountering the broader community, (c) experiencing intimacy and sexuality, (d) managing intergroup relations within the community, (e) venturing and moving into new communities; and (f) participating in collective events.

Acknowledging Family Life

The material outlined here begins with a consideration of relationships that develop around the family as a procreational context. It should be noted, however, that not only may "families" assume a variety of forms and become established in a multitude of ways,[1] but the relationships that develop in these contexts also lend themselves to a great many research arenas. Beyond the processes (and problematics) of establishing and maintaining procreational unions, social scientists could learn much about the human condition by examining the ways in which people accomplish all of the activities entailed in family life in various settings. Thus, matters of (a) people developing and managing procreational (and related) unions are highly consequential, as are (b) parent-child relationships (e.g., consider responsibility, companionship, trouble, and independence) and (c) children's encounters and dealings with parents and siblings and other caregivers.

Dealing with Procreational (Mate) Others[2]
>   Attending to, Establishing, and Sustaining (Mating) Contexts
>   Severing, Changing, and Reconstituting (Mating) Relationships

Having and Dealing with Offspring (Children, Adolescents, and Adults)
>   Experiencing Birthing Practices (and Making Other Arrangements)[3]
>   Defining[4] and Orienting (Responsibility,[5] Routines, Sacrifices) Self toward Offspring
>   Experiencing Offspring / Dealing with Offspring-related Trouble
>   Anticipating and Experiencing Offspring Independence (Leaving Home)
>   Dealing with Extended Offspring (e.g., Grandchildren)

Coming to Terms (As Offspring) with Parents, Siblings, Caretakers, Relatives[6]
> Learning about and Dealing with Parents (or Other Basic Caretakers)
> Managing Relations with Siblings (and Other Relatives and Early Intimates)
> Getting One's Own Way in the Setting
> Doing and Avoiding Duties
> Getting into Trouble in the (Familial) Setting

Encountering the Broader Community

The topics following draw attention to the great assortment of relationships that people may develop beyond those revolving more directly around family or procreational contexts. While children sometimes grow up more extensively within the confines of a (small-group) family setting, and may only gradually be introduced to "outsiders," for many others the experience of meeting others may be much more synonymous with their initial family lives as they are thrown into associations with outsiders in more sustained manners at very early ages. Acknowledging the processes involved in meeting people, making friends, and dealing with others who may be viewed as mentors, competitors, and enemies, as well as dealing with people who have established themselves more centrally as members of (outsider) groups, the material following suggests a great many valuable research sites.

Meeting (New) People (in One's Home Community)[7]
> Monitoring and Defining the Other(s)
> Attending to Associates' Definitions of the Other(s)
> Adjusting to (and Redefining) the Other(s) through Situated Association

Making, Interacting with, and Losing Friends[8]
> Meeting Others / Making Contacts with Others
> Experiencing (Defining) Attractions, Reservations, and Neutralizations
> Being Pursued by Others As Friends / Pursuing Others As Friends
> Dealing with Difficulties (with Friends)
> Encountering Interference from Outsiders
> Juggling Multiple Friends
> Losing, Disregarding, and Dropping Friends / Renewing Friendships

Dealing with Situated Associates[9,10]
    Defining Others (and Self) in the Situation
    Sustaining Encounters / Managing Intimacy and Distancing
    Dealing with Disruptions
    Terminating Encounters (and Relationships)

Encountering Instructors, Advisors, Managers, Directors
    Obtaining Access to (Informal and Organizationally Embedded)
        Instructors
    Receiving Instruction / Attending to the Other / Learning
        Techniques and Procedures
    Encountering Difficulties (Task, Relationship, Enthusiasm)
    Being Dismissed

Facing Competitors
    Defining Competitive Contexts / Attending to Objectives and
        Constraints
    Looking for Advantages / Encountering Set-backs / Sustaining
        Enthusiasm
    Experiencing Success / Dealing with Defeat / Disengaging from
        Competition

Having Enemies (and Adversaries)
    Being Disliked by Others / Disliking Others
    Encountering Ill-treatment from Specific Others (Individuals or
        Groups)
    Becoming Indignant about Others' Treatment of Self
    Disrespecting Disliked Others
    Experiencing Embittered Encounters / Escalating Confrontations[11]
    Deescalating Confrontations
    Developing and Maintaining Civil, Congenial Relations

Encountering and Dealing with Group-based Associations
    Forming Associations with Others in (Preexisting) Group
        Contexts[12]
        Having "buddies" (cliques) within groups
        Getting support from others in the group
        Managing intimacy and distancing in group settings
    Dealing (as Group Members) with Outsiders (and Rival Groups)

Experiencing Intimacy and Sexuality

Although somewhat redundant with the topics just outlined in
"Encountering the Broader Community," considerations of intimate

relations and sexuality merit more focused attention. This material may also be useful in highlighting some other research topics for those interested in comprehending family life since these two sets of topics intersect at so many points.

Matters of intimacy and sexuality are often blended, and when merged in our own society most often assume heterosexual dimensions, but the two topics have been separated to reflect the diverse orientations and practices that people may develop with respect to these relational themes.

Developing and Sustaining Intimate Relationships
> Experiencing "Courtship" (Intimacy-related) Situations[13]
>> Learning about prevailing practices for expressing intimacy
>> Encountering (and assessing) prospective partners
>> Managing intimacy and distancing in relationships
>> Dealing with obstacles, setbacks, and disenchantments[14]
>> Juggling multiple (partner) involvements
>> Breaking up / Becoming reinvolved with particular others
> Establishing more Enduring Unions ("Mate-like")[15]
>> Going steady, becoming engaged, getting married,[16] living together
>> Making adjustments to one another
>> Dealing with relatives, friends, other associates
>> Dealing with relational difficulties
>> Severing unions[17] / Reestablishing unions
> Acting as Union Facilitators ("Matchmakers"), Disruptors[18]

Experiencing Sexuality[19,20]
> Learning about "Sexuality" (As a Social Phenomenon) in the Community
> Encountering Ambiguities, Dilemmas, Disenchantments, and Problems in Sexual Matters
> Experiencing Continuity, Disinvolvements, and Reinvolvements in Sexual Matters
> Encountering Ambiguities, Dilemmas, Disenchantments, and Problems with Sexual Partners
> Experiencing Continuity, Disinvolvements, and Reinvolvements with Sexual Partners[21]

Managing Intergroup Relations within the Community

Intergroup relations may reflect any variety of "human differences," including demarcations such as families, clans, gangs, tribes, nations, races, languages, genders, and possessions to which groups of people may attend. As with other [objects], ingroup and outgroup definitions become *objectified* (Berger and Luckmann, 1966) when (and because) people act toward these categorizations *as if* they were consequential.

While understandings of human relationships more generally are absolutely fundamental to an appreciation of intergroup relations, the latter situation is typically confounded by the two broader life-worlds implied (or brought into existence) by (the socially) distinguished categories of people. Interpersonal encounters between members of two groupings reflect the more basic processes outlined in "Encountering the Broader Community," but any attentiveness on the part of the interactants to matters of ingroup-outgroup differences may significantly affect the situation at hand. In addition to any distinctive life-world features that any collectivity may develop over time, people encountering others in these types of circumstances also have to come to terms with the images of "these others" to which they have been exposed through their respective ingroup associations.

In contrast to a tendency on the part of many scholars to develop mystiques around particular substantive realms (e.g., race and ethnic relations, social classes, gender) and to approach intergroup relations in prescriptive and conceptually exclusionary terms, the processes outlined here are sufficiently generic that they could be applied across any realm of intergroup relations. Another implication is that much can be learned about intergroup relations in particular contexts by examining parallel processes in other settings.

Unfortunately, to date, social scientists have contributed very little to an understanding of intergroup relations in a direct interactive sense. Despite a great deal of talk about "undesirable aspects" of intergroup relations and concerted efforts to uncover "factors" deemed responsible for these situations, these scholars have embarked on very little research (i.e., ethnographic inquiry) that directly attends to participant experiences (situated viewpoints and practices) with intergroup relations. If we are to achieve a more informed understanding of the ways that intergroup relations are accomplished in practice, then it will be necessary to focus on processes such as the following:

Defining and Attending to "Insider" and "Outsider" Group "Boundaries"[22,23]

Developing, Maintaining, and Changing Images of "Insider" and "Outsider" Groups

Encountering Outsiders on a First-hand Basis

Anticipating (and getting prepared for) encounters with outsiders / Encountering outsiders

Distancing oneself from, and opening oneself to, outsiders

Experiencing fleeting and more enduring interactions with outsiders

Assessing, adjusting to, and anticipating subsequent encounters with outsiders

Monitoring, Shaping, and Regulating Insider-Outsider Contact Occurrences

Developing Collective Practices and Policies Regarding Insider-Outsider Relations[24]

Venturing and Moving into New Communities

The material outlined here focuses on people's relocations of both a temporary and more enduring sort. Although not everyone embarks on these ventures, these episodes (solitary and group-based) offer social scientists instructive vantage points to examine matters more directly revolving around (a) travel and (b) people's experiences with novelty, as well as opportunities to consider issues pertaining to (c) the accomplishment of intersubjectivity and object-definitions, maintaining presence, and (d) the development of a wide range of relationships.

Being Tourists (Temporary Ventures)
Contemplating Travel / Getting There
Touring Alone / Touring in a Group
Using Tourist Support Industries[25]
Encountering Difficulties Away from Home
Getting Home / Assessing and Reliving Tourist Experiences

Moving into New Communities (More Enduring Relocations)[26]
Contemplating Relocations / Leaving Home Territories
Finding New Places
Fitting In with the "Locals" / Learning and Developing New Routines
Maintaining (or Severing) Ties with Former Associates

Participating in Collective Events

The term *collective event* is used here to address the more dynamic or emergent features of human encounters, assemblies, episodes, occasions, and the like.[27] Collective events draw attention to the processual aspects of people's experiences with others in the more highly situated or particularized instances in which human group life takes place.

Some of these events will be much more extensive (participant-wise) and dramatic than others, but all collective interchanges entail some uncertainty since the people involved have to work out each situation anew. In some instances, as with a family coming together for a meal or a parent getting a child ready for school, the participants may know each other very well, work within fairly familiar frames of reference, and jointly possess seemingly well-defined sets of expectations about how the event will transpire. Still, even in these settings, the ensuing interchanges may take a variety of forms that might have been unanticipated by anyone in attendance. A relaxed family meal may develop into a confrontation, for example, or a parent may become very frustrated with a child who insists on wearing an item the parent deems inappropriate.

In other cases, the participants in the setting may not know the other people involved in the event at hand, how many others might be involved in the event, what the other participants might be doing at any point in time, exactly when or how the event started, or even the geographical parameters of the event they are (somehow) experiencing "with these others." Minimally, though, the participants are aware of some other participants and see themselves as acting in manners that are mindful of those of whom, in some capacity, they are aware.

Some collective episodes or occurrences may be focused around particular individuals or groups (e.g., birthdays, funerals, weddings, reunions) within a larger assemblage, but other events may be more thematic (e.g., festivals, contests, demonstrations) in emphasis. Likewise, some events may be more cyclical or repetitive (e.g., annual, weekly, daily events), whereas others may be one-time occurrences or assume uneven sequences of sorts.

Some collective events revolve around the interchanges characterizing particular instances of *relatively routine occurrences*. This would include things such as family meal assemblies; encounters with service specialists, salespeople, and friends; exchanges involving co-workers or neighbors; romantic interludes between dating or married couples; people going out for meals or to the theater; or (even) motorists encountering others during rush-hour traffic. This is not to overlook the emergent, constructed, or potentially problematic nature of these episodes, only to indicate that (because of their more repetitive nature) people expect that their participation in these (more routine) events will proceed in relatively feasible, reasonable, and manageable manners.

Other major variants of collective events might include people's participation in *festive occasions,* such as Halloween, New Year's Eve celebrations, birthday or house parties, wedding receptions, family picnics, high-school reunions, and religious festivities; *confrontational episodes,* such as debates, arguments, fights, and court cases, as well as protests and demonstrations, union strikes, race riots, political elections, and military skirmishes;[28] *contests,* of the sort one finds in competitive sports events, chess tournaments, scholastic competitions, art competitions, auctions, lotteries, bingo, and other zero-sum games;[29] *honorific ceremonies,* such as graduation exercises, funerals, recognitions of visiting dignitaries, displays of artwork, awards nights, and other meritorious acclamations; *situated performances,* of the type commonly associated with written and oral examinations, public speeches and presentations, band concerts and theatrical productions, or engineering projects and medical operations; *facilitating assemblies,* like staff, departmental, or board meetings as well as conferences and trade exhibits; *recruitment (and influence) ventures,* ranging from requests for favors and companionship, to attempts to control or direct other people's behaviors in various ways, to membership drives, fundraising endeavors, advertising programs, and political campaigns; and *responses to emergency situations,* such as floods, earthquakes, fires, traffic accidents, and other threatening situations involving two or more persons. Regardless of the number of people involved in or the substantive nature of particular collective events, these interchanges draw attention to the necessity of social scientists focusing on human interchange (and enterprise) as processual phenomena.[30]

Some of these events may be highly planned and extensively coordinated both at the outset and throughout the duration of the event, as people attempt to assemble and direct others in both very broad and highly detailed manners. In some other cases (e.g., many gatherings, celebrations of popular events), the basic themes may be fairly well defined at the outset but only loosely planned. In still other instances, people may find themselves in collective episodes in which they may have great difficulty articulating dominant themes.

It should also be observed that collective events may be characterized by multiple themes (e.g., consider, variously, the commercialism, gifting, family-life sentimentality, and religious themes associated with "Christmas"), with people often attending to these themes in quite different manners. As well, (intended) central themes may be displaced as interventions (e.g., accidents, abrupt challenges, unruly behavior) occur. It is worth noting, too, that people may (a) enter situations with a wide assortment of interests, (b) adopt a variety of (more central and more peripheral) roles as collective events take place, and (c) become more or less caught up in the central "spirit of the occasion" as events transpire. People may also (d) encounter or develop an assortment of secondary agendas as they interact with others in the setting. For example, although a group of people may approach a funeral as an occasion to mourn their losses, they may also find themselves particularly enjoying the presence of certain others or engaging in disruptive and unpleasant confrontations with their kinsfolk or other presumed mourners.

As well, some collective events may rather routinely subsume a variety of other collective endeavors in their broader constitution. For example, more extended confrontational episodes or festive occasions may encompass some honorific ceremonies, situated performances, facilitating assemblies, recruitment ventures, and responses to emergency situations. Further, while many of these subevents may be intended as enabling, other subevents may be intended as disruptive, embarrassing, or otherwise disabling vis-à-vis the central event. The implication is that people may define and experience any collective episode in multiple respects, both somewhat simultaneously and at various points during their participation in that event.

Acknowledging both (a) the shifting parameters of collective events and (b) the "transemergence" of interconnected or embedded subevents within the focal event, scholars also would find it productive to attend to people's differing awareness of particular (major and secondary) events in the setting, as well as their diverse modes of involvement in, and varying levels of participation in, specific episodes within the broader arena in which they are situated.

Likewise, it is important that analysts appreciate the human enterprise (and ambiguity) entailed in matters of coordinating activities, developing interpretations, maintaining enthusiasm, achieving centrality of presence, and invoking distancing practices, as well as people's manners of opposing, concluding, and assessing collective events. The listings that follow draw attention to notions of these sorts (and some of the options they entail), but sustained, ethnographic examinations of particular collective events are essential if social scientists are to arrive at more adequate understandings of community life in the making.[31,32]

Becoming Aware of, and Involved in, Collective Events[33]
> Finding Oneself in the Midst of Collective Events Begun by Others
> Being Recruited by Others Initiating or Encouraging Collective Events

Seeking Out Collective Events
Initiating Events Involving Others in the Community

Coordinating and Sustaining Collective Events[34]
Developing (and Articulating) a Sense of Purpose or Mission
Promoting (via Influence Work) the Collective Event to Others[35]
Developing Agendas (Plans of Action) / Developing Associations[36]
Accessing Funding and Other Supplies / Receiving Support and
    Cooperation from Others
Encountering Isolated, Widespread, and Coordinated Resistance
    (From Insiders and/or Outsiders)

Making Sense of Collective Events[37]
Defining Events as Familiar or Novel Forms
Obtaining Definitions of the Situation from Others (and Their
    Activities)[38]
Dealing with Multiple (Diverse) Themes or Definitions of the
    Situation
Watching Things Take Place over Time (Developing Processual
    [Re]Interpretations)
Engaging the Situation at Hand
Attending to the Reactions of Others

Becoming Caught Up in Collective Events
Attending to the Enthusiasm of Others / Encountering Encourage-
    ment to Participate
Anticipating, Defining, and Experiencing Intriguing Aspects of
    the Situation
Feeling a Sense of Obligation to Participate in the Event
Encouraging (Successfully) Others to Participate in the Event
Feeling Freed Up from External Restraints (or Prohibitions)
Developing Affective Bonds with Enthusiastic Participants
Making Commitments (Public and Personal) to Pursue the Event
    at Hand

Assuming More Central Roles in Collective Events
Assuming Greater Initiative or Responsibility / Being Assigned
    Positions of Prominence

Avoiding, and Withdrawing Participation from, Collective Events
Experiencing Reservations about Participating in the Collective
    Event
Depreciating the Central Themes Envisioned in the Collective
    Event

Attending to Other (External, Incompatible) Interests
Encountering Criticism
Being Displaced, Disregarded, or Treated as Inconsequential
Being Distracted from the Central Collective Theme by Others
in the Setting

Resisting Collective Events (Also Particular Themes, Activities, and People)[39]
Putting Limits on the Scope of One's Involvement
Discouraging Others from Participating in the Focal Event
Resisting Collective Events on One's Own
Resisting (Opposing, Containing, Eliminating) Collective Events
with Others

Concluding Collective Events
Being Informed of Event Endings by Others
Announcing Conclusions to Events
Facing Funding or Other Operational Limitations
Becoming Weary (e.g., Bored, Fatigued)
Witnessing Gradual Dispersal (e.g., Waning Interest) on the Part
of Others
Encountering Resistance or Competition from External Sources
Resurrecting Collective Events (See "Coordinating and Sustaining
Collective Events"

Reviewing, Reliving, Redefining, and Readjusting to Collective Events
Dismissing or Disattending to the Aftermath of the Event[40]
Reassessing Collective Events (Alone and with Others)
Experiencing Controversy
Attending to Accountability and Culpability
Making Adjustments to the Event, Subsequent Events, One's
Circumstances

Managing Morality

Both reflecting and shaping community definitions of objects (and practices), people's concerns with morality or community propriety are woven into virtually all arenas of human endeavor. Indeed, although only some areas of human involvement are viewed in "religious" terms, all realms of enterprise that attain some endurance tend to be characterized by sets of understandings that are generally expected to be acknowledged by ordinary participants in those settings. It is mindful of people's concerns with propriety or the moral order of the human community that discussions of (a) participating in religious movements, (b) defining propriety (and deviance), (c) identifying deviants and regulating deviance, and (d) becoming involved in deviance are presented.

Participating in Religious and Cultic Movements

Only some concerns with morality are rooted in religious themes in a more direct sense, but these realms of human enterprise are often among the most crystallized and intensely held of community moralities. What seems most notable about religious movements in general (as opposed to other moral viewpoints and cultic involvements) is an attempt on the part of people to explain central human experiences (and dispositions) by reference to outside (usually nonhuman) "agencies" and "supernatural" interventions.[41] Clearly, not all supernatural or mystifying experiences are cast or interpreted in religious terms. For our purposes, though, the primary concern is not over whether something is "truly religious" or not, but rather with the ways in which people develop life-worlds around "phenomena" that they deem worthy of devotion in some more enduring respect.[42]

Likewise, while the terms *cult* and *cultic* are often used to refer to more marginal religious movements, it may be useful (Klapp, 1969:138–201) to envision these notions more generically, as denoting certain kinds of practices on the part of particular groups regardless of their religious or supernatural orientations. Klapp lists six qualities that define groups as more "cult-like" in their operations: enthusiasm of the members; a sense of mystique and inner knowledge; reaffirmation of group perspectives in regularized gatherings; the organization of members' lives around group routines; an emphasis on identity change; and solidarity expressed through ingroup association. Viewed in these terms, virtually all sustained subcultures ("religious" and secular) may be seen as "cultic" in some respects (albeit in varying degrees). Thus, we may use this material both to encompass religious movements and to develop more fundamental appreciations of the ways in which groups express and sustain their viewpoints (and the moral orders implied therein) on both a "here-and-now" basis and over time.[43]

Experiencing the Supernatural (Religous and Secular Interpretations)
  Observing (and Defining) [Exceptional Objects]
  Acknowledging Bewilderment (Mystification, Awe)
  Envisioning Particular Objects in Religious (or Sacred) or Other
    (Secular) Terms[44]
  Sustaining Fascinations with Particular Objects

Developing Religious Interpretations and Associations
> Expressing and Elaborating Perspectives on Sacred Objects (and Supernatural Agents)
> Recognizing Spokespeople, Interpreters, Mediums, Ministers of the Faith[45]
>> Providing evidence, testimonials regarding sacred objects
>> Developing and promoting religious practices
>> Transmitting (sharing, training) religious or mystical capacities to others
>> Acquiring resources (funds, materials, properties) to sustain devotional programs
>> Monitoring and regulating member behavior

Attaining Cultic Dimensions of Association[46]
> Achieving Enthusiasm on the Part of Members
> Displaying Mystique and Inner Knowledge
> Reaffirming Group Perspectives in Regularized Gatherings
> Organizing Members' Lives around Group Routines
> Emphasizing Identity Change on the part of Members
> Attaining Solidarity through Ingroup Association

Recruiting and Maintaining Followers[47]
> Engaging in Proselytizing (Recruitment, Promotional) Activity
> Providing Instruction and Encouragement for Newcomers
> Dealing with Questions, Doubts, Resistances, Departures, Splinter Groups

Dealing with Outsiders
> Encountering Prospects, Supporters, Detractors, Competitors, Adversaries[48]

Experiencing Cultic (and Religious) Involvements (as Participants)[49]
> Becoming Initially Involved in Cultic Movements[50]
> Maintaining Continuity
> Becoming Disinvolved / Being Reinvolved

Defining Propriety (and Deviance)

Regardless of whether they are inspired by concerns with religious devotion, family practices, property relations, business transactions, conceptions of hygiene, the maintenance of human resources, or other matters, the development of notions of propriety or moral order appear fundamental to all sustained human groups.[51] Groups may be very uneven with respect to the particular themes they emphasize (centrality, intensity, duration), but collectively achieved understandings enable people to define and act toward one another in meaningful manners. As well, since they denote collectively verified (objectified) realities, moralities may be invoked as very powerful rationales for highly diverse treatments of particular people within the community (or pertinent subcommunity). Thus, the question of how groups define and manage morality becomes an issue of significance across the human sector.

It may be tempting to focus on the development of moralities and regulatory practices of the more formalized control agencies that one finds in our own society, but it is also important to appreciate the pervasiveness of the matters of defining and regulating morality across societies as well as within the subcommunities or subcultures that constitute particular societies. Thus, social scientists interested in the definition and regulation of morality may find it productive to attend to the ways in which morality is accomplished in *all* interactional settings and contexts (including the definition and regulation of morality within communities identified as "deviant" by others in the community).

While a number of "natural history" accounts of the emergence of legislation have made important contributions to the understanding of public acceptance of deviance definitions,[52] the most effective model developed in this area is the one proposed by Herbert Blumer. In "Social Problems as Collective Behavior," Blumer (1971) delineates five sub-processes or stages through which situations become publicly treated as "social problems" or threats to the moral order of the community: (a) emergence (initial awareness and publicity); (b) legitimation (public and official acknowledgement); (c) mobilization for action (recruiting, assembling, engaging situations); (d) formation of an official plan; and (e) implementation of the official plan. Clearly, only some "problems" are pursued through all of these "stages" (and the stages may overlap in actual practice). At each point, however, Blumer emphasizes that the process is negotiable and problematic, with outcomes reflecting collective enterprise and a myriad of knowledge, beliefs, resources, resistances, and political maneuverings, as persons and groups endeavor to ascertain and promote their interests relative to the issues at hand.[53] The following material addresses these matters:

Creating Awareness of a [Troublesome] Situation[54]
   Defining Situations as More Troublesome, Threatening, Disruptive

Dramatizing Conditions[55] / Spreading Information about "the Problem"
Using, Enlisting, and Battling with the Media[56]

Legitimating Definitions of the Situation
Pursuing Acknowledgements and Support of Influential Members of the Community
Providing "Evidence" from Experts / Credentialing Spokespeople

Mobilizing for Action[57]
Emphasizing Necessity of Immediate, Effective Action
Coordinating Efforts with Others
Neutralizing Alternative Viewpoints / Developing Alliances
Confronting Opponents

Formulating an Official Plan[58]
Defining and Promoting Preliminary Agendas
Encountering Obstacles, Resistances, Blockages
Negotiating, Redefining and Finalizing Agendas

Implementing the Official Plan[59]
Announcing Policies and Programs
Establishing Rule Enforcers and Control Agendas
Assigning Responsibility and Culpability
Encountering Resistances (from Targets, Rule Enforcers, Outsiders)
(Re)Assessing the Official Plan / Adjusting the Official Plan

Identifying Deviants and Regulating Deviance

Concerns with certain practices may become prominent only once instances of trouble are detected, but once "rules" and other definitions of propriety are developed within a community, attention may quickly shift to the definition and treatment of "troublemakers." It is here that considerations may be directed to the *labeling process* (Lemert, 1951, 1967; Becker, 1963; Prus, 1975a, 1975b) and the "denunciation ceremonies" (Garfinkel, 1956) implied therein, as people attempt to apply their images of morality to the situation (and actors [targets]) at hand.[60]

In the course of pursuing other aspects of human group life, a great many bothersome episodes may be dismissed as inconsequential, *handled informally*, or referred to situationally prominent third parties for action. However, members of communities (and groups within) may also establish specialized agents (and agencies) whose explicit task it is to deal with troublesome cases. In contemporary society, these *control agencies* have assumed major proportions, both financially and in their (state-sanctioned) abilities to intervene in people's lives.[61] Albeit only in outline form, the following listings address these matters:

Defining Deviants
    Developing Private Typings (Images, Definitions, Stereotypes) of (Troublesome) Target(s)
    Disclosing (Disreputable) Typings to Others (Targets and Other Audiences)
    Assessing Target Designations (by Targets, Others)
    Resisting Target Designations (by Targets, Others)
    Revising Earlier Target Images (by All Parties)[62]

Handling Trouble Informally[63]
    Overlooking Trouble
    Changing One's Own Practices to Minimize Disruptions
    Attempting to Change Troublesome Targets (Instruction, Sanctions, Treatment)
    Referring Troublesome Cases to Third Parties

Establishing and Maintaining Control Agencies[64,65]
    Setting Up Control Agencies
        Conceptualizing control agencies
        Legitimating particular control agencies
        Obtaining funding
        Locating, training, and maintaining personnel
    Running Control Agencies[66]
        Developing (and changing) agendas
        Accessing cases / Classifying cases / Processing or working with cases[67]
    Maintaining Control Agencies
        Assessing effectiveness / Maintaining internal order[68]
        Experiencing accountability[69] / Displaying competence
        Encountering outsider challenges[70]
        Dealing with (outside) competition

Developing Careers in Deviance Regulation (Control, Rehabilitation Work)[71]
    Becoming Involved in Control Work / Sustaining Involvements (and Performing Activities)
    Becoming Disinvolved from Control Work / Renewing Involvements in Control Work

Becoming Involved in Deviance

Although it may seem inappropriate in certain respects to include a discussion of "becoming involved in deviance" in the discussion of constructing and regulating morality, this material is rather consequential for comprehending the ways in which morality is experienced (and shaped) by those who find themselves at odds with those endorsing community or group-sanctified positions. As well, it is these "deviants" who represent focal (and resistance) points in the development and administration of rules and other control practices on the part of those who have assumed the task of maintaining the moral order of the community.

Mindful of these concerns, the emphasis here is on (a) people's participation in situations that others would consider deviant or disreputable and (b) people's experiences as targets of disrepute. The two themes are related but far from synonymous. In the first instance, only some of those participating in "deviant activities" may be detected by those concerned about culpability and, of those whose wrongdoings attract attention, only some may be processed in more consequential manners. On the other hand, some people may be subjected to extended denigrations (disrespectability, stigma, embarrassment, shame) without having knowingly or intentionally acted in disreputable manners.

The matter of people's involvements in deviance also may be considered with respect to *solitary* and *subcultural* ventures. Distinctions between the two are often blurred in practice since there are many activities in which people engage either on their own or in the company of like-minded participants (as in gambling [Lesieur, 1977], cheating at card games [Prus and Sharper, 1977], drinking [Prus, 1983], or getting tattoos [Sanders, 1989]). Still, some instances of deviance may be more clearly envisioned as isolated pursuits (as in much embezzlement [Cressey, 1953] and naive check forgery [Lemert, 1953]), while other involvements denote more extensive group-based or subcultural ventures (e.g., consider people's participation in "professional theft" [Sutherland, 1937; Maurer, 1964; Prus and Sharper, 1977]; jazz life-worlds [Becker, 1963]; bottle-gangs [Rubington, 1968]; religious cults [Lofland, 1966; Van Zandt, 1991]; or street [Keiser, 1969] and biker [Wolf, 1991] gangs).

Becoming Involved in Deviance on a Solitary Basis. Generally speaking, it seems more difficult for people to sustain [deviant] involvements on their own, since they typically lack (a) well-developed rationales, (b) clearer definitions of themselves as "practitioners," (c) supportive relationships, (d) ongoing instruction, and (e) activity-related assistance. At the same time, though, to the extent that their activities remain undetected by others, those engaged in solitary endeavors may have no immediate detractors, and no other participants with whom to become disenchanted. Further, practitioners need not define their activites as "deviant," especially in the absence of explicit challenges from others. Thus, so long as these activities enable people to achieve certain desired states or meet pressing obligations, solitary actors may continue these involvements indefinitely.

Although people may engage in [deviant] activities on their own, it should be noted that people's involvement in solitary activities still may reflect multiple routings, including explicit encouragements (i.e., initial recruitment, temptation) from others, independent attentiveness to the activities of others, improvisation, seekership, and closure. Further, because these people are faced with the prospects of implementing practices on their own, it may be exceedingly worthwhile to attend to the developmental aspects of the involvement process. Finally, since these practitioners are apt to endeavor to conceal their (conventionally discreditable) activities from others, research in this area may generate valuable insights into secrecy concerns, individualized forms of creativity (in practice), and the dynamics of disclosure (and discreditation). Reflecting matters of this sort, the following processes seem basic to studies of solitary deviance:

Learning about or Creating Conceptualizations of [Deviant] Activities

Developing Fascinations with Particular [Deviant] Involvements

Experiencing Closure (Defining Problems as Resolvable Only through [Deviant] Pursuits)

Overcoming Reservations

Developing and Sustaining [Deviant] Practices

Maintaining Secrecy / Disclosing Involvements to Others

Being Discovered / Dealing with Disrespectability[72]

Becoming Disinvolved

Renewing Involvements

Becoming Involved in Deviance on a Subcultural (Group-related) Basis. In contrast to those involved in [deviance] on a more isolated basis (who have to "do everything on their own"), deviant subcultures represent contexts in which participants may find that a great many aspects of their involvements have already been worked out by others.

Thus, not only are newcomers apt to be provided with perspectives (ideologies, justifications, rationales), sets of relevant identities (for self and others), fairly well articulated patterns of behaviors, and linguistic devices and modes of emotional expression, but (if accepted by the others) they may also be the recipients of social support (relationships) in all phases of what is a more thoroughly *collective* venture.

Because of the multifaceted or multidimensional nature of people's involvements in subcultures, it is often instructive to differentiate participants with respect to association with other deviants in the setting *from* their involvements in the central activities of the subculture. Some people may spend a lot of time "hanging around" others in the setting but never become very involved in the activities that are seen as deviant by outsiders.[73]

As well, although there is often a tendency to divide people involved in subcultures as either "leaders" or "followers," it is important to be attentive to everyone's involvements in situations as both *targets* (with respect to the recruitment activities of others) and *tacticians* (encouraging others' involvements in particular pursuits). This "dualistic" nature of people's involvements [in deviance] is often overlooked in the quest by many "analysts" to assign culpability to particular people. This is not to imply that people's influence endeavors are necessarily equal or highly mutual in most occasions, but to draw attention to people's abilities to influence (and resist) others on either a concurrent or sequential basis, relative to their own involvements.[74] The points following reflect these matters.

Becoming Involved With (Disreputable) Others and Group Practices[75]
  Making Contact with (Disreputable) Others
    Seeking others out / Being recruited by others
    Experiencing obligations to associate with others
    Overcoming any reservations
  Encouraging (Recruiting) Others to Become Involved in (Disreputable) Associations
    Fostering interests or creating obligations on the part of others (to become involved)
    Neutralizing reservations that others may have regarding participation
  Developing Mutual Interests and Practices with (Disreputable) Others
  Encountering Difficulties with (Disreputable) Insider Associates or Practices

Fading Away from, or Dropping Out of, (Disreputable) Associations
or Practices

Renewing (Disreputable) Associations or Practices

Experiencing Community Reactions (Target Perspectives). Regard-less of whether they (a) knowingly engage in activities [thought to be deviant by others] on a solitary basis or in subcultural contexts, or (b) simply find themselves in circumstances that others view offensive in certain ways, everyone whose "deviance" is detected by others in the community may find themselves targeted for special treatment by these "outsiders."

Some [deviants] will encounter audiences who for one reason or other may be willing to overlook the situation or at least not pursue the matter further, but other people will find themselves subject to some, and possibly quite extensive, losses of esteem (and ensuing sanctions) in the communities whose moralities they are thought to have violated.

Since solitary practitioners and other isolated targets are more apt to have to deal with any "degradation ceremonies" (Garfinkel, 1956) on their own, they seem particularly vulnerable to community indig-nation. In comparison, those involved in subcultural deviance may feel the wrath of community condemnation, but they may be able to draw upon the experiences and support of others in the subculture. At the same time, though, this indebtedness to members of the deviant subculture may also foster continuity in deviance.[76]

Community definitions of "deviants" and members' ensuing reactions to these targets are sometimes qualified by inferences of intentionality (of act, appearance, outcome), extenuating circum-stances, evidence, and such, but actual tolerances, notions of accep-table defenses, and ensuing treatments of any "deviants" may vary extensively. It should be noted, however, that while more intense community reactions (against the deviant) may represent particularly disruptive concerns at certain points in [deviants'] lives, it is unwar-ranted to presuppose that these will continue to be matters of uniform, primary, or pressing concern to all of those [deviants] encountering "righteous indignation." Rather, other than those subjected to exten-sive ostracism (e.g., incarceration, banishment, extended community denigration), the impact of many community degradations is apt to be episodic and situated in nature even if seen as devastating in certain (often more immediate) respects. As matters of human enterprise, community reactions to deviance are not only problematic, negotiable, and processual in their application, but are also uneven in their interpretation and implications for people's longer-term experiences. The following subprocesses suggest lines of inquiry attentive to people's experiences with community reactions:

> Having One's Involvements Overlooked, Tolerated, or Dismissed by Others
>
> Being More Explicitly Labeled or Identified by Others as a "Deviant"
>
>> Off-setting, minimizing, or resisting denigrations
>>
>> Attempting to change
>>
>> Dealing with more sustained rejection
>>
>> Encountering new associates and options
>
> Getting and Experiencing Treatment (Being Sanctioned, Reformed, Rehabilitated)[77]
>
>> Encountering and dealing with like-situated (disreputable) others
>>
>> Living with disrespectability and vulnerability[78]
>
> Being Reinstated in the Community

Emphasizing Community Presence

An appreciation of "community presence" is essential to a viable understanding of any aspect of the human condition, but, as used here, the term represents a means of focusing attention on three other aspects of community life: (a) the development of governing practices applied across communities at large, (b) the pursuit of military agendas, and (c) people's attempts to achieve communication across broader stretches of the community.

Implementing Political (Governmental) Forums

Although human groups sometimes develop very explicit and extensive political or governmental forums and practices, the matters addressed therein revolve around the relatively basic concerns of *coordinating, representing, and regulating group members.* In many respects, these pursuits are rather unexceptional. They appear to take place in all more enduring group contexts, ranging from family and play groups to all manners of formal organizations, including massive national and international forums.

Political forums, thus, at base only represent the more explicit arrangements that members of communities (or subcultures) develop for making decisions pertaining to the collectivity under consideration.

Much may be learned about "influence processes" in any setting (educational, recreational, familial, business, religious) in which people interact, but "governments" (denoting instances of more explicit regulatory mandates applied across particular community settings) also represent consequential and intriguing realms of study on their own.

While governments may be developed in any variety of community levels, from small-group associations to "city halls" (and the various branches within [e.g., zoning, utilities, development]) to regional, federal, and international arrangements, neither "political scientists" nor "political sociologists" have generated much research that depicts the ways in which groups of people in any context, forms, or levels of government actually *accomplish* their tasks on a day-to-day basis.

What is required is a research agenda that attends to human experiences and endeavors in the collective spheres of the community under consideration. This will entail replacing an emphasis on "factors," surveys, and "learned speculation" with ethnographic data that examines the ways in which "political behavior" is implemented on a day-to-day, here-and-now, and more sustained basis.

Mindful of this objective, five aspects of the larger political process are outlined here. These involve: (a) developing and maintaining governing arrangements; (b) governmental concerns with community conditions and policy implementation; (c) governmental practices regarding foreign policy; (d) people challenging existing governing practices; and (e) people's careers as participants in political forums. These topics are much more interlinked or interdependent in actual practice than these listings imply.

Developing and Maintaining Governing Arrangements
> Developing Visions of Governing Arrangements
> Promoting and Coordinating Associations for Governing Purposes
> Initiating and Sustaining (Governing) Associations, Arrangements, and Practices
> Financing Governmental Agencies and Ventures
> Extending Jurisdictions and Realms of Influence
> Establishing and Maintaining (Internal) Subagencies[79]
> Encountering and Dealing with Resistance and Competition
>> Facing challenges from (a) insiders, (b) others in the community, (c) external sources
>>> Encountering dissatisfaction, contenders, offensives
>>> Making concessions in the face of resistance, opposition, attack

Initiating offensives to neutralize, contain, or eliminate resistance or opposition

Turning Office (Government) over to Others (Competitors, Outsiders)

Dissolving Existing Governments

Assessing Community Conditions and Implementing Policies[80,81]
Defining Situations as Troublesome / Legitimating Problems
Mobilizing for Action
Forming an Official Plan / Implementing the Official Plan
Establishing agendas (and rules) and agencies (and enforcers)
Encountering and dealing with resistance
Adjusting policies and practices[82]

Developing and Sustaining Foreign Policy
Defining Outsider Communities (and Territories), Governments (and Spokespeople)
Developing Foreign Policy(ies) and Agencies (e.g., Trade, Diplomacy, Military)
Implementing Foreign Policy / Adjusting to Outsider Communities

Challenging Existing Governing Practices from Within Communities[83]
Defining Discontent with Present Governing Practices
Initiating Individual Challenges
Developing Collective Challenges[84]
Encountering Resistance from Governing Agencies (and Others)
Achieving Success (Attaining Desired Governing Positions)
Effecting the transition in governing arrangements
Consolidating a governing position
Anticipating challenge (any front) / Defending against challenges

Becoming Involved in Political Forums
(People's Careers of Participation)[85]
Becoming Initially Involved in Political Matters (Any Level, Arena, Capacity)
Sustaining Involvements (and Performing Activities) in Political Matters
Becoming Disengaged from Political Matters / Renewing Involvements in Politics

Creating Military Agendas and Agencies

Military agendas may be most centrally defined by a community (or subcommunity within) that uses physical force and related resources to defend, maintain, or assert one's interests with respect to others.[86] This definition encompasses a wide range of adversarial or confrontational stances, many of which are rooted in, or interlinked with, governing practices and policies (by means of direction and coordination concerns, as well as matters of resource allocation).

Although people may develop military-like agendas to deal with other species of life (e.g., wild animals, insect infestations, viruses) that may be seen as threats or obstacles to human existence and pursuits, the emphasis here is on matters pertaining to external group relations involving human targets. As well, in addition to military operations that attend to outsiders or matters of establishing an external (community) presence, military-like agendas may be deployed to dealing with matters of internal security[87] (consider actual or hypothetical threats from within the community to the government at hand).[88] The concern here is not with the rights or proprieties of any military endeavors, but rather with the processes by which people develop agendas involving military agencies and the ways in which they deal with their situations.

Attending to Defensive and Expansionary Concerns
>   Defining Problems or Objectives That Entail (Offensive or Defensive) Military Agendas
>   Envisioning, Promoting, and Establishing Military Programs and Policies

Developing and Maintaining Military Agencies (and Technologies)[89]
>   Recruiting and Staffing Military Organizations
>   Generating Funds / Obtaining Supplies, Equipment, Facilities
>   Establishing and Maintaining Centrality of Command
>   Consolidating Communication Channels
>   Developing Military Tactics / Providing Training
>   Maintaining Order within Day-to-Day Military Agencies and Operations

Pursuing Military Agendas
>   Maintaining Internal Security (Dealing with Citizens)
>   Deploying Military Agencies (Confronting Outsiders)
>   Encountering Other Military Agencies
>>   Defining and dealing with adversaries
>>   Invoking tactics and making ongoing adjustments in the field of operations
>>   Generating allies (and coordinating activities with allies)
>   Defining and Dealing with Success and Defeat on the Field
>   Managing Accountability (and Resistances) on the Home-Front

Becoming Involved in Military Agencies
(Careers of Participation)[90,91]
    Becoming Initially Involved in the Military (Varying Arenas, Levels, Capacities)
    Sustaining Involvements (and Performing Activities) in the Military
    Becoming Disinvolved from the Military / Becoming Reinvolved in the Military

Enhancing Communications (and Generating the Media)

While the "mass media" have become a very prominent feature of contemporary urban society, it is important to recognize that both group-wide and long-distance communications have represented long-standing, albeit often sporadic, concerns in human societies. The electronic media have been expanded greatly over the past century and we seem to be inundated with new variants and enhancements of existing (most notably computerized) technology in this area. However, versions of the graphics media have existed in some form for as long as people have been able to make communicative marks on surfaces. Likewise, as long as people have been able to send messages or enhance sounds with other objects, they may be seen to have transcended the limitations of the human voice (consider smoke signals, drums, horns and whistles). As well, where communities are smaller and members can more readily achieve co-presence, group assemblies, theatrical productions, and routine rumor transmission may offset many of the effects of "contemporary media transmissions."

What may be more unique and consequential about contemporary mass communications than any particular technology is (a) the heightened cultural diversity of the messages people may encounter through the media; (b) the development of a more sustained set of industries that create, use, and foster communication technologies and forums; and (c) the extensive overlap of the media (communications) process with other realms of human enterprise, such as trade, entertainment, religion, politics, and education. Thus, while social scientists may have much to learn about the ways in which people enhance communications within and across societies more generally, the development of media-related industries and media applications in contemporary society provides scholars with a great many research sites.

Despite the massive participation of contemporaries in the media process, social scientists have given remarkably little consideration to people's actual experiences in developing, using, and promoting media technology, or to people's attempts (as communicators) to use the media with respect to any realm of enterprise. Likewise, the matter of people experiencing (and using) the media as consumers has been almost entirely neglected. This is not to say that social scientists have been entirely mute on matters pertaining to the media, for this certainly is not the case. However, almost all discussions of the media have been largely speculative, often moralistic, and have been only minimally attentive to the ways in which people as reflective, enterprising entities are involved in the media process on a first-hand basis.

What is required are intensive, situated examinations of the experiences and practices of people (a) producing media technology, (b) using the media to send messages to others, and (c) encountering the media. While very sketchy, the material following draws attention to five different but interrelated sets of activities that address essential features of the media as matters of human experience. Sustained ethnographic inquiries into these realms of enterprise is essential for a fuller understanding (and an ensuing demystification) of the "media process":

Developing, Maintaining, and Using Communication Concepts and Products[92]

    Developing Communications Concepts

    Creating (e.g., Making, Financing, Assembling) Prototypic Communications Devices

    Testing, Revising, Promoting, and Dropping Communications Concepts and Prototypes

    Marketing Media Concepts, Technologies, and Services

    Encountering Resistances (from Potential Financiers, Users [in the Trade], Consumers)

    Encountering Competitors (Promoting Similar and Alternative Communication Concepts and Products)

Using Mass Communication Forums for "Broadcasting" Purposes[93]

    Directing Messages to Multiple Others[94]

    Generating Public Assemblies and Theaters[95]

    Using the Print and Electronic Media

        Developing specific media forums and message formats

        Selling others on using particular media concepts (forums and messages)[96]

        Employing media forums to send messages

            Generating and formatting specific media messages

        Sending, funding, assessing the effectiveness of, and adjusting media messages

Experiencing the Media as Targets (Recipients, Consumers, Seekers)[97]
  Encountering, Interpreting, and Attending to Particular Media Forums and Messages
  Seeking, Managing, and Avoiding Particular Media Forums and Messages
  Using Media Materials for One's Own Purposes

Establishing, Accessing, and Using "Interactive" Media
  Establishing and Maintaining Interactive Media Products and Facilities[98]
  Learning about, Accessing, and Developing User Fluencies with Interactive Media
  Using Interactive Media for Specific Purposes[99]
  Becoming Disengaged from Interactive Media / Renewing Involvements

Developing Careers in the Media Industry[100]
  Becoming Initially Involved
  Sustaining Involvements (and Performing Activities)
  Becoming Disinvolved / Renewing Involvements in the Media

Endnotes:

1. Although the family as commonly depicted in contemporary, Western society (mother, father, children) may be far from universal and at variance, as well, from many actual instances in contemporary society (e.g., one-parent families), we can recognize that some family-like (or substitute-surrogate parenting) arrangements are practically unavoidable for the care of the human young.

2. There are surprisingly few ethnographic studies that deal with the formation, maintenance or dissolution of procreational (mating) unions. For indications of the potential of field research for understanding these situations, see Darling's (1977) study of bachelorhood; Gross's (1980) study of couples who live apart; Chester's (1995) examination of the wedding subculture; Rosenblatt et al.'s (1995) consideration of multiracial couples; Merten's (1996) study of adolescent romance; and a set of studies on divorce and remarriage by Waller (1930), Hunt (1966), Vaughan (1986), and Hopper (1993). Although presented in more of a narrative style, Aschenbrenner's (1975) depiction of the "lifelines of some black families in Chicago" is also relevant here. For some cross-cultural ethnographic contrasts on "wedding" related practices, see Uhl (1989), Meekers (1989), Applbaum (1995), and Rasmussen (1995).

3. Daly (1988, 1992), Sandelowski et al. (1991, 1993), Weger (1992), and March (1994) provide considerations of the adoption experience. McMahon (1995) attends to aspects of the mothering phenomenon.

4. Although gender assignments may be seen as one of the more obvious demarcations that groups may make with respect to newborns, other definitions such as healthy or diseased (also frail, premature, disabled), or wholesome or "possessed" (Sargent, 1988), may no less prominently enter into considerations of the ways in which newborns are viewed and treated in particular settings.

5. For indications of parental responsibility in the ethnographic litura-ture, see Rosier and Corsaro's (1993) study of "managing parenthood in poverty," Beach's (1989) consideration of the "home-working family," Knowles's (1991) study of parents operating home schools, Darrough's (1984) account of parent-probations officer interchanges, and Garey's (1995) and McMahon's (1995) statements on motherhood. Enrollment of children in adult-supervised afterschool activities (Adler and Adler, 1994) may be seen as an attempt to extend the "effective range of parental responsibility."

6. It would also seem advantageous to consider the ways in which offspring deal with parents, siblings, and other relatives over time as they move through the stages of being children, adolescents, adults, adults with children, adults with aging parents, as well as the eventual loss of parents.

7. Although sociologists seem somewhat intrigued with encounters between strangers (see Lofland [1989] for a review of this literature), very little field research has been conducted in this area. Gardner's (1986) consideration of aid in public places and Hunt's (1966) and Snow et al.'s (1991) glimpses into the single's scene are suggestive in this regard.

8. Since friendships are so bound up in people's involvements in many activities (deviant and otherwise), the matter of "making friends" often affects the course of people's subsequent life experiences in manners that they are quite unable to anticipate at earlier points in time. Consider people's (initial and continuing) involvements in delinquency (Shaw, 1930), drug usage (Becker, 1963), religious cults (Lofland, 1966), sexuality and bar life (Prus and Irini, 1980), biker gangs (Wolf, 1991), and feminism (Wolf, 1994).

9. Situated associates would include neighbors, coworkers, extended kin, and functionaries of various sorts. These people may also become friends, competitors, enemies, intimates, and the like.

10. With the emergence of communication facilitated computer tech-nology, we find yet other variants of "situated others." People (in a manner somewhat akin to "penpals") may communicate extensively, but need never meet "in person." The work of Correll (1995) on lesbian encounters and Harrington (1995b) on gossip on computer bulletin boards is suggestive of the ways in which people may use these mediums to pursue their interests in both more direct and more vicarious respects.

11. For interactionist materials dealing with interpersonal confrontations (and violent interchanges), see Emerson and Messinger (1977), Prus (1978), Keiser (1969), Athens (1980), Prus and Irini (1980), and Wolf (1991). In contrast to those inclined to reduce interpersonal conflicts to matters of

"factors" or "personalities," those assuming a more consistent interactionist viewpoint tend to be particularly concerned with people's definitions of the situation (and senses of self) as well as the emergent or processual nature of the human interchanges that take place (see Prus, 1995, forthcoming).

12. See chapter 3 ("Forming and Coordinating (Subcultural) Associations") for more processually oriented conceptual materials on groups.

13. Merten's (1996) ethnographic study of adolescent romance is note-worthy here, as are the insights into sexuality and intimacy generated by studying "the world of the formerly married" (Waller, 1930; Hunt, 1966; Vaughan, 1986); bar life (Roebuck and Frese, 1976; Prus and Irini, 1980); and interracial marriage (Rosenblatt et al., 1995).

14. Among the obstacles that couples may encounter is that of "achieving sustained co-presence." For an account of long-distance relationships, see Gross (1980).

15. Darling (1977) provides an instructive statement on the life-careers of the "never married."

16. These particular notions reflect contemporary Western world practices, but some "bond-signifying" practices appear common across societies.

17. For valuable ethnographic research on divorce, widowhood, and related experiences, see Waller (1930), Hunt (1966), Gerstel (1986), Vaughan (1986), and Hopper (1993).

18. *Facilitators* would include "matchmakers" of all sorts, as well as dating service agencies, marriage counselors, and the like. *Disruptors* refer to any third parties that attempt to discourage people from forming or maintaining intimate relationships (e.g., consider disaffected parents, competitors ["love triangles"], divorce lawyers, or even sectors of the feminist [especially lesbian feminist] movement that have attempted to reshape existing heterosexual relations in various manners.

19. Although people's involvements in friendship, courtship, and sexuality often overlap, there are substantial advantages to separating these topics for purposes of inquiry and analysis. Even when the same parties are involved, these activities need not be synonymous in their directions, contexts, opportunities, pursuits, or accomplishments. Likewise, while sexuality may be prominently associated with procreational contexts, notions of sexuality may be extended to encompass any variety of sensations and images that people associate with physical or symbolic genital or other sensory arousal. For an earlier, highly insightful interactionist statement on gender and sex-uality, see Manford Kuhn (1954). Kando's (1973) and Cahill's (1980, 1989) discussions of appearance, identity, and gender development are also very instructive in this regard.

20. Somewhat ironically, very little consideration has been given to main-stream (hetero)sexual involvements as human lived experience. Merten's (1996) work on adolescent romance is particularly noteworthy in this sense. Ethno-graphic research on sexuality has generally focused on "deviant" involvements, as in considerations of transsexuality (Kando, 1973), homosexuality (Reiss,

1960; Ponse, 1976), commercialized sexuality (Cressey, 1932; Reiss, 1960; Salutin, 1973; Rasmussen and Kuhn, 1976; Prus and Irini, 1980; Luckenbill, 1985; and Ronai and Ellis, 1989), and group sex (Bartell, 1971). Still, these materials could provide very valuable parallels for comparing and contrasting human experiences with heterosexuality more generally.

21. It would seem instructive for those embarking on research in the area of sexuality to allow for much openness with respect to people's involvements in particular interests, activities, partners, and relationships.

22. Despite the profound necessity of attaining intimate familiarity with people's experiences with respect to ingroup-outgroup relations, surprisingly little ethnographic work has actively been pursued along these directions. This is particularly interesting since Thomas and Znaniecki's *The Polish Peasant in Europe and America* (1918–1920) appears to have been fairly instrumental in drawing attention to the potential of ethnographic research for sociological inquiry. However, as Blumer's *Critiques of Research in the Social Sciences: An Appraisal of Thomas and Znaniecki's The Polish Peasant in Europe and in America* (1939) indicates, a central flaw in their work (and one that prominently plagues the field) revolves around the tendency for researchers to rely on content analysis of documents, demographic materials, and survey (often attitude) data, instead of pursuing intimate familiarity (through sustained interactive contact) with the people experiencing these life-worlds on a first-hand basis. Incidently, in responding to his critique of their work, Thomas and Znaniecki (Blumer, 1939) concur with Blumer regarding the lack of authenticity associated with "content analysis." For some instructive fieldwork in the area of "race or ethnic relations," see Cohen's (1991) account of the "coping strategies of live-in domestic workers" and Rosenblatt et al.'s (1995) study of interracial couples.

23. Although often not so envisioned, some of the more insightful work on "intergroup relations" is that involving encounters between "deviants" and "respectables" in the community. See, for instance: Goffman's (1963) statement on stigma; Becker's (1963) account of jazz musicians and squares; Lofland's (1966) and Van Zandt's (1991) studies of religious cults; Keiser's (1969) depiction of a street gang; Roebuck and Frese's (1976) and Prus and Irini's (1980) considerations of bar life participants; Sanders's (1989) study of tattooed people; and Wolf's (1991) portrayal of outlaw bikers. Police contact with suspected troublemakers is also relevant here. See, for instance, Bittner (1967), Rubinstein (1973), and Meehan (1992).

24. Matters of policy presuppose centralized decision-making arrangements or the existence of spokespeople deemed able to act on behalf of particular sets of people. Policies may also be imposed by third parties (e.g., federal governments). The development of social policy on insider-outsider relations takes researchers in the realm of "constructing and regulating moralities" (later in this chapter).

25. Counts and Counts's (1992) study of "RVers" is noteworthy here.

26. Gold's (1994) depiction of Israeli immigrants in the United States is particularly instructive of the sort of work that needs to be done in this area,

as is Jones's (1980) account of the adjustment processes entailed in family relocations. Still, as with people moving in and out of differing subcultural contexts or life-worlds within the same community, not all mobility entails spatial relocation. Karp's (1986) study of social mobility suggests that people may also experience consequential orientation disruptures and disjunctions under these conditions. Although it could have been developed much more fully, Orser's (1994) study of "blockbusting" is suggestive of the insights that might be gleaned from more intensive field research along these lines. Given the (often extensive) geographical relocations that people in our own society experience as a consequence of work roles, marriage, advanced studies, and retirement, the matter of moving into, and adjusting within, new communities is a topic of widespread relevance.

27. Although the term *collective events* encompasses much of what has been considered *collective behavior*, I've resisted using the latter term in order to avoid inferences of "group minds" or other related stereotypes of crowd behavior. In this regard, I am particularly indebted to Carl Couch (1968), who takes issue with the tendency on the part of sociologists (following Gustave LeBon) to emphasize the simplistic, negativistic, and pathological nature of collective behavior by dwelling on images of suggestibility, destructiveness, irrationality, emotionality, mental disturbances, lower-class participation, spontaneity, creativity, lack of self-control, and antisocial behavior. While acknowledging elements of openness, emergence and unpredictability associated with crowd behavior, Couch draws attention not only to the importance of attending to the ways in which people define (and redefine) their situations through interaction with others, but also to the importance of focusing on people's plans, ongoing adjustments, and ensuing interactions. Collective behavior is socially constructed, and it requires a recognition of the differing (and potentially shifting) viewpoints, definitions, actions, and adjustments of all participants.

As well, I've built quite centrally on the notions of generic social process (chapter 3) in formulating the material presented here. Beyond that, I've simply tried to recast aspects of emergent group life in ways that would more readily lend themselves to ethnographic analysis. The result, it appears, is not only a demystification of collective behavior, but also a set of departure points for a very wide range of projects that focus on particularly (analytically) revealing instances of human experience.

28. In addition to those events that may be centrally intended as confrontational in particular manners, many otherwise intended collective events may become "confrontational episodes." In these latter instances, some of these confrontations may be handled as subthemes within other occasions (and possibly may be unnoticed by many of the people in the setting), while other adversarial encounters may extensively disrupt, effectively dominate, or even totally displace the original agenda for the collective gathering.

29. The distinction between confrontational episodes and contests is somewhat blurred in practice. Contests (and competitions) lend themselves

to confrontational episodes when the participants engage each other in more direct tactical manners.

30. Many other activities, such as reading a book to oneself, watching television or playing videogames on the computer by oneself, dining or consuming alcohol on one's own, or getting dressed, may be seen as social activities since they are done mindfully of the intersubjective other in certain respects, but they would be excluded from "collective events" as such, or at least not considered part of a collective event until tied into a particular interactive situation in a more direct sense. Thus, reading a book as part of a preparation for an exam may be seen as part of a collective event. Likewise, watching television in order to participate in anticipated discussions of celebrities with others, or getting dressed with the intention of meeting someone or making an appearance in a particular setting could be seen as part of a collective event, just as might someone drawing up plans for an impending gathering or demonstration. Indeed, although not all solitary pursuits have this quality to them, researchers would miss a great deal of information vital to collective events were they to disattend to the more solitary preparations (and restorations) that are associated with those events.

31. Although it has been necessary to represent collective events in more prototypic (and optional) forms for conceptual purposes, ethnographers in the field will encounter (and should carefully attend to) *collective events embedded within larger collective events*. While many of these embedded events will be implemented because of, and take orientational shape from, more encompassing collective events, these subevents can both contribute to as well as distract from (and, in some cases, effectively replace) earlier, more central events.

32. Ethnographers will likely find it instructive to attend to the sequential flows of sets (or series) of collective events in terms of developing particular "careers" of relationships or groups, for instance. See "Experiencing Relationships" and "Forming and Coordinating (Subcultural) Associations" in chapter 3.

33. The earlier discussion (chapter 3) of becoming involved in subcultural enterprises is exceedingly relevant to people's participation in collective events, both at the outset and in reference to subsequent continuities, disinvolvements, and reinvolvements.

34. As indicated by Momboisse's (1969) analysis of "the structure and tactics of professional (agitator) mobs" and Sharp's (1973) guru-like depictions of the strategies of nonviolent resistance (in which he delineates nearly two hundred methods of embarking on nonviolent resistance), a great deal of enterprise (preliminary and situated) may be involved in coordinating events that might assume relatively spontaneous (and bewildering) appearances to outsiders. For some ethnographic depictions of the extensive background work involved in some collective events, see Karsh et al.'s (1953) account of union organizers, Festinger et al.'s (1956) and Lofland's (1966) study of doomsday cults, Prus's (1989a, 1989b) portrayals of marketing and sales ventures, Grills's (1989,

1994) account of political recruitment, Wolf's (1991) study of the social organization of the outlaw biker gang, and Chester's (1995) statement on the wedding subculture.

35. Influence work represents a vital feature of coordinating and sustaining collective events at almost all stages. See the discussion of influence work in chapter 3 as well as the (later) statement on invoking the tactical self (chapter 6).

36. The material on forming and coordinating (subcultural) associations (chapter 3) is exceedingly central to the matter of sustaining collective events in both the short and long terms.

37. For related materials (and sources), see "Acquiring Perspectives" (chapter 3) and "Developing Stocks of Knowledge" (chapter 4).

38. It might be appreciated that people may be working with very incomplete stocks of knowledge as they attempt to sort their ways through particular collective events. Indeed, their senses of ambiguity and tentativeness may greatly overshadow their senses of predictability.

39. For more materials along these lines, see the subsequent discussions of implementing political forums and establishing military agendas (this chapter) and invoking the tactical self (chapter 6).

40. Definitions of dramatic, consequential, or noteworthy events can vary extensively even among the participants most directly involved. Thus, events that some people deem highly consequential may be quickly dismissed or effectively forgotten by others involved in the (seemingly same) event. This is another reason why analysts should avoid imputing (and imposing) their own meanings to events.

41. These "agents," it seems, may take any [object] form, visible or invisible, and may include inanimate (as we might define them) objects, as well as any biological life-forms (including living and deceased humans) and extraterrestrial or "otherworld" beings. Central to most religious movements is an assertion of a uniquely powerful essence(s) that possesses (mindful) capacities to intervene in human affairs, but which is, nonetheless, somewhat amenable to appropriately expressed human suggestion (and dedication).

42. Working with participant definitions of "religious" phenomena may bother some readers, but it allows researchers to focus on the ways in which people develop and act toward themes that they define in religious (sacred, devotional) terms. Not only may this foster greater comparability across "religious" settings with respect to social process, but this material also may be useful in providing a framework of sorts for comparing people's involvements in religion with their involvements in other realms of activity.

43. People's involvements (careers) in cultic (and religious) movements and the matters of forming and coordinating (cultic) associations can be readily located within the generic social processes introduced in chapter 3.

44. As Sutherland and Nash (1994) observe, the mystification of animals by the Animal Rights Movement appears to be assuming religious proportions.

The earlier discussion of "Dealing with Objects" in chapter 4 is most relevant to a consideration of religiously and secularly defined objects.

45. Although Weber's (1968) work on "charismatic leadership" is instructive in certain manners, as even more so are Klapp (1964, 1969) and Couch (1989), we have very few ethnographic accounts of aspects of the leadership process. Festinger et al. (1956), Lofland (1966), Shepard (1987), and Shaffir (1993, 1995) represent valuable exceptions to this realm of neglect. The predominant tendency (also see Willner, 1984) is to speculate extensively (as did Weber) on cases from historical accounts and the media, embarking on various kinds of imputations of strategies and motives to leaders, (organizational) supporters, and other followers generally in attempts to arrive at typifications of leaders or processes.

46. The material listed here is taken from Klapp (1969:138–210). For instances of cultic themes in religious and supernatural contexts, see Lofland (1966), Shaffir (1974, 1993, 1995), Lindenbaum (1979), Keesing (1982), Jorgensen (1984, 1992), Rochford (1986), and Van Zandt (1991). Also see Peven (1968) and Prus and Frisby (1990) for considerations of home party plans as instances of cultic involvement. Clearly, any group (e.g., recreational, military, political, sales agency) may develop cult-like qualities along these dimensions.

47. For ethnographic portrayals of religious recruitment, see Festinger et al. (1956), Lofland (1966), Shaffir (1973), Prus (1976), Rochford (1986), and Van Zandt (1991). As suggested in chapter 3, those interested in "religious prosletyzation" would find it productive to examine recruitment (and involvement) practices in a variety of other settings.

48. The material on forming and coordinating associations (chapter 3) is relevant not only to the matter of dealing with outsiders, but the entire consideration of religious and (other) cultic associations.

49. These notions are applicable to followers as well as those who become involved in religious orders in more central (e.g., leader, minister, assistant) roles. See Lofland (1966), Prus (1976), and Wallace (1992) for ethnographic examinations of the roles of local religious leaders.

50. The works of Festinger et. al. (1956), Lofland, (1966), Shaffir (1974), Prus (1976), Ebaugh (1988), Kleinman (1984), Van Zandt (1991), and Wallace (1992) are particularly relevant with respect to people's involvements in religious orders, but substantive encounters with [the supernatural] aside, the processes operative here would seem to parallel those occurring in other focused associations (see chapter 3).

51. For instances of moral order in seemingly minimalist (presumed disreputable) contexts, see Anderson's (1923) depiction of the "hobo" life-style, Goffman's (1961) account of the underlife of mental hospitals, Rubington's (1968) and Spradley's (1970) considerations of skid-row drunks, Roebuck and Frese's (1976) and Prus and Irini's (1980) studies of bar life, and Wolf's (1991) portrayal of outlaw biker gangs.

52. Among the more instructive natural history accounts of legislation are Cressey's (1932) statement of taxi-dance halls; Sutherland's (1950) depiction

of sexual psychopath legislation, Gusfield's (1955, 1963) portrayal of social movements opposing alcohol consumption, Lindesmith's (1965) and Becker's (1963) work on drug legislation; and Platt's (1969) and Rains and Teram's (1992) analyses of child-saving (delinquency) movements.

53. Although attending to only some of the subprocesses that Blumer delineated in his very seminal statement on social problems, additional insight into the ways in which social problems are produced can be gleaned by examining Kitsuse and Spector (1977), Gusfield (1981, 1989), and Best (1989, 1990). An edited collection, the Best (1989) volume is organized around the social construction of social problems, including materials on child abuse (Johnson), missing children (Best), elderly abuse (Baumann), aids (Albert), learning disabilities (Scritchfield), drug use (Reinarman and Levine; Staudenmeir), smoking (Troyer), drunk driving (Ross), music (Gray), and immigration (Bilderback). Gould's (1993) work on the problematics of mobilizing for environmental concerns is also pertinent here. Working in somewhat similar venues, Wiseman (1979) and Estes and Edmunds (1981) make concerted pleas for a "theory of policy analysis and implementation" (vs. interventionist sociology). Still, despite the overall contributions of this literature, it should be noted that most of these studies are based on the use of historical documents and media accounts rather than (being supplemented by or based extensively on) first-hand examinations of the social problems process. It would seem that even richer, more instructive materials could be obtained by extended ethnographic studies of aspects of the processes that Blumer (1971) outlines.

54. As Blumer (1971) emphasized, social problems reflect definitional processes rather than the presence of some set of "objective conditions." There is no guarantee, either, that people's attempts to define situations as consequential problems will be acknowledged and acted upon within the broader community.

55. Crusades represent only one aspect of the construction of community morality, but these events are nonetheless very noteworthy phenomena, particularly with respect to dramatizing "troublesome" situations. Crusades seem especially consequential when the proponents of particular positions find themselves in competition with other groups or agendas in the quest for control of community practices. Klapp (1969:257–311) observes that moral crusades typically reflect matters of achieving a vigorous sense of mission, emphasizing urgency of remedial action, expressing righteousness and moral indignation, indicating and countering evils, and maintaining an unwillingness to compromise.

56. A subsequent discussion of "enhancing communications" (this chapter) is relevant to an appreciation of "the emergence of social problems" (Blumer, 1971), as are notions of marketing and selling objects (chapter 4) more generally.

57. The material (earlier in this chapter) on "participating in collective events" is highly pertinent here. As well, since many instances of collective behavior (however spontaneous these may first appear to outsiders) have been

fostered by preexisting associations, considerations of "forming and coordinating associations" (chapter 3) are very relevant here. Likewise, it is most
instructive to be attentive to the associations that emerge in the process (and
in the aftermath) of pursuing particular lines of action within the context
of collective events.

58. Because "official plans" are often interfused with government offices
and practices, the discussion of "political forums" (later in this chapter) is
very relevant here.

59. This theme is extended in the next section, "Identifying and Regulating Deviance."

60. For a fairly extensive review of the "labeling" literature as it developed
from the works of Lemert (1951, 1967), Garfinkel (1956), Becker (1963), and
others, as well as a delineation of four aspects of the "naming process" (private
typings, designations, assessments, and resistances), see Prus (1975a, 1975b).

61. Beyond those agencies that have been more directly funded by the
state (or supported by other concerned subcommunities), people concerned
with particular moral issues may also establish any variety of "volunteer
agencies" to deal with (their versions of) troublesome situations. Typically,
control (including "volunteer") agencies endeavor to emphasize the centrality
of their representation of public interests in attempts to obtain funding from
government sources as well as support from the public at large.

62. Not all instances of labeling need reflect this fuller sequence. For
instance, people may never make their private typings of targets known to
others, or targets or others need not resist publicly imputed identities, and
so forth.

63. Emerson and Messinger's (1977) statement on "the micro-politics of
trouble" is very instructive with respect to the informal regulation of deviance.
Although much regulation of deviance by (formal) control agencies tends to
be much more "informal" than might first seem (e.g., Bensmen and Gerver,
1963; Bittner, 1967; Parnas, 1967; Emerson, 1969; Peyrot, 1985; Meehan, 1992),
most trouble is encountered and dealt with by people in informal settings.
See Lemert (1962), Prus (1978), Prus and Irini (1980), Irini and Prus (1982),
Sargent (1988), Prus (1989a:183–209), and Wolf (1991) for materials dealing
with the regulation of deviance in more casual contexts.

64. The scope of control agencies established to pursue versions of
community morality is exceedingly vast, as indicated in our own society.
Beyond the wide variety of control agencies represented by religious organizations and "volunteer agencies," state-sponsored control agencies can be found
in the following areas, among others: agriculture, fishing and hunting; business
(and trade); civil rights; communications; education and research; employment; entertainment; environmental (and pollution-control) issues; health-
related matters; land development; law enforcement, justice, and corrections;
migration and immigration; military; tourism; transportation; and welfare
and counseling. Not all of these agencies envision themselves in "control
terms," but control agencies are pervasive in contemporary society. While

ethnographic research would generate a better understanding of the operations of particular agencies, research in any of these settings would also foster a broader appreciation of control agency life-worlds.

65. The notions listed in this section would seem applicable to both governmentally funded and (privately developed) voluntary organizations. For ethnographic examinations of "volunteering activities" and the organizations providing "volunteer" services, see Gardner (1986), Daniels (1988), and Marks (1990).

66. While there is much to be learned, a considerable amount of ethnographic work has focused on control agencies and their operations. Ethnographic considerations of the police have been especially prominent, and include examinations of police work with respect to skid row routines (Bittner, 1967), juvenile encounters (Meehan, 1992), traffic wardens (Richman, 1983), domestic disturbances (Parnas, 1967; Davis, 1983), generating common-sense knowledge (McNulty, 1994), using normal force (Hunt, 1985), record-keeping practices (Meehan, 1986), detective encounters with criminals and victims (Stenross and Kleinman, 1989), undercover techniques (Jacobs, 1992a, 1992b, 1994), using lie-detector tests (Davis and McKenzie-Rundle, 1984), and internal affairs (Mulcahy, 1995). Rubinstein's (1973) study of city police provides some comprehensive background material.

Other research has focused on psychiatric practice (Goffman, 1961; Daniels, 1970; Pfohl, 1978; Emerson et al., 1983; Warren, 1983; Holstein, 1993), institutions catering to skid-row alcoholics (Wiseman, 1970), drug treatment (Peyrot, 1985), courtroom practices (Sudnow, 1965; Blumberg, 1967; Coleman, 1976; Warren and Phillips, 1976; Ulmer, 1994, 1995; McConville and Mirsky, 1995), presentence reports (Spencer, 1984), parole and probation practices (Emerson, 1969; Arnold, 1970; Prus and Stratton, 1976; Spencer, 1983; Darrough, 1984; Jacobs, 1990), and prison guards (Jacobs and Retsky, 1975; Andrews, 1983; Kauffman, 1988). Also noteworthy, more generally, are studies of teachers in the classroom (Hargreaves et al., 1975), water pollution control officers (Hawkins, 1984), front-line rehabilitation workers (Hall, 1983), women's shelters (Wharton, 1989), emergency services in hospitals (Roth, 1972), AIDS outreach programs (Broadhead and Fox, 1990; Cain, 1994), law interns (Winfree et al., 1984), and private investigators (Shulman, 1994).

67. For a theoretical statement on influence work in human service settings, see Prus (1992a).

68. Albeit focusing on police departments, Van Maanen's (1984) statement on "making rank" and Mulcahy's (1995) consideration of internal affairs depict but two of the many sets of issues pertinent to maintaining internal order in control agencies more generally.

69. Record keeping is a central feature of most control agencies. See, for instance, Meehan's (1986) study of police work and Olson's (1995) examination of record keeping in a public clinic. Although the somewhat related matter of "program evaluation" has received little attention from ethnographers to date, the works of Broadhead (1980b), Florez and Kelling (1984), and Loseke (1989) are relevant here.

70. Given the diverse origins and underlying sentiments that particular control agencies may represent, some control agencies may become targets of other control agencies. Consider police condemnations of vigilante groups, state opposition to unauthorized business cartels, or the work of "internal affairs" departments (Mulcahy, 1995).

71. *Deviance regulation* as used here would include all manners of rehabilitation, correctional, and policing activity. In addition to attending to (paid) work roles in this area, it would seem useful to consider the ways in which volunteer activities are interlinked with "paid practice." As well, it may be very instructive to attend to people's mobility across these contexts. Beyond the literature on control agencies, the discussion of involvement processes (career contingencies) in chapter 3 is also pertinent here.

72. Being discovered, particularly by those assuming more aggressive moral stances, typically takes the solitary [deviant] into a broader arena of community judgement and results in a more explicit identification of the actor as a *deviant*. For an extended treatment of "stigma," and people's attempts to move back and forth between more private and more public contexts, see Goffman (1963).

73. This distinction between "hanging around disreputable characters" and "engaging in disreputable practices" enables analysts to better capture variations in people's actual participation in situations. Whereas some people may be heavily involved in both respects, others' participation may be more adequately described as "associates" versus "doers" or vice-versa. Although not organized along these lines, Prus and Irini's (1980) study of the hotel community (and the multiple subcommunities embedded within) provides considerable evidence of the uneven nature of people's involvements with particular others in the setting and the variable involvements of those participants in the particular activities (e.g., drinking, smoking, violence, theft, commercial sexuality, and romance) in which people may be involved on a broader subcultural level.

74. While all of the material on influencing and recruiting others (chapter 3) is pertinent here, Becker's (1963) account of marijuana users, Lofland's (1966) examination of the "doomsday cult," and Prus's (1983) study of drinking as activity are particularly relevant.

75. The ethnographic literature on deviance is quite extensive, but the following sources may provide a viable starting point for people interested in pursuing research involving "disreputable" associations and practices. See, for instance, work on delinquency (Shaw, 1930), gangs (Keiser, 1969; Wolf, 1991), hustlers and thieves (Sutherland, 1937; Maurer, 1964; Ditton, 1977; Prus and Sharper, 1977), fences (Steffensmeier, 1986), burglary (Letkemann, 1973; Wright and Decker, 1994), commercial sexuality (Cressey, 1932; Rasmussen and Kuhn, 1976; Prus and Irini, 1980; Luckenbill, 1985; Ronai and Ellis, 1989), drinking and bar life (Rubington, 1968; Spradley, 1970; Roebuck and Frese, 1976; Prus and Irini, 1980; Prus, 1983; Donner, 1994), violence (Athens, 1974, 1977; Prus, 1978; Dietz, 1983; Wolf, 1991), drug use (Ray, 1961; Becker, 1963;

Adler and Adler, 1978; Wedow, 1979; Rosenbaum, 1981; Faupel, 1987, 1991; Biernacki, 1988; Waldorf et al., 1991; and Taylor, 1993), and drug dealing (Adler and Adler, 1980; Fields, 1984; Adler, 1985; Murphy et al., 1990; Williams, 1991; and Tunnell, 1993).

76. There seems considerable merit to the notion that community reactions to deviance may foster a perpetuation of the very activity that the community condemns as a consequence of (a) the "dramatization of evil" (Tannenbaum, 1938), (b) the development of a more explicit deviant identity, and (c) the possible removal of the "culprit" from mainstream opportunity structures (Lemert, 1951, 1967). However, it is also important to attend to (d) the various subcultural contexts within which [the deviant targets] operate and (e) the differing ways in which those experiencing negative community reactions interpret these events. The work of Shaw (1930), Sutherland (1937), Prus and Sharper (1977), Prus and Irini (1980), and Wolf (1991) are particularly relevant in this regard.

77. Schmid and Jones (1991, 1993) provide valuable accounts of the incarceration experience, while Fishman (1990) offers an account of the experiences of prisoners' wives. For some other depictions of people's experiences as they undergo "treatment" and posttreatment adjustment, see Goffman (1961, 1963), Ray (1961), Peyrot (1985), and Herman (1993). Still, the "treatment" phenomenon has been vastly understudied as a matter of lived experience and warrants extended ethnographic inquiry.

78. Readers interested in people's experiences with stigma or other notions of disrespectability are referred to (especially) Goffman (1963); Edgerton (1967); Kando (1973); Himmelfarb and Evans (1974); Petrunik (1974); Prus and Irini (1980); Petrunik and Shearing (1983); Lancaster (1988); Prus (1989a); Sanders (1989); Arluke (1991); Kretzmann (1992); and Herman (1993). By no means are people's experiences with stigma limited to those whose roles are more conventionally defined as "deviant."

79. In some politically more elaborated settings, this may also mean establishing secondary sets of practices (and agencies) to monitor and regulate the associations formed to deal with these very matters (i.e., "regulating the regulators").

80. Government policies may be developed with respect to any realm of human behavior, reflecting concerns with any area of task accomplishment or any manner of morality. See the preceding statements on defining propriety and deviance.

81. The points listed in this section are derived from Blumer's (1971) discussion, "Social Problems as Collective Behavior."

82. Rubin's (1987) account of rule-making exceptions in county land use is instructive here.

83. In those communities in which more enduring opposition parties are established, this may be a perpetually ongoing endeavor as the parties not "in power" may use whatever occasions they can to discredit, nullify, or otherwise displace the party in power.

84. For some ethnographic materials on collective challenges (i.e., creating and maintaining opposition associations) to prevailing "governing bodies," see Grills (1989, 1994) and Atkinson (1995), who deal with the problematics of establishing and maintaining political parties. Wolf's (1991) account of the internal governing practices of outlaw biker gangs is also instructive in this regard. The material on forming and coordinating associations (chapter 3) is pertinent here, as is the earlier discussion of "participating in collective events" in the present chapter.

85. Political careers encompass the somewhat interrelated and often overlapping notions of leaders and followers, contenders and supporters, distracters and mediators, promoters and voters. Scholars in political behavior could learn a great deal by examining people's careers in all of these facets, as well as all levels and arenas of the political process. See the earlier material on career contingencies (involvements) in chapter 3. For some ethnographic work pertaining to people's careers in politics, see Kinsey's (1985) study of congressional staff and Grills's (1989, 1994) inquiry into the recruitment practices of political parties. Readers may also find the autobiographical account of Louis Maisel (1982), a political scientist who ran for congress, of interest in this sense.

86. Clearly, the matter of defending, maintaining, or extending one's community vis-à-vis others is by no means limited to military involvements. While military confrontations may assume priorities in some instances and programs, such involvements may be viewed as last resorts in other cases. Thus, matters of diplomacy, trade, humanitarian appeals, and other tactical maneuverings may be seen as alternatives to, or resources to be used in conjunction with, military involvements in the "pursuit of presence."

87. It is, perhaps, worth noting that concerns with internal security are typically most acute during times of anticipated or actual military involvements with outsiders.

88. By the definition used here, police departments (all levels) could be viewed as military agencies whose central targets are those individuals and groups seen to act against the interests of the government or community at large. For purposes of conceptual convenience, however, the police are included under the (earlier) topic of "regulating deviance" along with other (internal) control agencies. Presumably, though, to a large extent the themes outlined here could be fairly readily applied to police departments, and vice-versa.

89. The material on forming and coordinating associations (chapter 3) is of central relevance to considerations of military agendas and agencies.

90. Beyond references to seemingly parallel materials on involvement processes (chapter 3), instructive instances of ethnographic work on the military are to be found in Zurcher's (1965) depiction of sailors, Cockerham's (1979) study of heroic symbolism among the Green Berets of the U.S. Army, Ingraham's (1984) account of "the boys in the barracks," Charlton and Hertz's (1989) account of security specialists in the U.S. Air Force, and Faulkner and McGaw's (1977) study of the reentry transition of Vietnam veterans. Also

relevant are some explorations of peace-keeping militia and their wives (Segal and Segal, 1993) and the life-worlds of military wives (Harrison and Laliberté, 1994).

91. In addition to those involved in the military in more direct (membership) terms, it would seem advisable to attend to those engaged in military support roles of various sorts (e.g., suppliers, civilian staff and volunteers, fund raisers, consultants) as well as those who benefit from direct contact with military personnel (e.g., civilian businesses in the vicinity of military bases) or whose lives may be influenced through other contact (e.g., friendships, romances, animosities) with the military.

92. Addressing objects in a more generic sense, the material in chapter 4 on "dealing with objects" is exceedingly relevant to people's experience with media concepts, technologies, and services.

93. Although only some of his (earliest) work has an ethnographic emphasis, David Altheide (1974, 1985; Altheide and Snow 1979, Altheide and Johnson, 1980) has contributed much thoughtful analysis of the media. The matter of "producing the media" has been given some ethnographic attention in studies of film composition (Faulkner, 1976; Mukerji, 1977), television drama (Mast, 1983), television news photography (Lindekugel, 1994), book publishing (Powell, 1985; Tomlinson, 1986a), and the marketplace (Prus, 1989b, especially 201–42). Best (1986) and Nelson and Robinson (1994) provide accounts of their own encounters with "celebrity status" in the media.

94. As suggested by "graffiti artists," any mark or sign intended for others "out there" may be seen as an instance of "mass communications." Likewise, any (verbal) statement intended to reach a broader set of others in the community would have this same quality.

95. For some ethnographic glimpses into the funding and coordination of theatrical performances, see Lyon (1974) and Gilmore (1987).

96. It should be appreciated that producers of particular media forums (and advertising agents) routinely "sell" advertisers (Prus, 1989b:201–42), educators, religious groups, political parties, and others on the desirability of using their versions of the media to accomplish influence work.

97. While the predominant tendency in the literature has been to view those exposed to the media as relatively passive recipients of messages, ethnographic research (Blumer, 1933; Blumer and Hauser, 1933; Frazer and Reid, 1979; Prus, 1993a; Harrington and Bielby, 1995a) indicates that people not only *interpret* and *selectively act toward* (accept, reject, alter) the messages they encounter in the media, but that they also assume active (tactical) roles in *pursuing* the media and *using* this material for their own purposes.

98. The emphasis here is on matters such as envisioning and developing technology, and related services that allow more direct modes of interchange, servicing these networks and components, and promoting these facilities and related products in the marketplace. These pursuits may be seen as "unique," product-wise, but since the interactive media represent only variants on more general matters of human enterprise, these endeavors are

best located within more generic notions of dealing with objects, developing stocks of knowledge, embarking on influence (and resistance) work, forming associations, dealing with competition, and the like. Similarly, all of the matters pertinent to other media also seem relevant to understanding the interactive media in very fundamental senses. In this regard, it is important that analysts permeate rather than promote an interactive media "mystique."

99. The interactive mediums signified by computer networks and computer "bulletin boards" of sorts allow people to participate in communication forums in an extended set of capacities. In addition to assuming roles as focused senders and direct recipients of messages, the openness of some of these mediums enables others to participate in emergent interactions as well as attend to these interchanges as audiences (perhaps vicariously, and often autonomously). For instances of people using these mediums for "gossip" and "lesbian pursuits," see Harrington and Bielby (1995b) and Correll (1995), respectively. While researchers should be very cautious about attributing any interactive uniquenesses to these computer-enabled mediums (e.g., as opposed to other human gatherings, for instance, in which people may assume a somewhat similar variety of roles), it is worth attending to the ways in which people use these mediums so that we might develop more comprehensive appreciations of the human communication process.

100. Just as one may have careers (strands of involvements—see chapter 3) in other lines of activity, the massive development of the media in our society encompasses a great many vocational themes (e.g., artists and entertainers, commentators and reporters, marketing and salespeople, technicians and engineers). As in other areas, people may move in and out of the media as well as achieve mobility across lines of work within the media. It should also be acknowledged that many "careers" (and a considerable realm of creativity) in the media may revolve around "amateur (and recreational)," "volunteer," or "part-time" pursuits.

6

Experiencing the [Intersubjective] Self

While the research agenda outlined to this point very much assumes the human capacity for reflectivity, or people's abilities to become "objects unto themselves" (Mead, 1934) as a consequence of symbolic interchange,[1] the material introduced in this chapter allows us to focus more directly on the senses of self that people experience in the course of their participation in the subcultural mosaic of community life. The notions of the self addressed herein clearly reflect an interactionist viewpoint, but the objective is to enable researchers to access the "self in process" rather than to present a theoretical statement on the self, per se. Hopefully, with extended ethnographic inquiry, we will be in a better position to elaborate on a pragmatically grounded theory of the self.

Acknowledging the Contextualized Self

As will become quickly apparent, people's sense of self, being, or identity is almost entirely a reflection of the activities outlined in the two preceding chapters. This means, that the ensuing discussion is to be envisioned in manners that are mindful of the various subcultural contexts in which people find themselves and their own relative states of involvement in those ventures.

The material following first acknowledges people's concerns, images, and actions (solitary and collective) as these apply to the *physical (physiological and imaged) self.*[2] Matters pertaining to other aspects of the self (e.g., as *ownership, proficient, relational,* and *tactical*) overlap to some extent with people's definitions of, and experiences with, the physical or embodied self, but focus on other aspects of the human condition that also merit careful attention.[3]

As with people's experiences with the physical self, these other arenas of human experience require an extended appreciation of the ways that people envision and *actively* incorporate themselves into particular social worlds. The "self," thus, denotes a community essence that is intersubjective not only in its origins or preliminary foundations but also in its ongoing realization. As Blumer (1969) stresses, the self is *not* a "structure" or some set of attitudes, values, dispositions, and the like. Rather, the self is an emergent, reflective process that is not only to be understood within a community of interacting others, but that achieves its central existence in situated activity. It is for this reason that the self is most productively studied both in process terms and within the social worlds in which people "do things."

Likewise, notions of a "consequential self" reflect the ways in which people attend to, and act toward, particular aspects of their social beings. For instance, concerns with one's physical well-being may seem basic across communities. However, people's attentiveness to aspects of their physical bodies varies significantly across life-worlds. Also, concern with one's well-being is apt to be a matter of only sporadic and occasioned focus for most people both within and across settings (i.e., as it interferes with other activities). People seem capable of sustaining a central focus in particular aspects of self for extended periods of time, but people's images of self appear to be quite multifaceted and vary considerably as people acknowledge (and become distracted from) particular senses of self over time and across inter-actional arenas. Thus, while Klapp (1969) draws explicit attention to fashions, cults, and crusades as routings through which people may strive to achieve consequential senses of identity, there are a great many other ways in which people may become "somebody," as suggested by notions of ownership, developing proficiencies, valuing relationships, consuming entertainment, and the like.

Beyond the matter of attaining consequential senses of self, analysts should also attend to people's experiences of *losing (or failing to attain) aspects of self that they may deem significant in certain regards*. With respect to all notions of (a consequential, inconsequential, or depreciated) self, though, it is essential to acknowledge that people's senses of self-worth are contextually situated, problematic in emphasis, and subject to ongoing (interactive and reflective) assessments as people engage, work their ways through, and become disinvolved from situations.

Also, even though there may be some overlap of people's senses of self (as people move from one life-world to another) along the lines delineated here (e.g., physical, proficient, entertaining), it seems much more productive for analysts to attend to the aspects of self that people experience in each social setting rather than striving for more comprehensive (averaging) or enduring ("personality" or "character") configurations.

People may fairly consistently employ certain modes of interacting with their associates as they move from one setting to another, but people generally find that highly consistent interactional styles do not bode well across differing contexts or even within the same settings over time. Not only are people apt to find that their associates expect different things of them as they move from one context to the next, but they are also likely to find that their associates expect them to shift and adjust their interactional styles (and senses of self) within particular settings over time.[4] Thus, while it may be tempting to envision certain people more exclusively with particular aspects of self, it is imperative that researchers maintain a stance of openness with respect to the *multiple senses of self* that people may experience and the ways in which people's various senses of self may be both selectively encouraged (and discouraged) by others and selectively invoked by themselves over time. To do otherwise is to violate, to a very large extent, the ways in which people "experience the [intersubjective] self" within the context of ongoing community life.

Attending to the Physical (Physiological and Imaged) Self

Although there is much more to one's embodied self than one's sense of physical well-being, people are biological entities whose abilities to deal with one another and other objects of their awareness may be affected by both their physical capacities and their senses of personal (physical) well-being. In addition to attaining notions of well-being, illness, and treatments by virtue of their embeddedness in a world of others, people also develop styles of relating to others that reflect the ways in which their relative physical conditions are viewed within these interactive settings.

Further, as self-reflective entities, people may also attempt to generate images or appearances of self that transcend concerns with their more immediate physiological conditions. Thus, while people's definitions of "feasible" or "desirable" appearances are apt to be centrally informed by their exposure to others in the community, people may endeavor to shape both their own senses of self and the manners in which others view them by recasting the ways in which they package or present (Goffman, 1959) their physical essences. The two themes following suggest many departure points for ethnographic inquiry.

Acknowledging the Physical (Embodied) Self
    Acquiring Images of the Physical (Embodied) Self[5]
    Monitoring and Maintaining the (Physical) Body

Developing Physical Abilities[6] / Engaging in Physical Activities
Encountering Illness[7] / Sustaining Accidental Injuries
Dealing with the Aging Process[8]
Dying (As a Personal and Group Experience)[9,10]

Achieving the Imaged Self (Appearances, Fashions, Looks, Styles)[11]
Attending to Images of Self and Others
Developing Preferred Images
Adopting Particular Styles of Appearance
Managing Appearances for Others[12,13]
Maintaining Appearances for Oneself[14]
Dealing with Image Problems (Disappointments, Disenchantments, Disrespectability)[15]

Developing an Ownership Self

Whereas one's physical condition and appearances contribute to some images of self, people may also define aspects of self by virtue of their possessions. Although people may be differentially concerned with possessions more generally, and the ownership of particular objects more specifically, people's sense of self (as Belk [1988] suggests) may be consequentially defined by the objects to which one has access. Further, while it may be tempting to define some people as more exclusively concerned about acquiring certain kinds of objects, even those with (comparatively) few possessions may envision these objects as consequential to their senses of self.

In addition to (a) any prestige that people (self and others) may associate with the possessor of certain items, it should be noted that objects also enable people (b) to do things in the here and now, (c) more explicitly plan for the future, and (d) maintain more enduring connections with their past (and earlier senses of self). Clearly, people do not incorporate all possessions equally into their notions of self, even when they define possessions as more consequential to their overall definitions of self-worth. Thus, it is useful to attend not only to the differing ways in which people come to define objects as more or less worthy of possession (and sacrifice), but also to the ways in which they envision their possessions (and their sense of self in relative terms) over time.

Emphasizing the Ownership Self (Defining Self by One's Possessions)[16]
Associating Prominence (Esteem) with Possessions
Developing Desires for (Mystiques, Fascinations with) Particular Objects

Envisioning Object Uses (Pursuing Interests, Attaining Objectives)
Pursuing, Obtaining, Owning, Collecting, and Caring for Objects
Losing and Disposing of Possessions (and Experiencing the Resultant Self)[17]

Appreciating the Proficient and Accomplished Self

The topics "Developing Proficiencies" and "Achieving the Accomplished Self" build upon and extend the preceding notions of the physical and ownership self in some respects, but they focus attention on (a) the acquisition of a sense of competence with respect to particular realms of activity and (b) the attainment of more specific goals or objectives that people might pursue in some context, respectively. The latter two themes are rather closely interrelated, as are their "flip sides," namely, the experiencing of ineptitude and failure, but they point to differences between achieving the abilities to accomplish some generalized set of tasks and establishing a sense of self-worth by virtue of meeting particular (socially established, but also self-defined on occasion) criteria of success, excellence, competition, and the like.

Developing Proficiencies[18]
   Learning Things and Developing Skills
      Acquiring linguistic fluency / Building stocks of knowledge
      Learning by doing (monitoring, practicing, and adjusting to ongoing performances)
      Engaging in solitary activities
      Attempting to coordinate activities with others
      Experiencing apprenticeships[19] and formal educations[20]
      Monitoring and assessing performances and accomplishments
   Producing Knowledge, Technology, and Other Community-directed Expressions[21]
   Dealing with Ineptitude (and Lack of Confidence)[22]
   Managing Failure

Achieving the Accomplished Self[23]
   Defining Challenges and Indicators of Attainment[24]
   Working toward Goals
   Making Sacrifices / Attaining Success
   Dealing with Set-backs, Failure

Attending to the Relational Self

As suggested in the earlier consideration of encountering the interpersonal other (chapter 5), the relational self encompasses a vast realm of human experience. However, in addition to matters pertaining to family interactions and encounters with the broader community (e.g., meeting people, managing intimacy and distancing, making friends and enemies, experiencing sexuality), it may be instructive to attend more specifically to matters of (a) affiliation and isolation, (b) helpfulness and helplessness, and (c) entertaining others and being entertained.

Achieving an Affiliated and Isolated Self. Focusing on people's sense of belongingness, bondedness or identification with others, the material outlined here acknowledges the senses of mutuality or integration that people experience with respect to the relational units (e.g., friendship, marriage, coworker exchanges) in which they find themselves. Conversely, one may speak of people's experiences of exclusion, rejection, or sense of loneliness with regard to the relational contexts in which they are situated. Although it may make sense, on occasion, to speak of people's overall sense of affiliation or isolation, it is important to recognize both the differential valuings that people may attach to any set of associations and the situated senses of self that people may experience with respect to each interactional context in which they locate themselves. Thus, some of these contexts may be more enduring for, and consequential to, particular people's overall sense of an affiliated (or disaffiliated) self, but attention is directed toward the senses of self that people experience with respect to particular interactive settings. It should also be recognized that people may experience somewhat concurrent senses of affiliation and isolation in particular settings as they relate to certain people and then others within broader contexts or even as the (same) people with whom they associate invoke varying degrees of distancing and intimacy over (sometimes very short periods of) time.

Achieving an Affiliated Self[25]
    Desiring Affiliation with the Other(s)
    Indicating Openness (Receptivity) to the Other(s)
    Envisioning the Other(s) as Receptive to Self
    Developing Mutuality (e.g., Activities, Confidences, Identities) with
        the Other(s)[26]
    Sustaining, Terminating, and Renewing Relations with the Other(s)[27]

Experiencing an Isolated Self[28,29]
    Desiring Affiliations with the Other(s)
    Indicating Openness to the Other(s)
    Encountering Inattention, Discreditation, or Rejection from the
        Other(s)
    Witnessing (Envying) Ongoing Associations amongst Others

Displaying the Helpful and Helpless Self. Only some situations involving assistance may be sufficiently dramatic for others to define the participants as "heroes" and "victims" (Klapp, 1962, 1964, 1971), but human relations lend themselves to a great many instances of helping or caring arrangements. Although the roles of "the helper" and "the helped" seem fairly clear on the surface, it should be noted that people may become concerned not only about who should give or decline help, but also what forms any assistance should assume, how much assistance should be given, and how grateful recipients should be to their benefactors. Consequently, various senses of self may develop around these interchanges. Indeed, beyond viewing themselves as benefactors, or recipients of aid, participants may see themselves as generous, taken advantage of, ignored, unappreciated, sympathy cases, stigmatized, and so forth. Hopefully, attention to the processes of the sort indicated here will result in a fuller appreciation of "helpers," the "helped," and the ensuing (and often problematic) realm of human interchange.

Endeavoring to Help the Other[30]
  Making Suggestions, Offering Assistance, Initiating Help, Responding to Other(s)
  Attempting to Coordinate (Helping) Activities with Recipients (and others)
  Encountering Reactions from the Recipients (and Others)
  Assessing and Readjusting to the Situation / Learning Lessons for the Future

Encountering Assistance from Others
  Indicating Desires for Assistance
  Having Expressions for Assistance Acknowledged
  Receiving Offers of Assistance / Accepting Offers of Assistance
  Dealing with Assistance Received / Acknowledging Assistance
  Assessing Assistance[31] / Making Adjustments and Revising Routines

Experiencing the Entertaining and Entertained Self. The term *entertainment*, as used herein, refers to all matters that people (as entertainers or the entertained) deem interesting or intriguing in some manner. There may be considerable disagreement as to what constitutes "entertainment" (as well as "good" or "acceptable" entertainment), but people may invoke notions of entertainment in all realms of activity. As well, while often envisioned in fictional,[32] playful, or pleasurable terms, it should be recognized that entertainment, at times, may be highly sincere, intense, shocking, or even clearly discomforting (mentally or physically) for the entertainers as well as the entertained.[33]

Although bounded by the broader notion of entertainment, it is important to distinguish the ways in which people develop senses of self as "entertainers" and "entertained" persons. These roles are interlinked by mutuality of interaction and appreciations of the other in some cases, but in other instances people may more exclusively assume performer or audience roles. Those attempting to entertain others need not be concerned about reciprocation of like kind, and those seeking out, using, or participating in their own entertainment need not be concerned about providing entertainment for the other.

Exhibiting the Entertaining Self (through Ongoing Productions)[34,35]
    Developing Symbolic Fluencies (Talk, Gossip, Humor, Stories)
        Informing (sincerely) others about situations
        Creating novel (artistic) representations (fictionalizing, fabricating, dramatizing)
    Locating Audiences / Presenting Entertainment / Dealing with Difficult Audiences
    Encountering and Dealing with Competition, Success, and Failure

Acknowledging the Entertained Self[36]
    Developing and Pursuing Solitary Fascinations
        Fantasizing[37]
    Seeking and consuming (other) solitary entertaining experiences
    Participating in Collectively (Situational, Emergent) Entertaining Venues
        Achieving, sustaining, losing, and regaining a mutuality of focus
    Participating in Established "Recreational" Subcultures[38,39]
        Becoming involved in "interesting" clubs, groups, associations
        Sustaining involvements / Dropping out / Becoming reinvolved
    Consuming Formalized (Systematic) Entertainment (As Targets, Audiences, Tacticians)[40]
        Attending to "entertainers" (acknowledged performers)
        Using the media (and the interactive media) for entertainment[41]
        Losing and regaining interest in particular forms and forums of entertainment

Invoking the Tactical (Target and Tactician) Self

The material outlined here focuses on people's abilities to embark on a wide variety of activities revolving around the influence process.

However, in contrast to most considerations of power and influence that tend to be structural in thrust and cast people into roles as tacticians or targets, the material outlined here not only assumes a definitional, processual, and interactional conceptualization of influence, but acknowledges people's capacities to assume roles as both targets and tacticians (on both a sequential and more or less simultaneous basis). The processes indicated here may be applied to any situation that one or other participants define in "influence," "control," or "power" terms,[42] but more fundamentally attest to the multiple senses of human agency that people may invoke in situations involving others.

The notion of an "influential self" focuses on the ways in which people attempt to "get their own ways" in dealing with others, both on their own and through various cooperative ventures with others. Thus, consideration is given to people's capacities for exercising persistence, invoking deception, attending to target interests and weaknesses, engaging in persuasive activity, and involving a variety of others (e.g., third-party referrals, mediators, coalitions) in their attempts to shape target behaviors and experiences.

The matter of "experiencing the receptive, vulnerable, restrained, elusive, and resilient self" draws attention to differing ways that the targets of particular influence endeavors may deal with those [tacticians] they envision as trying to influence them. Thus, although there will be times, when people (a) wish to be involved in the enterprises that may be proposed by others, or (b) see themselves as more amenable to certain kinds of influence work from others, [targets] may also (c) impose conditions on the nature of their participation in settings as well as (d) find ways of avoiding accountability and (e) assume active roles in resisting, acting back on, and tactically (on an individual or collective basis) attempting to influence those [tacticians] who initially sought to influence them in some manner.

Exercising the Influential Self[43]
 Assuming a Tactical Role (Alone or in Conjunction with Others)
  Being persistent / Shaping images / Invoking deception
  Focusing on target interests and vulnerabilities
  Bargaining with targets
  Attending to (preexisting, ongoing, and anticipated) relationships with targets
 Extending the Theater of Operations (Pursuing Influence through Cooperative Ventures)
  Consulting with third parties / Making referrals to third parties

Developing alliances and related associations
Pursuing strategic positional control within existing associations
Developing organizational principles and regulatory constraints
Using the media to influence targets
Developing political campaigns / Implementing political (governmental) forums
Creating military agendas and agencies / Pursuing military ventures

Experiencing the Receptive, Vulnerable, Restrained, Elusive, and Resilient Self[44]

Appreciating the Receptive Self / Experiencing the Vulnerable Self
Developing a Restrained Self / Invoking Situational Limitations
Averting (Tactically) Influence in Interpersonal Encounters
Embarking on Solitary (Tactical) Resistance (see "Exercising the Influential Self")
Engaging in Collective Resistance (see "Extending the Theater of Operations")

Managing the Centralizing and Fragmented Self

This last section deals with people's senses of personal coherence and disjointedness with respect to the situations in which they find themselves. People need not envision themselves in terms of these sorts, but those who do may apply these notions to their involvements in particular situations as well as to the overlapping realms of involvements that constitute their larger sets of experiences with the subcultural mosaic. Rather than presume that particular states of "diversity" or "unity" are more or less desirable in some ideal sense, the emphasis here is on the ways in which people become involved in more diversified or more centralized sets of activities and how they make sense of these situations. In this regard, it seems most feasible to consider people's tendencies towards more focused or diversified modes of involvement and to examine their ongoing experiences with (definitions of and adjustments to) these situations.

Experiencing the Centralizing (Unified, Coherent, Encapsulated) Self[45]

Developing More Singular Concentrations of Activity
Achieving Adequacy, Effectiveness, Competence within Particular Contexts
Being Encouraged to Focus / Disattending to Alternatives
Experiencing Problems (Distractions, Limitations) Focusing[46]

Assessing Centralized Emphasis and Making Adjustments

Experiencing the Overlapping (Diversified, Fragmented, Disjointed) Self[47]
 Encountering Opportunities for Diverse Involvements
 Becoming Immersed in Diverse Situations[48]
 Developing (and Failing to Achieve) Cross-Contextual Fluencies
   and Other Capabilities
 Juggling Multiple Involvements
 Encountering Difficulties Managing Diversity
 Assessing Diversity and Making Adjustments

Toward a Conclusion

The agenda outlined in chapters 4, 5, and 6 is exceedingly basic and massive. Effectively, it represents a "lifetime" of research arenas for the social sciences. Suggesting hundreds, if not thousands, of projects to which social science practitioners (researchers, instructors, and students) may direct their attention, this agenda allows for great diversity of inquiry reflecting people's interests, comfort zones, and opportunities for accessing particular aspects of the subcultural mosaic.

At the same time, though, there are some very humbling aspects to this material. First, while I've tried to be thorough in developing this set of topics, each reworking and rereading of this material has served to remind me of the inevitable sketchiness of the outlines presented here and of the difficulties involved in formulating a more precise, intersubjective, processually oriented framework for approaching the study of the human condition. A second realization revolves around the slow, fragmentary, and limited sense of progress that researchers are apt to make with respect to comprehending the human condition, at least in the short term.

Still, building on the conceptual material developed in the discussions of symbolic interaction and generic social processes, it is hoped that this set of contextualized themes may be used both as departure points for inquiry and anchorage points in which to situate instances of future ethnographic inquiry within the broader subcultural mosaic. As well, while subsequent ethnographic ventures will result in greater comprehensions of both substantive arenas and the particular generic themes from which they may have derived some preliminary inspiration, researchers are apt to find it most instructive to return to considerations of the fuller range of generic social processes outlined in chapter 3 and the ethnographic literature referenced in the bibliography as they (a) attempt to sort their ways through the subcultural contexts in which their research is embedded and (b) locate their findings in a more comparative (analytical) context.

Minimally, though, it is essential that social scientists move beyond broad images of culture and society on the one front and attempts to delineate "structures," "forces," and "factors" of various sorts that allegedly determine or produce human behavior on the other. If we are to comprehend the human condition in a more fundamental sense, then it is necessary to examine in extended, intimate, ethnographic detail the ways in which people distinguish, define, construct, and act toward all aspects of the world as they know it.

As the chapters following suggest, though, the pursuit of an agenda along these lines is a challenging venture. Ethnographic inquiry requires an ongoing openness and attentiveness to the intersubjective other on the part of the researchers, and a willingness on the part of ethnographic others to share their life-worlds in intimate detail with ethnographers. While hopefully instructive in suggesting a great many realms of human inquiry and providing a conceptual frame in which to build, this material will achieve its greatest worth as scholars embark upon and produce works that indicate in sustained substantive and conceptual detail the ways in which people engage the social worlds in which they find themselves.

Endnotes:

1. As a linguistic phenomenon or hermeneutic essence, the self is predicated on people's abilities (initially) to adopt the role (i.e., viewpoint) of the other with respect to one's being (presence, existence). This means that there can be no "pure" or "true" self apart from one's community or intersubjective context. At a minimum, *all* senses of self (however unique or "despised" these may be) are socially informed. There would be no self without the other, for it is only in establishing symbolic communication with the other that reference points allowing for a sense of self may be attained. These notions are developed in Dilthey [Ermarth, 1978], Mead (1934), and Blumer (1969), who observe that the self is more or less continuously "in the making;" i.e., denotes an emergent, reflective, active, and interactive essence as people engage the socially constructed (see Schutz, 1962, 1964; Berger and Luckman, 1966) world out there.

2. While people often take their physical states for granted, the obtrusiveness of physical ailments and the inevitability of injury and physical demise represent keen, if only individually sporadic, reminders of the very basic but enduring and problematic human struggle for survival.

3. At one point, this statement also included a discussion of the "emotional self." However, since some attention is given to emotionality as

a "generic social process" in chapter 3 of this volume and a more detailed consideration is available in Prus (1996:173–201), it seemed unnecessary to repeat this material. Rather than discount the matter of "experiencing the emotional self" or conceal its fundamentally intersubjective essence, it is hoped that this note may explicitly draw attention to the desirability of pursuing the study of emotionality through sustained ethnographic inquiry.

4. This is readily evident in family settings in which both "parents" and "children" find themselves developing an assortment of roles, not only over the family's life-span but also within particular contexts. This switching of identities and interactional styles can also be witnessed amongst childhood friends. Not only may children find themselves assuming a variety of roles revolving around situated playgroup pursuits, but as they age and move into other realms of endeavor, "childhood friends" also expect one another to change in manners (e.g., "Grow up!" and "Get real!") that are more fitting with their present situations. People may persist with particular styles of association across situations and over time, but this is often accompanied by some resistance and distancing on the part of one's associates.

5. For indications not only of some of the processes involved in acquiring images of physical limitations, but also some of the problems people encounter when they have physiological limitations, see Davis (1961, 1963), Roth (1962), Higgins (1979, 1980), Schneider and Conrad (1983), Evans and Falk (1986), Evans (1988, 1994), Charmaz (1991, 1994), and Robillard (1994).

6. See studies of bodybuilding (Gaines and Butler, 1974) and running (Altheide and Pfuhl, 1980) as cases in point.

7. Although some illnesses are easily defined and treated, people may encounter considerable ambiguity of symptoms and uncertainty regarding the ways in which they should deal with their situations. For some valuable ethnographic work along these lines, see Roth (1962), Davis (1963), Emerson (1970), Kotarba (1983), Bloor (1985), Gross (1986), Brooks and Matson (1987), Kutner (1987), McGuire and Kantor (1987), Mitteness (1987), Peyrot et al. (1987), Singer et al. (1987), Charmaz (1991, 1994), Karp (1992, 1993, 1994, 1996), Migliore (1993), Royer (1995), and Stouffer (1995).

8. Unruh's (1983) study of how elderly persons engage particular activities is especially suggestive of the sort of work that may be conducted along these lines. Also instructive in this regard is Snyder's (1986) account of (often elderly) people's involvements in shuffleboard.

9. For some instructive ethnographic materials on dying as a social process, see Glaser and Strauss (1965), Sudnow (1967), Matthews (1975), Unruh (1979a), Sandstrom (1990), and Charmaz (1991).

10. The contemplation of (suicide or) ending one's life is a very real prospect when people encounter what they envision as extensive and unavoidable negativity or meaninglessness. Here, as well, one may begin to examine this phenomenon in process terms. Although it is impossible to interview those who have actually taken their own lives, one may still ask others about times in which they may have considered ending their own lives and the

circumstances surrounding these occasions, being particularly mindful of people's definitions of their situations (and selves) and their interchanges with others over time. While much interactionist/ethnographic work could be done along these lines, readers may find suggestive the works of Douglas (1967), Jacobs (1967, 1971), and Henslin (1970).

11. The earlier discussion of developing and using clothing (chapter 4) is highly pertinent here.

12. Goffman's (1959, 1963) work on "impression management" is relevant not only to people's "appearances" but to the notion of a consequential self more generally (at least insofar as people are interested in having their images acknowledged or verified by others). Matters pertaining to fashion (Klapp, 1969; Davis, 1992) are noteworthy here, as are related concerns with hairstyles, cosmetics use, daily grooming practices, jewelry usage, dieting, bodybuilding (Gaines and Butler, 1974), and tattoos (Sanders, 1989).

13. People sometimes "put down" others' appearances as pretentious and the like, but analysts would want to attend carefully to the meanings that participants in various life-worlds associate with their presentations of self. Although (a) outsiders may impute any variety of meanings to people's appearances and (b) people may intentionally present deceptive or misleading images of self to others for various purposes, people (c) may be entirely sincere in affecting particular images (i.e., not inclined to be pretentious or deceptive). In actual practice, people cannot avoid "giving off" images of self to others and the matter of "genuine natural images" (e.g., does this mean *unbathed, unkempt, naked*) is a most elusive (if not somewhat absurd) concept in the human community. Some people may take much greater care in the images they assume (and "give off") than others, but even those least interested in attending to those aspects of self are likely to encounter some community pressures to "clean up their acts (images)" or otherwise attain minimal levels of community decorum.

14. This point acknowledges people's abilities not only to be "objects of their own awareness" (Mead, 1934), but also to develop and sustain "preferred" images of self, even in the absence of acknowledgment, or in the face of resistance, from others.

15. Goffman's (1963) statement on stigma is particularly relevant here.

16. Also see the earlier consideration of dealing with objects (chapter 4) to appreciate a fuller sense of one's involvements in things as an "owner."

17. While often taken for granted or otherwise not even envisioned as a "possession," the loss of one's heritage (as in the case of adopted children puzzling about and pursuing their biological roots [March, 1994]) provides an interesting instance of the interlinkage of identity and possessions.

18. The earlier material on acquiring stocks of knowledge (chapter 4) is particularly relevant here.

19. See Sutherland (1937), Prus and Sharper (1977), and Prus and Irini (1980) for indications of apprenticeship (and proficiency) in illicit pursuits. Haas's (1972, 1977) study of high-iron steel workers, Winfree et al.'s (1984)

consideration of law interns, Fine's (1985) examination of cook apprentices in trade school, Haas and Shaffir's (1987) study of medical students, and Hunt's (1995) exploration of learning about the risks of deep-sea diving are also instructive here. More generally, however, it is worth noting that learning "on the job" is an ongoing activity in all realms of (minded) activity.

20. For some valuable ethnographic research on student aspects of the university educational process, see Becker, Hughes et al. (1961, 1968), Bernstein (1972), Haas and Shaffir (1977, 1982, 1987), and Albas and Albas (1984, 1988, 1994).

21. For instances of technical proficiency in the art world, see Christopherson's (1974) and Schwartz's (1986) studies of photographic work.

22. The matter of ineptitude seems to plague all performers, from those viewed as "mentally retarded" to those considered among the "intellectual elite." For ethnographic considerations of competence and "the cloak of competence," see Edgerton (1967), Haas and Shaffir (1977, 1982, 1987), and Albas and Albas (1988, 1994). For further appreciations of the genuine struggle for competence on the part of some physiologically disadvantaged individuals, see Scott (1968, 1969), Higgins (1980), Evans (1988, 1994), and Robillard (1994). Although most stuttering does not appear to be physiologically based, Petrunik's (1974) and Petrunik and Shearing's (1983) work on stuttering is also valuable in depicting both the difficulties people may have and the strategies they may invoke in attempts to sustain a competent self in interactional contexts.

23. People's accomplishments may not only pertain to any realm of activity (work, recreation, religion, politics), but often attest to very highly focused incidents within those contexts. Consider, for instance, winning a "contest," sighting a "rare" object, overcoming a "significant" obstacle, being appointed to an "esteemed" position, or attaining some "noteworthy" standard.

24. For some ethnographic explorations of accomplishment, readers are referred to Gaines and Butler's (1974) study of bodybuilding, Altheide and Pfuhl's (1980) portrayal of long-distance running, Mitchell's (1983) account of mountain climbing, Dietz's (1994) study of ballet, and Donnelly's (1994) consideration of birding and mountaineering.

25. The material outlined in the earlier consideration of "encountering the intersubjective other" (chapter 5) is particularly relevant to people's senses of affiliation and isolation, as are ethnographic studies of people becoming involved in subcultural pursuits. Consider, for instance, Becker's (1963) study of jazz musicians, Scott's (1981) study of basketball players, Wolf's (1991) depiction of outlaw bikers, and Wolf's (1994) study of feminist involvements.

26. As Yoels and Clair (1995) indicate, humor may be seen to foster a sense of mutuality. At the same time, it is generally expected that humor will be managed relative to the objectives and proprieties of the setting (Bjorklund, 1985).

27. Merten's (1996) portrayal of adolescent romantic relations nicely depicts the ambiguity associated with many relationships. Also see "Experiencing Relationships" (chapter 3).

28. Although not all instances of isolation are directly related to stigma (see Lopata's [1969] portrayal of the loneliness associated with widowhood), stigma (Goffman, 1963) is often interconnected with people's sense of isolation. Studies of divorce (e.g., Waller, 1930; Gerstel, 1986; Vaughan, 1986) and adoptees' searches for their biological parents (March, 1994) are also relevant here.

29. Focusing on the interactional dynamics of "paranoia" (and reflecting more general practices of distancing, distrust, and spurious interaction), Lemert (1962) provides a particularly valuable set of insights on the ways in which people may find themselves subject to intensified notions of isolation in group contexts.

30. For some ethnographic work on volunteers and the situations that develop around these roles, see Gardner (1986), Daniels (1988), Marks (1990), and Wharton (1991).

31. Assistance is often received with diverse and mixed reactions, as indicated in studies of the unemployed (Burman, 1988; Engbersen et al., 1993; Rank, 1994; and Rogers-Dillon, 1995). Also see Smith and Belgrave's (1995) depiction of people's experiences with the devastation of a hurricane.

32. Since entertainment is often associated with novelty, intrigue, excitement, or other versions of exceptionality, fascination, and enjoyment, it seems generally much easier for people who wish to be entertaining on a more sustained basis to create fictional representations than to locate and sincerely portray "interesting things" on their own.

33. Consider the production and appreciation (entertainment-wise) of intense dramas, horror movies, contact sports, ballet (Dietz, 1994a), and mountaineering (Mitchell, 1983).

34. Some ethnographic depictions of people involved in forging entertainment for others can be found in studies of musicians (Becker, 1963; Faulkner, 1971, Sanders, 1974; Prus and Irini, 1980; Gilmore, 1987; MacLeod, 1993; O'Berick, 1993), comedians (Salutin, 1973; Stebbins, 1990), magicians (Stebbins, 1984; Prus and Sharper, 1991), erotic dancers (Cressey, 1932; Prus and Irini, 1980; Ronai and Ellis, 1989), theatrical productions (Lyon, 1974; Layder, 1984; Friedman, 1990), film composers (Faulkner, 1976; Mukerji, 1977), and television producers (Mast, 1983).

35. Instances of ethnographic work that more squarely address the "mutuality of entertainment" include considerations of factory work (Roy, 1959); shuffleboard (Snyder, 1986) and baseball (Fine, 1987); drug use (Becker, 1963); drinking and bar life (Rubington, 1968; Spradley, 1970; Roebuck and Frese, 1976; Prus and Irini, 1980; Prus, 1983; Katovich and Reese, 1987; Donner, 1993); group sex (Bartell, 1971); role-playing games (Fine, 1983); gang involvements (Wolf, 1991; Moore, 1994); and humor (Bjorklund, 1985; Yoels and Clair, 1995). Even here, however, people may shift back and forth in emphasis, between concerns with mutuality and more singular ventures as entertainers and the entertained.

36. Beyond (a) mutual entertainment encounters (in which participants attempt to entertain one another), those pursuing entertainment may do so

(b) on a more self-focused basis in the presence of others, or (c) on their own in a more complete solitary sense. Patrons at theaters (Blumer, 1933; Blumer and Hauser, 1933), taxi-dance halls (Cressey, 1932), and bars (Roebuck and Frese, 1976; Prus and Irini, 1980) generally are indicative of those seeking entertainment "amidst others" as are many of those who become "caught up" in shopping (Prus and Dawson, 1991), street or biker gangs (Keiser, 1969; Wolf, 1991), gambling (Lesieur, 1977), or soap operas (Harrington and Bielby, 1995a). On the other hand, people may also attend to entertainment more exclusively on their own by listening to music or watching television by themselves, by reading books, playing videogames, or accessing solitary-oriented entertainment venues on the computer, for instance.

37. Alfred Schutz (1962:234–244) provides some interesting conceptual work on fantasies and daydreams, as well as (and contrasted with) dreaming.

38. A considerable amount of ethnographic research has attended to recreational pursuits of one sort or another. Consider, for instance, M. Scott's (1968) depiction of "the racing game"; Fine's (1983, 1987) accounts of fantasy role-playing games and little league baseball; Lesieur's (1977) inquiry into heavy gambling; Scott's (1981) account of female basketball players; Mitchell's (1983) study of mountain climbing; Snyder's (1986) study of shuffleboard; Wolf's (1991) study of outlaw biker clubs; and Dietz's (1994a) portrayal of the ballet world. A small body of ethnographic literature has also developed around people's practices of hanging around "street corners" (Anderson, 1923; Whyte, 1943; Liebow, 1967; Rubington, 1968; Spradley, 1970; Wiseman, 1970; Anderson, 1976; and Snow and Anderson, 1993) and frequenting "drinking establishments" (Cavan, 1966; Roebuck and Frese, 1976; Prus and Irini, 1980; and Katovich and Reese, 1987).

39. The material on "becoming involved in subcultural enterprises" (chapter 3) is highly relevant to people's participation in recreational associations.

40. In considering the consumption of entertainment, even in the seemingly most sedentary forms (e.g., watching television, listening to music, dining out, going to the theater, or watching sports events), it is essential that analysts not assume inactive consumers! Some early work on theater patrons by Blumer (1933) and Blumer and Hauser (1933) remains particularly instructive in this regard. Also see Harrington and Bielby's (1995a) depiction of "Soap Opera" fans.

41. See "Enhancing Communications (and Generating the Media)" in Chapter 5 for other materials pertinent to using the media for entertainment.

42. The conceptualization of *power* as a *definitional, processual, interactive essence* is developed more fully in Prus (1995, n.d.). Rather than suggest that power is an omnipresent, objective, or structuralist phenomenon, it is posited that people situationally *invoke* definitions of power or influence in much the same way that they bring notions of beauty or deviance into effect in their daily interchanges.

43. Although very much informed by ethnographic research on marketing and sales (Prus, 1989) and hustling and magic (Prus and Irini, 1980; Prus and

Sharper, 1991), as well as the Chicago interactionist tradition more generally, the material presented here is developed in considerably more detail in an interactionist analysis of "power" (Prus, 1995; n.d.). For elaborations of the media and political campaigns, see chapter 5.

44. This outline was very much inspired by an ethnographic considera- tion of people's shopping practices (Prus and Frisby, 1990; Prus and Dawson, 1991; Prus, 1993a, 1993b, 1994a). It particularly acknowledges the ways in which consumers anticipate, resist, and attempt to shape vendor influences in the course of pursuing their own interests. For other indications of people's elusive and resilient selves in the ethnographic literature, see Roth's (1962) study of doctor-patient negotiations, Molstad's (1986, 1989) and Hodson's (1991) accounts of factory work, Wiseman's (1970) and Peyrot's (1985) portrayals of those targeted for rehabilitation work, Roebuck and Frese's (1976) and Prus and Irini's (1980) considerations of those caught up in bar life, Wolf's (1991) examination of outlaw bikers, and Frazer and Reid's (1979) study of children's encounters with television commercials. Williams et al.'s (1992) account of people's senses of vulnerability as fieldworkers and their adjustments to these situations is also relevant here.

45. It should be noted that some roles (ascribed and achieved) are expected to "center" people's lives in rather consequential manners. Consider, for example, people's involvement in marital roles (Waller, 1930; Vaughan, 1986), gender role assignments (Kuhn, 1954; Kando, 1973; Cahill, 1980, 1989), total institutions (Goffman, 1961), religious communities (Lofland, 1966; Shaffir, 1974; Kleinman, 1984; Rochford, 1986; Ebaugh, 1988; Van Zandt, 1991; Wallace, 1992), medical schools (Haas and Shaffir, 1987), the military (Cocker- ham, 1979), street and biker gangs (Keiser, 1969; Wolf, 1991), skinhead sub- cultures (Moore, 1994), and feminist associations (Wolf, 1994). While often not anticipated at the outset, these and other involvements may become highly centralizing themes in people's lives. Also consider people's participation in gambling (Lesieur, 1977; Rosencrance, 1985), fantasy role-playing games (Fine, 1983), street life (Anderson, 1923; Shaw, 1930; Snow and Anderson, 1993), theft and hustling (Sutherland, 1937; Prus and Sharper, 1977), drinking and bar life (Rubington, 1968; Spradley, 1970; Wiseman, 1970; Roebuck and Frese, 1976; Prus and Irini, 1980; Prus, 1983), and drug use (Ray, 1961; Becker, 1963; Wedow, 1979; Rosenbaum, 1981; Faupel, 1987, 1991; Biernacki, 1988; Waldorf et al., 1991; and Taylor, 1993).

46. Even when people seem fairly intent on pursuing particular roles, they may find this stance difficult to sustain as a consequence of both the criticisms and the distractions they encounter. Becker's (1963) study of jazz musicians is indicative of the dilemmas that many performers face between "doing things their way" and "making other people happy." Bernstein's (1972) account of "student fritters" and Nash's (1990) consideration of "computer fritters" illustrate the ease with which people may be distracted from more centralizing tasks. Reflecting aspects of both of these themes, Prus (1989a: 255–86) indicates that the matter of sustaining enthusiasm is a major concern

to those in sales on both a short- and long-term basis. Roth's (1962), Davis's (1963), Schneider and Conrad's (1983), and Charmaz's (1991, 1994) studies not only portray the very distracting and disruptive nature of long-term illness for people's involvements generally, but also show how an illness can become the centralizing feature of one's life.

47. While some diversification or fragmentation experiences may be highly valued, as when people seek out additional forms of entertainment, challenge, and the like, other tendencies toward fragmentation or decentralization may be much less welcome.

As Adler and Adler (1991) in their study of college athletes and Baroody-Hart and Farrell (1987) in their portrayal of prison artists suggest, people attempting to pursue two or more demanding, diverse lines of activity are apt to experience some fragmentation of self. Similar "ambivalences of identity" are experienced by those trying to juggle definitions of "deviance" and "respectability" (Goffman, 1963).

Another notable setting in which people tend to experience a heightened sense of personal fragmentation is during the process of disengagement from formerly central roles. Consider people in the process of undergoing divorce (Waller, 1930; Gerstel, 1986; Vaughan, 1986; Hopper, 1993), leaving the military (Faulkner and McGaw, 1977), becoming disengaged from religious orders (Ebaugh, 1988), anticipating release from prison (Schmid and Jones, 1993); or attempting to reconstruct their lives following an encounter with a natural disaster (Smith and Belgrave, 1995). Although less pronounced, somewhat similar notions of fragmentation are expressed by couples who live apart (Gross, 1980) and by people who have migrated to other communities (Jones, 1980).

48. Since people's lives are often intertwined with others in ways that are not readily disentangled at will, they may find themselves drawn into or placed in situations that they might very well wish to avoid. Ethnographic research on the wives of alcoholics (Jackson, 1954; Wiseman, 1991; Asher, 1992) and prisoners (Fishman, 1990) illustrates the predicaments and fragmentary senses of self that people in these circumstances may experience. By no means, of course, are these situations limited to drinking episodes or instances of incarceration, and those involved in families (and other more enduring relationships) are apt to encounter a variety of circumstances that may result in a sense of personal disjointedness. Experiences with personal bankruptcy, job loss, heavy gambling, criminal prosecutions, unwanted pregnancies, marital breakups, chronic illnesses, deaths, or cultic involvements, for instance, may result in somewhat parallel senses of fragmentation not only for those most centrally involved, but also for those more intimately involved (and interdependent) with these particular people.

Part III

Pursuing the Ethnographic Venture

7

Doing Ethnographic Research: Fieldwork as Practical Accomplishment

(with Mary Lorenz Dietz and William Shaffir)

> *No theorizing, however ingenious, and no observance of scientific protocol, however meticulous, are substitutes for developing a familiarity with what is actually going on in the sphere of life under study. (Blumer, 1969:39)*

> *The outstanding peculiarity of this method [field research] is that the observer, in greater or less degree, is caught up in the very web of social interaction which he observes, analyzes and reports. . . . This has a peculiar corollary. The problem of learning to be a field observer is like the problem of learning to live in society. (Hughes, 1961:xiv–xv)*

This chapter considers the major tasks and obstacles that people embarking on ethnographic research are apt to face.[1] In summary form, this statement depicts our experiences as field researchers and the sorts of strategies we employ in conducting ethnographic inquiry as well as the cautions we have developed regarding field research over the years. Although each of us has been involved in several ethnographies,[2] we've worked on these studies independently of each other and likewise have become involved in field research through rather different routings. Nevertheless, our overall approach to field research has been quite consistent with the tenets of (Chicago-style) symbolic interaction and very much typifies the ethnographic research tradition that is associated with the works of scholars such as Robert Park, Herbert Blumer, Everett Hughes, and their students.

This statement is not presented as a recipe for doing field research, but it is hoped that people embarking on field research will find it useful to reflect on the matters discussed in this chapter. Likewise, this material is not intended to replace other considerations of field research practices. Those doing qualitative research are very much encouraged to read as many statements of these sorts as they can,[3] and to examine as many actual studies (regardless of the substantive setting or the era in which these were written) as possible and do so before, during, and after conducting their own studies.[4] Indeed, while people may appreciate aspects of these statements before embarking on a particular study, it is often only when one is in the midst of a project or even after having completed it that certain observations made by others may be most helpful. As well, when ethnographic research is envisioned as an ongoing enterprise, it means that subsequent projects should be stronger as a result of attending to the ethnographic literature.

Following a consideration of (1) the objectives and assumptions of ethnographic research, this chapter focuses on (2) the problematics of accessing human lived experiences and (3) the tasks of analyzing ethnographic data.

Ethnographic Research

Ethnographic research (also commonly referenced as field research, qualitative research, participant observation, interactionist research, constructionist research, and naturalistic inquiry) might be most basically defined as the study of the life-worlds of particular groups of people through active interchange with the participants in those worlds. In doing ethnographic research, the investigator assumes the tasks of (a) permeating the social world of "the other" (the insiders), (b) achieving intimate familiarity with the other's lived experiences, (c) carefully and fully gathering and recording information about that life-world, and (d) conveying to others (outsiders) the life-worlds of the other (insiders) in ways which are both comprehensible to the outsiders and yet as closely as possible approximate the lived experiences of the insiders. This is the first and primary pursuit of the ethnographer: to achieve a thorough, sensitive, and fine-grained descriptive account of the life-world of the other. This is a major undertaking, and some ethnographers may limit their task to this objective.

However, there is a second and related objective that one may pursue as an ethnographer, and this involves the development of analytical concepts. Concepts are important, not only because they allow researchers to develop more precise understandings of the situation at hand, but also because they enable analysts to make comparisons across two or more ethnographic settings. While some might argue that concepts destroy the idiographic or unique features of this or that situation, this view is rather self-defeating, since some classifications or categorizations are essential if one is to attempt to make sense of any set of practices. Concepts of some kind are required when people ask even elementary questions, such as, "What is this thing? What does this object do? How does it work? How did this come about?"

Concepts do not destroy the exploratory process. Rather, as Blumer (1928:349) observes, they provide ways of focusing on various dimensions of the object at hand. However, not all concepts are equally viable. As Blumer also insists, the concepts we use in examining any object should be attentive to the essence of that phenomenon.[5] It is here, then, that our concepts should be sufficiently open and sensitive to the situation at hand that they allow us to address any idiographic or unique features of the object under study that are deemed noteworthy. Where no suitable concepts are available, we may tentatively pose one or other concepts to approximate these nuances. However, we should take great care to develop concepts that respect the subject matter under consideration.

As ethnographers, we would want to attend to the distinctions, categories, typifications, explanations, and other sense-making practices of those we study, and develop accounts of their worlds mindful of these categories. This "world of the other," for purposes of inquiry, is our paramount reality, and any investigatory or analytical activity should be attentive to this world.

At the same time, however, we may also find it useful to compare people's experiences (i.e., definitions and practices) across two or more ethnographic settings, asking when and how one set of people's experiences are similar to, or different from, those of others in seemingly parallel settings. Thus, we may observe, as does Weston LaBarre (1947) in his statement on the language of gestures and emotions, that different peoples may (a) engage in similar practices but do so with very different meanings, and (b) do very different things but attach very similar meanings to these activities. In all cases, the people LaBarre studied apparently felt that their own practices were entirely natural. Or we may find, as did Verne Ray (1953), who studied color perception across a range of North American cultural groups, that although each of the groups made definite color distinctions, their notions of both primary and other identifiable colors varied dramatically. Some groups have no terms for certain parts of the color spectrum despite normal physiological and perceptual tendencies and the relative presence of objects of those [colors] in their physical environments.

The point is not simply that differences and similarities exist, but rather that the use of concepts enables us to develop sharper apprecia- tions of the experiences of particular communities of others, as well as to achieve a fuller understanding of the concepts that we use to make comparisons. Thus, for instance, we may learn about this or that group by attending to the ways in which they express emotions or gesture to one another, but we also become more cognizant of "gestures" and "emotions" as concepts by attending to the ways in which these are dealt with in a variety of ethnographic contexts. Similarly, we may learn more about the ways in which colors, flavors, tastes, and other physical sensations are constructed by examining the ways in which these are experienced in different cultural settings. Not all comparisons will be equally central for helping us understand aspects of human lived experience in practice, but by being attentive to concepts that enable us to transcend a plurality of contexts, we seem to be in a better position to develop understandings both of particular or idiographic settings and of the concepts we are using to forge bridges across contexts. As this material develops, we will be addressing a set of "generic social processes" that ethnographers may find useful in dealing with the social construction of human group life,[6] but as with other concepts that we use as social scientists, it is important to remember that these also are instances of cultural constructions and should *not* be taken to be "more real" than the categories used by the participants in this or that setting.

The Ethnographic Advantage

Despite the remarkable potency of ethnographic research for examining and elaborating upon human lived experience, many scholars in the social sciences have been critical of ethnographic inquiry, often claiming that it is (a) unscientific or (b) atheoretical. These claims are largely unfounded, but they have tended to discredit ethnographic research as well as to divert attention from the considerable inade- quacy of alternative methodologies for studying human behavior.

Modeling their own versions of social science after what they assumed physical scientists were doing, positivist or factors-oriented social scientists (assuming notions of causality, objectification, and quantification) have felt justified in claiming that they were more scien- tific than were the ethnographers, who they saw simply as "hanging around people and talking to them in some loose, unstructured manners." Quantitative social scientists have sought to objectify human behavior, to measure it, to determine what caused it, to ascertain the factors responsible for it, and, where desirable, to reshape human behavior. Many experiments have been conducted, many surveys have been made, and many "facts" have been gathered. The argument is that the methods that had been seemingly so effective in dealing with physical objects could and should be transported to the study of humans.[7]

However, their thinking has been flawed in two major respects. First, none of the quantitatively oriented social scientists have conducted any careful, first-hand research into the ways in which "(physical) science is accomplished in practice." As more recent historical and sociological studies in this area indicate, *science itself is a social product and a social process*.[8] Science is a *human construction* and as such is subject to ongoing interpretation and negotiation. Accordingly, the processes underlying the social production of science have much in common with those characterizing political interchanges, family relations, school-ground activities, recreational pursuits, and marketplace exchanges, for instance. This "new sociology of science" literature in no way denies or denigrates the accomplishments of science, but it indicates that "science in practice" does not correspond with the images employed by those adopting a positivist paradigm in the social sciences. In short, the social sciences were modeled on mistaken inferences of how the scientific process is accomplished.

The second flaw is somewhat related to the first but is even more basic and consequential. Insofar as the scientific enterprise may be defined by the close, open, sustained examination of some phenomenon, and more particularly entails an approach that attempts to respect the subject matter of the phenomenon at hand, it may be argued that the positivists (for all their claims about being "scientific" in their theoretical and methodological emphases) are rather remiss with respect to the ways in which they approach their subject matter.

Should social scientists intend to approximate the objectives of scientific inquiry, they must employ (as Blumer [1969] posits) a methodology and conceptual approach that respects the nature of their subject matter. That is, they must develop a method that allows them to examine human group life *as it is constituted in practice*.

Thus, instead of viewing human behavior as the product of factors (internal and external) acting on people (i.e., viewing people as the mere mediums through which these factors find expression), as do quantitatively oriented social scientists, ethnographers generally attend to the ways in which people (as linguistic, thinking, interacting, adjusting, community-based beings) construct or accomplish their activities over time or in process terms.

While those conducting mainstream social science have been spewing out massive piles of rates and statistics, they have generated remarkably little insight into the actual production of human behavior. While purporting to isolate factors associated with this or that outcome, their models do not adequately approximate human lived experience.[9]

Not only do "factors" or "variables" not explain how behavior comes about, but social scientists using this type of data invariably turn to *paratheories* to explain the significance of this or that factor for the outcome under consideration.[10] Although these paratheories are typically introduced implicitly, they are necessary to "explain" this or that set of results or to tell us how some particular factor gets translated into actual practice in the world out there. Here, quantitative researchers are reduced to guesses and speculation. At best, these explanations are only marginally informed by their models and the data they have gathered. Consequently, the explanations they offer to account for the effects (or relative ineffectiveness) of particular variables in the study at hand rely centrally on paratheories that are built up in a much more haphazard fashion.

In discussing their results, quantitative researchers generally first turn to the paratheories that those preceding them have stated in the literature. They try to push these explanations as far as they can, since this published material is presumed to have a more objectified or legitimated quality (i.e., "What did Durkheim have to say about that? What about Weber, or Marx?" "What did someone suggest in this other study? Did they say anything that might help us explain this result?"). But almost inevitably, too, these researchers (as with those who preceded them) find themselves relying on the generalized stocks of knowledge that they build up as citizens in the community (by reading newspapers, watching television, and casually conversing with, or observing, other people in this or that setting). In actual practice, researchers using survey data (questionnaires and census data) or experimental designs are normally quite far removed from the people whose lives and situations they are discussing. Indeed, they may never have even met any of the people whose situations they spend their careers discussing, let alone conversed with them at length about their experiences in this or that realm of their lives.

For example, despite the millions of dollars that have been spent on research (mostly quantitative) on crime, delinquency, drinking, and drug use, social scientists have learned very little about the ways in which people become involved in these activities; how they go about doing these activities; the sorts of relationships or subcultures they develop; how they deal with their families, the police, the courts, and other control agencies; or how they become disinvolved from or re-involved in these same activities. And what we do know about these issues is almost entirely the product of a handful of researchers who have gone into the field to do ethnographic research on these matters. Unfortunately, this lack of intimate knowledge of the other is not limited to the study of deviance; it represents a major deficiency across the substantive fields of the social sciences. Despite a great deal of learned discourse, an abundance of well-intentioned advice, and much quantitative research activity (allegedly invoking scientific protocol), we know very little about the ways in which people go about their activities in reference to educational contexts, religious settings, politi-cal arenas, migration practices, business worlds, and so on.

Quite simply, without ethnographic research, we would have to rely almost entirely on journalistic accounts for most of our knowledge about the world of the other. The factors or variable-analysis approach that is so dominant in mainstream social science is not able to provide us with any sort of intimate knowledge about the other. And journal-istic accounts, despite being much more current than ethnographies (which normally take several months or years to develop), offer very uneven and unreliable accounts of human lived experience. This is not to dismiss journalistic accounts out of hand, but to recognize that ethnographers tend to be much more thorough, precise, and concep-tually oriented than are most journalists. Thus, although some journal-ists are very much concerned with arriving at careful, thorough, and open renderings of the viewpoints of the other, they lack the resources (time, literature, community of scholars) that ethnographers have in pursuing a more comprehensive and conceptually developed account of the life-worlds of the other. Further, even those journalists who more fully intend to take the role of the other and represent the views of the other as openly and completely as possible typically find them-selves scurrying to meet deadlines. As well, they often face intense competition from other journalists for "hot" materials and more sensationalistic angles. Further, those who strive for more comprehen-sive, balanced reports may find that their reports are dramatically cut and reconstructed by editors who likely are attentive to other matters (entertainment, readership, space, other articles). Given this uneven-ness, it becomes exceedingly difficult for the receiving audiences (readers, viewers, listeners) to sort out carefully developed and conveyed materials about the other from accounts that are much more hack-neyed and intended to provoke interest, entertainment, and rivet attention to the journalist or medium in question.

By contrast, quantitative social science is considerably more rigorous and much less sensationalistic than are most journalistic endeavors. However, its relevance to human lived experience is conveyed not so much through the factors that are presumably so central in the (structuralist) research design, but through the development of paratheories. These paratheories are not only shaped to fit whatever statistical results that the researcher in the study encounters,[11] but they are also developed somewhat haphazardly. Journalistic accounts tend to be unreliable, incomplete, and overly dramatized. Still, they often offer some first-hand insights into the lived experiences of the other, information that one typically does not obtain from a factors-oriented social science. Journalistic accounts also offer an immediacy (via an advanced communications network) that neither mainstream or ethnographic social science can possibly match.[12] Still, neither of these alternatives (quantitative social science or journalism) provides adequate insight into the ways in which human group life is accomplished. In these respects, there is no viable substitute for the careful, extended, and much more open accounts normally provided by ethnographers in the field.

Clarifying Ethnographic Assumptions

When people speak about embarking on ethnographic research, they assume the tasks of thoroughly examining the life-worlds and practices of those whose situations are being studied. Indeed, this is most basic. And yet, from the researcher's viewpoint, there is much more to ethnographic inquiry than simply going out to attend the world of people's lived experience in this or that setting. In their quest to be careful and thorough, and to communicate the information and insights they acquire to others, researchers are apt to find that ethnographic inquiry also encompasses concerns with clarifying one's assumptions and accessing worlds of human lived experience. As indicated in chapters 1–3, those taking an interactionist approach to the study of community life envision human lived experience as *intersubjective, (multi)perspectival, reflective, action-oriented, negotiable, relational, and processual.*

The research implications of these assumptions are highly consequential. It means giving full consideration to (1) the ways in which people achieve linguistic mutuality in particular life-worlds; (2) the viewpoints of those whose worlds one intends to examine; (3) the interpretations or meanings that people attach to themselves, other people, and other objects of their experiences; (4) the ways in which people accomplish or do things in the settings under consideration; (5) the attempts that people make to influence (as well as accommodate and resist) the inputs and behaviors of others; (6) the bonds that people develop with others over time and the ways in which they attend to these relationships; and (7) the natural histories or sequences of encounters, exchanges, and events that people develop and experience.

The study of human lived experience requires an examination of the ways in which people make sense of their situations and work out their activities in conjunction with others. Human experience is not to be dismissed as subjective, epiphenomenal, or nonfactual. Since people know the world only as they experience it, and people experience the world in an intersubjective manner, then this realm of inquiry (i.e., human experiences within a world of others) becomes the paramount reality to which researchers should attend in their investigations of human group life.

Accessing Human Lived Experience

The ethnographic task of accessing human lived experience involves a number of subthemes. While these notions overlap in a number of respects, we have outlined a number of issues that people embarking on field research would likely wish to consider as they attempt to achieve intersubjectivity with the other. Thus, attention is given to: methodological practices; substantive settings; analytical foci; making contact with the other; interacting with the other; managing oneself in the ethnographic context; recording information about the life-worlds of the other; and sampling concerns. This ordering should not be assumed to reflect priority of these particular matters, but rather attests to the practical limitation of not being able to talk about everything at once.

Methodological Practices

In their attempts to achieve intimate familiarity with the life-worlds of those they study, ethnographers rely primarily on three sources of data: observation, participant-observation, and interviews.

Observation encompasses not only those things that one witnesses through one's (primary, especially visual and auditory) senses, but also includes access to any documents, diaries, records, and the like that one may be able to obtain in a particular setting. While materials gathered in this way can be very valuable, it is imperative to recognize that the worth of any observation (or artifact) is contingent on researchers' abilities to achieve clear and accurate definitions of how that phenomenon or aspect of the situation was experienced and constructed by those participating in the situations under consideration.

Observational material, on its own, is much too limited (i.e., inadequate) a base on which to build an ethnographic study, because one would have to make extensive inferences regarding both the meanings that other people attribute to objects before, during, and after acting toward those objects in some manner. As well, observational data fails to consider other lines of action that people may have entertained but decided for one or other reasons not to implement.[13] However, observational materials can be very valuable in helping researchers formulate questions to be pursued in interviews, and is often useful as well in providing researchers with a means of assessing and contextualizing the information that one obtains through interviews and participant observation:

MLD: You know, we are doing observations all the time. In some ways, I think that "doing observations" is just a first phase in the fieldwork process. It is the stage in fieldwork where you start to develop ideas as you become aware of the uniqueness of a group, setting, or activity. It is a time when you begin to get an idea about relationships, whether this is from something you have been reading or seeing. Doing observation makes you aware of new ways of seeing things or things to be seen.

BP: I generally think of straight observation as so limited in comparison to what can be gleaned through participant-observation and interviews, but even simple observation can be very useful in helping people overcome preexisting images of this or that setting as well as picking up on certain features of the setting. While we often think of observation as a visual practice, it is also important to appreciate the verbal features. You can learn a lot just by listening, that is, assuming that you know the basic language and are able to remain in the setting for extended periods of time. I think people are often so struck by the visual features of a new situation that they overlook the verbal component. The other thing is this, though: observation should not be seen as a substitute for the sort of intersubjectivity that one attains through participant-observation and open-ended interviewing.

Field researchers will readily attest to the problems of making sense of their initial observations in new situations. Indeed, one's initial entry is apt to be especially confusing precisely because of the absence of an intersubjective context within which to situate one's observational data. However, this material can stimulate questions to be pursued as the researcher strives to become increasingly familiar with the setting and its participants. As field researchers discover sooner or later, all of the varied sources of data can provide "missing pieces" and become most valuable when compared and contrasted with data gathered through other means. While researchers typically gather observational data throughout the research, they tend to rely most heavily on this information during their initial involvements in settings when they feel least at ease and have yet to become better acquainted with the participants in those settings. Initially, then, researchers find it helpful to take note of all observations even though they might fail to understand their immediate relevancies. Objects and events that may appear trivial and insignificant to the research problem, in fact, may be later discovered to be intimately connected.

Participant-observation adds an entirely different and vital dimension to the notion of observation. Although this practice has often been (inappropriately) dismissed as "subjective" by positivist critics, the participant-observer role allows the researcher to get infinitely closer to the lived experiences of the participants than does straight observation. Like those doing straight observation, researchers engaged in participant-observation normally try to remain fairly unobtrusive or nondisruptive in the setting being studied. However, this research strategy entails a more active (and interactive) role as researchers attempt to fit into the settings at hand.

Insofar as participant-observation allows researchers to experience on a first-hand basis some aspects of the life-worlds of the other, it offers a rather unique and instructive form of data to those able and willing to assume the role of the other in a more comprehensive sense. Additionally, since it typically puts researchers in close, sustained contact with others, participant-observation generates further opportunities to gain insight into the viewpoints and practices of the other through ongoing commentary and other interactions. Participant-observation, thus, provides a doubly privileged form of contact with the other:

MLD: We have all done some interviewing where we are essentially outsiders. I certainly have not been a ballet dancer, or an urban lumberjack, or a felony killer, but in many of these cases, I had a sponsor or was able to relate in some way to the experience not as a total outsider. . . . I had the most difficulty with felony killers, because there was no way I could suggest that their activities were acceptable. When they asked me what I thought, I told them . . . I don't know if I would have had better data if I had been less honest.

BP: You can't always do participant-observation or at least not as fully as one might consider desirable. In the hotel community, for instance, there were some roles (e.g., hookers, exotic dancers) that we were physically unable to perform. There were other roles (e.g., drug dealing, loan sharking, pimping) that we deemed unwise to pursue. However, there were a number of roles (e.g., desk clerk, doorman, waiter, bartender, patron, friend) in the setting that were more accessible and provided us with a great deal of sustained contact with the people in the hotel community. . . . Similarly, I found my involvement in a craft enterprise was very helpful for the study I did on marketing and sales. Not only did I make contact with crafters (and other retailers), wholesalers, and manufacturers, as well as a wide range of customers, but I was also directly able to experience on a first-hand basis many of the ambiguities and dilemmas, frustrations and excitements associated with involvements in the business world.

In contrast to straight observation, participant-observation research is generally a very time-consuming and emotionally draining activity. In addition to one's concerns with (a) keeping records of the things that others say and do, one also (b) keeps track of one's own activities and experiences in the setting, (c) attempts to manage an active (presumably nondisruptive) role in the setting, (d) attempts to maintain viable working relationships with others in the situation, and (e) endeavors to acquire a thorough understanding of the life-worlds of the other through a variety of ongoing queries and involvements with the other. To be done effectively, participant-observation requires careful, concerted concentration. Insofar as one becomes immersed in a community of others, who attend in varying ways to the activities of the researcher, one is almost always "on" when in the field. However, in addition to fitting into roles that the others find acceptable for researchers to sustain, participant observers also attempt to pursue information about the ways in which community life is accomplished by the people in the setting. Thus, a considerable amount of ongoing concentration is required to sustain one's interpersonal and task-related presences in the field setting. In this latter regard, the researcher should also be alert to individuals previously encountered, conversations and exchanges with particular people, the general stock of knowledge yielded by the research to date, and specific kinds of data still sought. As a consequence of this concentrated focusing, extended periods of participant-observation (i.e., several hours) can generate considerable fatigue. When people are tired and distracted, the quality of the material collected tends to diminish, so it is important for researchers to approach the field with as much attentiveness and stamina as they can muster.

Unlike straight observational data, which can usually be collected at times more convenient to the researcher, participant-observation requires that the researcher attend to both the time frames of the other and the activities going on in that setting. Simply put, it is important not only to be where the action is, but to be there at the time when it is occurring. While this requirement sounds simple and straightforward, the logistics involved in executing it successfully may entail considerable sacrifice on the part of the researcher.[14] The simple rule is that if something significant is about to happen in the field, be there. Since it is impossible always to anticipate the development of important events, the researcher may be required to alter previously made commitments to family, friends, colleagues, and others as the project develops.

Finally, it is difficult to overemphasize the importance of the researcher sustaining a presence in the field. When the researcher is present in the field in more of an ongoing basis, higher levels of trust are apt to ensue. Since one's ongoing presence signals a commitment by the researcher to both understand and appreciate the participants' world from their perspective(s), it typically fosters their participation in the research.

Interviews represent the third major method of gathering ethnographic data, and under some circumstances may provide the primary source of data for field researchers. While those conducting interviews become participants of sorts in the life-worlds of the other, interviews in themselves should not be seen as substitutes for extensive involvements as participant-observers. At the same time, when researchers are able to establish a good working rapport with the other and can generate extended trust and openness, they may be able to obtain a great deal of information about the life-situations of the other through extended conversation. Ethnographers sometimes develop fairly extensive interview formats, but these normally take shape in the field as researchers learn more about the situations and the participants involved.

The process of conducting interviews, while seemingly elementary, involves the coordination of considerable skills. While so-called natural conversationalists may be eminently suited to this task, interviewing and conversing are not identical. Interviews can assume the form of an informal conversation, and may appear to be free-flowing and unconstrained, but such spontaneity typically belies a sustained concern about learning in intimate detail a great deal about the social world of the other. As the research proceeds, researchers typically develop general guides of issues to be pursued and the kinds of questions to be asked. Seasoned interviewers often mentally rehearse the interview encounter, anticipating the particular data that the interviewee may yield, and carefully consider the kinds of questions that particular individuals may be most able to discuss. In other words, what does the other know about best and when might the other be rightfully regarded as an expert in this or that realm of activity? While some of the questions may be carefully planned, the order in which they are asked and the manners in which they are formulated are less certain. Likewise, there is an ongoing adjustment to the other as researchers pursue unanticipated leads or realize that the other's stock of knowledge is more limited in this or that respect than earlier seemed the case. Herein lies the art of successful interviewing for ethnographic purposes. Each interviewee is not only unique but brings to the encounter different concerns, apprehensions, interests, and stocks of knowledge. On the one hand, there is a research agenda that should be acknowledged and addressed; but also, because of the openness of the ethnographic interview and the unexpected revelations and limitations one encounters in dealing with the other, exchanges with the other are inevitably problematic and adjustive in nature:

BP: Every interview is different and some will be so much more productive than others, but the best interviews, I think, are those in which you've established so much openness with the other that there is almost a little magic between the two of you whereby the other person takes you on a little trip into their world. And people can explain so much to you through the interview, so many things that you would never get otherwise. And, the more they share, explain, and elaborate in the process, the better it is for you. . . . I basically assume the role of a student who is there to learn about their world as they know it. I'm interested, inquisitive, and I try to be as patient as possible, letting them talk about their situations and experiences as fully as they are able. I try to pursue as much detail as I can and I ask them about specific instances. The instances are all different to some extent, but they are so important in enabling you to see how things are worked out in practice. Otherwise, you are asking them to develop generalizations for you and that data is typically much less instructive in the long run.

Typically, as I do more interviews or learn more about the field, I develop a list of things that seem important in understanding these people's situations and the things they do. I'll show people the list of things that I've come up with and ask them what things I've missed. Then add these things to this working list as well as other things that I might notice along the way. My basic approach is "What can you tell me about this topic?" Then, I pursue that topic with them as much as I can. Sometimes, I'll leave the list with those I'm interviewing in advance and ask them to add anything they can think of. Then I'll talk to them about these things the next day or whenever we get together. As well, since people normally end up discussing things in orders different from the way your list is organized, I've also observed that one useful way of beginning an interview, rapport-wise, is to ask them if there are any topics with which they might like to start and try to pick up other topics as we go along. You pretty well have to do that anyway, within a more free-flowing interview.

There is also the task of sustaining the interests and cooperation of the other. Researchers who expect to receive information from and about the other without reciprocating in some manner (if only by exhibiting genuine attentiveness) may discover that the pace and flow of the interview become stilted. The people we meet also develop definitions of the interview encounter and of our research interests and objectives. Thus, it is important to be vigilant to those concerns, while managing and directing the overall encounter within a limited time frame. The various interpersonal skills that must be marshaled during the interview, all in a seemingly informal and relaxed fashion, should indicate that this approach to collecting ethnographic data involves hard work. As with effective participant-observation, good interviewing requires a high level of attentiveness to the other. Seasoned researchers recognize that the ensuing fatigue and exhaustion are natural experiences of sustaining ethnographic interviews.

The ethnographic interview is characterized by careful and receptive listening, open-ended queries, and extensive probing. It reflects a generalized curiosity about the situation of the other and emergent sets of questions that develop as the researcher spends more time in the setting and the company of the other. Researchers in the field vary greatly in the ways in and extent to which they pursue interview materials, but a fuller openness to the other or greater receptiveness to letting the other "talk back" to the researcher is fundamental in achieving a more viable sense of intersubjectivity. Indeed, without this opportunity to uncover, ascertain, and qualify the meanings that others hold for objects in their life-worlds and the ways in which people go about accomplishing their activities in practice, it would make little sense to talk about studying human lived experience.

While each setting is somewhat different from the next (as is each encounter with the same person), and may necessitate some change in researchers' practices, there is little doubt about the generally enhanced quality (amount and depth) of the data one may obtain by spending more time in the setting and more fully participating in the life-worlds of the other. When researchers are able to gather observational, participant-observation, and interview data on a more or less simultaneous basis, this generally leads to a more complete understanding of the other. Researchers who become more immersed in the setting are not only more apt to be exposed to a wider and more intricate range of materials, but they are typically in a much better situation to inquire about, pursue, and assess incoming information gleaned in all of these manners:

BP: It's not always feasible to be a participant-observer in a fuller sense in some of the field research one does. I'm thinking here of the work I did on parole officers, the clergy, the hookers, the strippers, the hustlers, and the magicians. In each of these cases, I was centrally dependent on those I interviewed and their willingness to take me to this or that event with them. In contrast, the work I did on the marketing and sales project and consumer behavior had a very different dimension to it as a consequence of the opportunities I had for more extensive involvements in those settings. There are many things one can pick up from more cursory observations in particular settings, and one can also pick up on a lot of little things that people mention to you in the course of an interview and begin to really pursue those themes, but it's also very instructive to experience those things that people have told you about as well as to use your own experiences as a basis for asking them more about particular situations.

WS: When I began my research on the Lubavitcher hasidim in Montreal, I was immediately introduced to the importance of the rebbe in the lives of his followers. The hasidim, I learned, anxiously awaited opportunities to travel to Crown Heights, Brooklyn, in order to *farbreng* [celebrate] with their rebbe. It was only when I experienced a *farbrengen* first-hand that I began to appreciate the significance of this experience for the hasidim. I had read about farbrengens and they were always the subject of conversation when hasidim returned from New York, but witnessing the event provided a very different perspective on their relevance for my research. As a rule, I believe that there are immeasurable advantages to experiencing and participating in the range of activities of the people under study where this is both possible and feasible. Of course, it's sometimes neither of these and I would stress that participation is not a sine qua non of field research. It is simply the case, I've discovered, that when I've had opportunities to observe people going about their daily routines, and could engage them in informal conversation in the process, my understanding of their concerns and perspectives is greatly enhanced. For instance, there's a world of difference between interviewing medical students about their clinical skills experiences and following them on their clinical rounds in the hospital as Jack Haas and I did. In short, then, my principle is this: if it makes sense to hang around and hang out, do it, and don't worry much about safeguarding objectivity. It took some time for me to reach this position, although as I reflect on my experiences I realize that in my research on hasidic Jews, medical students, and the socialization of newcomers to Orthodox Judaism I was frequently discouraged by those I was studying from simply observing them from a distance. Finally, along this line, I have never become a complete participant either out of choice or circumstance, and in each project have learned to gauge the degree to which participation is both useful and feasible.

Substantive Settings

Some ethnographic research is undertaken to learn about the life-styles and practices of certain groups of people. This objective may be pursued in as many dimensions and with as much intensity as the researcher can manage over the course of the project. In other cases, researchers may focus on particular analytical themes, such as "achieving identity," "generating trust," and "settling disputes," and explore one or more of these notions in particular substantive settings.

Substantive settings refer to the contexts in which projects are situated. Ethnographers exploring substantive contexts may study particular communities or subcultures (communities within communities) or focus on more specific practices (e.g., settling disputes, drinking, using drugs) among particular groups of people. The research foci may be as broad or as narrow as the researchers desire, but the emphasis in substantive inquiry lies in examining and explaining the context at hand.

Like instances of people's involvements in other settings, researchers' attentiveness to substantive foci appear to reflect the routings (often combinations) of seekership, recruitment, and closure, and tend to be qualified by people's reservations about entering or becoming part of this or that setting. Thus, some studies reflect (a) preexisting interests (curiosities, fascinations) researchers may hold, but other projects denote (b) the opportunities and encouragements provided by other people and (c) pressing obligations (e.g., course requirements, pursuit of research contracts) researchers may pursue. Prospective topics also seem subject to some screening relative to (d) any reservations researchers may hold (e.g., costs, risk, time encumbrances, personal disaffections) about pursuing the study of particular topics:

BP: Every project that I've been involved in has come about in a different manner. I started doing research on parole officers not because I had any great interest in the parole system, but because I was interested in labeling theory and decided I would like to work with John Stratton (as my advisor in graduate school) who had a strong interest in the criminal justice system. . . . The study of the clergy started as a research assignment in a class on the sociology of religion with Steve Weiting. . . . I met C. R. D. Sharper in one of my classes and he introduced me to a world (card and dice hustling) of which I knew virtually nothing beforehand. . . . Styllianoss Irini dropped by my office one day to talk about deviance courses and we ended up doing a study of the hotel community. As with the study of card and dice hustling, I had no intention whatsoever of embarking on this study, but as I became more cognizant of the world Styllianoss knew and how different it seemed from the accounts of the underlife I had been reading in the literature, I began to realize the necessity of studying deviance as a community phenomenon. . . . As we were finishing the study of the hotel setting, I became increasingly aware that we had been studying a number of businesses and business people, that is the hookers, strippers, bar business, room rentals, and such, and I became attentive to the lack of attention that both sociologists and those in business schools had given to the ways in which business was conducted on a day-to-day basis. So I started talking to people in malls, at trade shows, craft shows, and the like and went on from there. . . . The study of consumer behavior emerged as a natural sequel, as I became more and more cognizant of the necessity of studying exchanges from their sides. . . . The research I did on magicians came about as a consequence of Bob Farmer's efforts to contact me, and the efforts he and Richard Kaufman expended to encourage and arrange for the republication of *Road Hustler*. . . . The other thing that I might add is that there are so many opportunities to get involved in research in so many other settings. I have on many, many occasions thought, "That would be very worthwhile studying, in depth, but I'm already overly committed." It's just that you meet people who are into this and that, and you notice things in the media, where you say, "That would be really interesting to study."

WS: The projects in which I've become involved reflect a combination of fortuitous circumstances and some measure of choice. My studies of hasidic Jews have extended over a twenty-year period. Malcolm Spector, my thesis advisor at McGill University, once suggested in passing that it would be interesting to study hasidic Jews. I had already begun researching a pool hall but, upon some reflection, elected to begin visiting hasidic yeshivas. Although my doctorate on a hasidic community was completed in 1972, I have continued with the general topic because of the personal gratification I derive from it. I enjoy the challenges it offers but most of all am fascinated by the dynamics by which the hasidim's distinctive lifestyle is maintained. The hasidic research provided the basis for some of my other projects on religion, notably those on newcomers to, and defectors from, Orthodox Judaism. The former project came about as I had to complete an application for a Leave Fellowship and knew I'd be spending a sabbatical in Israel. I had already studied newcomers to the Lubavitch hasidic community in Montreal, and realized that the process of becoming observant could easily be followed up in Jerusalem by visiting several religious institutions catering specifically to young unobservant Jews. A chance remark by a friend several years later led me to begin examining ultra-Orthodox Jews who left the confines of their closed communities to pursue a more liberal way of life. At the time I was in Israel, once again on sabbatical, but in the midst of a project on the immigration experiences of Canadian Jews who had recently moved to Israel to live. The data from this project were becoming somewhat repetitive, which diminished my interest in arranging further interviews, and I eagerly embarked on what became a most challenging and fascinating project.

My involvement in the study of the professionalization of medical students was a case of being in the right place at the right time. McMaster's medical school was new, it had embarked upon a radical curriculum for its undergraduates, and here were three freshly minted Ph.D.'s in the sociology department (Jack Haas, Victor Marshall, and I) eager to begin a new project. . . . My study of an ethnic riot in Toronto in 1933, with Cyril Levitt, really began as a study on ethnic violence for which we were unable to receive funding. The granting agency considered our proposal to be overly ambitious and recommended that we best begin with a case study and we settled on the Christie Pits riot. Upon the completion of this research, and realizing how enjoyable we found working together, Cyril and I began a study of Canadian Jews who, having immigrated to Israel, decided to return to live in Canada.

The study of the McMaster University Arts and Science Program, highly innovative in the liberal arts, came about as I realized that so much of my research called for me to travel to other cities, while the opportunity to study something new and exciting was right under my nose. What actually sparked the research were chance remarks by a faculty member who taught in that program that the students were significantly different and brighter than other undergraduates he had taught. . . . And finally, there are occasions when research opportunities are just too exciting to pass up. While I've maintained a somewhat dormant interest in the Lubavitch hasidic sect, my research arousal piqued when Lubavitch mounted a campaign heralding the Messiah's imminent arrival followed by a significant shift in the campaign's focus that the Lubavitcher rebbe was the actual Messiah. Generally speaking, I involve myself in several projects simultaneously, and often feel that I'm over-committed. I've never been one to search for research projects, and see the possibilities for potentially exciting research in the round of activities comprising social life.

Overall, it is generally much more productive for researchers to focus on substantive realms that they can readily access. And, if they have existing familiarities with particular settings, so much the better. If researchers don't have to spend as much time ascertaining accessibility or achieving rudimentary familiarity with this or that situation, they should be able to generate fuller and richer sets of data with the same time and effort.

Likewise, researchers (particularly novices) might be discouraged from seeking out topics simply because these are "exotic" (i.e., those characterized by the "deviant mystique") or when these involve substantive areas in which their analyses may be colored by their values (e.g., taking sides, crusading). A clean, careful, thorough analysis is so demanding in itself that this objective should have precedence over the selection of any particular substantive setting. Further, insofar as any substantive setting involves people working out their interests, dilemmas, and activities with others, every (or any) setting should hold some interest for researchers, regardless of how "banal" it may seem at the outset. Thus, while some people will undertake studies in this or that area because of strong preexisting interests or fascinations in that subject matter, people who are genuinely "interested in people" are apt to find that any ethnographic setting can yield fascinating insights into the world of the other (and the self):

MLD: It seems to me that once you begin to understand the complexities and changing nature of human social life, that you can't escape seeing everything as an interesting research possibility. One of the problems that I have is being interested in everything. It seems boring to me to stay on the same subject all the time, but I know that everybody doesn't feel that way.

Analytical Foci

Although some overlap seems inevitable, ethnographers have three major options in developing conceptual themes for their research: (a) postcontact analysis, (b) interim foci, and (c) focused entries. While beginning with the option that seems the least rigorous of the three, it is instructive to consider the strengths and dilemmas each option poses as well as their more common implications for analysis and conceptual development.

Postcontact Analysis. Postcontact analysis of field studies comes about in two major ways. In one routing, these statements reflect people's previous involvements in the situations being analyzed. People, thusly, build on experiences that predate their research interests. By utilizing diaries, letters, and other reconstructions of their earlier participant-based experiences, researchers may provide valuable insider accounts of the way of life of a group of people. While limited by their abilities to recall situations in full and "open" (descriptive and nonprescriptive vs. clipped and moralistic) manners as well as by their own role experiences (i.e., how much intimate awareness does someone have of various aspects of this social world?) in these settings, it should be noted that postparticipation analyses need not be so confined. To the extent these people have maintained viable relationships with other participants in their settings, they may be able to (re)turn to these associates for assistance (via interviews, further participant-observation) in developing analyses of these settings.

The second routing involves people who enter settings initially as researchers. To this end, they may engage in as extensive inquiries into all facets of the setting as possible, typically making comprehensive notes of their observations and experiences. These researchers may have entered with some preexisting foci and/or may develop certain analytical themes as they spend time in the field, but other possibilities exist. First, researchers may find their contact time in the field too brief (resources, cooperation) to complete their analyses while in the field, thus necessitating some postcontact analyses. Many researchers are fortunate enough to maintain contact with their settings throughout the course of their projects, but other analyses assume a postcontact quality. Secondly, researchers may find themselves using data collected earlier in the field to explore issues that occur to them at later points in time. Sometimes researchers have gathered data addressing these emergent issues; other times these remain as subjects for future inquiry. These points provide testimony to the advantages of selecting substantive settings to which one can return on an ongoing basis as one does the analysis. Sometimes, however, as in the case of anthropologists studying more distant societies, this simply is not feasible. Here, one must limit one's analysis more severely or postpone the consideration of certain issues until one can next venture into the field.

Interim Focus. Signifying the development of analytical themes in the midst of data collection, interim foci denote the essence of much ethnographic research. While these themes emerge in various ways, they typically reflect researchers' attempts to familiarize themselves with situations before drawing out particular matters for further inquiry. Researchers may spend several weeks or months becoming acquainted with settings (making records of all their observations and explorations, developing contacts, etc.) prior to selecting specific features of group life for more intensive study:

BP: Two quick examples come to mind. In the hotel project, Styllianoss Irini and I spent about six months in the field before we started to sketch out the directions we thought the project would take. We had gathered a lot of information to that point, but we weren't able to articulate the directions of the analysis earlier than that. . . . The research on magic came together a great deal quicker, but, even here, before I could begin to develop a more specific sense of an analytical direction, I had to come to one very simple, but one very, very fundamental realization. This was the recognition that "there could be no magic without the other (an audience)." Only after I began to appreciate the intersubjective nature of this phenomenon was I able to start sorting the material I had been gathering into analytical themes of some sort and relate the accomplishment of magic to other work on the influence process.

WS: I, too, can think of several examples illustrating this point. When I first began the hasidic project, the direction of the work wasn't immediately apparent. Indeed, at first I was absolutely overwhelmed by the hasidim's way of life and how it differed so radically from my own. My experiences were, perhaps, best characterized by the term "culture shock," and I spent several months familiarizing myself with these ultra-observant Jews' routine practices and ways of understanding the world. Gradually I narrowed the focus of the research to concentrate on patterns of identity maintenance. The focus for the medical student socialization research also crystallized gradually. It was clear from the outset that neophyte professionals were inundated by an enormous amount of knowledge which they felt compelled to master. In trying to understand the students' professionalizing experiences, we eventually realized the importance of situating them within the larger context of the profession they were seeking to enter. It soon became clear that medical students learned from their future colleagues to objectify patients, to contain their idealism, and to impress others of their competence, and enveloping themselves in a "cloak of competence."

While researchers may have missed earlier opportunities to collect data on some emergent analytical themes, subsequent contact with the field typically enables researchers to collect rich data on which to build an analysis. Hypotheses testers may find this unevenness disconcerting, but it attests to both the openness and the demand for flexibility which characterizes field research. It denotes a basic ethnographic concern with "letting the data talk back," as well as a profound appreciation that the study of group life should not be forced into "nice, neat little boxes":

MLD: It's funny, but when you talk about the analytic focus, I can't help but think of my work with the urban lumberjacks and how hard they had to work to modify the focus I thought was the key. Two things struck me as being really important when I was ready to start interviewing the lumberjacks. The first was the fact that they used deadly chemicals in their work and no one ever paid any attention to how the chemicals affected them. The second was how scary it must be to be up in a ninety or one hundred foot tree in the rain and the sleet with just a tiny rope holding you there. I kept asking them about the chemicals and the fear and they kept responding with disinterest. No matter how I phrased the questions or when I brought them up, they just didn't seem to think these two issues were important. Since I was presenting the work from their viewpoint, I finally had to see that in their worldview these were not major issues.

Focused Entries. Ethnographers planning to examine the existence and essence of particular concepts (e.g., impression management, recruitment, cooperation, deception) may be seen as making focused entries into the field. Those employing this approach may attend to single or multiple processes, but typically approach the field with a sense of openness vis-à-vis those concepts. Thus, while they may have engaged in extensive surveys of the literature prior to entry, an effort is made to "suspend this outside knowledge" in order that the phenomena to be examined may be given greater opportunity to "speak for itself," to be allowed to challenge existing formulations whenever and as much as this seems warranted. Insofar as focused inquiries address "generic" features of interaction, these projects allow researchers to (a) draw upon work on similar processes in other contexts and (b) evaluate and qualify these concepts more generally. Thus, these inquiries are more readily assimilated into a larger body of knowledge about the other. Attention to generic processes can dramatically increase the value of ethnographic research, but it should be emphasized that unless researchers are prepared to be patient, outreaching, and highly receptive to the other in their inquiries, they will miss much of the potential that ethnographic research offers:

BP: Whenever I embark on a new project, I try to find out what it is that people are doing in the situation. In addition to any observations I might make, I typically ask what the other does and how he or she goes about doing these things and how they work things out with others in the setting. I try to pick up on as much detail on things as I possibly can. This emphasis is something that I started doing increasingly as I've been involved in field research. The other thing I try to do is to follow the careers of people's involvements in this or that activity and the ways in which other people's activities and careers intersect with those of the focal other. It's been my experience that by focusing on activities and people's involvements in situations over time, that one inevitably picks up a great deal of information about people's perspectives, identities, and relationships, because all of these things seem to revolve around the things that people do. I'm always amazed, however, at how much we have to learn from people in the field. That is, if you let them explain their world and activities to you in detail. I'm a firm believer that one can learn a great deal from materials in the library, but I've also found that there is so much more that we can learn from the people out there.

WS: While the projects in which I've been involved were quite different from one another, they are all centrally focused on the processes that underlie peoples' interactions and behavior. I think I'm best off understanding how people go about doing what they do rather than becoming obsessed with the why's of their behavior. Moreover, activities and plans are coordinated with others, whether they are physically present or serve to channel how persons think and organize their actions. My underlying concern is with how people make sense of what they do, and how their behavior coincides with a particular perspective or set of perspectives they have acquired. Little is gained by inferring people's perspectives or guessing their explanations for their actions. The best way to understand people, and the events and activities in which they're involved, from their perspectives, is by listening to their stories. People seem to willingly share this information with me, and I allow them to do so at a pace convenient for them.

Making Contact with the Other

Since our subject matter involves people, researchers face the problem of making contact with others. We have four major options: (a) utilizing our own experiences, (b) accessing mutual settings, (c) finding sponsors, and (d) making "cold calls." Researchers in any given setting may find that one or other means of making contact predominates, but as with the three methods of gathering data (observation, participant-observation, interviews), researchers using all of these ways of making contact are apt to be advantaged over those not doing so:

BP: Here again, my experiences have been very varied, but I've received a lot of help from sponsors of different sorts. John Stratton, my Ph.D. supervisor, had good connections with the parole department and that paved the way for my initial contact with those people. . . . I started the study of the clergy by myself and went knocking on doors, but later I was assisted by Ken Jaggs and Harry Burstyn. . . . C. R. D. Sharper was an incredible contact and without him, I simply wouldn't have been able to access the world of the card and dice hustlers. . . . Styllianoss Irini was not as adept at generating contacts as was Sharper, but he was very instrumental in establishing my identity as a viable researcher in the hotel setting. . . . Bob Farmer, likewise, was pivotal in my introduction to the magic community, and that project just wouldn't have happened without his willingness to open this world up to me. . . . Many, many other people have been helpful in other ways, both in these studies and in the studies of the marketplace and consumer behavior, but a great deal more of the work in these other settings involved cold calls either on my part or the other people with whom I worked. So, I really don't have a set strategy for approaching the field. Basically, I realize that I'm going to need all the help I can possibly get, so I tend to be receptive and grateful to whoever might be able to help me in this or that manner.

WS: One of the best lessons that I learned early on was that I'd require others' assistance in order to do the work. In certain instances, I was forced to rely on others whether I wanted to or not. While these others can take the form of official gate-keepers, as they have in several of my studies, whose permission is required to secure initial access, I have generally relied on the good graces of ordinary persons to introduce me to their friends. In the cases of the medical school study, and the Arts and Science Program research, my colleagues and I were re-quired to convince administrative officials that our work was worthy of support. This required presentations concerning our intentions and answering numerous questions about our theo-retical orientation and methodology, which were sometimes irritating and frustrating. For the most part, however, I've simply asked people for help—either to explain something or to intro-duce me to others who could shed light on something I wished to know more about. Most of the hasidic research was carried out in this way. I have also learned that while I can always use help to meet people, that I, myself, can best explain both how and why I can use another's assistance. In fact, one of the very few times that I was refused the opportunity to meet someone was when I relied on a relative to explain my research instead of doing so myself. While my research on the newly observant Jews initially necessitated some explanation to those respon-sible for the respective yeshivas' programs, I soon, thereafter, relied upon the snowball technique for meeting new people. This same kind of reliance characterized the research on the Christie Pits riot, although here ads were placed in newspapers to help locate respondents. My research on the haredi defectors could not have been conducted without the assistance of one individual—an ex-haredi himself—who, when I began the work, was unique in that he kept a list of names of former ultra-Orthodox haredi Jews who left the fold. Without his coopera-tion, for which he was remunerated, I probably would not have been able to meet enough respondents to carry out the work. Generally speaking, I play things by ear and try figuring out who might best help me and when it is best to approach him or her to explain what I do. Little is gained by going at it alone, especially when I've seen so many times that people are pre-pared to help providing they understand that you aren't there to harm.

When one has been or presently is involved in a particular situation, one of the easiest methods of generating descriptive material is to *build on one's own experiences*. Here (as a participant-observer), more extensive accounts of one's own lived experiences are much more valuable than fleeting commentaries. It is also crucial that one be attentive to the desirability of generating materials that describe (rather than moralize) and openly depict (rather than selectively enhance) one's own activities. One strives for accounts that are thorough, careful, and brutally honest. A self-observer who is patient, willing to tolerate a great deal of ambiguity, open to everyone in the setting, and meticulous in maintaining detailed accounts of situations will fare much better overall. This mode of data collection denotes "an ongoing interview with oneself" and the same concerns apply to gathering data on (or from) oneself as from others. As with probing in an interview with another person, the more contextual depth provided in one's own journals, the more valuable is that material:

MLD: Most of us who learned to do research prior to the last decade tended to conceal our involvement in a research situation unless we were writing our field notes or methods specifically. In the past few years, it has become increasingly noticeable that if an event occurred while the researcher was present, that she or he was likely to have said or done something. In doing field research on street violence, I think my actions and responses were as much a part of the data as any of the other participants. For example, when I was "hanging out" at taverns known for frequent fights I wanted to observe what took place without getting hurt. On more than one occasion, when a fight broke out, I jumped over to the bartender's side of the bar where I could watch more safely. At one time, I did not report on this, but now I see this as part of the data that could have been used in "avoiding violent encounters."

BP: Some of your best data may very well come from your own observations and experiences. This isn't always evident in your papers, though, because usually you get so much material that you can't possibly use all of it, or even most of it in the form of quotations or extracts in your final statements. Generally speaking, I prefer to let other people talk about their experiences in the text, but the better your field notes, the easier it is to put a manuscript together because you just have so much more depth and understanding as a consequence. Good field notes can be such a valuable resource all along the way, and in ways that one could never anticipate in advance.

While one may describe a particular encounter in considerable detail, it is very valuable to also discuss any reservations one might have had along the way, as well as other lines of action one had contemplated as the encounter developed, and any adjustments or reflections one might have made after the encounter. It is also helpful to indicate how this encounter may have differed from or been similar to others in which one engaged or relative to those involving other people.

Utilizing one's own experiences does not necessarily mean that the researcher is engaged in a situation or setting at the time of the study, but can refer to previous involvements in the setting. In such instances, care must be taken to appreciate how the passage of time may have affected one's observations and reflections. Relying on one's personal experiences can enable the researcher to better understand the affective dimensions of the situation under investigation and, thereby, to more easily establish rapport with the other. However, it should not be assumed that one's experiences are necessarily representative of those of others in the setting. Thus, one's involvements and experiences should be used cautiously, as a tentative guide for approaching and pursuing the study:

MLD: One of the things that interested me in the ballet world was the position of the ballet parent. Prior to my son's ballet training, I had been involved in a number of sports and school activities. In many ways, though, I felt less competent and knowledgeable in the ballet world. It was necessary to examine my own relationship to that world, compared to the sport and academic worlds, before I could view it clearly.

A second type of situation that nicely lends itself to ethnographic inquiry is that in which *one has "natural contact" with others* whose worlds one would like to study. Thus, for instance, people who have friends, associates, or family members involved in this or that lifestyle may ask them to help with the research. Since these other people already know and presumably feel comfortable with the researcher, they are often willing to provide these researchers with a great deal of inside information as well as other opportunities to learn more about the situation at hand. There are genuine advantages to building on these sorts of network situations. These settings not only may offer considerable benefits in terms of time expediency, but also offer the advantages of substantive familiarity and minimized "stage fright." As well, insofar as these settings often are ones in which people may be employed, or enjoy particular activities and associates, these situations may afford researchers an opportunity to benefit doubly from the research application:

MLD: A lot of times, when people talk about doing participant-observation, they describe it as going into the field. For some people, that is accurate, but many times, it is more developing a sensitivity that some activity or setting that one is already involved in can be seen through a sociological perspective. Many times I have found that I was a participant and by seeing the situation sociologically, I became a participant-observer. My ballet research started that way. I was just there as a parent and I became more aware of the relationships in the ballet world and so I began to attend to them and was transformed into a participant-observer doing research. . . . I think that this is particularly true of women researchers who have child-care or other caregiving responsibilities, that we use the situations of natural contact. Many of the excellent studies on child-care, housework, home parties, children's parties, and other activities have resulted from making use of the opportunities provided by our everyday experiences. Not only has this filled a gap in research information, but it has allowed the researcher to take his or her responsibilities into account and fit the research into an existing life-style. I'm sure, in the next few years, we will develop a series of studies on hockey moms, cheerleading, school plays, and other kinds of everyday experiences that have been part of our everyday lives, but have not yet been studied and reported on. This is not to suggest that women researchers should be limited in their research, but there shouldn't be a premium placed on research done in rare or distant places. Certainly most of my research has had this opportunistic aspect to it. . . . Taking advantage of places where one has natural contacts is really important. This is particularly true if you can see your natural world as a research setting. . . . This is a little different, but the research I did on street violence was facilitated by my being known in the neighborhood. It was easy enough for people to check out not only if I was a cop, but also to find people who had known me for a long period of time. That doesn't mean that I was immune to warnings, but it allowed me to avoid some of the closing out and suspicion that occurs to strangers.

Although many associates are genuinely helpful, researchers may also encounter some associates who trivialize the nature of the work at hand. Sometimes, people who know the researcher very well may not take the researcher's questions seriously or may fail to spell out their answers more fully, assuming that the researcher can fill in the blanks. By failing to respond as seriously as one would hope, some associates may discourage the researcher from pursuing the project more fully.

Sponsors are people who in one way or other facilitate the researcher's contacts with those they would like to access. Sometimes people offer to serve as sponsors for researchers embarking on particular lines of inquiry, but other times researchers may approach particular people as a means of making contact with others. On some occasions, sponsors may be formal gatekeepers of sorts who provide permission and entry into certain research sites. In other cases, they may be friends and other associates who introduce researchers to those with whom they wish to make contact. Some sponsors are very "strong" and may also serve as key informants themselves, while others may provide researchers with an introduction or a name of another contact, possibly without much enthusiasm at all for the project. Indeed, the individual or organization approached for sponsorship must be carefully considered lest its endorsement impact negatively on the researcher's intentions.

While sponsors may help researchers overcome some of the problems of establishing contact and negotiating access to others, this strategy may also lull researchers into a false sense of security. Believing that others will be instrumental in facilitating access and securing cooperation, researchers may devote less attention to this critical dimension of the research than may be necessary. Those to whom we turn for assistance may help pave the way, but we should not substitute their help for the time and energy that are typically required in securing the approval and cooperation with others. Sponsors may facilitate access to others, but they are usually not in a position to guarantee the cooperation of others. Others, especially those unfamiliar with field research, may be unable to represent our interests and intentions as well as we might do ourselves.

Cold calls represent a fourth means of making contact with people. The term cold call is commonplace among salespeople (Prus, 1989b) who present themselves to relative strangers at their homes or places of business. The notion of cold calls is most applicable to some aspects of field research, as are the related concerns of initiating contact, managing stage fright, and obtaining an opportunity to present one's proposals to the other. Because of the outreaching nature of this enterprise and the uncertainty of the reactions of the people being approached, cold calls put the initiator in a more vulnerable or risky situation. However, because cold calls put salespeople or researchers in direct contact with people with whom they wish to make contact, cold calls can be extremely valuable. Thus, even when researchers have good overall contacts in the field, they are apt to find it productive to approach those they don't know as well. While some people may be reluctant to participate in the project once it is explained to them, others may turn out to be excellent sources of information and contacts.

Cold calls require the researcher to have an account for the research that can be delivered rather quickly in seeking the other's attention. The explanation should be worked out in advance and is generally best devoid of scientific jargon lest it sound too threatening or not be understood. Likewise, the initial call or encounter should not place excessive demands on the other but simply introduce one's interests generally, indicate how the other might help, and seek an opportunity to meet again. While approaching people in this manner may be somewhat disconcerting for the researcher, since one never knows how one will be received by the other, cold calls are a most common form by which contacts in the field are established:

BP: I usually approach people in rather straightforward manners: "Hi, my name is whatever and I'm interested in learning more about this or that. If you have a minute, I'll give you a better sense of what I'm up to and then you can decide if you'd like to help me with it." I try to pick times that are not too inconvenient for people and that don't seem as likely to interfere with their other activities. If people have questions, they usually don't hesitate to ask about things that are important to them, and people may put priorities on very different things when they meet you, so it's a matter of relating to them on that level. Most people, I've also found, are willing to give you a few minutes to explain your interests and how it relates to them. Sometimes, people may be evasive or brush you off, but if you seem reasonably affable and interested in what they have to tell you, most people are considerably more receptive. There are many ways of making contact with people, but what I like about cold calls is the fact that you don't have to sit around and wait and hope that someone will do something to help you meet someone. You can really help yourself if you take a little initiative in approaching others. The prospect of approaching strangers can generate a little stage fright and I'm probably as vulnerable to that as the next person, but if you think something is important, worth doing, then you try to concentrate on that and try not to be so concerned about how someone may see you or act toward you.

As will be appreciated, these four options for establishing contact are typically not exercised in their purest forms. As the research unfolds, variations of these options are shaped to suit the particular demands of the study. For instance, as the researcher becomes increasingly familiar with the setting and its participants, the participation of sponsors or the initiation of cold calls may be altered from the ways these were accomplished at earlier stages. As well, personal experiences in the field may be used to shape the manners in which various others may be approached. Ethnographic research does not contain a formula or set of rules to be strictly applied for meeting others. Instead, the process is much like the one characterizing everyday interaction in which people face a variety of uncertainties, dilemmas, and unexpected receptivities in pursuing particular lines of action:

BP: In practice, you have to expect the unexpected, if that makes any sense. You never know for sure just how people will respond when you approach them. Sometimes, people who you think will be genuinely helpful turn out exactly that way and similarly those who you might suspect to be of limited assistance may very well turn out to be of little help. But many other times, things turn out quite differently than you might expect. Someone who has been very open and friendly may become evasive, quiet, or distracted and the interview may end up being much less valuable than appeared at the outset. Whereas at other times, people who appeared more reticent or even hesitant to even listen to you may become very enthusiastic about the project and provide you with some of the best material in the entire study. Similarly, some people who profess to know a lot may quickly run out of information when you start to ask about specifics, while someone else who seemed less confident or more marginal may have a great deal of information to share about some topic. Likewise, while we think that researchers normally approach others with the idea of doing a study of their life-worlds, the suggestion may come from the other. On several occasions, for instance, while doing the hotel project or the study of marketing and sales, different people with whom I have been casually conversing have made comments along these lines, "You know, someone should do a study of this place. It would be very interesting!" To which I reply something to the effect, "Well, I'm glad you mentioned that. Guess what I'm doing!"

Interacting with the Other

Ethnographic research is not only an interpretive, cooperative, and interactive process, but it is also a mutual process! That is, both parties (researchers and community members) may assume roles as tacticians and as targets on a more or less concurrent basis. Not only do the people with whom we are working have capacities for reflectivity, but they can also act back on us as they endeavor to pursue any concerns that seem appropriate to them. We may not be selling people "a bill of goods" (which people sometimes very eagerly pursue on their own!), but we are seeking their cooperation and assistance. As researchers, we take people's time and encourage them to share their experiences with us. Many people find the interview process an interesting, stimulating, and enjoyable experience. Some people have also said that they would have paid for the opportunity to discuss their situations with an open-minded, patient, and interested person such as the researcher. Almost inevitably, though, ethnographers are apt to encounter some people who do not seem to appreciate the interview experience. They may have been skeptical or distracted in some way, but, generally speaking, they were people with whom one was not able to establish more meaningful dialogue. Fortunately, researchers generally are not wholly or exclusively dependent on a single individual in conducting ethnographic research and as a result are able to carry on with the research largely intact despite these sorts of setbacks.

In a study of salespeople, Prus (1989a) examines a set of processes that seem basic to considerations of the ways in which people pursue cooperation with others. Since field researchers are dependent on the cooperation of those they encounter, these will be considered here. While the immediate discussion is highly abbreviated, it may help draw the reader's attention to the various components of persuasion on which ethnographers are dependent in gathering data: formulating (preliminary) plans, role-taking (inferring/uncovering the perspectives of the other), promoting interest in one's objectives, generating trust, proposing specific lines of action, encountering resistance, neutralizing obstacles, seeking and making concessions, confirming agreements, and assessing "failures" and recasting plans.

While ethnographic research projects are quite open-ended at the outset, ethnographers still face the task of *formulating some preliminary plans* about the direction of their studies, the people to be approached, the roles that researchers assume, and the like. The ethnographer who insists on approaching the research as a tabula rasa fails to consider how theoretical inclinations and personal concerns may shape and influence the direction of the research. It is best to acknowledge such interests at the outset as this may facilitate the general directions in which the research plans are organized.

The concept of *role-taking* (or the task of achieving empathetic understanding with the other) is very much a part of everyday life as well as being the staple of the ethnographic inquiry. Researchers take the role of the other in attempting to uncover and comprehend the viewpoints, perspectives, or life-worlds of the other and to achieve intimate familiarity with their subject matter. Successful role-taking cannot be achieved without openness, receptivity, and curiosity. It requires the researcher to exercise patience and the other social skills underlying competent social interaction. Role-taking may be achieved rapidly or take considerable time, but without it the researcher cannot hope to experience, comprehend, or convey the life-world known to the other.

The notion of *promoting interest* in one's work may be among the subprocesses least explicitly pursued by field workers. Experienced researchers know that some interest on the part of those whose assistance is being sought is essential if one hopes to gain access to, and cooperation from, prospective respondents. Researchers are usually best able to generate such interest when they, themselves, are intrigued by their work. This sort of enthusiasm typically becomes contagious. It is mutually reinforcing and helps generate a commitment to pursuing the research. As well, most people tend to be interested in anything that pertains to them more personally:

WS: I don't think there's any specific approach that I've used to promote my work, but in studies of groups, as opposed to individuals who don't necessarily know one another, it is clear that actions speak loudest. The single best way to get others interested in my work is to show them that I take it seriously and this, I'm convinced, is best accomplished by being visible. While people may not recognize that you are present, or publicly acknowledge it, they will inquire as to your absence, especially if it seems prolonged. Medical students sometimes asked where we were. After all, if we were serious about our study, as we claimed, then why weren't we around on a regular basis? The key is to convince people that you are serious and are prepared to make sacrifices if necessary. I have sometimes remained at hasidic weddings until the very end—3:30 A.M.—to demonstrate that I wasn't satisfied with a fleeting glimpse of their world but wished to understand it as thoroughly as they'd allow. As well, however, I deliberately make it a point of informing people that I consider the research fascinating despite the fact that their activities, to them, are probably routine and uneventful. I actually view this as a way of instructing people about my research and helping them understand how they can help. And most of the time I really am fascinated, but some projects are clearly more enjoyable than others. I seem to find it easy to become interested in my work, and make it a point of informing people that I find what they do to be interesting.

MLD: I find that people are generally receptive to interest in themselves and their activities, including criminals, once they are sure that you are trustworthy according to their norms. The important thing in studying everyday life is for the researcher to be able to see everyday life from a research perspective. If the researcher does in fact look at others in the situation as collaborators, they usually don't face too much difficulty in making concessions. Other people are going to present their experiences in self-serving ways, whether they are criminals or not. But, in many cases, they are going to tell things that they do not want people to know about themselves or they are going to talk about others but want to be assured that the information is not attributed to them. This really isn't very different from everyday interaction in a family, department, or other work setting.

Although *trust* is often taken for granted in many qualitative projects, researchers fare much better when they are able to establish personal integrity among respondents. This generates confidence in their projects, and minimizes obligations respondents might associate with participation in these studies. Generating trust is an ongoing process; it is not completed at a particular point in time. Individuals may interpret and respond to the research differently as it unfolds and the researcher should attend to the ebbs and flows this generates among those whose trust otherwise may mistakenly be taken for granted.

BP: I think that every seasoned ethnographer realizes, at least implicitly, that trust is problematic and precarious. This is part of the reason that it is so important to try to maintain people's confidences within the setting relative to other participants. I was going to mention another thing, though, that I sometimes do now. I'll often carry a published ethnography or two with me and show it to people as I'm talking with them about participating in the study. This way, they can see how I deal with information of the sort they may provide to me. People generally find this interesting and appreciate seeing that they will maintain a sense of anonymity in the published work. If I was new to the field, I might take an ethnography that someone else did as a sample or model. I don't always use this, and I don't stick it out front, but something of this sort can help establish a sense of trust, especially with people who initially may be a little more reticent or skeptical about the project.

In asking for an interview, or an opportunity to observe or "hang around," researchers are proposing *specific lines of action.* And, they may *encounter resistances* pertaining to time, interest, skepticism, and the like. Resistance may take the form of outright refusal to tolerate the researcher's presence in the setting to more subtle reluctances to cooperate. Whether or not researchers obtain opportunities to gather data in particular contexts, or with certain people, may very well depend on their abilities to *neutralize the obstacles* that they encounter during the course of these preliminary exchanges. Researchers should be constantly alert to such obstacles and consider the most effective means for dealing with them. Once again, there are no established canons for organizing such efforts, and different techniques and approaches may be required for specific individuals and situations.

In part, researchers may find themselves *seeking and making concessions* with these others, as they attempt to *confirm agreements* or develop mutual understandings regarding the nature of the commitments they might achieve from prospective participants. Of course, the researcher will want to determine the range of concessions that may be offered without jeopardizing the integrity of the research. When others demand substantial concessions on the part of the researcher, the researcher must ensure that these will not unduly restrict or hamper one's abilities to pursue certain lines of inquiry.

When successful in their practices to date, researchers are apt to continue along much the same routes in dealing with those they encounter. However, when researchers experience setbacks in the field, they are apt to engage in some *recasting of plans* as they pursue their objectives. The nature of the recasting may range from elaborate to more minor adjustments, but ethnographic research, as a rule, compels the investigator to constantly monitor the research process and determine whether the objectives, and the planned strategies for obtaining them, require modification or even drastic change.

Because it involves attaining and maintaining the cooperation of other people, the research role is very much an exercise in dealing with the other. Although researchers differ from "moral entrepreneurs" (Becker, 1963) or salespeople (Prus, 1989a) in that they do not try to shape the life-styles or financial situations of those they contact, some enterprise or promotional activity seems inevitable as researchers endeavor to obtain the cooperation of others in assembling materials pertinent to their studies. As has been observed repeatedly, while successful ethnography requires the execution of research skills, the management of interpersonal skills is equally critical. In fact, experienced ethnographers know all too well that their abilities to secure trust and cooperation are less a reflection of the scientific merits of the research than their abilities to interact with the other in ways that the other considers acceptable and worthwhile. In brief, since others respond to researchers beyond their research roles, researchers must learn to manage themselves as persons in the ethnographic context.

Managing Oneself in the Ethnographic Context

In contrast to those who work with questionnaire or experimental data, people doing ethnographic research very much put themselves on the "front lines." Not only do they deal with people and all the uncertainty that human interaction entails, but they also are highly dependent on these others for their cooperation and overall well-being. This very fact bears directly on how ethnographic research evolves. Stated briefly, since ethnographers are always dependent on the other, they are much less able to control the pace of the research than would be the case were the primary data sources located in the library or contained on completed questionnaires. As well, since ethnographic research requires the display of human interactional skills, the degree of cooperation from others is generally tied directly to the researcher's comportment in the setting.[15]

Encounters with strangers or others upon whom one is dependent, may engender some "stage fright" on the part of fieldworkers.[16] One does not know how receptive others will be when approached for their assistance on various matters, or how extensively they will pursue these matters with the researchers over extended periods of time. While many of these reservations later prove to have been unfounded, ethnographers simply do not know that their interests will be received in the manner in which they had intended. Unable to anticipate accurately how others will respond to the ethnographer's interests can intensify the anxiety that typically accompanies the initiation of the research. Feelings of uncertainty and apprehensiveness do not characterize only novice ethnographers but typically appear as the emotional companions of even the most experienced ethnographers as they embark on new projects or encounter new people.

Depending on others for cooperation and information, ethnographers find that concerted role-taking (or empathizing) effort is essential in obtaining in-depth materials, as are patience and perseverance. Much more important than the specific questions researchers ask is the development of trust, especially as this pertains to the participants feeling comfortable with the researcher. Indeed, it is essential that participants be given opportunities to elaborate on their positions in full and open manners. Herein lies much of the art, not to mention strain, inherent in this research approach. One must learn to role-take effectively, and how the skill is exercised is not identical with each participant. Unlike precise mathematical formulae, which are applied uniformly where particular values are sought, effective role-taking requires that one attend to the dynamics of the situation:

MLD: You can carry this kind of person the researcher is supposed to be too far. Each of us has to work within our own strengths and weaknesses. We can work to become better listeners or to have more empathy, but it comes down to each researcher developing a style of eliciting information that is comfortable for her.

BP: The problem, in part, is that of trying to connect, in an open, trusting manner, with each person with whom you make contact. Can you develop that relationship, bond, or openness with the other, where that person feels comfortable with you?

That they feel comfortable with me is much more important than whether or not I feel comfortable with them. If the other person is not willing to open up and share their experiences with you, then your interview is not going to be very valuable. This is where the interviewer subjects oneself to the other, and strives to comprehend the viewpoints and experiences of the other as fully as possible. If the researcher insists on maintaining a strong presence or persona in the situation, the interview is not apt to be as valuable. You learn more about the situation of the other when you let the other dominate the encounter. You can still ask questions and make probes of various sorts, but the other person is the star as far as I'm concerned. A deferential style combined with a persistent curiosity and a genuine interest in the life-situation of the other is so important. However, since everyone is different, one continually faces the task of adjusting both to each new person one encounters and to each person as the encounter unfolds. If you wish to role-take more effectively, or to achieve empathy with a cross-section of people, you have to be a mental chameleon of sorts, but I think that that is a skill that can be developed.

To be a good listener is vital, as is open-ended and nonjudgmental inquiry. Thus, the researchers most likely to obtain extensive interview materials are those who both are more "chameleon-like" in their demeanor and more intensively pursue elaboration and clarification. The interview is an ongoing exercise in fitting in. It requires an ongoing set of adjustments to the other. It entails sustaining participants' interests in the discussions at hand. It necessitates sympathetic understanding of sorts, but also requires that the researcher invoke some distance (i.e., that one not be too understanding or helpful) so that the other is encouraged to detail the events being discussed. In this respect, a very "helpful" interviewer can effectively destroy an interview by taking things for granted or assisting the respondents in formulating or summarizing their positions on things:

MLD: These taken-for-granteds can also pose dilemmas for researchers when they attempt to convey knowledge of the setting to readers. Researchers have to be careful of what they take for granted and what they make explicit to the reader. Good researchers seem able to attend to the taken-for-granteds and make them explicit and interesting to the reader.

BP: As a researcher, and this may sound a little odd to some people, you don't want to be very helpful or understanding in certain respects. Even worse, of course, is to pretend that you know or understand the things that people are talking about when you don't. You may have to do these things in order to fit in on occasion, but what you really want in the course of doing an interview is to have people explain things to you as fully and as completely, in their own words, as they possibly can. So, it's always, "Can you tell me more?" "Can you give me an instance or example of that?" "How did that work out?" "You say that you had a good time, or that so and so is very helpful, or that you really enjoy doing this, can you tell me a little more what you mean by that?" You need that depth! Then you turn it over, as much as you can, "Are there times when you didn't have a good time, or when so and so is not very helpful, or times you don't enjoy doing this?" or "What about this other situation, this other person, or this other activity?" Hopefully, you will be able to encourage people to explain things to you in great detail very early in the interview. Then, if you can sustain that mode of communication throughout, you may end up with some very good material. Basically, when you're talking with someone in this situation, you want to know every thought, every hesitation, every inclination that that person has at the time. You want to know the world as they know it and as they engage it, and this is where the taken-for-granteds, assumed meanings, or attempts to be helpful as an articulator can definitely get in the way. If you look at your transcripts and see that you are talking as much or more than the other person, or notice that you are helping them articulate their ideas or finishing off their thoughts, you're probably not obtaining very much viable material. Further, although it might seem as though you are dwelling on the obvious and the participants might become offended or bored by that, my experience suggests that the people with whom we speak generally appreciate the opportunity to explain their situations in detail. This seems most likely when someone else appears sincerely interested in their life-worlds. The biggest obstacle, in that regard, may be the researcher's own reluctance to probe "the obvious." . . . As a postscript, I might add that if you look over your transcripts and see that you are getting a lot of "because's" from the people you are interviewing, this likely means that you are asking people "why they do things" or to justify their practices. It's really very important to avoid doing that. Asking "why" may seem like a more direct or incisive form of inquiry, but people sometimes feel that they are "on trial" when you do that or they may feel obliged to give you "good reasons" for doing something. They may also feel that that they are being rushed or channeled through the interview. When these sorts of things happen, people's explanations are more apt to be more limited or clipped, so you can lose a lot of valuable information. This type of questioning may represent another taken-for-granted on the researcher's part. That's something else you want to watch out for, that you don't presume too much when asking people questions or rush people through interviews. It's really important to be patient with people and to give them every opportunity to be open with you. This, I think, is a failing with a great deal of journalism or so called investigative reporting. There, people typically just want a story or what they term "the facts" and then rush off to meet some deadline or be the first to come out with something "hot." As ethnographers, we have to take the time to develop a much fuller understanding of people's situations and experiences, and this requires a rather different intellectual stance and another set of ways of relating to people. And that's part of what makes ethnography so uniquely valuable.

Quite clearly, the development of trust and rapport requires the execution of a delicate balancing act in which researchers must neutralize perceptions of aloofness on the part of the other while simultaneously ensuring that the researcher's sense of empathy does not unnecessarily cloud their abilities to rigorously pursue all facets of the study. Rather than becoming a convert to the way of life being studied, it may be more accurate to envision an effective researcher as one who takes on the situated role of an apprentice in the world of the other. In somewhat parallel terms, researchers often find that insiders who adopt roles of teachers, guides, or research partners of sorts are particularly effective in communicating their experiences with the researcher. Under these conditions, the achievement of intersubjectivity on the part of the researcher tends to be greatly enhanced.

In addition to encouraging a sense of enthusiasm on the part of respondents, researchers are also faced with the task of maintaining their own motivation. Indeed, the process of involvement in and commitment to the research is somewhat dialectic and mutual.

Generally speaking, the greater the amount of time researchers spend in the setting, the more comfortable and at ease the researchers feel in those arenas. When researchers become more familiar with the situation and take greater interest in learning about the situation of the other, the insiders seem more willing to take the time and effort to share more of their life-worlds with researchers.

Ethnographic research is demanding! Fieldwork is often interesting, and may be quite fascinating at times, but it can be very gruelling in many respects. In addition to overcoming any stage fright one might experience along the way, as well as managing any difficult or disquieting situations that may emerge, one has to deal with a great deal of ambiguity and a willingness to put one's fate in the hands of others. Not only do researchers not know how projects will work out in the end, but so too are they uncertain of how much work will be entailed or when their projects might be considered "completed." This sense of "open-endedness" is further complicated by a realization that beyond the efforts that one might be willing to devote to a project, one is ultimately dependent on the schedules and willingness of others to participate in this endeavor:

BP: I think that every serious ethnographic project is a gruelling experience, in part because it is so labor intensive. In many respects, your work can be likened to that of a traveling salesperson because you're more or less continually trying to locate, make contact with, and develop relationships with others out there, but there is so much more involved than that. You have to consider the actual time in the field, doing interviews or dealing with the situation at hand. Then there's the note-taking afterwards and transcribing the tapes and sorting out all this information and trying to see where you and the project are headed. Each project is different, but basically you do these sorts of things. Plus, you have the analysis where you try to put all of these things together and, if you're lucky, you can go back to the field to check things out with the people you've been working with and perhaps do some more interviews and spend more time in the setting, and transcribe some more tapes, make some more notes, try to sort things out further, and so forth, because you realize that there's always more to be learned. So it's challenging, for sure, and frustrating in those respects as well, because you're trying to do all of these things at once. As well, you have to work things around other people's schedules, interests, and disruptions. The hotel project was really tough that way, because many of the people we were dealing with had rather erratic life-styles (drinking, drug use, work habits, residences) in one or other ways. The study of marketing and sales was also a problem in that respect, but for somewhat different reasons. In dealing with salespeople, for instance, you might find yourself adjusting your schedule to their situations while they might be attempting to do the same with their customers. In retrospect, the cooperation that we received from the people in both studies was really quite remarkable, but the point is that even when others are very willing to help you with your research, you have to expect to make accommodations and be prepared to find other things to do in those time frames. Patience and perseverance are genuine virtues in field research, but you also have to be fairly well organized so that you can do other things if something falls through. Otherwise, you can have a lot of unproductive down time.

WS: While the projects I've done have been interesting and rewarding, they have also been draining, some more so than others. The real problem has less to do with anxieties of being rejected, or the challenges of locating respondents and establishing relations with them, than feelings of guilt that I really ought to be doing more than I am—more informal interviews, more analysis of the data, more note-writing, and so on. The point is that there is always more that could be done to reach a more complete understanding of the phenomenon under investigation. I can still recall the gruelling pace I set for myself when I first began the hasidic research. For a time, I served as a secretary in a hasidic yeshiva from 9:00 in the morning till 4:30 P.M., and would then visit another hasidic sect to collect more, and different, data. I wouldn't get home until 9:00 or 10:00 at night and would then feel obligated to record the day's field notes. This alone could take a few hours if done properly. Since I was single at the time, adjusting my schedule to fit the hasidim's was quite easy, even if at times inconvenient. Perhaps because this was my first project, I devoted myself to it completely, and temporarily sacrificed, on occasion, my non–research-related interests and relationships. The problem, in large measure, was that I wasn't in a position to exercise any control over the pace of the work, or so I honestly believed. Gaining some control over the pace is one of the essential differences between ethnographic and other types of research.

Ethnographic research, I've found, requires a measure of flexibility because we must accommodate the schedules of those we're observing. It just isn't all that easy to plan when people will have time to chat or when certain events will unfold for which we really ought to be around. As well, interacting with people can also be quite strenuous: Do they understand what I'm doing? Will they cooperate, are they suspicious? Am I doing everything I can to generate friendly relations, am I sufficiently sensitive to their expectations? These are the kinds of questions that can pop into my head at any given time, even when I'm involved in an activity that has nothing to do with my research. The point is that what works in one project doesn't necessarily apply in another. The demands of studying hasidic Jews were quite different from those pertaining to medical students; in fact, in this regard, each project is different from the preceding ones. The hasidic and the medical school studies were by far the most time-consuming. My work on the religious recruits in Jerusalem could have gone this route as well, but I simply didn't allow it. The fact is that I've also changed over the years and approach the research with different priorities and expectations.

The ethnographic process is also complicated by an awareness that in some respects one is almost always "on" while in the field. This requires that the researcher always be aware of what is new, and what continues as routine, in the setting and for its participants. As well, an interest and enthusiasm for the work must be exuded, however tired or distracted the researcher might feel. The other people in the setting tend to react to the researcher in manners paralleling those of the researcher attending to them. Thus, although researchers may find themselves relaxing in this or that setting, it may be at some cost to the overall project.

As well comes the realization that the typically massive amounts of material emerging from ethnographic inquiry tends to complicate rather than simplify the researcher's understandings. And, unlike questionnaire or experimental data, which can be readily slotted into variable analysis, the expansive type of data that ethnographic research entails does not lend itself to highly distilled sets of findings for analyses and eventual publication. This is mentioned not to discourage people from doing ethnographic research, but rather to assure them that these sorts of experiences are quite typical. Perhaps among the most important benefits served by the numerous accounts of field research is not that they provide a set of prescriptive rules for conducting ethnographic research, but that they enable researchers to recognize that problems and challenges that seem unique have likely been experienced and addressed by others and are, therefore, more routine and resolvable than might be supposed.

Recording Information in Ethnographic Contexts

So far, we have discussed a number of tactical practices and interactional styles that one might implement in doing ethnographic research, as well as several obstacles ethnographers are apt to face in the course of pursuing their studies. As should be apparent, an ongoing interest in learning about the other is fundamental to gathering information in ethnographic contexts. The objective is to be as thorough, careful, and curiously attentive to the life-worlds of the other as possible. The subsequent question becomes one of "How do I record all this material?" Here again, there is no simple formula. In realistic terms, first of all, one can't record everything that one might encounter. Even the extensive use of audiovisual recorders would not solve that problem. Records of more sights and sounds may be very useful in certain respects, but this "data" is not in itself inherently meaningful. Information about the other must always be contextualized, and that is something that can only be accomplished as one establishes intersubjectivity with the other:

MLD: There is another thing about tape recording we should note, or two things, actually. One is that when you record on tape, you can concentrate on the person talking and not on writing things down. The other is the opposite. Sometimes, when you are not writing things down, when you trust the tape recorder to record, you may not pay as close attention to what the person is saying, per se, as you should. The result, and this may happen when you're more tired, especially, is that you relax too much and the interview isn't as good because of that.

To pursue intersubjectivity with the other is to seek intimate familiarity with the life-worlds of the other as known to the other. While ethnographers generally try to develop records (written notes, tape recordings) that are as comprehensive as they can without disrupting the integrity of the situation at hand, these materials cannot and should not be substituted for concerns with permeating the life-worlds or lived experiences of the other. One has to interrelate with the other, to delve sufficiently deeply into the experiences of the other that one obtains as good a sense as one can of the other's thoughts and concerns, as well as any second thoughts and hesitations the other might have regarding this and that matter. It means, too, that one would pursue both the consistencies as well as the contradictions the other experiences, as well as the varying qualifications the other imposes on the situations at hand.

Sometimes, it will be convenient to tape or video record encounters with the other. While many people are somewhat "equipment shy," this is often overcome when researchers use less equipment (e.g., tape recorders vs. video recorders) and provide the other with justifications that seem feasible. For example, if it's convenient to tape record, one might ask, "Is it okay if we tape the interview," perhaps adding something to the effect of "I wouldn't want to miss anything," or "It would be really helpful if I could capture the way you express your ideas," or "If I don't have to worry about taking notes, I can enjoy the conversation a whole lot more," or "This little unit has a lot better memory than I do." Researchers may add something like, "But if you find yourself feeling uncomfortable, we can switch it off":

WS: I haven't developed any hard and fast rules with respect to recording conversations and interviews. For the most part, it just isn't a big deal because I've learned to recall much of conversations, even lengthy ones. I prefer recording interviews if only because it makes the encounter less draining, and I can concentrate on the conversation instead of continually reminding myself of what I shouldn't forget, such as a choice turn of phrase or a new twist to understanding certain situations or events. I just downplay the importance of the cassette recorder and don't fuss over it during the conversation. It's there but ignored. Unlike others I've spoken to, I haven't found that the presence of the recorder impedes the conversation flow or its contents. I certainly don't see the need to record everyone, and I don't walk around with a recorder on my person in case I meet someone interesting. In general, I've usually been surprised at the relatively few people who have refused permission to be recorded. It's important, I find, to set people at ease and I can do this by starting off by talking about things that people know something about and showing that I'm interested in what they have to offer.

If it doesn't seem feasible to tape, one might ask, "Do you mind if I take a few notes? It'll help me recall our conversation a lot better and I'd like to remember more of what you're telling me." If neither tape-recording or note-taking seems appropriate at the time, one faces the task of trying to recall as much about the situation or conversation as possible at another point in time. Here, again, ethnographers try to be as thorough and careful as they can be when reconstructing (notes, written or self-taped) accounts of earlier situations and exchanges. Likewise, they generally try to reconstruct these materials as soon as they can afterwards and review these with an eye to detail and accuracy of what they have recorded. Although one may lose some precision as one moves in these directions, this material can be extremely valuable and often takes on significances that researchers could not possibly have anticipated at the time. Similarly, while ethnographers tend to place more emphasis on fuller accounts of situations, even fragments of observations, insights, and questions are worth noting as one goes about doing the research. The metaphor of the sponge, picking up everything in the area, is not inappropriate for the seasoned ethnographer.

As well, regardless of whether one is working with tapes or records of other sorts, it is also most instructive to *keep reviewing one's materials* along the way. Not only does this alert the researcher to new areas and missing items, but it will also allow the researcher to better contextualize (and recontextualize) one's existing stock (and fragments) of knowledge within the setting. Indeed, this review process is much more vital that might first seem and enables the researcher to pursue more, different, and better information than what one has gathered to date. In these respects, the recording of ethnographic materials should not be seen as a clearly defined point on route to one's analysis, but as part of the ongoing process of accessing and interpreting the life-worlds of the other.

Sampling Concerns

One of the more common questions that one encounters from novices contemplating ethnographic research runs along the lines of "How many people should I talk to?" Another common variant is "How long should I spend in the field?" Unfortunately, there are no good, simple answers to any questions of these sorts. First, so much depends on how intensively researchers approach the situation, how adept they are at fitting in with those they encounter, and the extent to which they are accepted by the people in the setting. Not only are these intensities and interpersonal skills not uniformly distributed across the population of scholars, but even when researchers are more willing to apply themselves to the situation at hand and possess generally good sets of interpersonal skills, they may still encounter obstacles as they attempt to relate to, be accepted by, and gain cooperation from a particular set of others in the field. So much, too, depends on the others one encounters—their stocks of knowledge and their willingness to share this information with the researcher. Some people are remarkably knowledgable, insightful, and able to communicate their insights with others. Some other people may be very proficient at this or that role but may not be willing or able to communicate their experiences as openly or precisely to researchers. Another consideration revolves around the capacities of the researchers to carefully and thoroughly investigate, track, document, and sort out the materials they encounter in the field. These and other matters, including the depth and breadth one wishes to achieve in a particular study, can greatly affect notions of "adequate samples and time frames."

It is also the case, when discussing ethnographic research, that "one interview" does not equal "one interview." Even under the most ideal conditions, researchers are apt to find considerable variation exists from interview to interview and that some interviews are immeasurably more valuable than others. One would like to obtain as many of these highly productive interviews as possible, but one cannot tell in advance just which participants will be most helpful or in what capacities they will be more or less instructive in revealing aspects of their worlds to the interviewer either on an overall basis or with respect to this or that particular aspect of the study. Thus, while one might suggest that a student might do five or ten interviews for a course assignment, for instance, there is no way of judging in advance the adequacy of this material even for a course project. Given a chance to talk openly and at great length, one person might make the entire study worthwhile, or a researcher might come up relatively impoverished after interviewing a hundred people (including this same individual; not realizing the potential that people generally represent):

MLD: I don't think that I can emphasize enough the importance of a researcher's abilities to probe, pursue, record, and synthesize. Maybe the person you are talking with is not the most informed person in the setting, but a good interviewer, by probing and pursuing topics more fully, being more thorough, can get a lot of information from that interview, where someone else wouldn't have come up with much even with the most informed person in the group.

BP: I am often amazed at what people can tell you about their
        situations and experiences when given an opportunity to do
        so. In this regard, I'd encourage researchers to try to talk to as
        many people in a particular setting as possible, including those
        who seem more marginal or peripheral to the situation as a
        consequence of their work roles, newness, disrepute in the
        setting, etc. Anyone who focuses more exclusively on particular
        people because they appear more central, more educated, more
        experienced, and the like, may miss a great deal of insight and
        information that might be obtained from others in the setting.
        I'm not saying that some people won't be more informative
        overall, but I think we should be as resourceful and thorough
        as possible and talk with everyone we can.

    In like terms, not all of one's time in the field is equally productive.
In addition to the uneven experiences researchers may have in
attempting to familiarize themselves with the basic features of the
setting, there is also the problem of coming to terms with the events
taking place in the setting. Sometimes, researchers encounter more
action in certain time frames than at others, so that the hours spent
in a setting can be richer or less productive in that sense alone. Or
one may witness an event that becomes a central matter of concern
for those in the field and to have missed this episode may put even
very conscientious ethnographers at a disadvantage in dealing with
those in the setting. Sometimes, too, so much is going on that one
cannot possibly attend to everything, while at other times one can
deal with particular events in great detail because they unfold much
more slowly. As well, while busy (group) times may appear interesting
on the surface, researchers may find that quieter times present much
greater opportunities to engage others in extended conversations about
matters pertaining to the study. These sorts of things simply cannot
be foretold in advance.
    In general terms, ethnographers readily sacrifice numbers for
quality. Thus, to use the metaphor of the natural biologist, one would
rather study a small band of geese in great detail over an extended
period of time than watch thousands winging their way overhead. At
the same time, to follow the metaphor along, it would be more valuable
to study the same (as if they were unchanging) band of geese over the
course of a year or two as opposed to one summer's outing. Likewise,
much more could be learned by studying additional bands of geese
or ducks or other comparable species in the same sorts of extended
detail for purposes of analytical comprehension.

There is no magic number of interviews or hours in the field that somehow can be defined as sufficient. Some very powerful ethnographies have relied on "samples" (and that term is appropriate in only the vaguest sense when considering participant-observation research) as small as one, while others have involved well over a hundred intensive interviews. While ethnographers would not sacrifice numbers for quality, they are in agreement that anytime researchers are able to supplement their existing, in-depth materials with more interviews and more time in the field, they are considerably advantaged as a consequence of this additional awareness of the other.

As we sometimes observe to our students, though, practical limitations often become established by the necessity of completing field research within these or those time parameters. Then, it becomes a matter of establishing closure within these time-frames and sorting out the material that one has to the best of one's ability. Ethnographers experiencing these sets of time restrictions are often painfully aware of many of the shortcomings of their data and attempt to qualify their statements accordingly. However, the adequacy of the ethnography depends not on the time-frame (either time expended or time limits), but rather on the depth and breadth with which researchers are able to achieve (and convey) intersubjectivity with the other. At a minimum, novices should appreciate that ethnographic research can be as time consuming and demanding as anything else they might consider doing:

WS: My experiences in leaving the field have varied with the various projects. The hasidic research that I began in the late 1960s continues, albeit in a different form and at a different pace. I've continued writing about facets of their way of life, but feel free to focus on different sects as I please. So while my involvement in the field has changed, I haven't left it at all. The very opposite is the case with the medical school study. When the class we were observing graduated, the research essentially came to an end. The difference is partially reflected in the nature of the research bargain with regard to these projects: we had agreed on a set period for studying the medical students, whereas no such formal bargain characterized the hasidic research. In most of the projects, the opportunity to return for additional data is available and in this sense I regard the projects as on-going more or less. Much seems to depend on my interest in the work and whether I can think of new things about the setting and its people that are worth studying. Of course, this isn't always the case. For example, Cyril Levitt and I said everything we could say about the Christie Pits riot, and following the publication of the book there was no reason to search for more data. There have been a few cases where the changing times have added new dimensions to the problems I investigated at an earlier period and I returned to the field to see what was different. In this sense, then, I don't always leave for good but seem to drift in and out. Where possible I keep in touch both because of relationships I've formed as well as the opportunity to continue the work at some future date.

Some field researchers suggest that one might define a project as complete when one stops encountering significant new materials. While this may sound quite reasonable, as practical advice, this is problematic as well. There may well come a point at which researchers feel that they have more than enough data with which to generate a viable analysis, but this suggested guideline may also foster a certain "nearsightedness" on the part of researchers or constrain inquiry to a more immediate and superficial or commonplace awareness. Often, this rule of thumb fails to take into account the richness, diversity, and emergent nature of the life of the other. As well, it overlooks the capacities of researchers to increasingly understand and become aware of more features of the world of the other. It may be an appealing justification for these researchers who have become impatient with themselves or the time field research consumes and want to find ways of moving their project to the next stage.

Perhaps a more viable approach is to keep accumulating materials until one is convinced that one has much more than enough material to complete a written analysis of the life-world of the other with respect to this or that topic. Then begin the analysis, being attentive to weaknesses and shortcomings that become evident as one works on the analysis, and *plan to go back* to the field to learn more about these gaps as well as variants in the more established areas of the analysis.

As well, even in the most extended involvements in the field comes the realization that one can never totally comprehend the world of the other, and that some ambiguity and incompleteness is inevitable, no matter how conscientious or thorough one may be. In these respects, the best one may be able to do at some point is to indicate the questions or issues that the researcher was unable to examine adequately or didn't realize were important until much later in the project.

Analyzing Human Lived Experiences

When discussing ethnographic research it is essential to appreciate that the analysis doesn't begin as a distinct stage in the project after the data are collected, but more typically extends throughout the entire research process. Ethnographic analysis is grounded in the human lived experience of the other. Thus, by pursuing intimate familiarity with the other and recording this material in more complete and detailed manners, ethnographers lay the foundations for their analysis. This is why it is so very important to gather as much intimate detail as possible about the life-worlds of the other.

The materials following have a summary quality to them, since they very much build on the preceding discussions of the objectives and assumptions of ethnographic research as well as the problematics of accessing the life-worlds of the other. It is hoped that readers may also find helpful the following discussions of (a) coding ethnographic materials and (b) conceptualizing ethnographic research.

Coding Ethnographic Materials

It may seem odd to leave a discussion of coding toward the end of this statement on ethnographic research. There are two rationales for doing so. First, before one "codes" something, one has to think (i.e., coding or classifying is a cognitive demarcation of "reality"; it presumes an interpretation and definition of a field of "objects"), and it is helpful if one is more aware of the situation at hand before one attempts to code, objectify, or "conceptually freeze" the objects that one encounters. Indeed, if more thought had gone into coding efforts beforehand, we likely would have had a great deal less useless research (the products of one's analysis can be no better than the codes one uses to structure the objects one encounters).

In contrast to quantitative research, in which one generally sets up codes or scales (indicators of this or that factor) in advance of contact with the other, ethnographic research is characterized by a much greater sensitivity to "what is going on in the setting." This concern is reflected in the entire ethnographic enterprise, but it is also evident in the ways in which one codes or formats information gleaned about the life-worlds of the other.

The second reason for leaving a discussion of coding to this point is that in developing codes one is effectively organizing the presentation of the ethnographic statement. One's codes or concepts serve as mediums for connecting the intersubjectivities of the three parties to the ethnographic enterprise: the insider, the researcher/writer, and the outsider who examines the ensuing ethnographic statement. It is for this reason that one's coding of the material is so important and, for this reason as well, it is essential that the codes that ethnographers use be subject to ongoing revision or adjustment so that one might more fully and accurately develop concepts that better approximate the situations of the other.

In general, ethnographers tend to work from vague to more specific understandings of the other, and even more basic understandings are seen as subject to revision as one learns more about the other through the pursuit of intimate familiarity with the life-worlds of the other. This means, too, that one must find some way of conveying the general parameters of the world of the other (insider) to the outsider in order to set the stage for more focused statements of the central features of the life-worlds of the other. Typically, too, since one cannot talk about everything in the world of the other, one should also alert readers to the themes central to this particular portrayal of the other. The matter of coding (and organizing) ethnographic materials is developed further in chapter 8, but it may be useful to comment explicitly on two other topics that also bear directly on the task of conducting field research.

Toward an Interactionist Analysis

While ethnographers working on their own or in less well defined theoretical perspectives may develop some important insights into the world of the other, it is much more difficult for these scholars to develop an analysis comparable to those achieved by scholars working more extensively in the interactionist tradition. First, although most ethnographers would likely accept premises of the sorts outlined at the beginning of this volume, many of those working outside the interactionist tradition have not thought much about or dealt with these concerns at a more explicit level.[17] This means that their conceptual foundations are apt to be less well formulated and of less assistance to them throughout the entire ethnographic enterprise. They also tend to lack conceptual resources for locating ethnographic research with respect to mainstream (quantitative) social science and dealing with the critiques of ethnographic inquiry commonly made by mainstream social scientists. Those working more on their own, thus, tend to be more vulnerable to these criticisms and may spend considerable time and effort attempting to come to terms with issues that may already have been dealt with by others in the interactionist tradition (and likely expressed more effectively than they could be by someone working on his or her own). Third, and this is reflected in the first two points as well, those working on their own typically lack the resources, literature, and interpersonal exchanges that normally accrue to members of a community that has focused on these and related matters (i.e., through ongoing explorations, conceptual development, debates) for over seventy years. It's not that people working on their own are less competent intellectually than are those in the interactionist community; however, one can do only so much on one's own. Likewise, while there is considerable variation and debate within the interactionist community across a range of issues pertaining to ethnographic research and theoretical matters, there is also considerable coherence within the tradition, as well as a great many opportunities for scholars to articulate ongoing concerns and practices pertaining to theory, method, and research with others in the community.

There may be an infinite number of ways in which one may approach and analyze settings ethnographically, but those assuming an interactionist approach tend to focus most specifically on the ways in which people do things (and work things out with others). There is a central emphasis on *process*, or more precisely on depicting the social processes characterizing practices in this or that community or subcultural setting. Thus, although researchers strive for highly detailed accounts of how people view their life-situations, define themselves and others, become involved in particular behaviors, conduct their activities, develop relationships, and the like in practice, there is also an attempt to derive a set of concepts or themes that centrally address the processes involved in doing these things. In this manner, researchers move from a more situated or individualized set of instances of human behaviors to more generalized sets of understandings, which nonetheless are firmly grounded in the day-to-day practices of those whose activities constitute the life-worlds under consideration.

Those presently working within the interactionist tradition are very fortunate in that the researchers who preceded them not only provided some extremely valuable accounts of people's practices in a wide variety of life-worlds, but have also helped formulate a set of concepts that have great importance for approaching subsequent ethnographic inquiry. As a result, we are able to define more precisely the assumptions that people make as ethnographers. Likewise, as part of this legacy, we have a body of concepts and a stock of knowledge about the other on which to build in approaching and analyzing subsequent ethnographic projects. Although there is a clear understanding that our findings in the field must maintain priority over our concepts, the availability of this ethnographic literature and the conceptual material that has accompanied it not only provide us with a set of contexts for comparing and contrasting our present inquiries with those developed earlier, but it also means that we can dialogue with, and contribute to, this body of literature in much more dynamic manners as our inquiries develop.

Contextualizing Human Lived Experience

Ethnographic work is very much concerned about achieving situated descriptions of instances of human lived experiences. However, unless ethnographers are content to pile up little islands of isolated studies, then we need to develop concepts that will allow us to transcend the contextual uniqueness of each research setting. We need concepts which will enable us to link (via comparisons, contrasts, assessments, refinements) ethnographic inquiries with one another.

Although one could develop conceptual material along any set of dimensions, the concept of "action" or the notion of "human behavior as ongoing accomplishment" appears to be the single most valuable avenue for pursuing ethnographic research and for drawing comparisons across contexts. A fuller statement on the emergence and forms of "generic social processes" is available in chapter 3, but these trans-situational or transcontextual concepts offer considerable advantages to those doing ethnographic research. In addition to (a) summarizing a number of themes that have emerged in ethnographic research to date, this material also (b) enables researchers to dialogue with the literature that addresses materials parallel to the issues they may be examining in their own work, and (c) affords researchers opportunities to assess the viability of these conceptual notions and thus contribute their own grounded appraisals (and reconstructions) of these notions to the literature.

When conducting research, ethnographers normally put their sensitizing concepts in suspension. First and foremost, ethnographers have an objective of achieving intimate familiarity with the setting at hand. The data of human lived experiences should have primacy over our concepts and it should be used to reshape and otherwise inform our conceptual developments to date. But researchers can still use conceptual notions derived from any earlier inquiry (regardless of substantive context) as a source of stimulation in developing material on any research setting, and they can use the material from each new setting to assess the viability of concepts developed in other contexts. In this way, by building a conceptual frame increasingly rigorously grounded in research on people's lived experiences, we may develop a social science that is genuinely attentive to everyday life.

Endnotes:

1. In contrast to those who may be inclined to assume a "postmodernist orientation" to the human sciences, the position taken in chapters 7 and 8 (as in this volume more generally) attends to the notion of an "obdurate reality" as formulated by Herbert Blumer (1969) and makes explicit claims to the "privilege of presence." The issues involved are clearly beyond the scope of the present volume, but are dealt with in extended detail in Prus (1996, especially 203–57) along with a critique of "postmodernist representations." Very simply expressed though, and at variance from the postmodernist (poststructuralist) cynicism associated with language and all forms of knowing, the position taken here is that the human struggle for existence presupposes intersubjectively formulated notions of reality in which certain claims "about the world" will be prioritized over others in order that things may be accomplished. Far from representing "the first and great lie" (as defined by Nietzschean skepticism), language is the uniquely enabling feature of the human condition. The underlying message, here, is an insistence that researchers strive for extended and sincere role-taking (Mead, 1934) encounters with the ethnographic other and endeavor to develop accounts of those encounters that provide third-party readers with representations of the ethnographic other that sincerely, openly, and comprehensively portray the lived experiences (viewpoints and practices) of the other.

2. Our work has included studies of felony killers (Dietz, 1983), ballet dancers (Dietz, 1994a), urban lumberjacks (Dietz, 1994b), and high-school athletes (Dietz and Cooper, 1994); clergymen and their congregations (Prus, 1976), parole officers and their clients (Prus and Stratton, 1976), hookers, entertainers, bar staff, and patrons (Prus and Irini, 1980), marketing and sales activities (Prus, 1989a, 1989b; Prus and Frisby, 1990), road hustlers and magicians (Prus and Sharper, 1991), consumer behavior (Prus and Dawson, 1991; Prus, 1993b, 1994a), and business development officers (Prus and Fleras, 1996); orthodox Jewish religious communities (Shaffir, 1974), medical students (Haas and Shaffir, 1987), ethnic riots (Levitt and Shaffir, 1989), innovative educational programs (Pawluch et al., 1994), and anticipations of the Messiah (Shaffir, 1993). For other statements we have written on the problematics of doing field research, see Shaffir, Dietz, and Stebbins (1994), Prus (1980, 1989a, 1989b, 1991, 1996) and Shaffir (1980, 1985, 1991).

3. Readers are referred to the collections of articles in Shaffir, Stebbins, and Turowetz (1980) and Shaffir and Stebbins (1991) for other accounts of field research. Also see Becker (1970), Bogdan and Taylor (1975), Johnson (1975), Douglas (1976), Lofland and Lofland (1984, 1995), and Jorgensen (1989) for other valuable methodological statements.

4. The bibliography at the end of this volume provides an excellent starting point for those wishing to track down ethnographic studies. For ethnographic materials dealing with specific substantive topics, see chapters 4–6.

5. While all knowledge is perspectival or defined with respect to the frames of reference people bring into the situation, this should not negate an openness with respect to the things we study. Thus, although people may never experience anything in a "pure" form, we can attempt to be sensitive to the resistances that [objects] offer to people's current conceptualizations, and the ways in which they alter their earlier images of [the objects] in question to accommodate disjunctures between their earlier images of [those objects] and the additional information they've acquired through their encounters with [those objects]. Indeed, much of what constitutes the process of scientific inquiry revolves around the reconstitution (or rejection and reformulation) of people's perspectives with respect to this or that object of inquiry. By no means, however, is this processual view of knowledge limited to the realm of "scientific knowledge" (see Prus, 1996; Prus and Dawson, 1996). See "Developing Stocks of Knowledge" and "Dealing with Objects" in chapter 4.

6. See chapter 3 in this volume for a fuller statement on the origins, variations, and ethnographic literature pertaining to generic or transsituational social processes.

7. For a much more sustained examination of the positivist (structuralist) —interpretivist debate, see Prus (1996:3–9, 203–16, 245–57).

8. As much as anyone, Thomas Kuhn (1962) has been instrumental in alerting social scientists to the socially constructed nature of the physical science enterprise. For an elaboration of the sociology of science as it applies to the development of an intersubjective social science, see Prus (1996: especially 94–98, 203–17). Also see "Developing Stocks of Knowledge" in chapter 4.

9. Readers are also referred to Blumer's (1969) statements, "Sociological Analysis and the 'Variable' " and "What is Wrong with Sociological Theory," for further elaborations of the problems engendered by a factors-oriented approach to the social sciences.

10. We are grateful to Robert A. Campbell for suggesting this term to us. *Paratheory* denotes the development of a second, more implicitly recognized theory that is parallel to, but effectively outside of, the theory or model which "officially" is intended to explain the phenomenon at hand.

11. The implication, in part, is that differing results, however these might be attained (e.g., obscure questions, coding mistakes, mislabeled variables, misread outputs, differing statistical procedures, or bogus data), could result in the construction of remarkably different paratheories to explain the relationships of the variables considered in the study.

12. We are aware that opinion polls and other census and tracking data may be input electronically and that statistical computations may be achieved almost instantaneously when variables and codes are predefined. This in itself,

however, does not constitute quantitative social science. It overlooks the intellectual enterprise and the academic interchange that undergirds this realm of activity.

13. Those who might be tempted to rely heavily on observational materials (i.e., as in "content analysis") are encouraged to examine Blumer's (1939) critique of Thomas and Znaniecki's classic (1918–1922), *The Polish Peasant in Europe and America*, a critique which these same authors subsequently endorsed.

14. Like other people, researchers in the field are apt to have many other obligations (e.g., families, children, work roles) and unanticipated obstacles to which to attend on a day-to-day basis. These other involvements may compete and interfere with fieldwork activities as well as be put on hold as a consequence of researcher pursuits. Researchers often experience fragmented selves (chapter 6).

15. For a more extended discussion of emotionality as a generic social process (and emotionality and the ethnographer self), see Prus (1996:173–201).

16. Lyman and Scott (1989) provide an insightful statement on stage fright and the problem of identity.

17. Elvi Whittaker (1994) elaborates on this point. While most anthropologists seem quite amenable to interactionist assumptions, many of these people have had to work out variations of these premises largely on their own, without the assistance of statements such as those provided by Mead (1934) or especially Blumer (1969).

8

Writing Ethnographic Research Reports: Some Practical Considerations for Students

(with William Shaffir and Mary Lorenz Dietz)

While ethnographic research is demanding in many ways, the production of ethnographic text may represent a challenge no less formidable than gathering the data used as a base for the text.[1] Whether writing generally seems to come easy for people or not, the development of ethnographic texts entails a certain discipline and commitment that other forms of writing need not. Ethnographers may assume a wide variety of styles and practices in presenting their material, but they are faced with the tasks not only of representing the (ethnographic) other in a way that adequately reflects the experiences of the other, but also of fostering a comprehensive understanding of the other for readers. As well, ethnographers often assume the additional objective of dialoguing with existing concepts and studies in the literature pertaining to the study of human group life.

These undertakings are considerably compounded by the complexity of the data that detailed examinations of social worlds generate. In contrast to quantitative research that takes survey or experimental data and distills these into statistical units revolving around independent and dependent variables, ethnographic inquiry assumes a highly expansive quality as these researchers attempt to detail and comprehend the complex life-worlds in which human behavior takes place.

Although ethnographers realize that they will never be able to produce the perfect account of the life-world of the other, this does not and should not prevent them from striving for a careful, thorough, balanced account of the other. Indeed, despite the inabilities of researchers to achieve complete intersubjectivity with the other or to find ways of conveying information about the other that insures that readers will fully comprehend all aspects of people's life-worlds, there is no more viable way of accessing and comprehending human lived experience in the social sciences than through ethnographic inquiry.

The discussion following is not intended as a magic potion for producing ethnographic text, but rather is presented as an epilogue of sorts for students and other novices embarking on this undertaking. Simply put, these are the sorts of things we routinely attempt to convey to our students when they ask us how they might go about writing up their studies.

The discussion following is divided into two parts: formatting the ethnographic text and assembling the ethnographic text. These two statements are very much interrelated, but draw attention to different aspects of producing ethnographic text. Hopefully, this statement will provide newcomers with a framework of sorts that may help them to better anticipate their own statements as they work their way through these projects:

BP: Even as we talk about this, I realize that one can set up a project in so many different ways. In fact, every ethnographic text I've written has been somewhat different in that respect. In the hotel book, for example, although each chapter deals with somewhat parallel processes for a different set of actors, we set up each chapter somewhat differently just to generate some variety for the reader as well as for ourselves. In that same book, as well, our major methodological statement is presented at the end of the book. The big thing is not exactly how the text is set up, but rather what it contains on an overall basis.

WS: I try to disabuse students of the idea that there is but one correct way to write up their research. This is usually a difficult idea for them to appreciate and stems, in some measure, from their uncertainty and insecurity in doing ethnographic research. I try to explain that, sociologically speaking, the same material can be organized in different ways when viewed through various lenses. I ask them to consider the story they wish to tell and the aspects of it that their data can illuminate. . . .

There isn't any formula that I regularly apply in organizing the material in any given project. There are numerous exigencies that influence the organization, including deadlines, fatigue, and the range of data that are available. In my own case, I wouldn't underestimate the advice that I've received from colleagues and editors. In *The Riot at Christie Pits*, coauthored with Cyril Levitt, the storyline flips back and forth between Toronto and Germany. This idea, a superb one we thought, was suggested by the editor. It turned out to be a most effective device for telling the story of the riot and of the events leading to it. My first ethnography of a hasidic community emphasizes certain aspects of community life while ignoring or omitting others. There are times when I simply don't have all of the data that I'd like and this, too, influences the shape of what follows. The simple point is that there isn't any one way of doing things, and that any way has its advantages and disadvantages.

Formatting the Ethnographic Text

The actual headings that people use in presenting ethnographies may vary considerably, but it is useful to provide a couple of variants for conceptual purposes. This allows us to discuss a number of components of the ethnographic research paper and indicate some of the ways these may be developed.

Set-up 1	Set-up 2
Title	Title
Introduction	Introduction
Data and Analysis	Theoretical Approach
Conclusion	Literature Review
Epilogue	Research Setting and Methods
	Data and Analysis
	Theme A
	Theme B
	Theme C
	Conclusion

Although set-up 2 is longer and appears more complex, a good paper using set-up 1 normally would contain the same sorts of materials noted in set-up 2. This simply is not made explicit in the first instance. For this reason, most people may find it easier both to write and to read ethnographies when more explicit outlines are used.

The Title: Providing Preliminary Directions

Since the title conveys the first set of images that readers might ordinarily associate with a paper, the author(s) may like to develop a title that depicts the setting under consideration, indicates the approach taken to the study, and focuses the reader's attention on a particular social process. The title may also be seen as introducing the central "thesis" or "conceptual issue" being pursued in the paper, but for an ethnographic paper it is also helpful to establish the context as soon as possible. Although not necessary, further attention may be drawn to the paper by adding a little color, creativity, irony, and the like.

The following examples provide some indications of how these concerns might be expressed as well as indicate some possible realms of ethnographic inquiry: "Flatfoot: An Ethnographic Study of Social Order among Street Patrol Officers," "Quick Pics: An Interactionist Analysis of Sidewalk Artists," "Striking Out Alone: A Social Constructionist Account of Life in the Singles Scene," "Bottoms Up!: Drinking As Negotiated Activity," "Censorship Incorporated: A Natural History of a Morals Campaign," and "Being Your Own Manager: A Participant-Observation Study of the Ambiguities, Dilemmas, and Practices of the University Student."

Paper titles may be developed before, during, or after the paper has been written, but even a tentative working title is apt to be useful in moving projects along:

MLD: Titles are important for me because I often do them first and then use them to help keep me on track or rather to keep me from getting sidetracked. The title should really say what you're talking about.

BP: Most of the titles I have for ethnographic papers are focused on activities, and I really try to do two things. One is to emphasize the particular activity and context under consideration. The other is to locate this topic within a more generic social process, so that readers might be better able to appreciate the underlying conceptual significance of the issue being considered. I have to admit, though, that I like to have a little fun with titles, too.

WS: I tend to choose the title at the end and I select from several possibilities that I've jotted down along the way. I almost never have the title before I start writing. What is important, for me, is to have a sense of the paper's focus and the larger conceptual issues it might address. At times, seemingly out of nowhere, catchy titles for a paper pop into my head. Titles aren't invented that easily, and I'm always revising what I have for what, I think, is catchier and better. For the most part, though, I don't fuss over them.

The Introduction: Contextualizing the Study

In some ways, it may be useful to think of ethnographic statements as having three major components: an introduction, a presentation (and analysis) of the data collected, and a conclusion. In actual practice, however, it is often unwieldy to attempt to limit oneself to three headings or sections. This is particularly true for larger projects, but even statements about smaller studies may benefit from further divisions.

Introductions vary greatly in length and the tasks assumed in this first part of the paper. In general, however, the purpose of the introduction is to set the stage or generate a sense of direction, to provide the readers with an overview of what they might expect from the paper. Insofar as it is longer than the title, the introduction is generally viewed as the place to define the thesis, purpose, or objective of the paper for the reader:

MLD: There isn't any question that a title and introduction create an important first impression about what is going to follow. Introductions usually set off the problem or issue as unique and give the reader an idea of what to expect in the paper. Many authors write their intros after they conclude the paper. This has an up and a down side. On the down side, the author may not have developed a guiding statement to work with from the beginning, but on the plus side, writing the introduction last often makes for a truer description of the contents. One can, of course, do a tentative introduction and then rewrite it after doing the rest of the paper.

WS: I usually begin by sketching the introduction where I identify the main substantive issue(s) that I'll address in the paper and the larger conceptual theme(s) to which it can be related. This comes quickly but only because I've thought about it for some time beforehand. I then leave this and return to it once I have completed the entire draft. Although it is challenging to situate the material conceptually and theoretically, I don't especially enjoy writing introductions, but it is necessary work. This is probably why I keep them short.

Since the introduction provides an opportunity for the author to establish a preliminary base or reference point for the reader, some consideration of the theoretical approach employed in developing the study is particularly valuable in this respect. Here, authors normally locate their statement within a tradition or field as they talk about the approach they are taking and the concepts and literature that they see as pertinent to the paper at hand. Ideally, as well, authors will frame the paper around some "conceptual issue" and draw some tentative parallels between the present inquiry and other seemingly similar studies. The amount of detail presented in the introduction will vary somewhat with one's objectives, but the author normally has some obligation to insure that the reader will be able to locate these efforts within some scholarly tradition.

Establishing the Theoretical Approach. Even if the author intends to develop a separate discussion (section or chapter) of the theoretical approach later in the text, it is important to provide the reader with a preliminary overview of the approach in the introduction. To establish a theoretical approach, authors normally locate their project within some scholarly paradigm or tradition. Here, they may wish to make note of the figures most central to the development of these notions, outline the major thrusts and assumptions of this approach, and indicate the sorts of issues or questions that are seen to be more pertinent. In the process, authors attempt to indicate where their projects fit into some overall scheme. Regardless of whether this material is presented in the introduction per se, or whether it is developed as a section or chapter on its own, this material is very important in framing the project for the reader:

MLD: Students sometimes get bogged down in theoretical discussions. They tend to see theory as grand theory that explains all of human conduct. As a result, they sometimes are unable to find an appropriate place for their own research. The interactionist approach provides sufficient theoretical framework for most ethnographic studies and allows student ethnographers to work on the development of key concepts without trying to build a grand, abstract scheme. In some cases as well, theoretical discussions could be embedded in the analysis section or presented at the end, after the data analysis. Students should show that they know what theoretical perspective they operate from, some place in their overall statement, but good ethnographic work does not necessarily require massive theoretical discussion prior to the data presentation.

WS: I'll generally advise students doing ethnographic research to familiarize themselves with the symbolic interactionist perspective because the conceptualizations of social life contained therein offer useful vantage points from which to analyze the research problem. A formulation of the theoretical orientation enables the reader to better appreciate how and why the data are analyzed as they are. At the same time, however, I've encountered too many instances where preoccupation over theoretical fit and relevance stymie creative and powerful ethnography. In my own work, for instance, I regard the theoretical contribution to be largely pedestrian and have increasingly concentrated on offering rich description and paying careful attention to the dynamics of the social process I'm examining.

BP: A statement on the theoretical orientation is invaluable in alerting the reader to the viewpoint of the author, but it is important for the author, too. In defining the approach for the reader, the author is also more explicitly attending to the sorts of assumptions or premises that one is utilizing in developing the study. Individual authors may find it useful to contrast their approach with those that others have taken to the same topic, but a statement of this sort should also help the author to maintain a more consistent and more productive focus throughout the project.

If papers are written as class assignments of sorts, then it is generally highly advisable for the authors to show the instructor in some detail that they are familiar with *the approach* (e.g., symbolic interaction) used in the course as well as using this material to build a launching pad for the ensuing project. Indeed, insofar as instructors are normally in a position to give people credit for everything they generate in their written texts, students also may be able to use these other parts of course projects as buffers of sorts against what sometimes amounts to a less compelling set of materials from the field.

The Literature. A discussion of the literature may also be presented in the introduction, or it may be located in a section or chapter of its own. In either event, authors should be attentive to both the *substantive* and the *conceptual* dimensions of the literature and sort these out as well as they can in developing their statements.

In generating *substantive reviews* of the literature, people usually discuss the materials that others have written on the same topic. Typically, this involves some sort of cataloguing or classifying activities, wherein authors make references to the types of work that have been done on the same topic and show where and in what ways these other studies differ from, or are similar to, one another. In this way, authors may begin to claim some expertise of sorts on matters pertaining to the police, bars, censorship, or whatever topic they are investigating. In actuality, however, the only thing that these studies may have in common is that they all deal with a particular topic in some respect. Beyond that, this literature may be a rather hopeless muddle of assumptions, conceptualizations, methodologies, data, and analyses of whatever people have done on this topic. It should not be presumed that this material can or should be fitted into some rational, viable, holistic synthesis. The main value of substantive literature reviews to ethnographers may simply be that of indicating what other people have done and showing where and how their research contrasts with and is similar to these other statements:

WS: The substantive literature review is important for purposes of establishing some measure of credibility. It is essentially to indicate that you are familiar with the material that is relevant and pertinent to your topic. This shouldn't be taken to mean that one must digest all of the relevant material prior to setting out for the field, or that the findings are either similar or identical to others'. Familiarizing oneself with the available literature needn't always be time-consuming. In the case of my work on the hasidic Jews, the task was fairly simple: not much sociological or anthropological work had been published when I started out. And when I studied defectors from ultra-Orthodox (haredi) Judaism, virtually nothing was available. By contrast, the topic of professional socialization enjoyed an extensive literature by the time Jack Haas and I conducted our study of medical students. I should say that I've never felt compelled to master a body of literature before writing and publishing on a topic.

The other literature, the *conceptually oriented material*, is much more pertinent and instructive. This material builds very centrally around one's approach to the study at hand and generally treats the study at hand as a particular instance of a broader category of some phenomenon. Thus, people embarking on studies of police-citizen encounters, buyer-seller interactions, or dating episodes, for instance, may review any ethnographic literature that deals with negotiation or relationships. Similarly, people considering doctor-patient encounters, life in the singles scene, or student roles may examine any ethnographic study that discusses ambiguity or impression management, for example. Likewise, people interested in others' involvements in drug usage, religious cults, or gambling may examine any studies that deal with people's careers (as school teachers, bikers, police officers, or hustlers, for instance).

Those taking a conceptual approach, thus, attend to parallel (generic) processes and other transcontextual features of human group life. Instead of reviewing study after study of the police, doctors, factory workers, or students, for instance, one may draw upon any studies (regardless of the context) that one is able to find that focus on the particular conceptual theme (e.g., acquiring perspectives, negotiating outcomes, developing relationships) pertinent to one's research. It should be recognized that this type of literature review implies a very different way of approaching the materials in the library. It is the more difficult type of library research to generate as well, since most library and indexing codes are substantively rather than conceptually oriented. The payoffs for the additional work can be highly consequential, however, and begin to establish the student as a much more resourceful and analytical thinker. It might also be observed that this type of literature review is much more instructive in enabling the reader to anticipate and appreciate aspects of the analysis than are most substantive references. Indeed, the closest conceptual pieces of research in the literature may have nothing whatsoever to do with the particular substantive setting in which one is working. But unless authors think processually, they may very well miss the very powerful analytical resources represented by studies of other settings as well as an opportunity to raise their own studies to a more consequential conceptual level:

BP: We are speaking here of instances of conceptual fertilization as well as more abstract conceptual awareness and resourcefulness. Often, the most powerful and relevant concepts are those developed by researchers who have been working in other topical areas. Indeed, this seems quite likely, since people have done ethnographic research on so many different topics but not all that much on any one topical area. A couple of examples come readily to mind. First, a lot of the conceptual material I've been using in studying buyers and sellers in the marketplace, such as that pertaining to career contingencies, recruitment practices, and interpersonal influence, is rooted in the works of scholars working in the areas of deviance and religion. Second, in studying medical students who are presumably among the most mentally competent people in our society, Jack

Haas and Bill Shaffir relied very heavily on the "cloak of competence," an analytical theme introduced by Robert Edgerton in his study of the lives of those labeled mentally retarded. The point is not to emphasize the ironies of these instances, but rather to indicate the importance of thinking generically, processually, transcontextually, rather than limiting oneself to particular substantive literatures.

The Setting: Here's the Situation at Hand. Authors also may use the introductory segment of the text to provide readers with a more extended introduction into the setting or the context in which the study took place. If the study involves life in a halfway house, a church, or a university residence, for instance, it is generally helpful if the author informs the reader about the setting at hand and tells how the author/ethnographer became involved in the study. Where possible, authors may describe settings (of this type) in more general terms as well as indicate the more unique features of the particular settings in which they conducted their research. Ethnographers vary greatly in the amount of information they provide, but if one envisions a description of the context as setting the stage for the ensuing analysis, then it becomes apparent that this material is essential for enabling the reader to comprehend the larger project being developed:

WS: A comprehensive description of the setting is relevant insofar as it shapes and influences the nature of the activity under consideration. In some of my research—for example, immigrants' decisions to alter their citizenship, or the immigration and emigration of Canadian Jews to and from Israel—a discussion of the setting was inconsequential to the behavior I wished to explain. On the other hand, my research on hasidic communities, the McMaster medical school, defections from the ultra-Orthodox Jewish fold, and newcomers to Orthodox Judaism immediately revealed that the setting was critical both for shaping persons' definitions of situations and the organization of their subsequent behavior.

MLD: When I wrote about urban lumberjacks in Detroit, the city itself was an important part of examining the work that these men did. The setting was also important in my work on the ballet world because so much of a dancer's life is either in a classroom or a theatre. In contrast, settings for interpersonal violence can be anywhere. Still, however, particular types of settings can

enter importantly into the dynamics of the interaction surrounding episodes of violence. People's definitions of different
settings can be related to how people relate to each other.
Violence occurring in private settings, for instance, is normally
conducted in different manners from that occurring in public
settings.

BP: Some ethnographic contexts are so particular that one needs
to spend considerable time just "setting the stage" so to speak.
The work Sharper and I did on card and dice hustlers, or the
study I did with Styllianoss Irini on the hotel community was
like that. Other research, such as the study of the marketing
and sales activity I did or the study of consumer behavior that
I'm presently working on are much more generic, but even here,
one has to establish some conceptual parameters and common
understandings for the reader.

The Method. Since the "what" and "how" of doing ethnographic
research can vary greatly from one instance to the next, it is important
for ethnographers to provide readers with a greater sense of how the
field research was accomplished in each particular instance. Discussions of the method often overlap with considerations of the conceptual approach and the setting, but specific attention should be
given to matters of contacts and continuities; procedures and practices;
and shortcomings and qualifications. While these research issues are
sometimes encompassed in the introduction or the data and analysis
sections, they generally are more appropriately developed as a chapter
or section on their own.

The notion of *contacts and continuities* draws attention to the
importance not only of telling the reader how the researcher became
involved in this particular study, but also how the researcher made
contact with the people whose life-worlds were being studied and how
the researcher sustained a presence in that setting over the duration
of the study. In addition to outlining initial concerns and conditions
of encountering the other, authors typically comment on obstacles
and difficulties they encountered as well as the dilemmas and adjustments they made along the way. Here, as well, researchers enter into
more specific discussions of their sampling practices and related
concerns as these took shape over the course of the project.

A discussion of *research procedures and practices* provides the
reader with more information about how the study was conducted
and may involve more extended discussions of field observations,

interview questions, participant-observer roles, recording field notes, sorting out the data, developing analytical schemes, and such.

Since researchers know their own field experiences better than anyone else, this may also be a good place to indicate any *shortcomings and qualifications* that ethnographers associate with the inquiry at hand. What things would they like to be able to do differently? What things were left undone? What advice might they have for others embarking on similar tasks? If authors are concerned about this discussion interrupting the overall flow of the paper, they may talk about these sorts of issues later in the text, possibly in the conclusion or an epilogue or appendix:

BP: This is one place where published works and student papers and theses often differ. If you are preparing something for a journal editor or a book publisher, they often limit you and sometimes very sharply to so many pages of text. As a result, the discussion of methods is often highly abbreviated because this material is played off against other things that one might wish to include. Now, some faculty set very stringent limits on student papers as well, but other instructors very much appreciate extended discussions of methodological matters so that they can better see what their students did and learned in the process. I think that it is also entirely desirable that students develop this material in greater detail so that they can more explicitly reflect on these vital aspects of the project.

WS: I believe that discussions of data collection and, more generally, the natural history of the project should be as thorough as possible. As we know, the processes by which relationships in the field are established, or fail to be maintained, can critically influence the kind of data to which we gain access. Quite understandably, the amount of space available for such consideration varies with the particular publication; a journal-length article in contrast to a monograph will include a synopsized account of matters pertaining to field research methods. The main problem, however, is that many accounts of how field research is executed follow a prescribed formula for how such work ought to proceed while neglecting to attend to more subjective aspects of the research experience. These subjective components, while seemingly incidental and of little consequence, are more often than not integral to the kind of analysis that is produced.

The Data and Analysis

As the preceding discussion indicates, there are many ways that an ethnographic text might be presented. However, when we move to a consideration of the data and analysis, the options become more diverse. To this point, we've been able to maintain a greater sense of coherency because the objectives of most ethnographic research have been more parallel to this point. However, differing conceptual emphases generate more diverse presentational strategies.

To this end, it may be useful to delineate five different processual emphases that ethnographers may employ in developing their analyses. These reflect (1) natural history approaches; (2) studies of career involvement; (3) analyses of role performance; (4) analyses of particular subcultural (or community) life-worlds; and (5) generic social processes studies. Some overlap in these different approaches is inevitable, but each implies a somewhat different mode of organizing one's materials. Not all projects will fall into these categories, and a great many projects represent combinations of these analytical themes as one or more of these themes is embedded within a more dominant or overriding analytical issue. Still, considerations of each of these may help students gain a greater sense of some of the routes and options they may employ in their own projects.

Taking a Natural History Approach (Studying Events). Natural history approaches are organized around chronological sequencings or processes of sorts. If a single event is involved, the analysis often follows a moment-to-moment, day-to-day, month-to-month, etc., accounting of the production of the event under consideration. Researchers adopting a natural history approach may focus on an encounter, an involvement, a relationship, an occasion, a social problem, a social movement, or something of that sort. Ethnographic accounts generally differ from historical statements in that particular attention is given to the ways in which the people involved experience, define, act, and adjust to one another. Compared to those doing historical analysis, ethnographers have the clear advantage of being able to spend time with people, to observe them, to experience some of their roles directly, and, most importantly, to talk to them about their experiences. This is vastly superior to relying on material that one may find in journals, letters, newspapers, committee reports, and the like, since (a) these have generally been developed with very little if any interest in facilitating an ethnographic appreciation of the other and (b) analysts must make so many unsubstantiated inferences of meaning.

An ethnographic natural history approach depicts people's lived experiences and the human enterprise involved in producing this or that state of affairs.

In addition to outlining as many of the episodes and interchanges that constitute the larger event as possible, ethnographers normally direct attention to those activities and occasions that seem particularly consequential for understanding the emergence of the event under consideration. However, it is also important to provide readers with a good sense of the more routine or banal practices taking place at this and that point in time because this material represents an essential background for understanding the more dramatic episodes along the way.

Since authors adopting a natural history approach work within sequential presentational schemes, other analytical themes (e.g., considerations of people's careers, activities, or relationships) are generally introduced here and there, within the context of an unfolding account of the event. Ethnographers commonly discuss the perspectives used by the people in the setting under consideration and the meanings that those people attach to objects, as well as the processes by which they work out their identities, relationships, and activities with one another.[2]

If more than one event is covered in the analysis, then the "natural history" presented tends to take the form of the "typical" case. Here, a generalized conceptual sequence is developed with the understanding that actual cases need not follow this model precisely at this or that point. Instead, each stage or subprocess of the typical case normally becomes the site for presenting (and analyzing) a multitude of cases. The analyst tries to give readers a sense of the range, variations, and prominence of the cases under consideration as well as indicating qualifications of these processes as they pertain to the cases at hand. While analysts are typically able to provide more contextualizing detail when single cases are featured, the use of multiple cases fosters stage-by-stage comparisons and contrasts that single cases may not be able to offer:[3]

BP: The two books I wrote on marketing and sales employ variations of a multiple-case, natural history approach. The study was not developed around a single business or product line. Instead, I talked with people selling everything from ice cream and candy to shoes, factory products, real estate, and advertising. While each chapter was organized around some activity associated with the overall task of marketing and sales, both books were presented with an eye toward a natural sequencing of events. Thus, although readers will appreciate that marketing and sales represent an ongoing and interrelated set of activities, one simply cannot talk about everything at once. As a result, the books were organized around a natural sequence of events. *Pursuing Customers* depicted "stage-setting activities" and was organized with this flow: setting up business, doing management, purchasing products for resale, setting prices, and doing promotional activity (media, showrooms, in the field). *Making Sales*, which dealt with interpersonal influence, was organized with this sense of chronological sequence: presenting products, generating trust, neutralizing resistance, obtaining commitments, encountering troublesome customers, developing loyalty, holding sales, and maintaining enthusiasm.

In actual practice, cases needn't follow these orderings, and one could have rearranged the order of these activities quite extensively and still maintained the essence of the sales context because, in many respects, all of these activities can take place more or less simultaneously in "up and running business." For example, both the products one orders for resale and one's pricing practices may be done in manners mindful of one's existing customers. Likewise, salespeople presenting products or generating trust may approach prospects differently depending on whether they are dealing with repeat customers or have just made some significant sales and experience a greater sense of enthusiasm. Still, a stage-by-stage presentation allows us to focus on a natural ordering that tends to hold for a large portion of cases.

In both instances, the single case study and the multiple case account, there is normally some emphasis on delineating a set of processes central to the development and direction of the event under consideration.

Studying Careers of Involvement. "Career contingency" studies, or those that depict people's involvements in particular situations over time, represent a subtype of the natural history approach. If one envisions people's participation in situations in "career" terms (e.g., a sequence of involvements as doctors, thieves, drug users, cultic members, magicians, or ballerinas), then one may ask about the ways people (a) become involved in, (b) continue and intensify involvements in, (c) become disengaged from, and (d) possibly reinvolved in some career or line of involvement. As with natural history projects more generally, studies of this sort may focus on a single person or may examine the involvements of multiple people as they work their way through particular situations.

Instead of asking why someone did this or that or what caused or made them do something, interactionists ask *how* people become involved in situations. They ask about people's definitions of the situations at hand and their experiences with others at this and that point of the involvement. In addition to attending to initial routes of involvement, consideration is also given to continuance and the ways in which people become more (or less) intensively involved in particular situations:

BP: If you look at *Road Hustler*, you'll see that we focused on issues regarding the ways in which people became involved in card and dice hustling and when they were likely to continue and become more fully involved in these pursuits. As well, we asked when and how people were likely to become disinvolved from these activities, and, if they did quit, we wanted to know when and how they became reinvolved. Obviously, we were very much influenced by Sutherland's *The Professional Thief,* but we also benefitted from Howard Becker's work on jazz musicians and marijuana users. Interestingly, although I didn't know this at the time that Sharper and I wrote *Road Hustler,* our work was also very similar in thrust to Clifford Shaw's *The Jack-Roller.* I mention that book in part because although it was written over sixty years ago, it remains the single best account of juvenile delinquency that we have in the literature.

WS: Questions pertaining to process or the sequential steps by which persons become involved in, and committed to, particular lines of activity reflect what the focus of our work ought to be. In my own case, understanding why someone elects to radically alter their lifestyle either by, say, becoming observant or abandoning an ultra-Orthodox way of life is best accomplished by appreciating the stages or steps through which such changes are negotiated. Such decisions are typically organized around persons' interactions with others and it is, therefore, necessary to comprehend the range of their involvements and the latters' subsequent impact on persons' identities. This idea was pursued in the study of medical students. Jack Haas and I tried to show that the career route of the medical student

necessarily involves a complex set of interactions and involvements with a multitude of others who, at various times, critically affect the students' attitudes and behavior.

Examining Role Performance (Activity). While studies of role
performance often overlap with the career contingency type of analysis
just discussed, analyses of role performance generally put heavier
emphasis on the ways in which people go about doing or accomplishing the activities that their role involvements entail. Thus, although
ethnographers may locate people's practices within a career contingency or natural history sequence of some sort (to better contextualize
people's activities), the predominant emphasis here is on detailing the
what and how of the role under consideration. Here one might ask
what people *do* as managers, thieves, drug users, students, or in
whatever roles or situations they happen to find themselves, and then
embark on a more concerted analysis of all of the activities this or
that role entails. This means attending to all the things that people
involved in performing these activities experience on a day-to-day,
moment-to-moment basis. However, in addition to attending to what
people actually do on a here-and-now basis, it is also important to
provide some sense of how people learn to do, and adjust to, these
activities over time. This means that some recognition of a natural
history is inevitable even in this mode of analysis:

BP: What I like about a role performance analysis is that the
        emphasis is on activity, the doing or the "what and how" aspects
        of some role or set of activities associated with someone in a
        particular situation or life-style. Although I've done a lot of
        career contingency analysis in my research, I think I've become
        increasingly attentive to the importance of focusing on activity
        at a more concerted level. Whereas my earlier work attended
        to activities within the context of career contingencies, I've
        noticed that the work I've been doing more recently has em-
        bedded considerations of career contingencies within a larger
        focus on activities.

MLD: In the study I did on killers, I found that their roles as killers
        evolved from both their activities that they considered essential,
        i.e., whether they killed as part of a robbery, sex crime, or doing
        a contract, and to some degree the interpersonal style they used
        in interacting with the victims. These interactions developed
        in part from their own sense of role identity or self.

Exploring Subcultural Life-Worlds. While the analysis of particular subcultures should reflect the organizational complexity of the subculture or community under consideration, the exploration of subcultural life-words commonly builds on the natural history, the career contingency, and the role-performance themes just discussed. If the subculture is quite homogenous, then an analysis of this group is apt to more closely approximate the role-performance type of project just discussed, although some consideration is apt to be given as well to the comings and going (i.e., careers) of participants and to the ongoing interpersonal adjustments made by those who constitute the community at this and that point in time.

If the subculture is more diversely constituted and contains people involved in differing sets of activities (i.e., involves a number of more distinguishable roles), then analysis would not only entail some portrayal of the different roles that participants in the setting may assume, but also provide some indication of how people fit these roles (activities) together as they go about their activities on a day-to-day basis in conjunction with the others whose lives intersect therein.

BP: In studying card and dice hustlers, C. R. D. Sharper and I very much maintained a focus on one group of practitioners. We indicated here and there how these people's lives intersected with those of others such as their targets, the police, their families, sponsors, and such, but we presented the analysis very much from the road hustlers' perspectives. This tendency to focus on single role or category of people is quite typical of ethnographic analysis dealing with deviance involvements and in sociology more generally.

In contrast, when Styllianoss Irini and I embarked on the study of the hotel community, we found ourselves dealing with an assortment of people who were involved in that setting in very different ways (i.e., hookers, strippers, patrons, bar staff, desk clerks, musicians, etc.). We recognized this and wanted to see how all of these people fitted into the hotel community from their perspectives. In that sense, while we benefitted enormously from the earlier study with C. R. D. Sharper, we effectively produced a series of accounts from these different participants, each of which was like a smaller version of the text Sharper and I developed in *Road Hustler*. It meant, however, that we had come much closer to portraying an entire community in process and we were much better able to indicate the ways in which all the parties whose lives intersected within were able to work out their lines of action *in conjunction with one another.*

In developing analyses of subcultures or communities, it also is important to be attentive to the tasks of (a) depicting the elements that seem more distinctive or characteristic of particular life-worlds, (b) indicating the factions and divisions within those life-worlds and (c) showing the interconnections (blending, spill-overs, affinities) between subcultural involvements and people's participation in and contacts with mainstream community life (and vice-versa). One of the more viable ways of doing this is to approach subcultures not as single units but as reflecting a number of generic social processes. Minimally, it appears instructive for analysts to be attentive to people's *perspectives, activities, identities, relationships, communicative styles, and emotional experiences* as these take shape within particular life-worlds. These generic social processes are developed in some detail in chapter 3 and substantively contextualized (as research agendas) in chapters 4, 5, and 6. While the concept of subcultures or (multiple) life-worlds is fundamental to the ethnographic enterprise, the generic social processes delineated here not only provide students with a set of themes that cut across diverse settings and foster a more transcontextually informed approach to the study of any setting, but also enable researchers to better appreciate the unevenness of people's participation in particular settings. As well, although some subcultural analyses may represent more comprehensive, multifocused ventures, other inquiries may focus more explicitly on perspectives, identities, or activities, for instance:

BP: The subculture, that's where it all comes together—perspectives, identities, activities, relationships, commitments. It's a blending of people, activities, and the objects that they are working with or producing in the process. That's where reality is defined, shared, challenged, changed. That's where things are done, accomplished, and where people get frustrated, experience ambiguity, confusion, success, excitement. The subculture is where the action is. But it is also the pivot point for people's identities or the sense of self and other. It's where people experience pride, humor, embarrassment, and feel like they're a "somebody" or a "nobody." The subculture also draws our attention to the affiliations people have with others, the interconnections that they develop with others as they enter, intermingle, depart, and perhaps return to associate with particular others. We can talk, too, of the commitments people make and the ways in which, and the extent to which, they organize their lives around some or all of these features of the subculture. This also has important implications for disinvolvement, because the things that foster participation in a particular setting may serve to intensify the problems of disentanglement, even when the participants so desire. Plus, all of these elements are interlinked, so that any analysis of activities or identities, for instance, requires some appreciation of people's perspectives, their relationships, their commitments, and so on.

WS: For the ethnographer, disentangling the dynamics of a subculture is both challenging but also very time consuming. In my research, accessing the subculture and gaining an intimate familiarity with the goings-on has not come easily. As part of their survival strategy and effectiveness, subcultures establish boundaries separating insiders from outsiders. My research among the hasidic Jews offers a case in point. I quickly discovered that while gaining access to their places of worship was simple—after all, anyone can walk in off the street—acquiring some measure of their trust was an entirely different matter. Hasidim subscribe to a set of norms governing interactions with outsiders. My study of them alerted me to the centrality of socialization processes enabling the sects to remain distinct. I have also witnessed the intricate dynamics of how the subculture actively organizes and shapes the socialization of newcomers in my studies of medical students and newly observant Jews. In all three studies, the subculture (or community) could be characterized as a people-processing institution, and appreciating the manifold actions within it, interwoven as these were with Prus's generic social processes, helped make the research all the more interesting.

Developing Generic Social Process Projects. While the preceding discussions of perspectives, activities, identities, relationships, and commitments associated with particular subcultural (and role) involvements are very central to discussions of generic social processes (GSPs), ethnographers may also examine particular social processes across a variety of social contexts or subcultural settings. Someone interested in persuasion practices, for example, may examine instances of influence and resistance in playgrounds, medical schools, factories, churches, family settings, and the like, regardless of where these processes seem evident. Similarly, ethnographers may focus on such things as acquiring perspectives, achieving identities, developing relationships, and making commitments. Those doing research in subcultural contexts that involve several diverse roles may be in an excellent position to develop a series of GSP papers as a consequence of contact with people assuming different roles. Other researchers may move across unlimited contextual settings in attempts to examine the variations, complexities, and qualifications of human behavior associated with particular GSPs:

BP: GSP projects are multicontextual inquiries. They are not bound as readily by a single context or setting the same way that many other ethnographies are. One focuses on a particular process and examines these wherever they occur. A significant problem, of course, is being able to contextualize each episode within its local setting and then to compare this instance with seemingly parallel instances in other contexts. Now, one does this to some extent when one focuses on a particular setting as well, since all instances of human group life occur in contexts. Thus, for example, were one to examine disputes within a single family, it may be easier to convey a generalized setting to the reader, but each episode is somewhat different and may require some further contextualization as a result. Someone doing a GSP project on disputes might attend to disputes in families, in hospital settings, in the marketplace, and so forth. Although the GSP ethnographer would want to situate each dispute within a particular setting, prior to asking about the similarities and differences in the ways in which disputes might arise, intensify, or dissipate, for instance, the task is not so fundamentally different. GSP ethnographers may face greater obstacles in shifting frames for themselves and their readers, as they strive to comprehend and appreciate participant viewpoints than do those focusing on one site. However, some very powerful contrasts and similarities are apt to emerge when seemingly parallel processes are examined across a set of diverse settings.

People doing GSP projects generally organize their analysis around a natural flow or developmental sequence of a particular GSP (see chapter 3 for elaborations of several basic GSPs). While the subthemes developed around each GSP were attained by reviewing the ethnographic literature, they may provide a sense of the ways in which people may begin to conceptualize process in reference to specific research projects and develop more specific themes for analysis.

Regardless of whether one is doing a natural history or career contingency inquiry, a role performance analysis, a subcultural analysis, a GSP study, or some combination thereof, the importance of attending to *social process* should be underscored when doing an interactionist analysis. Although some contextual material is essential for grounding the analysis in the actual situations in which people find themselves, analyses that centrally concentrate on developing content-based typologies (e.g., four or seven kinds or types of bars, prostitutes, cults, social movements, etc.) not only tend to overlook the features that transcend these (allegedly) different types of phenomena, but they fail to tell us how people work their ways through the settings in which they find themselves. These context-based typifications may be useful in allowing people to place particular people, groups, places, and so forth in some category (for whatever that is worth), but we should be careful not to substitute classification for explanation of the emergence, change, and demise of this or that mode of association, setting, and the like. Content-based classifications also offer little transcontextual relevance. Not only may we be unable to develop understandings of similar processes in different contexts, but we may be unable to appreciate the "same contexts" at other points in time since (ongoing) change may make both the classification scheme and the location of particular people or things in that scheme obsolete.[4]

When developing a GSP analysis (or when working with other concepts or frames), one more caution is essential. Conceptual material is intended primarily as a means of organizing thoughts to date on some set of processes and instances of human experience. It is not something to be "proven" or used as a convenient frame for "filling in illustrations." The data gathered in the field must retain priority over our concepts, and the concepts must be adjusted to the material that we encounter in the field and not vice-versa.

The Conclusion

The conclusion (also summary, discussion, in perspective) represents an opportunity for the author to summarize the major concerns or themes in the paper and to highlight insights emerging from the study. It is also a place in which one may suggest future lines of inquiry as well as to note things that might be done differently were one to embark on a similar project (knowing what one knows now). The conclusion may be used, as well, to address some conceptual qualifications that have been overlooked elsewhere or to stress certain features of the approach or methodology that are thought important. If the reader has examined the larger paper more extensively, then the conclusion may be less consequential overall. If that has not happened, then the conclusion may represent the last major occasion for the author to develop points that seem important for appreciating the study at hand or even the last chance the author has to encourage the reader to go back and read the paper more carefully. In any event, many people like a conclusion because it recaps or highlights themes from the entire paper or book and helps refocus attention on central features of the preceding material.

Epilogues and Appendices

Only some ethnographic statements include epilogues. While epilogues may be used for a wide variety of purposes, they tend to be used either for "add-on" features that emerged after the initial study was conducted or for discussing matters that seem less direct to the larger text. On occasion, ethnographers use epilogues to update an earlier study or analysis in some way. Sometimes ethnographers use an epilogue to discuss some of their dilemmas, setbacks, or other problems that emerged in the project. At other times, the epilogue may be used to address ethnographers' personal viewpoints or to give advice, make policy recommendations, and the like.

An appendix is normally used to provide readers with some body of information that may be considered important for some reason, but which, nonetheless, is apt to disrupt the flow of the text if it were inserted in the main body. Ethnographers sometimes use appendices to provide readers with diagrams, photographs, lists of questions, and other such things that they think might help readers better contextualize the overall project.

References

Indicating the works on which one has built in developing, pursuing, and analyzing one's data, the "references" or "bibliographic sources" section represents another integral aspect of the research report. In addition to providing readers with a better sense of the conceptual framework(s) authors have used in developing the present statement, bibliographies may also provide readers with other sources that they may find of value in pursuing particular topics of study. While undergraduates tend to concentrate almost exclusively on the most recently published works they can find in a certain field, some of the earliest and "middling" works may be extremely consequential for a variety of purposes (e.g., foundational statements, differing emphases, unique contributions). An attentiveness to the literature on a more enduring basis is particularly consequential for ethnographic research. Because of the highly detailed depictions of aspects of the human condition one finds in more fully developed ethnographies, these materials not only maintain an "evergreen" quality but represent extremely valuable resources both as comparison points and for developing more generic (i.e., theoretical) appreciations of human community life.

The actual mode of representing biographical material is much less consequential than the contents provided within, but as general sources for ethnographic works, readers may refer to journals such as the *Journal of Contemporary Ethnography, Qualitative Sociology*, or *Symbolic Interaction*.

While the preceding discussion of formatting the ethnographic text has introduced a number of elements central to assembling the ethnographic paper, attention in the following section is focused more directly on the task of putting an ethnographic statement on paper.

Assembling the Paper

Since most ethnographies are too large to treat as single units, one way to begin putting an ethnography together is to envision the project as consisting as a number of parts, units, modules, or components. Probably the best way to start is simply to list or outline the themes, stages, issues, processes, or whatever the units with which one is working. Typically, this list or outline takes rudimentary shape as people venture into the field and then is developed more explicitly as one achieves greater familiarity with the situation at hand.

The list or outline represents an ethnographic "road map," and field researchers normally attempt to develop an outline that is, first and foremost, sensitive to the world of the other and secondly can be used to organize one's thoughts and the materials one gathers about the ethnographic other.

The outline is a way of managing one's project and should be viewed as a tentative, emergent indication of "where one's mind is" with respect to the project. Rather than representing a concrete form to be rigidly followed, the outline should be viewed as a dynamic, ongoing representation of how the project is taking shape. It should be *revised* more or less continuously as the ethnographer becomes more familiar with the life-world of the other. As the project gets larger, the outline becomes even more consequential, and great care should be taken not only to keep the outline up to date but also to provide as much detail as possible regarding the contents of each subtheme as is feasible.

In conjunction with an outline that overviews the project and provides the ethnographer with a working road map of the current status of the project, people attempting to manage (i.e., code) the materials they gather will likely find it valuable to create a separate file or package of material for each heading and subheading (and more precise files if necessary) the project entails. Not only does this help people organize their materials, but it also enables researchers to more carefully inspect and compare materials they've gathered on particular topics. As well, it might be observed that one effectively is "writing" the ethnography as one goes about sorting and assembling material pertaining to this and that theme and developing an outline which reflects those themes and the variants therein:

WS: Such filing is invaluable and, like all good things, requires a strong dose of discipline to execute consistently. Although I subscribe to the idea whole-heartedly, I haven't been as successful in practice. In those studies where I have created files, sorted the data into them, and have written memos of a theoretical and conceptual nature, the process of assembling the material for publication was facilitated enormously.

If each section of the text is treated as a separate module or component, then people may work on this or that part of the text as time and materials allow. As well, when the larger ethnographic text is approached as a series of files or components, researchers encountering difficulties with one or other sections can switch off to other parts and return to the troublesome sections at later points in time. This tends to reduce people's "down time" and sense of frustration, because issues sometimes get resolved in people's minds in effective ways when they are working on different but related things. Likewise, simply by looking at the material from a different angle on another occasion, researchers may see better ways of sorting out or expressing the materials at hand. A more detailed outline is helpful here, too, since one can not only quickly locate the various components of the project but can more effectively maintain continuity over the entire spectrum (and various complexities) of the project.

The task of actually fitting the various components together into a text is normally pursued later, as authors move toward a final copy of the manuscript. Often, as well, ethnographers find themselves moving topics around in differing sequences or with differing emphasis, so it is only toward the end that one may have the clearest sense of appropriate transition or linkaging statements.

Managing the Data

Although people sometimes write ethnographies with relatively little data, it is generally much easier to work with more data than one in the end may require. In this respect, people who have kept better field notes and who have pursued interviews more extensively tend to be greatly advantaged over others.

People working with tape-recorded interviews have two major options in dealing with this material on a more systematic basis. The first is that of transcribing all tapes. Although this is more work, it results in both the richest and most viable form of data with which to work. As well, researchers who type or write up their own interviews end up learning this material much better than do those who do not. This can result in a more effective analysis later on. The second option is to relisten to the tapes and make an indexed, sequential listing (a digitized tape counter is desirable here) of all of the topics that someone discusses, hopefully with enough detail that one can recall with some accuracy what was being discussed at this and that point in (what will become) one's catalogue of tapes. Although this is the quickest route in the short run, it tends to become more time-consuming when one goes on to use this material, since much time is apt to be spent changing, rewinding, and relistening to tapes. As well, one is faced with the eventual task of copying out these materials when they are to be used. This second option is recommended only as an alternative to not developing an index. Researchers who simply try to remember materials without using transcripts or (minimally) indexes are courting disaster. In short, if it was worthwhile to do the interview, it will likely be worthwhile to transcribe the tapes from the interview, even though this may seem like a lot of work along the way:

WS: Much of my time these days (at the time this chapter is being written) is spent transcribing tape-recorded interviews on messianic proselytization. I can't imagine a more tedious task, especially since I have the funds to hire someone. I'm quite convinced that much is gained by doing this work myself. My recall of specific points, topics, expressions, and turns of phrase becomes much sharper. As well, I achieve an intimacy with the data which doesn't measure up as well by reading someone else's transcription.

BP: It may sound funny, but until we have other technologies available, I would very much encourage student ethnographers to take a typing course. Occasionally, one is able to secure grant money for the purposes of transcribing tapes, but there are genuine advantages to being able to transcribe your interview materials with some proficiency on your own. My own typing is quite weak and it's truly frustrating for me to sit down and type out transcripts. But I've done it and I would do it again if necessary, because I find the full transcripts are just such invaluable resources with which to work. I have been fortunate, in a number of projects, in securing research money so that I could pay someone to type tapes for me, but this still means sitting down and listening to the tapes afterwards with the transcripts in front of you. All in all, I think you're advantaged, though, if you can do the transcribing yourself.

Sometimes it is not feasible to tape-record interviews with respondents. Here, ethnographers normally take notes, which they rewrite into much more detailed forms as soon thereafter as possible, trying to preserve as much of the interchanges and conversation as possible. If note-taking is not feasible, then ethnographers typically attempt to write out as full accounts of their experiences as possible from memory as soon as they are able to do so. These notes, as well as any journal entries, are treated in manners paralleling one's tape-recorded materials, albeit with the recognition of the appropriate limitations of note-taking and recall.

People transcribing tapes (or recreating interchanges) by hand or with typewriters are encouraged to use only one side of the page and to make carbon copies or photocopies of intact transcriptions (one copy will be cut up in developing the data base). When materials are written on only one side of the page, the transcriptions can be cut up and taped together here and there. This way, people needn't spend time rewriting materials as they move pieces of information around in the process of sorting out the material and assembling the text in a more coherent fashion.

Those working on computers will likely also want to work with a hard copy that they can cut up as they begin sorting out their materials. It is very easy to miss materials (and the interconnections within) when working with screen versions. Presumably, they will save copies of their files so that they can obtain other intact copies whenever they wish, as well as incorporate quotations from their transcriptions already on the system into their analytic subfiles.

When transcribing interviews and notes, it is highly desirable to tag each piece of conversation or topic with a code that allows the researcher to identify the source when a piece of material is moved from its original context. Ethnographers generally give each interviewee a code number. It is very useful to insert this code either before or after each topic or piece of information one encounters in transcribing the interview.

Some researchers like to add other codes or comments to their materials as they type out their interviews. These codes and comments may be useful in helping the researcher later to find materials that deal with this or that topic as well as in alerting the researcher to other things one might consider in pursuing the analysis or subsequent interviews. Still, codes attached to interviews as these are being transcribed should be seen as tentative and incomplete, as well as only partially informed. Indeed, coding is seen better as an ongoing, ethnographic mapping process in which people are better able to define both the direction and significance of particular materials as one gains greater familiarity with the situation at hand.

Some ethnographers use computer programs that have been written expressly for ethnographers to code their data. Here, people typically rely on codes that they insert at the time of data entry or later do word searches of sorts in attempts to call up particular contents from the transcripts in which these words are embedded. However, word searches are only partially reliable, and codes inserted at the time the interviews were transcribed tend to be too limited for many later uses. People may insert codes in transcribed materials at later dates, but unless one is prepared to review entire manuscripts this is apt to be less than satisfactory as well. In short, while these are designed to help make interview materials more manageable, it is important to emphasize that no program will or should do your thinking for you. This is an especially important concern with respect to coding, sorting, and otherwise interpreting your field data.

As with the overall paper, researchers are apt to find it desirable to organize their field materials and data analysis around certain major and more minor themes or files (thereby creating a series of components or modules). It is desirable to recast these topics and subtopics into one's outline as one goes along, since these begin to serve as focal points for building up files. Thus, it may be instructive to review one's material several times before attempting to settle on a coding scheme and, even then, coding schemes should be reworked over time to better reflect the life-world of the other.

Our own preference is to read through and review the hard-copy field notes and transcripts in order to obtain a better sense of the various issues that are dealt with in that material. When one has a working sense (outline) of the issues, then some global sorts may be done, wherein one begins to put materials dealing with this topic in file A, materials dealing with this other topic in file B, and so forth. While some subtopics may become evident as one attempts to sort the material at that first level, the next step is to go through the material in file A seeing how this material might be sorted around any variants on that theme (i.e., A1, A2, A3, etc.). The same is done for file B and so forth. Third and subsequent sorts may be done on subfiles A1, A2, and so on. In this way, one becomes increasingly aware of, and attentive to, the complexities of the data: one becomes more aware of the range of data one has, as well as its depth, limitations, and holes. Highly detailed outlines become increasingly valuable as researchers sort out materials in this manner. Otherwise, it is very easy to become overwhelmed with the complexity of the material with which one is working.

Ethnographers have different styles of incorporating quotes or extracts into their written text, although it has become increasingly common to see author-generated text supplemented with explicit passages from interviews and field notes. Some journal editors and book publishers have sometimes been reluctant to see manuscripts "lengthened" with what they may envision as "only talk" (as opposed to tables and statistics), but this material can be extremely valuable in enabling readers to gain an appreciation of the ethnographic other. It also seems most instructive when ethnographers let the people they study talk at some length about their experiences in this and that area:

BP: When C. R. D. Sharper and I first started working on *Road Hustler*, I tried to assume much the sort of role and writing style that Ed Sutherland did in *The Professional Thief*, the book he wrote with Chic Conwell. Our book is a sequel to their work in many, many respects. However, as I wrote and rewrote the material, I became increasingly disenchanted with the copy I was producing. I had taken a fascinating life-world and was flattening it with sociological jargon. I knew that we had to keep the sociological profile because the concepts and parallels seemed very powerful, but at the same time we had to do something more than that. Essentially, we had to let Sharper speak for himself. He was very colorful and articulate. It was my job to organize the material into a book and do the sociological framing, but Sharper had to be the real star, because it was his lived experiences that we were examining. Certainly, we weren't the first to extensively use participant quotations, but as someone who hadn't been trained in Chicago-style interaction or ethnographic research, I've had to learn some of these things the hard way. All my fieldwork since has benefitted from this experience. I try to pursue interviews as fully and openly as I can and then build the text around the life-worlds that those people have shared with me, and I let them explain their viewpoints to others as much as I possibly can.

WS: Since my objective is to tell the story from the perspectives of those that I'm studying, I include numerous excerpts from our conversations in the text. Far from detracting both from the analysis or the flow, such excerpts enrich the presentation and provide it with a "life"—a quality that is often lacking in sociological reports. Moreover, the use of participants' quotations fortifies the credibility of the analysis. As I generally circulate my written work to the study's participants, some are occasionally surprised to discover that I have included their remarks verbatim. When the group studied is small, and/or where people occupy prominent positions such that their views are well known, such verbatim accounts may compromise promises of confidentiality and anonymity. Such was my experience on a few occasions, once with serious consequences. Generally, however, participants appreciate that their viewpoint is represented more than just in passing.

Beyond using interview materials and quotes to arrive at one's analytical themes, one faces the task of selecting quotes that one might use in the body of the text. In general, we prefer to work with as many quotes as we can at each point of the analysis. Some of these will likely be dropped as one goes along because they are unclearly or inadequately expressed. Other times, people's statements are mixed with other themes or highly redundant. As well, too, a number of people may have stated the same point in similar manners. In moving toward the final selections, ethnographers generally attempt to provide a wider range of styles or emphases in the extracts, albeit with the usual recognition that "one-liners" and other really short quotes tend to be the least valuable overall. Ethnographers may also encounter some practical limitations (e.g., instructor- or publisher-imposed page limits) and thus may end up deleting a great many instructive quotations from the final copy.

If ethnographers see their task as one of contextualizing the study and indicating the linkages and variations of the different themes that they've encountered in this or that life-world, then their work as writers may become more relaxed. The implication, as well, is that in organizing the study and gathering the data, sorting it out, developing analytical categories, and framing these discussions, ethnographers are essentially writing the paper. The tasks of conveying the life-worlds of the other to the reader and dialoguing with the conceptual literature are much more important than producing "entertaining prose."

A highly detailed outline can also be invaluable in writing up one's text. While one may write to the outline, the outline should also be altered as one writes in order to reflect what one is learning in the process of trying to express the issues at hand. By working in this way, researchers are also more apt to become aware of gaps in their studies, and if they are able to go back to the field, they now have some more specific matters to investigate.

Although some ethnographers like to isolate themselves from others and other materials while writing their texts, others find it very helpful to continue to read other ethnographies and discuss their research with other people (in the field, other academics, and others). Likewise, while some ethnographers are reluctant to let others read their materials until they think they have something approaching final copy, other ethnographers may find it useful to get readings of their materials along the way.

BP: When I'm working on something, I like to talk to people about it. It's on my mind, and for the most part I find everything about ethnographic research to be interesting in some respect. I've found talking with other people very helpful, overall. Sometimes, people make very good suggestions or ask you about things you hadn't thought of: "Well, that's a good point! Very interesting! I'll have to find out more about that." Likewise, while I've received many good suggestions from my colleagues and other sociologists, I've found it helpful to talk with almost anyone who's been willing to talk to me about the topic. Sometimes, too, you find ways of expressing your thoughts on paper just by attempting to explain things to other people. Often, as you're struggling to express something, things will become more crystalline in your mind. . . . I also find it helpful to read new ethnographies and reexamine earlier ones, especially ones with some sort of conceptual, processual thrust, while I'm working on the analysis. If it's something that's parallel to what you're working with, that can be really, really helpful because someone might have already developed a term or a concept that fits with the material on which you're working.

WS: To the extent that it's possible, I circulate drafts of my work to selected respondents—those who have expressed an interest in reading it or those whose advice and criticisms I consider would be helpful. These are usually the same people. Jack Haas and I regularly distributed drafts of our material to medical students, and I pursued this practice in my study with Pawluch et al. of a distinctively organized undergraduate program. Not only were the students appreciative of this gesture, but their feedback helped to assure us that the analysis we were evolving was credible. So both they and we benefitted from the exchange. Quite interestingly, but not surprisingly, in both cases the administrators who saw our work were displeased with it, which contrasted sharply with the students' more favorable evaluations. I've also sent drafts of my work to hasidic Jews. As they are generally suspicious of outsiders, I conceived of the gesture as a disarming device. In fact, it always turns out to be much more than that. Some have offered incisive comments about where my material doesn't adequately represent their viewpoint, and factual errors have been quickly brought to my attention. I correct the latter and meet to discuss their concerns over the former. This approach works for me, but may not be appropriate for everyone.

Another important aspect of generating ethnographic text is to stay composed. Ethnographers often find themselves feeling overwhelmed by the complexity of the social world of the other. Here, patience and perseverance are major advantages. It is important to be thorough and careful, but ethnographers should be prepared to deal with considerable ambiguity. Likewise, if people can keep active and continue to work away at this or that aspect of the larger project, it will eventually take shape. When one encounters difficulty with one aspect of the analysis, it may be wise to move on to another area and do some work there before resuming the earlier task. Researchers may also find it helpful to discuss problem areas with others, because even if they are not able to help directly, the dialogue they provide may be useful in other ways.

When developing ethnographic text, it is usually advisable to write (or rewrite) one's introduction to the paper after the analysis, and often after the conclusion has been written. At least this way, one has a better sense of what exactly is being introduced. In general terms, as well, ethnographers tend to rewrite their manuscripts, often several times, as they struggle for statements that are both stronger conceptually and that better represent the life-world of the ethnographic other for the reader:

WS: I find that discipline is the key to writing. Before I begin writing a paper, I have usually spent some time thinking about the argument I'll present and the possible ways in which the material could be organized. I then commit myself to writing between one or two pages each day. This is my self-imposed limit. This daily task is sometimes completed quickly, but can also take several hours. My goal must be met by the day's end. Writing doesn't come easily for me, and I find that this approach minimizes the struggle. The important thing is to complete a draft of the work which I then leave for several days before beginning the arduous process of revision.

BP: This may sound funny, but I really have no idea how many times I rewrite materials. I write in modules, and while some modules or parts of them flow fairly easily, I genuinely struggle with other parts. I don't worry about how many times I've rewritten something. I generally don't even think about that. I'm much more inclined to put some ideas out on a page with the intention that I will keep working them over until I can put them in the sort of shape I would like. Doing an ethnography is not like writing a letter or something of that sort. It's very, very different, I think in part because you're trying to find a way of expressing in a very balanced and hopefully comprehensible manner some very complex understandings and processes.

Writing for the Other

Although this discussion of writing for the other has been left to the last, it should be appreciated that the purpose of an ethnography is to communicate an understanding of the life-world of the ethnographic other to some third-party reader or audience. Thus, while the researcher-author assumes the tasks of accessing, comprehending, conceptualizing, and representing the ethnographic other, ethnographies are developed for third-party audiences. Despite all the ambiguities besetting researchers in the field, the task of writing for the other is apt to be one of the realms in which researchers experience the most ambiguity.

First, with the exception of those ethnographic inquiries that are conducted with a specific reader in mind (e.g., funding agency, instructor), ethnographers may only have a vague idea of who may end up reading the materials they generate. Most ethnographies are written for what at best may be a vaguely defined audience. As well, ethnographers cannot be certain just how third parties will attend to their work even when they have been able to target specific readers. However, since they provide the major conduit between the ethnographic and third-party other, ethnographers have an obligation to maintain the integrity of the ethnographic other while attempting to express these viewpoints and practices in manners that third-party audiences not only find comprehensible but on whose part it invokes empathetic or shared experiences.

The task of communicating images of the ethnographic other to third parties is compounded in part by the differing stocks of knowledge, levels of empathetic understanding, and constellations of interests with which third parties approach ethnographic texts. As well, beyond attempts to foster more widely generalized understandings of the ethnographic other, researchers may use ethnographic inquiry to develop better understandings of the generalized other. While some readers may wish to focus more exclusively on the immediate ethnographic other, the introduction of more abstract concepts or processes allows the researcher to communicate with and tie the immediate project into a body of materials produced by people studying the ethnographic other in other settings:

BP: As an ethnographer you encounter a great deal of uncertainty. Even when you think that you have a research site or good contacts, you never know just how you will be received by this or that person or group of people in the field. Likewise, you can't be sure if you will be able to develop an adequately detailed and appreciative understanding of the viewpoints and practices of the other. As well, you have the problem of conceptualizing the information you encounter in the field with the literature and indicating just what the implications of the material you've collected are for the literature, and vice versa. But you are also writing for a community of scholars, and although you might dialogue with some of these people along the way, you never know just how they will view the material you've produced. . . . Minimally, though, I think one should be attentive to the matter of "respecting the ethnographic other," of trying to achieve an intimate appreciation of the life-world of the other and of trying to convey this in a careful, thorough manner that reflects the viewpoint of the other to third-party readers. If you can do these things, then I think you've given the community something very worthwhile, something very precious! An ethnography like that is something that we can use as a foundation piece in pursuing a social science that is genuinely attentive to the human condition.

Endnotes:

1. For some other statements that address the writing of ethnographic text as a matter of practical accomplishment, see Spradley (1972, 1980), Wolcott (1990), and Emerson et al. (1995).

2. See Karsh et al's (1953) discussion of the tactics of a union organizer for an instructive case-study of a particular work setting.

3. Cressey's (1932) analysis of taxi-dance halls and Sutherland's (1950) depiction of the emergence of sexual psychopath legislation represent two valuable illustrations of a multiple-case, natural history approach to the study of community life. For conceptual material that could be applied to natural history approaches to the study of deviance, see Blumer's (1971) portrayal of social problems as collective behavior and the statement on defining propriety (and deviance) in chapter 5.

4. For an instructive statement on the importance of process versus typologies of people, see Gibbons's (1975) reflections on his own typologies of criminals and delinquents.

References

Adler, Patricia. 1985. *Wheeling and Dealing.* New York: Columbia University Press.

Adler, Patricia, and Peter Adler. 1978. "Tinydopers: A Case Study of Deviant Socialization." *Symbolic Interaction* 1 (2): 90–105.

———. 1980. "The Irony of Secrecy in the Drug World." *Urban Life* 8 (4): 447–465.

———. 1983a. "Relationships Between Dealers: The Social Organization of Illicit Drug Transactions." *Sociology and Social Research* 67: 260–278

———. 1983b. "Shifts and Oscillation in Deviant Careers: The Case of Upper-Level Dealers and Smugglers." *Social Problems* 31: 195–207.

———. 1991. *Backboards and Blackboards: College Athletes and Role Engulfment.* New York: Columbia University Press.

———. 1994. "Social Reproduction and the Corporate Other: The Institutionalization of Afterschool Activities." *Sociological Quarterly* 35 (2): 309–328.

Albas, Daniel, and Cheryl Albas. 1984. *Student Life and Exams.* Dubuque, IA: Kendall/Hunt.

———. 1988. "Aces and Bombers: The Post-Exam Impression Management Strategies of Students." *Symbolic Interaction* 11 (2): 289–302.

———. 1994. "Studying Students Studying." Pp. 273–289 in Mary Lorenz Dietz, Robert Prus, and William Shaffir (eds.), *Doing Everyday Life: Ethnography as Human Lived Experience.* Toronto: Copp Clark Longman.

Alley, Kelly D. 1994. "Ganga and Gandagi: Interpretations of Pollution and Waste in Benaras." *Ethnology* 33 (2): 127–45.

Altheide, David L. 1974. *Creating Reality: How TV News Distorts Events.* Beverly Hills: Sage.

———. 1985. *Media Power.* Beverly Hills: Sage.

Altheide, David L., and John M. Johnson. 1980. *Bureaucratic Propaganda.* Boston: Allyn and Bacon.

Altheide, David L., and Erdwin H. Pfuhl Jr. 1980. "Self-Accomplishment Through Running." *Symbolic Interaction* 3 (2): 127–142.

Altheide, David L., and Robert P. Snow. 1979. *Media Logic.* Beverly Hills: Sage.

Anderson, Elijah. 1976. *A Place on the Corner.* Chicago: University of Chicago Press.

Anderson, Nels. 1923. *The Hobo.* Chicago: University of Chicago Press.

Andrews, Florence Kellner. 1983. "A Case Study of Two Types of Officer-Inmate Interaction in a Correctional Establishment." *Symbolic Interaction* 6 (1): 51–68.

Applbaum, Kalman D. 1995. "Marriage with the Proper Stranger: Arranged Marriage in Metropolitan Japan." *Ethnology* 34 (1): 37–51.

Applebaum, Herbert A. 1981. *Royal Blue: The Culture of Construction Workers.* New York: Holt, Rinehart and Winston.

Arluke, Arnold. 1991. "Going into the Closet with Science: Information Control Among Animal Experimenters." *Journal of Contemporary Ethnography* 20 (3): 306–330.

———. 1994. " 'We Build a Better Beagle': Fantastic Creatures in Lab Animal Ads." *Qualitative Sociology* 17 (2): 143–158.

Arnold, David O. 1970. *The Sociology of Subcultures.* Berkeley, CA: Glendessary Press.

Arnold, William R. 1970. *Juveniles on Parole.* New York: Random House.

Aschenbrenner, Joyce. 1975. *Lifelines: Black Families in Chicago.* New York: Holt, Rinehart and Winston (Reprint, 1983) Prospect Heights, IL: Waveland.

Asher, Ramona M. 1992. *Women with Alcoholic Husbands: Ambivalence and the Trap of Codependency.* Chapel Hill: University of North Carolina Press.

Athens, Lonnie H. 1974. "The Self and the Violent Criminal Act." *Urban Life* 13 (1): 98–112.

———. 1977. "Violent Crime: A Symbolic Interactionist Study." *Symbolic Interaction* 1 (1): 56–70.

———. 1980. *Violent Criminal Acts and Actors: A Symbolic Interactionist Study.* Boston: Oxford University Press.

Atkinson, J. Maxwell. 1971. "Societal Reactions to Suicide: The Role of Coroner's Definitions." Pp. 165–191 in Stanley Cohen (ed.), *Images of Deviance.* Baltimore: Penguin.

Atkinson, Michael. 1995. "Toeing the Party Line: An Ethnographic Study of Political Parties and the Political Process as Human Lived Experience." Paper presented at the Qualitative and Ethnographic Research Conference. McMaster University, Hamilton, Ontario.

Barley, Stephen R., and Beth A. Bechky. 1994. "In the Backrooms of Science: The Work of Technicians in Science Labs." *Work and Occupations* 21 (1): 85–126.

Barnes, Barry. 1974. *Scientific Knowledge and Social Theory*. London: Routledge and Kegan Paul.

Barnes, Barry, and David Edge. 1982. *Science in Context: Readings in the Sociology of Science*. Cambridge, Mass.: MIT Press.

Baroody-Hart, Cynthia, and Michael P. Farrell. 1987. "The Subculture of Serious Artists in a Maximum Security Prison." *Urban Life* 15 (3–4): 421–448.

Barth, Fredrik. 1992. "Toward Greater Naturalism in Conceptualizing Societies." Pp. 17–33 in Adam Kuper (ed.), *Conceptualizing Society*. New York: Routledge.

Bartell, Gilbert. 1971. *Group Sex*. New York: Signet.

Bass, Jay. 1983. "Dunners and Defaulters: Collectors' Work as a Context for Naming." *Urban Life* 12 (1): 49–73.

Baumann, Eleen. 1991. "Negotiating Respectability in Ambigous Commerce: Selling Sex Paraphenalia at Home Parties." *Canadian Review of Sociology and Anthropology* 28:377–392.

Beach, Betty. 1989. *Integrating Work and Family Life: The Home-Working Family*. Albany: State University of New York Press.

Becker, Howard S. 1963. *Outsiders*. New York: Free Press.

———. 1966. "Introduction." Pp. v–xviii in Clifford Shaw, *The Jack-Roller*. Chicago: University of Chicago Press.

———. 1967. "Social Bases of Drug Induced Experiences." *Journal of Health and Social Behavior* 8:163–76.

———. 1970. *Sociological Work: Method and Substance*. Chicago: Aldine.

———. 1982. *Art Worlds*. Berkeley: University of California Press.

———. 1995. "The Power of Inertia." *Qualitative Sociology* 18:301–309.

Becker, Howard S., Blanche Geer, David Reisman, and Robert Weiss. 1968. *Institutions and the Person*. Chicago: Aldine.

Becker, Howard, Everett Hughes, and Blanche Geer. 1968. *Making the Grade: The Academic Side of Student Life*. New York: Wiley.

Becker, Howard, Everett Hughes, Blanche Geer, and Anselm Strauss. 1961. *The Boys in White*. Chicago: University of Chicago Press.

Belk, Russell. 1988. "Possessions and the Extended Self." *Journal of Consumer Research* 15:139–168.

Bensmen, Joseph, and Israel Gerver. 1963. "Crime and Punishment in the Factory: The Function of Deviancy in Maintaining the Social System." *American Sociological Review* 28:588–598.

Berger, Peter, and Thomas Luckmann. 1966. *The Social Construction of Reality*. New York: Anchor.

Bernstein, Stan. 1972. "Getting it Done: Notes on Student Fritters." *Urban Life and Culture* 2:275–292.

Best, Joel. 1986. "Famous for Fifteen Minutes: Notes on the Researcher as Newsmaker." *Qualitative Sociology* 9 (4): 372–382.

———. 1989. *Images of Issues: Typifying Contemporary Social Problems.* New York: Aldine de Gruyter.

———. 1990. *Threatened Children: Rhetoric and Concerns.* Chicago: University of Chicago Press.

———. 1995. "Lost in the Ozone Again: The Postmodernist Fad and Interactionist Foibles." Pp. 125–130 in Norman K. Denzin (ed.), *Studies in Symbolic Interaction* 17. Greenwich, CT: JAI.

Biernacki, Patrick. 1988. *Pathways from Heroin Addiction: Recovery without Treatment.* Phildelphia: Temple University Press.

Bigus, Odis E. 1972. "The Milkman and His Customer: A Cultivated Relationship." *Urban Life and Culture* 1:131–165.

Bittner, Egon. 1967. "The Police on Skid Row: A Study of Peace Keeping." *American Sociological Review* 32:699–715.

Bjorklund, Diane. 1985. "Dignified Joking: Humor and Demeanor in a Public Speaking Club." *Symbolic Interaction* 8 (1): 33–46.

Blake, Joseph A. 1974. "Occupational Thrill, Mystique and the Truck Driver." *Urban Life and Culture* 3 (2): 205–220.

Bloor, Michael J. 1985. "Observations of Abortive Illness Behavior." *Urban Life* 14 (3): 300–316.

Blum, Nancy S. 1991. "The Management of Stigma by Alzheimer Family Caregivers." *Journal of Contemporary Ethnography* 20 (3): 263–284.

Blumberg, Abraham. 1967. "The Practice of Law as a Confidence Game: Organizational Cooptation of a Profession." *Law and Society Review* 1:15–39.

Blumer, Herbert. 1928. "Method in Social Psychology." Doctoral dissertation. University of Chicago.

———. 1931. "Science Without Concepts." *American Journal of Sociology* 36:515–533.

———. 1933. *Movies and Conduct.* New York: Macmillan. (Reprint 1970, New York: Arno).

———. 1939. *Critiques of Research in the Social Sciences: An Appraisal of Thomas and Znaniecki's The Polish Peasant in Europe and America.* New York: Social Science Research Council, Bulletin 44.

———. 1969. *Symbolic Interactionism.* Englewood Cliffs, NJ: Prentice-Hall. (Reprint, 1986, Berkeley: University of California Press).

———. 1971. "Social Problems as Collective Behavior." *Social Problems* 18:298–306.

Blumer, Herbert, and Hauser, Philip. 1933. *Movies, Delinquency and Crime.* New York: Macmillan. (Reprint 1970. New York: Arno Press).

Bogdan, Robert, and Stephen J. Taylor. 1975. *Introduction to Qualitative Research Methods.* New York: Wiley.

Broadhead, Robert S. 1980a. "Individuation in Facework: Theoretical Implications from a Study of Facework in Medical School Admissions." *Symbolic Interaction* 3 (2): 51–68.

———. 1980b. "Qualitative Analysis In Evaluation Research: Problems and Promises of an Interactionist Approach." *Qualitative Analysis* 3 (1): 23–40.

Broadhead, Robert S., and Kathryn J. Fox. 1990. "Takin' It to the Streets: AIDS Outreach as Ethnography." *Journal of Contemporary Ethnography* 19 (3): 322–348.

Brooks, Nancy A., and Ronald R. Matson. 1987. "Managing Multiple Sclerosis." *Research in the Sociology of Health Care* 6:73–106.

Burman, Patrick. 1988. *Killing Time, Losing Ground: Experiences of Unemployment.* Toronto: Wall and Thompson.

Cahill, Spencer E. 1980. "Directions for an Interactionist Study of Gender Development." *Symbolic Interaction* 3 (1): 123–138.

———. 1989. "Fashioning Males and Females: Appearance Management and the Social Reproduction of Gender." *Symbolic Interaction* 12 (2): 281–298.

———. 1995. "Some Rhetorical Directions of Funeral Direction: Historical Entanglements and Contemporary Dilemmas." *Work and Occupations* 22 (2): 115–136.

Cain, Roy. 1994. "Managing Impressions of an AIDS Service Organization: Into the Mainstream or Out of the Closet?" *Qualitative Sociology* 17 (1): 43–61.

Calkins, Kathy (Charmaz). 1970. "Time: Perspectives, Marking and Styles of Usage." *Social Problems* 17: 487–501.

Caplow, Theodore, and Reese J. McGee. 1958. *The Academic Marketplace.* New York: Science Editions.

Cavan, Sherri. 1966. *Liquor Licence: An Ethnography of Bar Behavior.* Chicago: Aldine.

Chagnon, Napoleon A. 1992. *Yanomano.* New York: Harcourt Brace Jovanovich.

Charlton, Joy, and Rosanna Hertz. 1989. "Guarding Against Boredom: Security Specialists in the U.S. Air Force." *Journal of Contemporary Ethnography* 18 (3): 299–326.

Charmaz, Kathy Calkins. 1975. "The Coroner's Strategies for Announcing Death." *Urban Life* 4 (3): 296–316.

————. 1983. "The Grounded Theory Method: An Explication and Interpretation." Pp. 109–126 in Robert M. Emerson (ed.), *Contemporary Field Research: A Collection of Readings.* Prospect Heights, IL: Waveland.

————. 1991. *Good Days and Bad Days: The Self In Chronic Illness.* New Brunswick: Rutgers University Press.

————. 1994. "Identity Dilemmas of Chronically Ill Men." *The Sociological Quarterly* 35 (2): 269–288.

————. 1995. "Between Positivism and Postmodernism: Implications for Methods." Pp. 43–72 in Norman K. Denzin (ed.), *Studies in Symbolic Interaction* 17. Greenwich, CT: JAI.

Charon, Joel. 1979. *Symbolic Interactionism.* Englewood Cliffs, NJ: Prentice-Hall.

Chayko, Mary. 1993. "What is Real in the Age of Virtual Reality? 'Reframing' Frame Analysis for a Technological World." *Symbolic Interaction* 16:171–181.

Chester, Tina Westlake. 1995. "The Processes and Problematics of Coordinating Events: Planning the Wedding Reception." Paper presented at the Qualitative and Ethnographic Research Conference. McMaster University, Hamilton, Ontario.

Christopherson, Richard W. 1974. "From Folk Art To Fine Art: A Transformation in the Meaning of Photographic Work." *Urban Life and Culture* 3 (2): 123–157.

Clark, Colin, and Trevor Pinch. 1995. *The Hard Sell: The Language and Lessons of Street-wise Marketing.* London, GB: Harper Collins.

Clarke, Adele, and Joan H. Fujimara. 1992. *The Right Tools for the Job: At Work in Twentieth Century Life Sciences.* Princeton: Princeton University Press.

Clarke, Adele, and Elihu Gerson. 1990. "Symbolic Interactionism in Social Studies of Science." Pp. 179–214 in Howard Becker and Michal McCall (eds.), *Symbolic Interactionism and Cultural Studies.* Chicago: University of Chicago Press.

Cockerham, William C. 1979. "Green Berets and the Symbolic Meaning of Heroism." *Urban Life* 8 (1): 94–113.

Cohen, Rina. 1991. "Women of Color in White Households: Coping Strategies of Live-in Domestic Workers." *Qualitative Sociology* 14 (2): 197–215.

Coleman, Ronald V. 1976. "Court Control and Grievance Accounts: Dynamics of Traffic Court Interactions." *Urban Life* 5 (2): 165–188.

Collins, Harry, and Trevor Pinch. 1982. *Frames of Meaning: The Social Construction of an Extraordinary Science.* London: Routledge and Kegan Paul.

———. 1993. *The Golem: What Everyone Should Know about Science.* Cambridge: Cambridge University Press.

Cooley, Charles Horton. 1922. *Human Nature and the Social Order* (Second edition). (Reprint, 1964) New York: Shocken.

Coombs, Robert H. and Pauline S. Powers. 1975. "Socialization for Death: The Physician's Role." *Urban Life* 4 (3):250–271.

Conner, Walter D. 1972. "The Manufacture of Deviance: The Case of the Soviet Purge, 1936–1938." *American Sociological Review* 37:403–413.

Conrad, Peter, and Joseph W. Schneider. 1980. *Deviance and Medicalization: From Badness to Sickness.* St. Louis: Mosby.

Correll, Shelley. 1995. "The Ethnography of an Electronic Bar: The Lesbian Cafe." *Journal of Contemporary Ethnography* 24 (3): 270–298.

Couch, Carl. 1968. "Collective Behavior: An Examination of Some Stereotypes." *Social Problems* 15:310–322.

———. 1975. "Obdurate Features of Group Life." Pp. 237–254 in C.J. Couch and R. Hintz (eds.) *Constructing Social Life: Readings in Behavioral Sociology from the Iowa School.* Champaign, IL: Stipes.

———. 1984. "Symbolic Interaction and Generic Sociological Principles." *Symbolic Interaction* 7:1–14.

———. 1989. "From Hell to Utopia and Back to Hell: Charismatic Relationships." *Symbolic Interaction* 12:265–279.

Counts, Dorothy Ayers, and David R. Counts. 1992. " 'They're My Family Now': The Creation of Community among RVers." *Anthropologica* 34:153–182.

———. n.d. *Over the Next Hill: An Ethnography of RVing Seniors in North America.* Peterborough, Ontario: Broadview (in press).

Cressey, Donald. 1953. *Other People's Money: A Study in the Social Psychology of Embezzlement.* Glencoe, IL: Free Press.

Cressey, Paul G. 1932. *The Taxi-Dance Hall.* Chicago: University of Chicago Press.

Daly, Kerry. 1988. "Reshaped Parenthood Identity: The Transition to Adoptive Parenthood." *Journal of Contemporary Ethnography* 17 (1): 10–66.

———. 1992. "Toward a Formal theory of Interactive Resocialization: The Case of Adoptive Parenthood." *Qualitative Sociology* 15 (4): 395–417.

Daniels, Arlene Kaplan. 1970. "The Social Construction of Military Diagnoses." Pp. 181–208 in H.P. Dreitzel (ed.), *Recent Sociology* 2. New York: Macmillan.

————. 1988. *Invisible Careers: Women Civic Leaders from the Volunteer World*. Chicago: University of Chicago Press.

Darling, Jon. 1977. "Bachelorhood and Late Marriage: An Interactionist Interpretation." *Symbolic Interaction* 1 (1): 44–55.

Darrough, William D. 1984. "In the Best Interest of the Child: Negotiating Parental Cooperation for Probation Placement." *Urban Life* 13 (2–3): 123–153.

Davis, Fred. 1959. "The Cabdriver and His Fare: Facets of a Fleeting Relationship." *American Journal of Sociology* 65:158–165.

————. 1961. "Deviance Disavowal: The Management of Strained Interaction by the Visibly Handicapped." *Social Problems* 9 (2): 120–132.

————. 1963. *Passage through Crisis*. Indianapolis: Bobbs-Merrill.

————. 1968. "Professional Socialization as Subjective Experience: The Process of Doctrinal Conversion among Student Nurses." Pp. 235–251 in Howard S. Becker et al., (eds.), *Institution and the Person: Papers Presented to Everett C. Hughes*. Chicago: Aldine.

————. 1992. *Fashion, Culture and Identity*. Chicago: University of Chicago Press.

Davis, Fred, and Virginia L. Olesen. 1963. "Initiation into a Women's Profession: Identity Problems in the Status Transition of Coed to Student Nurse." *Sociometry* 26 (1): 89–101.

Davis, Phillip W. 1983. "Restoring the Semblance of Order: Police Strategies in the Domestic Disturbance." *Symbolic Interaction* 6 (2): 261–278.

Davis, Phillip W., and Pamela McKenzie-Rundle. 1984. "The Social Organization of Lie-Detector Tests." *Urban Life* 13 (2–3): 177–205.

Dawson, Lorne and Robert Prus. 1993a. "Interactionist Ethnography and Postmodernist Discourse: Affinities and Disjunctures in Approaching Human Lived Experiences." Pp. 147–177 in Norman K. Denzin (ed.), *Studies in Symbolic Interaction* 15. Greenwich, CT: JAI.

————. 1993b. "Human Enterprise, Intersubjectivity, and the Ethnographic Other: A Reply to Denzin and Fontana." Pp. 193–200 in Norman K. Denzin (ed.), *Studies in Symbolic Interaction* 15. Greenwich, CT: JAI.

————. 1995. "Postmodernism and Linguistic Reality Versus Symbolic Interactionism and Obdurate Reality." Pp. 105–124 in Norman K. Denzin (ed.), *Studies in Symbolic Interaction* 17. Greenwich, CT: JAI.

Denzin, Norman K., and Yvonna S. Lincoln. 1994. *Handbook of Qualitative Research*. Thousand Oaks, CA: Sage.

Derrida, Jacques. 1976. *Of Grammatology.* Translated by G. Spivak. Baltimore, Md.: John Hopkins University Press.

———. 1978. *Writing and Difference.* Translated by A. Bass. London: Routledge and Kegan Paul.

Desroches, Frederick J. 1995. *Force and Fear: Robbery in Canada.* Toronto, Ontario: Nelson.

Diamond, Timothy. 1992. *Making Gray Gold: Narratives of Nursing Home Care.* Chicago: University of Chicago Press.

Dietz, Mary Lorenz. 1983. *Killing for Profit: The Social Organization of Felony Homicide.* Chicago: Nelson-Hall.

———. 1994a. "On Your Toes: Dancing Your Way into the Ballet World." Pp. 66–84 in Mary Lorenz Dietz, Robert Prus, and William Shaffir (eds.), *Doing Everyday Life: Ethnography as Human Lived Experience.* Toronto: Copp Clark Longman.

———. 1994b. "He's a Lumberjack and He's Not Okay: The Fall of the Urban Treeman." Pp. 377–397 in Nancy Herman and Larry Reynolds (eds.), *Symbolic Interaction: An Introduction to Social Psychology.* Dix Hills, NY: General Hall.

Dietz, Mary Lorenz, and Michael Cooper. 1994. "Being Recruited: The Experiences of 'Blue Chip' High School Athletes." Pp. 109–125 in Mary Lorenz Dietz, Robert Prus, and William Shaffir (eds.), *Doing Everyday Life: Ethnography as Human Lived Experience.* Toronto: Copp Clark Longman.

Dietz, Mary Lorenz, Robert Prus and William Shaffir. 1994. *Doing Everyday Life: Ethnography as Human Lived Experience.* Toronto: Copp Clark Longman.

Dingwall, Robert. 1987. "The Certification of Competence: Assessment in Occupational Socialization." *Urban Life* 15 (3–4): 367–393.

Ditton, James. 1977. *Part-Time Crime: An Ethnography of Fiddling and Pilferage.* London: Macmillan.

Donnelly, Peter. 1994. "Take My Word for It: Trust in the Context of Birding and Mountaineering." *Qualitative Sociology* 17 (3): 215–241.

Donner, William W. 1994. "Alcohol, Community, and Modernity: The Social Organization of Toddy Drinking in a Polynesian Society." *Ethnology* 33 (3): 245–60.

Donovan, Francis. 1920. *The Woman Who Waits.* Boston: Gorham. (Reprint 1974, New York: Arno.)

———. 1929. *The Saleslady.* Chicago: University of Chicago Press.

———. 1939. *The Schoolma'am.* New York: Stokes. (Reprint 1974, New York: Arno.)

Dordick, Gwendolyn A. 1996. "More than Refuge: The Social World of a Homeless Shelter." *Journal of Contemporary Ethnography* 24 (4): 373–404.

Douglas, Jack. 1967. *The Social Meanings of Suicide*. Princeton: Princeton University Press.

———. 1976. *Investigative Social Research*. Beverly Hills: Sage.

Dubin, Steven C. 1985. "The Politics of Public Art." *Urban Life* 14 (3): 274–299.

Eayrs, Michele A. 1993. "Time, Trust and Hazard: Hairdressers' Symbolic Roles." *Symbolic Interaction* 16 (1): 19–37.

Ebaugh, Helen Rose. 1988. *Becoming an EX: The Process of Role Exit*. Chicago: University of Chicago Press.

Edgerton, Robert. 1967. *The Cloak of Competence: Stigma in the Lives of the Mentally Retarded*. Berkeley: University of California Press.

Einstadter, Werner J. 1969. "The Social Organization of Armed Robbery." *Social Problems* 17:64–83.

Emerson, Joan. 1970. "Behavior in Private Places: Sustaining Definitions of Reality in Gynecological Examinations." Pp. 74–97 in Hans Peter Dreitzel (ed.) *Recent Sociology* 2. New York: Macmillan.

Emerson, Robert M. 1969. *Judging Delinquents*. Chicago: Aldine.

———. 1981. "On Last Resorts." *American Journal of Sociology* 87:1–22.

Emerson, Robert M., and Sheldon L. Messinger. 1977. "The Micro-Politics of Trouble" *Social Problems* 25:121–134.

Emerson, Robert M., E. Burke Rochford Jr., and Linda L. Shaw. 1983. "The Micropolitics of Trouble in a Psychiatric Board and Care Facility." *Urban Life* 12 (3): 349–367.

Emerson, Robert M., Rachel I. Fretz, and Linda L. Shaw. 1995. *Writing Ethnographic Fieldnotes*. Chicago: University of Chicago Press.

Engbersen, Godfried, Kees Schuyt, Jaap Timmer, and Frans Van Waareden. 1993. *Cultures of Unemployment: A Comparative Look at Long-Term Unemployment and Urban Poverty*. Boulder, CO: Westview Press.

Ermarth, Michael. 1978. *Wilhelm Dilthey: The Critique of Historical Reason*. Chicago: University of Chicago Press.

Estes, Caroll, and Beverly Edmunds. 1981. "Symbolic Interaction and Social Policy Analysis." *Symbolic Interaction* 4:75–86.

Evans, A. Donald. 1987. "Institutionally Developed Identities: An Ethnographic Account of Reality Construction in a Residential School for the Deaf." Pp. 161–184 in *Sociological Studies of Child Development*. Greenwich, CT: JAI.

———. 1988. "Strange Bedfellows: Deafness, Language and the Sociology of Knowledge." *Symbolic Interaction* 11:235–255.

———. 1994. "Socialization into Deafness." Pp. 129–142 in Mary Lorenz Dietz, Robert Prus, and William Shaffir (eds.), *Doing*

Everyday Life: Ethnography as Human Lived Experience. Toronto: Copp Clark Longman.

Evans, Donald, and W.W. Falk. 1986. *Learning to be Deaf.* Berlin: De Gruyter.

Faulkner, Robert R. 1971. *Hollywood Studio Musicians: Their Work and Careers in the Recording Industry.* Chicago: Aldine-Atheron.

———. 1976. "Dilemmas in Commercial Work: Hollywood Film Composers and Their Clients." *Urban Life* 5 (1): 3–32.

Faulkner, Robert R., and Douglas B. McGaw. 1977. "Uneasy Homecoming: Stages in the Reentry Transition of Vietnam Veterans." *Urban Life* 6 (3): 303–328.

Faupel, Charles E. 1987. "Heroin Use and Criminal Careers." *Qualitative Sociology* 10 (2): 115–131.

———. 1991. *Shooting Dope: Career Patterns of Hard-Core Heroin Users.* Gainesville: University of Florida Press.

Festinger, Leon, Henry Riecken, and Stanley Schacter. 1956. *When Prophecy Fails.* New York: Harper and Row.

Fields, Allen B. 1984. " 'Slinging Weed:' The Social Organization of Streetcorner Marijuana Sales." *Urban Life* 13 (2–3): 247–270.

Fine, Gary Alan. 1983. *Shared Fantasy: Role Playing Games as Social Worlds.* Chicago: University of Chicago Press.

———. 1985. "Occupational Aesthetics: How Trade School Students Learn to Cook." *Urban Life* 14 (1): 3–31.

———. 1987. *With the Boys: Little League Baseball and Preadolescent Culture.* Chicago: University of Chicago Press.

———. 1996. *Kitchens: The Culture of Restaurant Work.* Berkeley: University of California Press.

Fine, Gary A., and Sherryl Kleinman. 1979. "Rethinking Subculture: An Interactionist Analysis." *American Journal of Sociology* 85:1–20.

Fishman, Laura T. 1990. *Woman at the Wall: A Study of Prisoners' Wives Doing Time on the Outside.* Albany: State University of New York Press.

Florez, Carl P., and George L. Kelling. 1984. "The Hired Hand and the Lone Wolf: Issues in the Use of Observers in Large-Scale Program Evaluation." *Urban Life* 12 (4): 423–443.

Foucault, Michel. 1967. *Madness and Civilizations.* London: Tavistock.

———. 1970. *The Order of Things.* London: Tavistock.

———. 1972. *The Archaeology of Knowledge.* London: Tavistock.

———. 1977. *Discipline and Punish.* New York: Vintage.

Frazer, Charles, and Leonard N. Reid. 1979. "Children's Interaction With Commercials." *Symbolic Interaction* 2 (2): 79–96.

Freidson, E. 1961. *Patients' Views of Medical Practice.* New York: Russell Sage.

———. 1970a. *Profession of Medicine.* New York: Harper and Row.

———. 1970b. *Professional Dominance.* Chicago: Aldine.

———. 1975. *Doctoring Together.* New York: Elsevier.

———. 1986. *Professional Powers.* Chicago: University of Chicago Press.

Friedman, Norman L. 1990. "The Hollywood Actor: Occupational Culture, Career, and Adaptation in a Buyers' Market Industry." *Current Research on Occupations and Professions* 5:73–89.

Friedman, Raymond A. 1994. *Front Stage, Backstage: The Dramatic Structure of Labor Negotiations.* Cambridge: The MIT Press.

Gaines, Charles, and George Butler. 1974. *Pumping Iron: The Art and Sport of Bodybuilding.* New York: Simon and Schuster.

Gamst, Frederic C. 1980. *The Hoghead: An Industrial Ethnology of the Railroad Engineer.* New York: Rinehart and Winston.

Gardner, Carol Brooks. 1986. "Public Aid." *Urban Life* 15 (1): 37–69.

Gardner, Peter M. 1993. "Dimensions of Subsistence Foraging in South India." *Ethnology* 32:109–144.

Garfinkel, Harold. 1956. "Conditions of Successful Degradation Ceremonies." *American Journal of Sociology* 61:420–424.

———. 1967. *Studies in Ethnomethodology.* Englewood Cliffs, NJ: PrenticeHall.

Garey, Anita Ilta. 1995. "Constructing Motherhood on the Night Shift: 'Working Mothers' as 'Stay-at-Home Moms.'" *Qualitative Sociology* 18 (4): 415–437.

Gerstel, Naomi. 1987. "Divorce and Stigma." *Social Problems* 34 (2): 172–186.

Ghidina, Marcia J. 1992. "Social Relations and the Definition of Work: Identity Management in a Low-Status Occupation." *Qualitative Sociology* 15 (1): 73–85.

Gibbon, Heather M. Fita. 1987. "From Prints to Posters: The Production of Artistic Value in a Popular Art World." *Symbolic Interaction* 10 (1): 111–128.

Gibbons, Donald. 1975. "Offender Typologies—Two Decades Later." *British Journal of Sociology* 15:140–156.

Gilderbloom, John I. 1985. "Social Factors Affecting Landlords in the Determination of Rent." *Urban Life* 14 (2): 155–179.

Gilmore, Samuel. 1987. "Coordination and Convention: The Organization of the Concert World." *Symbolic Interaction* 10 (2): 209–227.

Glaser, Barney, and Anselm Strauss. 1965. *Awareness of Dying.* Chicago: Aldine.

———. 1967. *The Discovery of Grounded Theory: Strategies for Qualitative Research.* Chicago: Aldine.

Goffman, Erving. 1959. *The Presentation of Self in Everyday Life.* New York: Anchor.

———. 1961. *Asylums.* New York: Anchor.

———. 1963. *Stigma.* Englewood Cliffs, NJ: Spectrum.

Gold, Steve. 1994. "Israeli Immigrants in the United States: The Question of Community." *Qualitative Sociology* 17 (4): 325–363.

Goldstein, Michael S., Dennis T. Jaffe, Dale Garell, and Ruth Ellen Berke. 1985. "Holistic Doctors: Becoming a Nontraditional Medical Practitioner." *Urban Life* 14 (3): 317–344.

Gould, Kenneth A. 1993. "Pollution and Perception: Social Visibility and Local Environmental Mobilization." *Qualitative Sociology* 16 (2): 157–178.

Gould, Kenneth A., Adam S. Weinberg, and Allan Schnaiberg. 1993. "Legitimating Impotence: Pyrrhic Victories of the Modern Environmental Movement." *Qualitative Sociology* 16 (3): 207–246.

Granfield, Robert. 1991. "Making it by Faking It: Working-Class Students in an Elite Academic Environment." *Journal of Contemporary Ethnography* 20 (3): 331–351.

———. 1992. *Making Elite Lawyers: Visions of Law at Harvard and Beyond.* New York: Routledge.

Grills, Scott. 1985. The Social Process of Essay Construction. M.A. Thesis, University of Waterloo.

———. 1989. "Designating Deviance: Championing Definitions of the Appropriate and Inappropriate through a Christian Political Voice." Doctoral dissertation, McMaster University.

———. 1994. "Recruitment Practices of the Christian Heritage Party." Pp. 96–108 in Mary Lorenz Dietz, Robert Prus, and William Shaffir (eds.), *Doing Everyday Life: Ethnography as Human Lived Experience.* Toronto: Copp Clark Longman.

Gross, Edward. 1986. "Waiting at Mayo." *Urban Life* 15 (2): 139–164.

Gross, Harriet Engel. 1980. "Couples Who Live Apart: Time/Place Disjunctions and Their Consequences." *Symbolic Interaction* 3 (2): 69–82.

Grove, Kathleen. 1992. "Career Change and Identity: Nurse Practitioners' Accounts of Occupational Choice." *Current Research on Occupations and Professions* 7:141–155.

Gubrium, Jaber F. 1975a. "Death Worlds in a Nursing Home." *Urban Life* 4 (3): 317–338.

———. 1975b. *Living and Dying at Murray Manor.* New York: St. Martin's.

——. 1993. *Speaking of Life: Horizons of Meaning for Nursing Home Residents*. New York: Aldine de Gruyter.

Gusfield, Joseph R. 1955. "Social Structure and Moral Reform: A Study of the Woman's Christian Temperance Union." *American Journal of Sociology* 61:221–232.

——. 1963. *Symbolic Crusade: Status Politics and the American Temperance Movement*. Urbana: University of Illinois Press.

——. 1981. *The Culture of Public Problems*. Chicago: University of Chicago Press.

——. 1984. "On the Side: Practical Action and the Social Constructionism in Social Problems Theory." Pp. 31–51 in Joseph W. Schneider and John I. Kitsuse (eds.), *Studies in the Sociology of Social Problems*. Norwood, NJ: Ablex.

——. 1989. "Constructing the Ownership of Social Problems: Fun and Profit in the Welfare State." *Social Problems* 26:431–441.

Haas, Jack. 1972. "Binging: Educational Control among High Steel Ironworkers." *American Behavioral Scientist* 16:27–34.

——. 1977. "Learning Real Feelings: A Study of High Steel Ironworkers' Reactions to Fear and Danger." *Sociology of Work and Occupations* 4:147–170.

Haas, Jack, and William Shaffir. 1977. "The Professionalization of Medical Students: Developing Competence and a Cloak of Competence." *Symbolic Interaction* 1 (1): 71–88.

——. 1980. "'Fieldworkers' Mistakes at Work: Problems in Maintaining Research and Researcher Bargains." Pp. 244–255 in W. Shaffir, R.A. Stebbins, and A. Turowetz (eds.), *Fieldwork Experience: Qualitative Approaches to Social Research*. New York: St. Martin's Press.

——. 1982. "Taking on the Role of Doctor: A Dramaturgical Analysis of Professionalization." *Symbolic Interaction* 5 (2): 187–203.

——. 1987. *Becoming Doctors: The Adoption of a Cloak of Competence*. Greenwich, CT: JAI.

Habenstein, Robert W., and William Lamers. 1960. *Funeral Customs the World Over*. Milwaukee: Bulfin.

——. 1981. *The History of American Funeral Directing*. Milwaukee: Bulfin.

Hall, Ian. 1983. "Playing for Keeps: The Careers of Front-line Workers in Institutions for Developmentally Handicapped Persons." M.A. thesis, University of Waterloo.

Hall, Oswald. 1946. "Informal Organization of Medical Practice." *Canadian Journal of Economics and Political Science* 12:30–41.

Hall, Peter. 1972. "A Symbolic Interactionist Analysis of Politics." Pp. 35–76 in Andrew Effrat (ed.), *Perspectives in Political Sociology.* Indianapolis: Bobbs-Merrill.

Hannerz, Ulf. 1992. "The Global Ecumene as a Network of Networks." Pp. 35–56 in Adam Kuper (ed.), *Conceptualizing Society.* New York: Routledge.

Hargreaves, David, Stephen Hestor, and Frank Melor. 1975. *Deviance in Classrooms.* London: Routledge and Kegan Paul.

Harrington, C. Lee, and Denise D. Bielby. 1995a. *Soap Fans: Pursuing Pleasure and Making Meaning in Everyday Life.* Philadelphia: Temple University Press.

———. 1995b. "Where Did You Hear That? Technology and the Social Organization of Gossip." *The Sociological Quarterly* 36 (3): 607–628.

Harrison, Deborah, and Lucie Laliberté. 1994. *No Life Like It: Military Wives in Canada.* Toronto: James Lorimer and Company.

Hawkins, Keith. 1984. "Creating Cases in a Regulatory Agency." *Urban Life* 12 (4): 371–395.

Hearn, H.L., and Patricia Stoll. 1975. "Continuance Commitments in Low-Status Occupations: The Cocktail Waitress." *Sociological Quarterly* 16:105–114.

Henderson, Kathryn. 1995. "The Political Career of a Prototype: Visual Representation in Design Engineering." *Social Problems* 42 (2): 274–299.

Henslin, James. 1968. "Trust and the Cabdriver." Pp. 138–158 in Marcello Truzzi (ed.), *Sociology and Everyday Life.* Englewood Cliffs, NJ: Prentice-Hall.

———. 1970. "Guilt and Guilt Neutralization: Responses and Adjustment to Suicide." Pp. 192–228 in Jack Douglas (ed.), *Deviance and Respectability.* New York: Basic.

Herman, Nancy J. 1993. "Return to Sender: Reintegrative Stigma-Management Strategies of Ex-Psychiatric Patients." *Journal of Contemporary Ethnography* 22 (3): 295–330.

Hickrod, Lucy Jen Huang and Raymond L. Schmitt. 1982. "A Naturalistic Study of Interaction and Frame: The Pet as 'Family Member.' " *Urban Life* 11 (1): 55–77.

Higgins, Paul C. 1979. "Outsiders in a Hearing World: The Deaf Community." *Urban Life* 8 (1): 3–22.

———. 1980. "Societal Reaction and the Physically Disabled: Bringing the Impairment Back In." *Symbolic Interaction* 3 (1): 149–156.

Himmelfarb, Alexander, and John Evans. 1974. "Deviance Disavowal and Stigma Management: A Study in Obesity." Pp. 221–232 in Jack

Haas and William Shaffir (eds.), *Decency and Deviance*. Toronto: McClelland and Stewart.

Hodson, Randy. 1991. "The Active Worker: Compliance and Autonomy at the Workplace." *Journal of Contemporary Ethnography* 20 (1): 47–78.

Hoffman, Joan Eakin. 1974. " 'Nothing Can Be Done': Stroke Patients in a General Hospital." *Urban Life and Culture* 3 (1): 50–70.

Holstein, James A. 1993. *Court-Ordered Insanity: Interpretive Practice and Involuntary Commitment*. New York: Aldine De Gruyter.

Hood, Jane C. 1988. "From Night to Day: Timing and the Management of Custodial Work." *Journal of Contemporary Ethnography* 17 (1): 96–116.

Hopper, Joseph. 1993. "Oppositional Identities and Rhetoric in Divorce." *Qualitative Sociology* 16 (2): 133–156.

Hughes, Everett. 1961. "Introduction: The Place of Fieldwork in the Social Sciences." Pp. v–xiv in B. H. Junker. *Fieldwork: An Introduction to the Social Sciences*. Chicago: University of Chicago Press.

Hunt, Jennifer. 1985. "Police Accounts of Normal Force." *Urban Life* 13 (4): 315–341.

———. 1995. "Divers' Accounts of Normal Risk." *Symbolic Interaction* 18 (4): 439–462.

Hunt, Morton. 1966. *The World of the Formerly Married*. New York: McGraw Hill.

Ingraham, Larry H. 1984. *The Boys in the Barracks: Observations on American Military Life*. Philadelphia: Institute for the Study of Human Issues.

Irini, Styllianoss, and Robert Prus. 1982. "Doing Security Work: Keeping Order in the Hotel Setting." *Canadian Journal of Criminology* 24 !1): 61–82.

Jackson, Joan. 1954. "The Adjustment of the Family to the Crises of Alcoholism." *Quarterly Journal of Studies on Alcohol* 15:564–586.

Jacobs, Bruce A. 1992. "Undercover Deception: Reconsidering Presentations of Self." *Journal of Contemporary Ethnography* 21 (2): 200–225.

———. 1992. "Undercover Drug-Use Evasion Tactics: Excuses and Neutralization." *Symbolic Interaction* 15 (4): 435–453.

———. 1994. "Undercover Social-distancing Techniques." *Symbolic Interaction* 17 (4): 395–410.

Jacobs, James B. and Harold G. Retsky. 1975. "Prison Guards." *Urban Life* 4 (1): 5–29.

Jacobs, Jerry. 1967. "A Phenomenological Study of Suicide Notes." *Social Problems* 15:62–72.

———. 1970. "The Use of Religion in Constructing the Moral Justification of Suicide." Pp. 229–251 in Jack Douglas (ed.), *Deviance and Respectability*. New York: Basic.

———. 1971. *Adolescent Suicide*. New York: Wiley-Interscience.

Jacobs, Mark D. 1990. *Screwing the System and Making It Work: Juvenile Justice in the No-Fault Society*. Chicago: University of Chicago Press.

Johnson, John M. 1975. *Doing Field Research*. New York: Free Press.

Jones, Wendy L. 1980. "Newcomers' Biographical Explanations: The Self As an Adjustment Process." *Symbolic Interaction* 3 (2): 83–94.

Jorgensen, Danny L. 1984. "Divinatory Discourse." *Symbolic Interaction* 7 (2): 135–153.

———. 1989. *Participant Observation*. Newbury Park, CA: Sage.

———. 1992. *The Esoteric Scene, Cultic Milieu, and Occult Tarot*. New York: Garland.

Kalab, Kathleen A. 1987. "Student Vocabularies of Motive: Accounts For Absence." *Symbolic Interaction* 10 (1): 71–83.

Kando, Thomas. 1973. *Sex Change: The Achievement of Gender Identity among Feminized Transsexuals*. Springfield, IL: Charles C. Thomas.

Karp, David A. 1986. " 'You Can Take the Boy out of Dorchester, But You Can't Take Dorchester out of the Boy': Toward a Social Psychology of Mobility." *Symbolic Interaction* 9 (1): 19–36.

———. 1992. "Illness Ambiguity and the Search for Meaning: A Case Study of a Self-Help Group for Affective Disorders." *Journal of Contemporary Ethnography* 21 (2): 139–170.

———. 1993. "Taking Anti-Depressant Medications: Resistance, Trial Commitment, Conversion, and Disenchantment." *Qualitative Sociology* 16:337–359.

———. 1994. "Dialectics of Depression." *Symbolic Interaction* 17:341–366.

———. 1996. *Speaking of Sadness: Depression, Disconnection and the Meanings of Illness*. New York: Oxford University Press.

Karp, David A., and William Yoels. 1979. *Symbols, Selves, and Society: Understanding Interaction*. New York: Lippincott/Harper and Row.

Karsh, Bernard, Joel Seidman, and Daisy M. Lilienthal. 1953. "The Union Organizer and His Tactics: A Case Study." *American Journal of Sociology* 59:113–122.

Katovich, Michael A., and William A. Reese II. 1987. "The Regular Full-Time Identities and Memberships in an Urban Bar." *Journal of Contemporary Ethnography* 16 (3): 308–343.

Kauffman, Kelsey. 1988. *Prison Officers and Their World*. Cambridge: Harvard University Press.

Keesing, Roger M. 1982. *Kwaio Religion: The Living and the Dead in a Solomon Island Society.* New York: Columbia University Press.

Keiser, R. Lincoln. 1969. *The Vice Lords: Warriors of the Streets.* New York: Holt, Rinehart and Winston.

Kielhofner, Gary. 1983. "'Teaching' Retarded Adults: Paradoxical Effects of a Pedagogical Enterprise." *Urban Life* 12 (3): 307–326.

Kinsey, Barry A. 1985. "Congressional Staff: The Cultivation and Maintenance of Personal Networks in an Insecure Work Environment." *Urban Life* 13 (4): 395–422.

Kitsuse, John I. and Malcom Spector. 1977. *Constructing Social Problems.* Menlo Park, CA: Cummings.

Klapp, Orrin. 1962. *Heroes, Villains and Fools.* San Diego: Aegis.

———. 1964. *Symbolic Leaders.* Chicago: Aldine.

———. 1969. *The Collective Search for Identity.* New York: Holt.

———. 1971. *Social Types: Process, Structure and Ethos.* San Diego: Aegis.

Kleinman, Sherryl. 1983. "Collective Matters As Individual Concerns: Peer Culture among Graduate Students." *Urban Life* 12 (2): 203–225.

———. 1984. *Equals before God: Seminarians As Humanistic Professionals.* Chicago: University of Chicago Press.

Kling, Rob, and Elihu Gerson. 1978. "Patterns of Segmentation and Intersection in the Computer World." *Symbolic Interaction* 1 (2): 24–43.

Knorr-Cetina, Karin. 1981. *The Manufacture of Knowledge: An Essay on the Constructivist and Contextual Nature of Science.* Oxford: Permagon.

———. 1983. "New Developments in Science Studies: The Ethnographic Challenge." *Canadian Journal of Sociology* 8:153–177.

———. 1995. "Laboratory Studies: The Cultural Approach to the Study of Science." Pp. 140–166 in Shiela Jasanoff, Gerald E. Markle, James C. Petersen, and Trevor Pinch (eds.), *Handbook of Science and Technology Studies.* Thousand Oaks: Sage.

Knowles, J. Gary. 1991. "Parents' Rationales for Operating Home Schools." *Journal of Contemporary Ethnography* 20 (2): 203–230.

Kohler, Robert E. 1994. *Lords of the Fly: Drosophila Genetics and the Experimental Life.* Chicago: University of Chicago Press.

Kotarba, Joseph A. 1975. "American Acupuncturists: The New Entrepreneurs of Hope." *Urban Life* 4 (2): 149–177.

———. 1983. *Chronic Pain: Its Social Dimensions.* Beverly Hills: Sage.

Kretzmann, Martin J. 1992. "Bad Blood: The Moral Stigmatization of Paid Plasma Donors." *Journal of Contemporary Ethnography* 20 (4): 416–441.

Kroeber, Alfred Louis, and Clyde Kluckhohn. 1952. *The Nature of Culture.* Chicago: University of Chicago Press.

Kuhn, Manford. 1954. "Kinsey's View on Human Behavior." *Social Problems* 1:119–125.

Kuhn, Thomas S. 1962. *The Structure of Scientific Revolutions* (revised edition, 1970). Chicago: University of Chicago Press.

Kunda, Godown. 1992. *Engineering Culture: Control and Commitment in a High-Tech Corporation.* Phildelphia: Temple University Press.

Kuper, Adam. 1992. *Conceptualizing Society.* New York: Routledge.

Kurtz, Lester R. 1984. *Evaluating Chicago Sociology: A Guide to the Literature, with an Annotated Bibliography.* Chicago: University of Chicago Press.

Kutner, Nancy G. 1987. "Social Worlds and Identity in End-Stage Renal Disease (ESRD)." *Research in the Sociology of Health Care* 6:33–71.

LaBarre, Weston. 1947. "The Language of Emotions and Gestures." *Journal of Personality* 16:49–68.

Lancaster, Roger N. 1988. "Subject Honor and Object Shame: The Construction of Male Homosexuality and Stigma in Nicaragua." *Ethnology* 27:111–125.

Latour, Bruno. 1987. *Science in Action.* Cambridge: Harvard University Press.

Laub, John H. 1983. *Criminology in the Making: An Oral History.* Boston: Northeastern University Press.

Laurer, Robert H., and Warren H. Handel. 1977. *The Theory and Application of Symbolic Interaction.* Boston: Houghton Mifflin.

Layder, Derek. 1984. "Sources and Levels of Commitment in Actors' Careers." *Work and Occupations* 11 (2): 147–162.

Lee, Richard B. 1992. *The Dobe Ju/'Hoansi* (2nd ed). New York: Harcourt Brace.

Lemert, Edwin. 1951. *Social Pathology.* New York: McGraw-Hill.

———. 1953. "An Isolation and Closure Theory of Naive Check Forgery." *The Journal of Criminal Law, Criminology and Police Science* 44:296–307.

———. 1962. "Paranoia and the Dynamics of Exclusion." *Sociometry* 25:2–25.

———. 1967. *Human Deviance, Social Problems and Social Control.* Englewood Cliffs, NJ: Prentice-Hall.

Lesieur, Henry. 1977. *The Chase.* New York: Anchor.

Letkemann, Peter. 1973. *Crime as Work.* Englewood Cliffs, NJ: Prentice-Hall.

Levitt, Cyril, and William Shaffir. 1987. *The Riot at Christie Pits.* Toronto: Lester and Orphen Dennys.

———. 1989. "The Swastika as Dramatic Symbol: A Case Study in Ethnic Violence." *The Jewish Journal of Sociology* 31:5–24.

Liebow, Elliot. 1967. *Tally's Corner: A Study of Negro Streetcorner Men.* Boston: Little, Brown.

Lindebaum, Shirley. 1979. *Kuru Sorcery: Disease and Danger in the New Guinea Highlands.* Palo Alto, CA: Mayfield.

Lindekugel, D.M. 1994. *Shooters: TV News Photographers and Their Work.* Westport, CN: Greenwood.

Lindesmith, Alfred. 1965. *The Addict and the Law.* New York: Vintage.

Lofland, John. 1966. *The Doomsday Cult.* Englewood Cliffs, NJ: Prentice-Hall.

———. 1969. *Deviance and Identity.* Englewood Cliffs, NJ: Prentice-Hall.

———. 1970. "Interactionist Imagery and Analytic Interruptus." Pp. 35–45 in Tamotsu Shibutani (ed.), *Human Nature and Collective Behavior: Papers in Honor of Herbert Blumer.* Englewood Cliffs, NJ: Prentice-Hall.

———. 1976. *Doing Social Life.* New York: Wiley.

———. 1993. *Polite Protesters: The American Peace Movement of the 1980s.* Syracuse: Syracuse University Press.

———. 1995. "Analytic Ethnography: Features, Failings, and Futures." *Journal of Contemporary Ethnography* 24 (1): 30–67.

Lofland, John, and Lyn Lofland. 1984. *Analyzing Social Settings* (2nd edition). Belmont, CA: Wadsworth.

———. 1995. *Analyzing Social Settings* (3rd edition). Belmont, CA: Wadsworth.

Lofland, Lyn. 1989. "Social Life in the Public Realm: A Review." *Journal of Contemporary Ethnography* 17 (4): 453–482.

Lopata, Helena Znaniecki. 1969. "Loneliness: Forms and Components." *Social Problems* 17:248–262.

Loseke, Donileen R. 1989. "Evaluation Research and the Practice of Social Services: A Case for Qualitative Methodology." *Journal of Contemporary Ethnography* 18 (2): 202–223.

Lu, Shun, and Gary Alan Fine. 1995. "The Presentation of Ethnic Authenticity: Chinese Food As a Social Accomplishment." *The Sociological Quarterly* 36 (3): 535–553.

Luckenbill, David F. 1985. "Entering Male Prostitution." *Urban Life* 14 (2): 131–153.

Lyman, Karen A. 1993. *Day in, Day out with Alzheimer's: Stress in Caregiving Relationships*. Philadelphia: Temple University Press.

Lyman, Stanford, and Marvin Scott. 1989. *A Sociology of the Absurd* (2nd ed.). Dix Hills, N.Y.: General Hall.

Lyon, Eleanor. 1974. "Work and Play: Resource Constraints in a Small Theatre." *Urban Life and Culture* 3 (1): 71–91.

Lyotard, Jean Francois. 1984. *The Postmodern Condition*. Translated by Geoff Bennington and Brian Massumi. Minneapolis: University of Minnesota Press.

MacAndrew, Craig, and Robert Edgerton. 1969. *Drunken Comportment*. Chicago: Aldine.

MacLeod, Bruce A. 1993. *Club Date Musicians: Playing the New York Party Circuit*. Urbana: University of Illinois Press.

Maisel, Louis Sandy. 1982. *From Obscurity to Oblivion: Running in the Congressional Primary*. Knoxville: University of Tennessee Press.

Malinowski, Bronislaw. 1922. *Argonauts of the Western Pacific*. New York: Dutton.

Mandell, Nancy. 1984. "Children's Negotiation of Meaning." *Symbolic Interaction* 7 (3): 191–211.

March, Karen. 1994. "Needing to Know: Adoptees' Search for Self Completion." Pp. 213–225 in Mary Lorenz Dietz, Robert Prus and William Shaffir (editors), *Doing Everyday Life: Ethnography as Human Lived Experience*. Toronto: Copp Clark Longman.

Marks, James Thomas William. 1990. "Volunteering: Patterns of Interaction and the Process of Helping." M.A. thesis, University of Waterloo.

Marshall, Victor W. 1975. "Organizational Features of Terminal Status Passage in Residential Facilities for the Aged." *Urban Life* 4 (3): 349–368.

Martin, Wilfred. 1975. "Teacher-Pupil Interactions: A Negotiation Perspective." *Canadian Review of Sociology and Anthropology* 12:529–540.

Mast, Sharon. 1983. "Working for Television: The Social Organization of TV Drama." *Symbolic Interaction* 6 (1): 71–83.

Matthews, Sarah. 1975. "Old Women and Identity Maintenance: Outwitting the Grim Reaper." *Urban Life* 4 (3): 339–348.

Maurer, David. 1964. *The Whiz Mob*. New Haven, Conn.: College and University Press.

McCall, Michal M. 1977. "Art Without A Market: Creating Artistic Value in a Provincial Art World." *Symbolic Interaction* 1 (1): 32–43.

McConville, Mike, and Chester Mirsky. 1995. "Guilty Plea Courts: A Social Disciplinary Model of Criminal Justice." *Social Problems* 42 (2): 216–234.

McGuire, Meredith B., and Debra J. Kantor. 1987. "Belief Systems and Illness Experiences: The Case of Non-Medical Healing Groups." *Research in the Sociology of Health Care* 6:221–248.

McMahon, Martha. 1995. *Engendering Motherhood: Identity and Self-Transformation in Women's Lives.* New York: Guilford.

McNulty, Elizabeth W. 1994. "Generating Common Sense Knowledge among Police Officers." *Symbolic Interaction* 17 (3): 281–294.

Mead, George H. 1934. *Mind, Self and Society.* Ed. by Charles W. Morris. Chicago: University of Chicago Press.

Meehan, Albert J. 1986. "Record-Keeping Practices in the Policing of Juveniles." *Urban Life* 15 (1): 70–102.

———. 1992. "'I Don't Prevent Crime, I Prevent Calls': Policing as a Negotiated Order." *Symbolic Interaction* 15 (4): 455–480.

Meekers, Dominique. 1993. "The Noble Custom of Roora: The Marriage Practices of the Shona of Zimbabwe." *Ethnology* 32:35–54.

Mehan, Hugh, and Houston Wood. 1975. *The Reality of Ethnomethodology.* New York: Wiley.

Merten, Don E. 1996. "Going-with: The Role of a Social Form in Early Romance." *Journal of Contemporary Ethnography* 24 (4): 462–484.

Migliore, Sam. 1993. " 'Nerves': The Role of Metaphor in the Cultural Framing of Experience." *Journal of Contemporary Ethnography* 22 (3): 331–360.

Miller, Gale. 1978. *Odd Jobs: The World of Deviant Work.* Englewood Cliffs, NJ: Spectrum.

Miller, Gale, and James A. Holstein. 1995. "Dispute Domains: Organizational Contexts and Dispute Processing." *The Sociological Quarterly* 36 (1): 37–59.

Mitchell, Richard G. Jr. 1983. *Mountain Experience.* Chicago: University of Chicago Press.

———. 1993. *Secrecy and Fieldwork.* Newbury Park, CA: Sage.

Mitteness, Linda A. 1987. "So What Do You Expect When You're 85?: Urinary Incontinence in Late Life." *Research in the Sociology of Health Care* 6:177–219.

Molstad, Clark. 1986. "Choosing and Coping with Boring Work." *Urban Life* 15 (2): 215–236.

———. 1989. "Coping with Alienation in Industrial Work: An Ethnographic Study of Brewery Workers." Doctoral dissertation, University of California, Los Angeles.

Momboisse, Raymond M. 1969. *Confrontations, Riots, Urban Warfare.* Sacramento, CA: MSM Enterprises.

Moore, David. 1994. *The Lads in Action: Social Process in an Urban Youth Subculture.* Brookfield, VT: Ashgate.

Morrione, Thomas. n.d. *The Collected Papers of Herbert Blumer: Fundamentals of Symbolic Interaction.* Berkeley: University of California Press (in preparation).

Morris, Charles. 1970. *The Pragmatic Movement in American Philosophy.* New York: Braziller.

Mukerji, Chandra. 1977. "Film Games." *Symbolic Interaction* 1 (1): 20–31.

———. 1989. *A Fragile Power: Scientists and the State.* Princeton: Princeton University Press.

Mulcahy, Aogán. 1995. " 'Headhunter' or 'Real Cop?': Identity in the World of Internal Affairs Officers." *Journal of Contemporary Ethnography* 24 (1): 99–130.

Murphy, Sheigla, Dan Waldorf, and Craig Reinarman. 1990. "Drifting into Dealing: Becoming a Cocaine Seller." *Qualitative Sociology* 13 (4): 321–345.

Nash, Jeffrey E. 1975. "Bus Riding: Community on Wheels." *Urban Life* 4 (1): 99–124.

———. 1990. "Working at and Working: Computer Fritters." *Journal of Contemporary Ethnography* 19 (2): 207–225.

Nelkin, Dorothy. 1970. "Unpredictability and Life Style in a Migrant Labor Camp." *Social Problems* 17:472–487.

Nelson, E. D. (Adie), and B. W. Robinson. 1994. " 'Reality Talk' or 'Telling Tales'? The Social Construction of Sexual and Gender Deviance on a Television Talk Show." *Journal of Contemporary Ethnography* 23 (1): 51–78.

Nelson, Richard K. 1969. *Hunters of the Northern Ice.* Chicago: University of Chicago Press.

Olson, Lynn M. 1995. "Record Keeping Practices: Consequences of Accounting Demands in a Public Clinic." *Qualitative Sociology* 18 (1): 45–70.

O'Berick, Gary. 1993. *Getting Tall: Cocaine Use in the Subculture of Canadian Professional Musicians.* Toronto: Canadian Scholars' Press.

Orser, W. Edward. 1994. *Blockbusting in Baltimore: The Edmondson Village Story.* Lexington: University Press of Kentucky.

Ouellet, Lawrence J. 1994. *Pedal to the Metal: The Work Lives of Truckers.* Philadelphia: Temple University Press.

Palmer, C. Eddie. 1983. "'Trauma Junkies' and Street Work: Occupational Behavior of Paramedics and Emergency Medical Technicians." *Urban Life* 12 (2): 162–183.

Parnas, Raymond. 1967. "The Police Response to Domestic Disturbances." *Wisconsin Law Review*: 914–960.

Paules, Greta Foff. 1991. *Dishing It Out: Power and Resistance among Waitresses in a New Jersey Restaurant.* Philadelphia: Temple University Press.

Pawluch, Dorothy, Roy Hornosty, R.J. Richardson, and William Shaffir. 1994. "Fostering Relations: Student Subculture in an Innovative University Program." Pp. 340–353 in Mary Lorenz Dietz, Robert Prus and William Shaffir (eds.), *Doing Everyday Life: Ethnography as Human Lived Experience.* Toronto: Copp Clark Longman.

Peretz, Henri. 1995. "Negotiating Clothing Identities on the Sales Floor." *Symbolic Interaction* 18 (1): 19–37.

Pestello, Fred P. 1991. "Discounting." *Journal of Contemporary Ethnography* 20 (1): 26–46.

Petrunik, Michael. 1974. "The Quest for Fluency: Fluency Variations and the Identity Problems and Management Strategies of Stutterers." Pp. 201–220 in Jack Haas and William Shaffir (eds.), *Decency and Deviance.* Toronto: McClelland and Stewart.

Petrunik, Michael, and Clifford Shearing. 1983. "Fragile Facades: Stuttering and the Strategic Manipulation of Awareness." *Social Problems* 31:125–138.

Peven, Dorothy. 1968. "The Use of Religious Revival Techniques to Indoctrinate Personnel: The Home Party Organizations." *Sociological Quarterly* 9:97–106.

Peyrot, Mark. 1985. "Coerced Voluntarism: The Micropolitics of Drug Treatment." *Urban Life* 13 (4): 343–365.

Peyrot, Mark, James F. McMurry, Jr., and Richard Hedges. 1987. "Living With Diabetes: The Role of Personal and Professional Knowledge in Symptom and Regiment Management." *Research in the Sociology of Health Care* 6:107–146.

Pfohl, Stephen J. 1978. *Predicting Dangeruosness: The Social Construction of Psychiatric Reality.* Lexington, MA: D.C. Heath.

Pickering, Andrew. 1990. "Knowledge, Practice and Mere Construction." *Social Studies of Science* 20:682–729.

———. 1992. *Science As Practice and Culture.* Chicago: University of Chicago Press.

———. 1993. "The Mangle of Practice: Agency and Emergence in the Sociology of Science." *American Journal of Sociology* 99:559–589.

———. 1994. *The Mangle of Practice. Chicago:* University of Chicago Press.

Platt, Anthony. 1969. *The Child Savers.* Chicago: University of Chicago Press.

Pollner, Melvin, and Robert M. Emerson. 1983. "The Dynamics of Inclusion and Exclusion in Fieldwork Relations." Pp. 235–252 in Robert M. Emerson (ed.), *Contemporary Field Research: A Collection of Readings.* Prospect Heights, IL: Waveland.

Ponse, Barbara. 1976. "Secrecy in the Lesbian World." *Urban Life* 5 (3): 313–338.

Powell, Walter. 1985. *Getting into Print: The Decision-Making Process in Scholarly Publishing.* Chicago: University of Chicago Press.

Prus, Robert. 1975a. "Labeling Theory: A Reconceptualization and A Propositional Statement on Typing." *Sociological Focus* 8:79–96.

———. 1975b. "Resisting Designations: An Extension of Attribution Theory into a Negotiated Context." *Sociological Inquiry* 45:3–14.

———. 1976. "Religious Recruitment and the Management of Dissonance: A Sociological Perspective." *Sociological Inquiry* 46:127–134.

———. 1978. "From Barrooms to Bedrooms: Towards a Theory of Interpersonal Violence." Pp. 51–73 in M. A. B. Gammon (ed.), *Violence in Canada.* Toronto: Methuen.

———. 1980. "Hustling the Hustlers: The Dynamics of Acquiring Information." Pp. 132–145 in W. Shaffir, R. Stebbins, and A. Turowetz (eds.), *The Social Experience of Fieldwork.* New York: St. Martin's Press.

———. 1982. "Designating Discretion and Openness: The Problematics of Truthfulness in Everyday Life." *Canadian Review of Sociology and Anthropology* 18:70–91.

———. 1983. "Drinking as Activity: An Interactionist Analysis." *Journal of Studies on Alcohol* 44 (3): 460–475.

———. 1987. "Generic Social Processes: Maximizing Conceptual Development in Ethnographic Research." *Journal of Contemporary Ethnography* 16 (3): 250–291.

———. 1989a. *Making Sales: Influence as Interpersonal Accomplishment.* Newbury Park, CA: Sage.

———. 1989b. *Pursuing Customers: An Ethnography of Marketing Activities.* Newbury Park, CA: Sage.

———. 1990. "The Interpretive Challenge: The Impending Crisis in Sociology." *Canadian Journal of Sociology* 15 (3): 355–363.

———. 1991. "Encountering the Marketplace: Achieving Intimate Familiarity with Vendor Activity." Pp. 120–130 in William Shaffir and Robert A. Stebbins (eds.), *Experiencing Fieldwork: Qualitative Research in the Social Sciences*. Newbury Park, CA: Sage.

———. 1992a. "Influence Work in Human Service Settings: Lessons from the Marketplace." Pp. 41–56 in Gale Miller (ed.), *Current Research on Occupations and Professions* 7. Greenwich, CT: JAI.

———. 1992b. "Producing Social Science: Knowledge as a Social Problem in Academia." Pp. 57–78 in Gale Miller and James Holstein (eds.), *Perspectives in Social Problems* 3. Greenwich, CT: JAI.

———. 1993a. "Encountering the Mass Media: Consumers as Targets and Tacticians." Paper presented at Studying Human Lived Experience: Symbolic Interaction and Ethnographic Research '93. University of Waterloo, Waterloo, Ontario.

———. 1993b. "Shopping With Companions: Images, Influences and Interpersonal Dilemmas." *Qualitative Sociology* 16:87–109.

———. 1994a. "Consumers as Targets: Autonomy, Accountability, and Anticipation of the Influence Process." *Qualitative Sociology* 17 (3): 243–262.

———. 1994b."Generic Social Processes: Intersubjectivity and Transcontextuality in the Social Sciences." Pp. 393–412 in Mary Lorenz Dietz, Robert Prus, and William Shaffir (eds.), *Doing Everyday Life: Ethnography As Human Lived Experience*. Toronto: Copp Clark Longman.

———. 1995. "Envisioning Power as Intersubjective Accomplishment: Acknowledging the Human Enterprise Entailed in Tactician-Target Interchanges" Paper presented at the Society for the Study of Symbolic Interaction. Washington, DC, August 20–21.

———. 1996. *Symbolic Interaction and Ethnographic Research: Intersubjectivity and the Study of Human Lived Experience*. Albany: State University of New York Press.

———. n.d. Power as Intersubjective Accomplishment (ms. in preparation)

Prus, Robert, and Lorne Dawson. 1991. "Shop 'til You Drop: Shopping as Recreational and Laborious Activity." *Canadian Journal of Sociology* 16:145–164.

———. 1996. "Obdurate Reality and the Intersubjective Other: The Problematics of Representation and the Privilege of Presence." Pp. 245–257 in Robert Prus, *Symbolic Interaction and Ethnographic Research: Intersubjectivity and the Study of Human Lived Experience*. New York: State University of New York Press.

Prus, Robert, and Augie Fleras. 1996. " 'Pitching' Images to the Generalized Other: Promotional Strategies of Economic Development

Officers." Pp. 99–128 in Helena Znaniecki Lopata (ed.), *Current Research on Occupations and Professions: Getting Down to Business 9.* Greenwich, CT: JAI.

Prus, Robert, and Wendy Frisby. 1990. "Persuasion as Practical Accomplishment: Tactical Manoeuverings at Home Party Plans." Pp. 133–162 in Helena Znaniecki Lopata (ed.), *Current Research on Occupations and Professions: Societal Influences 5.* Greenwich, CT: JAI.

Prus, Robert, and Grills, Charles Scott. n.d. *The Deviant Mystique* (ms. in preparation).

Prus, Robert, and Styllianoss Irini. 1980. *Hookers, Rounders, and Desk Clerks: The Social Organization of the Hotel Community.* Toronto: Gage. (Reprint 1988, Salem, WI: Sheffield.)

Prus, Robert, and C. R. D. Sharper. 1977. *Road Hustler: The Career Contingencies of Professional Card and Dice Hustlers.* Lexington, MA: Lexington Books.

———. 1991. *Road Hustler: Hustlers, Magic and the Thief Subculture.* New York: Kaufman and Greenberg.

Prus, Robert, and John Stratton. 1976. "Parole Revocation Related Decision Making: Private Typings and Official Designations." *Federal Probation* 40:48–53.

Rains, Prue, and Eli Teram. 1992. *Normal Bad Boys: Public Policies, Institutions, and the Politics of Client Recruitment.* Montreal, Que.: McGill-Queen's University Press.

Ralph, Jack. 1950. "Junk Business and the Junk Peddler." M.A. thesis, University of Chicago.

Rank, Mark Robert. 1994. *Living on the Edge: The Realities of Welfare in America.* New York: Columbia University Press.

Raphael, Ray. 1985. *Cash Crop: An American Dream.* Mendocino, CA: Ridge Times.

Rasmussen, Paul K., and Lauren L. Kuhn. 1976. "The New Masseuse: Play for Pay." *Urban Life* 5 (3): 271–292.

Rasmussen, Susan. 1995. "Zarraf, A Tuareg Women's Wedding Dance." *Ethnology* 34 (1): 1–16.

Ray, Marsh. 1961. "The Cycle of Abstinence and Relapse among Heroin Addicts." *Social Problems* 9:132–140.

Ray, Verne. 1953. "Human Color Perception and Behavioral Response." *Transactions of New York Academy of Science* 16:98–102.

Reid, Margaret. 1982. "Marginal Man: The Identity Dilemma of the Academic General Practitioner." *Symbolic Interaction* 5 (2): 325–342.

Reimer, Jeffrey. 1979. "Working Setting and Behavior: An Empirical Examination of Building Construction Work." *Symbolic Interaction* 2 (2): 131–151.

Reiss, Albert J. Jr. 1960. "Sex Offenses: The Marginal Status of the Adolescent." *Law and Contemporary Problems* 25 (2): 309–333.
———. 1961. "The Social Integration of Queers and Peers." *Social Problems* 9:102–120.

Richman, Joel. 1983. *Traffic Wardens: An Ethnography of Street Administration.* Manchester, UK: University of Manchester Press.

Robillard, Albert B. 1994. "Communication Problems in the Intensive Care Unit." *Qualitative Sociology* 17 (4): 383–395.

Robins, Douglas M., Clinton R. Sanders, and Spencer E. Cahill. 1991. "Dogs and Their People: Pet-Facilitated Interaction in a Public Setting." *Journal of Contemporary Ethnography* 20 (1): 3–25.

Rochford, E. Burke. 1986. *Hare Krishna in America.* New Brunswick: Rutgers University Press.

Rock, Paul. 1973. *Making People Pay.* London: Routledge and Kegan Paul.

Rodabough, Tillman, and Carolyn Rodabough. 1981. "Nurses And The Dying: Symbolic Interaction As a Precipitator of Dying 'Stages.' " *Qualitative Sociology* 4 (4): 257–278.

Roebuck, Julian B., and Wolfgang Frese. 1976. *The Rendezvous: A Case Study of an After-Hours Club.* New York: Free Press.

Rogers, Jackie Krasas. 1995. "Experience and Structure of Alienation in Temporary Clerical Employment." *Work and Occupations* 22 (2): 137–166.

Rogers-Dillon, Robin. 1995. "The Dynamics of Welfare Stigma." *Qualitative Sociology* 18 (4): 439–456.

Rollinson, Paul A. 1990. "The Story of Edward: The Everyday Geography of Elderly Single Room Occupancy (SRO) Hotel Tenants." *Journal of Contemporary Ethnography* 19(2): 188–206.

Ronai, Carol Rambo, and Carolyn Ellis. 1989. "Turn-Ons For Money: Interactional Strategies of the Table Dancer." *Journal of Contemporary Ethnography* 18 (3): 271–298.

Rosecrance, John D. 1985. *The Degenerates of Lake Tahoe: A Study of Persistence in the Social World of Horse Race Gambling.* New York: Peter Lang.

Rosenbaum, Marsha. 1981. *Women on Heroin.* New Brunswick: Rutgers University Press.

Rosenblatt, Paul C., Terri A. Karis, and Richard D. Powell. 1995. *Multiracial Couples.* Thousand Oakes, CA: Sage.

Rosenhan, David L. 1973. "On Being Sane in Insane Places." *Science* 179:250–258.

Rosier, Katherine Brown, and William A. Corsaro. 1993. "Competent Parents, Complex Lives: Managing Parenthood in Poverty." *Journal of Contemporary Ethnography* 22 (2): 171–204.

Ross, H. Lawrence. 1980. *Settled Out of Court*. New York: Aldine.

Roth, Julius A. 1962. "The Treatment of Tuberculosis as a Bargaining Process." Pp. 575–588 in A. Rose (ed.), *Human Behavior and Social Process*. Boston: Houghton-Mifflin.

———. 1972. "Staff and Client Control Strategies in Urban Hospital Emergency Services." *Urban Life and Culture* 9:39–60.

Roy, Donald. 1953. "Work Satisfaction and Social Reward in Quota Achievement: An Analysis of Piecework Incentive." *American Sociological Review* 18:507–514.

———. 1959. "Banana Time—Job Satisfaction and Informant Interaction." *Human Organization* 18 (4): 158–168.

Royer, Ariela. 1995 "Living with Chronic Illness." *Research in the Sociology of Health Care* 12:25–48.

Rubin, Herbert J. 1987. "Rule Making, Exceptioning, and County Land Use Decisions." *Urban Life* 15 !3–4): 299–330.

Rubington, Earl. 1968. "Variations in Bottle-Gang Controls." Pp. 308–316 in Earl Rubington and Martin Weinberg (eds.), *Deviance: The Interactionist Perspective*. New York: Macmillan.

Rubinstein, Jonathan. 1973. *City Police*. New York: Ballantine.

Salutin, Marilyn. 1973. "The Impression Management Techniques of the Burlesque Comic." *Sociological Inquiry* 43:159–168.

Sandelowski, Margarete, Betty G. Harris, and Diane Holditch-Davis. 1991. " 'The Clock Has Been Ticking, the Calendar Pages Turning, and We are Still Waiting': Infertile Couples' Encounter with Time in the Adoption Waiting Period." *Qualitative Sociology* 14 (2): 147–173.

———. 1993. " 'Somewhere Out There:' Parental Claiming in the Preadoption Waiting Period." *Journal of Contemporary Ethnography* 21 (4): 464–486.

Sanders, Clinton R. 1974. "Psyching Out the Crowd: Folk Performers and Their Audiences." *Urban Life and Culture* 3 (3): 264–282.

———. 1989. *Customizing the Body: The Art and Culture of Tattooing*. Philadelphia: Temple University Press.

———. 1993. "Understanding Dogs: Caretakers' Attributions of Mindedness in Canine-Human Relationships." *Journal of Contemporary Ethnography* 22 (2): 205–226.

———. 1994. "Annoying Owners: Routine Interactions with Problematic Clients in a General Veterinary Practice." *Qualitative Sociology* 17 (2): 159–170.

———. 1995. "Stranger than Fiction: Insights and Pitfalls in Postmodern Ethnography." Pp. 89–104 in Norman K. Denzin (ed.), *Studies in Symbolic Interaction* 17. Greenwich, CT: JAI.

Sandstrom, Kent L. 1990. "Confronting Deadly Disease: The Drama of Identity Construction among Gay Men with AIDS." *Journal of Contemporary Ethnography* 19 (3): 271–294.

Sargent, Carolyn F. 1988. "Born to Die: Witchcraft and Infanticide in Bariba Culture." *Ethnology* 27:79–95.

Schmid, Thomas, and Richard S. Jones. 1991. "Suspended Identity: Identity Transformation in a Maximum Security Prison." *Symbolic Interaction* 14 (4): 415–432.

———. 1993. "Ambivalent Actions: Prison Adaption Strategies of First-Time, Short-Term Inmates." *Journal of Contemporary Ethnography* 21 (4): 439–463.

Schneider, Joseph W., and Peter Conrad. 1983. *Having Epilepsy.* Philadelphia: Temple University Press.

Schutz, Alfred. 1962. *Collected Papers I: The Problem of Social Reality.* The Hague, Netherlands: Martinus Nijhoff.

———. 1964. *Collected Papers II: Studies in Social Theory.* The Hague, Netherlands: Martinus Nijhoff.

———. 1967. *The Phenomenology of the Social World.* Evanston: Northwestern University Press.

Schwalbe, Michael. 1995. "The Responsibilities of Sociological Poets." *Qualitative Sociology* 18:393–413.

Schwartz, Dona. 1986. "Camera Clubs and Fine Art Photography: The Social Construction of an Elite Code." *Urban Life* 15 (2): 165–195.

Scott, Lois. 1981. "Being Somebody: The Negotiation of Identities in a Community Context." M.A. thesis, University of Waterloo.

Scott, Marvin. 1968. *The Racing Game.* Chicago: Aldine.

Scott, Robert. 1968. *The Making of Blind Men: A Study of Adult Socialization.* New York: Russell Sage.

———. 1969. "The Socialization of Blind Children." Pp. 1025–1045 in David A. Goslin (ed.), *Handbook of Socialization Theory and Development.* Chicago: Rand-McNally.

Segal, David R., and Mady Wechsler Segal. 1993. *Peacekeepers and Their Wives: American Participation in the Multinational Force and Observers.* Westport, CT: Greenwood.

Semmes, Clovis E. 1991. "Developing Trust: Patient-Practitioner Encounters in Natural Health Care." *Journal of Contemporary Ethnography* 19 (4): 450–470.

Shaffir, William. 1974. *Life in a Religious Community: The Lubavitcher Chassidim in Montreal.* Toronto: Holt, Rinehart and Winston.

———. 1985. "Some Reflections on Approaches to Fieldwork in Hassidic Communities." *The Jewish Journal of Sociology* 27:115–134.

———. 1991. "Managing a Convincing Self-Presentation: Some Personal Reflections on Entering the Field." Pp. 72–81 in William Shaffir and Robert Stebbins (eds.), *Experiencing Fieldwork.* Newbury Park, CA: Sage.

———. 1993. "Jewish Messianism Lubavitch Style: An Interim Report." *The Jewish Journal of Sociology* 35:115–128.

———. 1995. "When Prophecy is Not Validated: Explaining the Unexpected in a Messianic Campaign." *The Jewish Journal of Sociology* 37:119–136.

Shaffir, William, Mary Lorenz Dietz, and Robert Stebbins. 1994. "Field Research as Social Experience: Learning to Do Ethnography." Pp. 30–54 in Mary Lorenz Dietz, Robert Prus, and William Shaffir (eds.), *Doing Everyday Life: Ethnography As Human Lived Experience.* Toronto: Copp Clark Longman.

Shaffir, William B., and Robert A. Stebbins. (eds.). 1991. *Experiencing Fieldwork: An Inside View of Qualitative Research.* Newbury Park, CA: Sage.

Shaffir, William B., Robert A. Stebbins, and Allan Turowetz. 1980. *Fieldwork Experience: Qualitative Approaches to Social Research.* New York: St. Martin's Press.

Sharp, Gene. 1973. *The Politics of Nonviolent Action* (3 vols.). Boston: Porter Sargent.

Shaw, Clifford. 1930. *The Jack-Roller: A Delinquent Boy's Own Story.* Chicago: University of Chicago Press.

Shaw, Clifford, Henry McKay, and James McDonald. 1938. *Brothers in Crime.* Chicago: University of Chicago Press.

Shaw, Clifford, and M. E. Moore. 1931. *The Natural History of a Delinquent Career.* Chicago: University of Chicago Press.

Shepard, Gordon. 1987. "The Social Construction of a Religious Prophecy." *Sociological Inquiry* 57:395–413.

Shibutani, Tamotsu. 1955. "Reference Groups as Perspectives." *American Journal of Sociology* 60:522–529.

Shields, Renee Rose. 1988. *Uneasy Endings: Daily Life in an American Nursing Home.* Ithaca: Cornell University Press.

Shulman, David. 1994. "Dirty Data and Investigative Methods: Some Lessons from Private Detective Work." *Journal of Contemporary Ethnography* 23 (2): 214–253.

Simmel, Georg. 1907. *The Philosophy of Money.* (1978) Translated by Tom Bottomore and David Frisby. Boston, Ma.: Routledge and Kegan Paul.

———. 1950. The Sociology of Georg Simmel. Trans. and ed. by Kurt H. Wolf. New York: Free Press.

Simmons, Jerry. 1969. *Deviants*. Berkeley, CA: Glendessary Press.

Singer, Merrill, Maureen H. Fizgerald, Lyn Madden, Christa E. Voight von Legat, and Carol D. Arnold. 1987. "The Sufferer's Experience of Hypoglycemia." *Research in the Sociology of Health Care* 6:147–175.

Smith, Charles W. 1989. *Auctions: The Social Construction of Value.* Berkeley: University of California Press.

Smith, Kenneth J., and Linda Liska Belgrave. 1995. "The Reconstruction of Everyday Life: Experiencing Hurricane Andrew." *Journal of Contemporary Ethnography* 24 (3): 244–269.

Snow, David A., Cherylon Robinson, and Patricia L. McCall. 1991. " 'Cooling Out' Men in Singles Bars and Nightclubs: Observations on the Interpersonal Survival Strategies of Women in Public Places." *Journal of Contemporary Ethnography* 19 (4): 423–449.

Snow, David A., and Leon Anderson. 1993. *Down on Their Luck: A Study of Homeless Street People.* Berkeley: University of California Press.

Snyder, Eldon E. 1986. "The Social World of Shuffleboard: Participation by Senior Citizens." *Urban Life* 15 (2): 237–253.

———. 1994. "Getting Involved in the Shuffleboard World." Pp 85–95 in Mary Lorenz Dietz, Robert Prus, and William Shaffir (eds.), *Doing Everyday Life: Ethnography As Human Lived Experience.* Toronto: Copp Clark Longman.

Southard, P.A. Dee. 1996. "Uneasy Sanctuary: Homeless Campers Using Public Lands." Paper presented at the Pacific Sociological Association meetings. Seattle, WA.

Spencer, Jack William. 1983. "Accounts, Attitudes, and Solutions: Probation Officer-Defendant Negotiations of Subjective Orientations." *Social Problems* 30:570–581.

———. 1984. "Conducting Presentencing Investigations: From Discourse to Textual Summaries." *Urban Life* 13:207–227.

Spradley, James P. 1970. *You Owe Yourself a Drunk: An Ethnography of Urban Nomads.* Boston: Little, Brown.

———. 1972. *Culture and Cognition: Rules, Maps, and Plans.* San Francisco: Chandler.

———. 1980. *Participant Observation.* New York: Holt, Rinehart and Winston.

Spradley, James P., and Brenda J. Mann. 1975. *The Cocktail Waitress: Woman's Work in a Man's World.* New York: Wiley.

Stanton, Ester. 1970. *Clients Come Last.* Beverley Hills: Sage.

Star, Susan Leigh. 1989. *Regions of the Mind: Brain Research and the Quest for Scientific Certainty.* Stanford: Stanford University Press.

Stebbins, Robert. 1984. *The Magician: Career, Culture and Social Psychology in a Variety Art.* Toronto: Irwin.

———. 1990. *The Laugh Makers: Stand-up Comedy as Art, Business, and Life-Style.* Kingston, Ontario: McGill-Queen's University Press.

Steffensmeier, Darrell. 1986. *The Fence: In the Shadow of Two Worlds.* Totawa, NJ: Rowman and Littlefield.

Stenross, Barbara. 1994. "Aesthetics in the Marketplace: Collectors in the Gun Business." *Qualitative Sociology* 17 (1): 29–42.

Stenross, Barbara, and Sherryl Kleinman. 1989. "The Highs and Lows of Emotional Labor: Detectives' Encounters with Criminals and Victims." *Journal of Contemporary Ethnography* 17 (4): 435–452.

Stoddart, Kenneth. 1986. "The Presentation of Everyday Life: Some Textual Strategies for 'Adequate Ethnography.' " *Urban Life* 15:103–121.

Stouffer, Dennis J. 1995. *Journeys Through Hell: Stories of Burn Survivors' Reconstructions of Self and Identity.* Lanham, MD: Rowman and Littlefield.

Strauss, Anselm. 1952. "The Development and Transformation of Monetary Meanings in the Child." *American Sociological Review* 17:275–286.

———. 1954. "The Development of Conceptions of Rules in Children." *Child Development* 25:193–208.

———. 1970. "Discovering New Theory From Previous Theory." Pp. 46–53 in T. Shibutani (ed.), *Human Nature and Collective Behavior: Papers in Honor of Herbert Blumer.* Englewood Cliffs, NJ: Prentice-Hall.

———. 1978. "A Social World Perspective." Pp. 119–128 in Norman K. Denzin (ed.), *Studies in Symbolic Interaction* 1. Greenwich, CT: JAI.

———. 1982. "Social Worlds and Legitimation Processes." Pp. 171–190 in Norman K. Denzin (ed.), *Studies in Symbolic Interaction* 4. Greenwich, CT: JAI.

———. 1984. "Social Worlds and their Segmentation Processes." Pp. 123–139 in Norman K. Denzin (ed.), *Studies in Symbolic Interaction* 5. Greenwich, CT: JAI.

———. 1993. *Continual Permutations of Action.* Hawthorne, NY: Aldine de Gruyter.

Sudnow, David. 1965. "Normal Crimes: Sociological Features of the Penal Code in a Public Defender Office." *Social Problems* 12: 255–276.

———. 1967. *Passing On: The Social Organization of Dying.* Englewood Cliffs, NJ: Prentice-Hall.

Sutherland, Anne, and Jeffrey E. Nash. 1994. "Animal Rights as a New Environmental Cosmology." *Qualitative Sociology* 17:171–186.

Sutherland, Edwin. 1937. *The Professional Thief.* Chicago: University of Chicago Press.

———. 1950. "The Diffusion of Sexual Psychopath Laws." *American Journal of Sociology* 56:142–148.

Tannenbaum, Frank. 1938. *Crime and the Community.* New York: Columbia University Press.

Taylor, Avril. 1993. *Women Drug Users: An Ethnography of a Female Injecting Community.* Oxford: Clarendon.

Thomas, Robert J. 1992. "Organizational Politics and Technological Change." *Journal of Contemporary Ethnography* 20 (4): 442–447.

Thomas, William I., and Florian Znaniecki. 1918–1920. *The Polish Peasant in Europe and America* (vols. 1–4). Boston: Richard Badger.

Thorlindsson Thorolfur. 1994. "Skipper Science: A Note on the Epistemology of Practice and the Nature of Expertise." *Sociological Quarterly* 35 (2): 329–345.

Thrasher, Frederick M. 1927. *The Gang.* (Abridged version, 1963) Chicago: University of Chicago Press.

Tomlinson, Graham. 1986a. "The Social Construction of Truth: Editing an Encyclopedia." *Urban Life* 15 (2): 197–213.

———. 1986b. "Thought for Food: A Study of Written Instructions." *Symbolic Interaction* 9 (2): 201–216.

Trice, Harrison M. 1993. *Occupational Subcultures in the Workplace.* Ithaca, NY: ILR Press.

Tuchman, Gaye, and Harry Gene Levine. 1993. "New York Jews and Chinese Food: The Social Construction of an Ethnic Pattern." *Journal of Contemporary Ethnography* 22 (3): 382–407.

Tunnell, Kenneth D. 1993. "Inside the Drug Trade: Trafficking from the Dealer's Perspective." *Qualitative Sociology* 16 (4): 361–381.

Tylor, E.B. 1871. *Primitive Culture.* London: J. Murray.

Uhl, Sarah. 1989. "Making the Bed: Creating the Home in Escalona, Andalusia." *Ethnology* 28:151–166.

Ulmer, Jeffery T. 1994. "Trial Judges in a Rural Court Community: Contexts, Organizational Relations, and Interaction Strategies." *Journal of Contemporary Ethnography* 23 (1): 79–108.

———. 1995. "The Organization and Consequences of Social Pasts in Criminal Courts." *The Sociological Quarterly* 36 (3): 587–605.

Unruh, David R. 1979a. "Doing Funeral Directing: Managing Sources of Risk in Funeralization." *Urban Life* 8 (2): 247–263.

———. 1979b. "Influencing Common Sense Interpretations of an Urban Setting: The Freeway Coffee Shop." *Symbolic Interaction* 2 (1): 27–42.

———. 1983. *Invisible Lives: Social Worlds of the Aged*. Beverly Hills: Sage Publications.

Valdez, Avelardo. 1984. "Chicano Used Car Dealers: A Social World in Microcosm." *Urban Life* 13 (2–3): 229–246.

Valentine, Catherine. 1982. "The Everyday Life of Art: Variation in the Valuation of Art Works in a Community Art Museum." *Symbolic Interaction* 5 (1): 37–47.

Van Maanen, John. 1984. "Making Rank: Becoming an American Police Sergeant." *Urban Life* 13 (2–3): 155–176.

Van Zandt, David E. 1991. *Living in the Children of God*. Princeton: Princeton University Press.

Vaughan, Diane. 1986. *Uncoupling: Turning Points in Intimate Relationships*. New York: Oxford.

Waldorf, Dan, Craig Reinarman, and Sheigla Murphy. 1991. *Cocaine Changes: The Experiences of Using and Quitting*. Philadelphia: Temple University Press.

Wallace, Ruth A. 1992. *They Call Her Pastor: A New Role for Catholic Women*. Albany: State University of New York Press.

Waller, Willard. 1930. *The Old Love and the New*. Carbondale: Southern Illinois University Press (1967).

Warren, Carol A. B. 1983. "The Politics of Trouble in an Adolescent Psychiatric Hospital." *Urban Life* 12 (3): 327–348.

Warren, Carol A. B., and Stephen W. Phillips. 1976. "Stigma Negotiation: Expression Games, Accounts, and the Drunken Driver." *Urban Life* 5 (1): 53–74.

Weber, Max. 1968. *Economy and Society: An Outline of Interpretive Sociology*. Guenther Roth and Claus Wittich (eds.), New York: Bedminster Press.

Wedow, Suzanne. 1979. "Feeling Paranoid: The Organization of an Ideology about Drug Use." *Urban Life* 8 (1): 72–93.

Weger, Katarina. 1992. "The Sociological Significance of Ambivalence: An Example from Adoption Research." *Qualitative Sociology* 15:87–103.

Wharton, Carol S. 1989. "Splintered Visions: Staff/Client Disjunctions and Their Consequences for Human Service Organizations. *Journal of Contemporary Ethnography* 18 (1): 50–71.

———. 1991. "Why Can't We Be Friends?: Expectations Versus Experiences in the Volunteer Role." *Journal of Contemporary Ethnography* 20 (1): 79–106.

White, Leslie A. 1973. *The Concept of Culture*. Minneapolis: Burgess.

Whitehurst, Robert N. n.d. "Marriage as a Total Institution." Unpublished paper. Sociology Department, University of Windsor, Windsor, Ontario, circa 1980.

Whittaker, Elvi. 1994. "The Contribution of Herbert Blumer to Anthropology." Pp. 379–392 in Mary Lorenz Dietz, Robert Prus, and William Shaffir (eds.) *Doing Everyday Life: Ethnography As Human Lived Experience.* Toronto: Copp Clark Longman.

Whyte, William Foote. 1943. *Street Corner Society: The Social Structure of an Italian Slum.* (Enlarged edition, 1955) Chicago: University of Chicago Press.

Wierzbicka, Anna. 1994. "Apples are not a Kind of Fruit: The Semantics of Human Categorization." *American Anthropologist* 11:313–328.

Williams, Terry. 1991. *The Cocaine Kids: The Inside Story of a Teenage Drug Ring.* Boston: Addison-Wesley.

Williams, Terry, Eloise Dunlop, Bruce D. Johnson, and Ansley Hamid. 1992. "Personal Safety in Dangerous Places." *Journal of Contemporary Ethnography* 21 (3): 343–374.

Willner, Ann Ruth. 1984. *The Spellbinders: Charismatic Political Leadership.* New Haven: Yale University Press.

Winfree, L. Thomas Jr., Lawrence Kielich, and Robert E. Clark. 1984. "On Becoming a Prosecutor: Observations on the Organizational Socialization of Law Interns." *Work and Occupations* 11 (2): 207–226.

Wiseman, Jacqueline. 1970. *Stations of the Lost: The Treatment of Skid Row Alcoholics.* Englewood Cliffs, NJ: Prentice-Hall.

———. 1979. "Towards a Theory of Policy Intervention in Social Problems." *Social Problems* 27:3–18.

———. 1991. *The Other Half: Wives of Alcoholics and Their Social-Psychological Situation.* New York: Aldine de Gruyter.

Wolcott, Harry Fletcher. 1990. *Writing Up Qualitative Research.* Newbury Park, CA: Sage.

Wolf, Charlotte. 1994. "Conversion into Feminism." Pp. 143–157 in Mary Lorenz Dietz, Robert Prus, and William Shaffir (eds.), *Doing Everyday Life: Ethnography As Human Lived Experience.* Toronto: Copp Clark Longman.

Wolf, Daniel. 1991. *The Rebels: A Brotherhood of Outlaw Bikers.* Toronto: University of Toronto Press.

Wood, Juanita. 1975. "The Structure of Concern: The Ministry in Death-Related Situations." *Urban Life* 4 (3): 369–384.

Wright, Richard T., and Scott Decker. 1994. *Burglars on the Job: Streetlife and Residential Break-ins.* Boston: Northeastern University Press.

Yoels, William C., and Jeffrey Michael Clair. 1994. "Never Enough Time: How Medical Residents Manage a Scarce Resource." *Journal of Contemporary Ethnography* 23 (2): 185–213.

————. 1995. "Laughter in the Clinic: Humor as Social Organization." *Symbolic Interaction* 18 (1): 39–58.

Zurcher, Louis. 1965. "The Sailor aboard Ship: A Study of Role Behavior in a Total Institution." *Social Forces* 43:389–400.

Index of Names

Index of Terms